FACE TO THE VILLAGE

The Riazan Countryside under Soviet Rule, 1921–1930

In the summer of 1924, the Bolshevik Party called on scholars, the police, the courts, and state officials to turn their attention to the villages of Russia. The subsequent campaign to 'face the countryside' generated a wealth of intelligence that fed into the regime's sense of alarmed conviction that the countryside was a space outside of Bolshevik control.

Richly rooted in archival sources, including local and central-level secret police reports, detailed cases of the local and provincial courts, government records, and newspaper reports, *Face to the Village* is a nuanced study of the everyday workings of the Russian village in the 1920s. Local-level officials emerge in Tracy McDonald's study as vital and pivotal historical actors, existing between the Party's expectations and peasant interests. McDonald's careful exposition of the relationships between the urban centre and the peasant countryside brings us closer to understanding the fateful decision to launch a frontal attack on the countryside in the fall of 1929 under the auspices of collectivization.

TRACY MCDONALD is an associate professor in the Department of History at McMaster University.

Face to the Village

The Riazan Countryside under Soviet Rule, 1921–1930

TRACY McDONALD

UNIVERSITY OF TORONTO PRESS
Toronto Buffalo London

Toronto Buffalo London
www.utppublishing.com

Reprinted in paperback 2016

ISBN 978-1-4426-4082-5 (cloth) ISBN 978-1-4875-2169-1 (paper)

Library and Archives Canada Cataloguing in Publication

McDonald, Tracy, 1966–
Face to the Village : The Riazan countryside under Soviet rule, 1921–1930 / Tracy McDonald.

ISBN 978-1-4426-4082-5 (bound) ISBN 978-1-4875-2169-1 (paper)

1. Riazan' Region (Riazanskaia oblast', Russia) – History. 2. Riazan' Region (Riazanskaia oblast', Russia) – Politics and government. 3. Peasants – Soviet Union – History – 20th century. 4. Soviet Union – Rural conditions – History. 5. Soviet Union – History – 1917–1936. 6. Soviet Union – Politics and government – 1917–1936. I. Title.

DK511.R9M43 2011 947'.33 C2010-905238-2
DK511*

This book has been published with the help of a grant from the Canadian Federation for the Humanities and Social Sciences, through the Aid to Scholarly Publications Program, using funds provided by the Social Sciences and Humanities Research Council of Canada.

The University of Toronto Press acknowledges the financial assistance to its publishing program of the Canada Council for the Arts and the Ontario Arts Council, an agency of the Government of Ontario

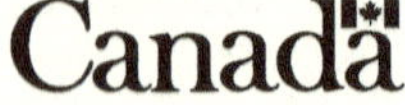

For my father,
Kenneth George McDonald
(1918–2006)

Trust me, this will take time but there is order here,
very faint, very human.

Michael Ondaatje, *In the Skin of a Lion*

Contents

List of Illustrations and Maps

Illustrations

Maps

Word Choice and Translation

I have endeavoured to use English translations where possible and feasible throughout the text. Russian is used for all titles in the appropriate references and notes. Thus, in the text, *guberniia* becomes 'province,' *volost'* becomes 'district,' and *sel'sovet* becomes 'rural soviet.' For the pre-Revolutionary references to '*volost'* scribes' I have retained the Russian. Where accuracy would be sacrificed, in terms of measure such as *desiatina* or *pud* or in less frequently used geographic divisions such as *uezd*, which were more difficult to translate, I have retained the Russian. Desiatina is a unit of measure for land; one desiatina is equivalent to about one hectare. Pud is a unit of weight; one pud is approximately 16.4 kilograms. I have retained some Russian words that lose much in their translation, such as *samosud*, which I used interchangeably with 'vigilante justice' and sometimes *samogon* interchangeably with 'moonshine' and 'homebrew.' The first mention of the Russian word is in italics with a brief translation; subsequent references are in regular type. I have used the English method of creating a plural; for example, the plural of *raion* would be *raions* rather than *raiony*, *okrugs* rather than *okrugy*. I have also avoided the soft sign in anglicized spellings at the end of frequently used words, so Riazan rather than Riazan'. The Library of Congress system of transliteration is used. For well-known names such as Trotsky or Tolstoy, the more familiar transliteration is retained unless it is spelled differently in a direct quotation from another author. All translations are my own unless otherwise noted.

Acknowledgments

I am grateful for this opportunity to thank all of the people and the institutions that helped me in the course of writing this book. I know there are many more than are named here. The book began as a dissertation at the University of Toronto, where the Ontario Graduate Scholarship, Social Sciences and Humanities Research Council, and the Department of History provided generous financial assistance. The University of Toronto and the Department of History were always extremely supportive, and a special thank you is in order to Kim Donaldson, Vicky Dingillo, and Marion Harris. The Stalin Era Research and Archives Project and the Centre for Russian and East European Studies provided me with generous funding for research travel and research experience. The University of Utah's Arts Research Council provided funding for additional research on the police in the Riazan countryside. McMaster University's Arts Research Board granted funds for a new chapter on forests and wood theft. This book has been published with the help of a grant from the Canadian Federation for the Humanities and Social Sciences, through the Aid to Scholarly Publications Program, using funds provided by the Social Sciences and Humanities Research Council of Canada. Molly Malloy at the Hoover Library helped me a great deal at the very beginning of this project and even gave an interloper a desk in the library.

The University of Utah took in an ABD scholar and gave her an academic haven and home. I want to take this opportunity to thank my friends and colleagues there, in particular, Beth Clement, Ben Cohen, Ron Colemen, Nadja Durbach, Larry and Gail Gerlach, Anne Keary, and Ron and Ruth Smelser. Many of my students at Utah made those years extremely rewarding, especially Julie Koo and Larry Staten. I also thank those colleagues at McMaster and in Hamilton who supported me and some read chapters, in particular, Megan Armstrong, Nancy Christie, Ken Cruikshank, Ruth Frager, Michael Gauvreau, Vladimir Goneharove, and Debbie Lobban. Deb aided and abetted above and beyond the call. John Weaver is an outstanding mentor and role model and has fairly decent taste in films except for an indefensible liking for Eric Rohmer.

Peter Holquist read through the entire manuscript at a very early stage and generously offered his time and numerous suggestions in the midst of the busiest schedule imaginable. David Hoffmann did the same at a much later stage. They are true scholars and gentlemen. Stephen Kotkin and Alain Blum encouraged a very uncertain graduate student by asking for copies of the first paper that I ever presented at the AAASS; their positive feedback probably convinced me to stay in the field. That paper was the foundation for the final chapter of this book. Fellow historians of the Russian, Soviet, and post-Soviet countryside have given their time and wisdom generously over the years. I would especially like to thank Jessica Allina-Pisano, Ben Eklof, David Hoffmann, and Aaron Retish. A still anonymous reader early on in the process helped me immensely in refining my arguments.

Many people made my numerous research trips to Russia a very human experience. Special thanks to the Koloskov family for feeding and sheltering me in the summer of 1993 and for much friendship beyond. I would like to thank my friends in Moscow, Sergei Kapterev, Zhenia Kravchenko, Jen O'Shea, and Sergei Zhuravlev. I would like to thank the staff at RGAE, GARF, and RGASPI for the times that they were generous and helpful. Valentina Osepian was a source of constant support and encouragement in Riazan. Viacheslav Egorkin and Natasha Zhuravleva shared their intimate knowledge of Sasovo Raion and Riazan Province and welcomed us into their homes and families. Evgeny Kashirin always provided a magical place to be in the city of Riazan amidst his students, his photo laboratory, and his haunting photographs. Andrei Mel'nik helped me a great deal at the Riazan archives. The loss of Andrei and Zhenia is felt deeply. The reading room staff graciously assisted me in an often very cold archive. I will always remember them for their laughter and their honesty, especially when responding to the fire marshal. He very seriously pointed out that an ancient wood-burning stove, in an ancient church, now full of old paper and false wooden floors, was quite the fire hazard. When he asked them what they would do in the event of a fire, they answered, 'We would run.' They wondered why I 'wasted my youth,' sitting in their archive. I frequently ask myself the same question.

I was fortunate enough to have outstanding professors at the University of Toronto who continue to inspire me. Bob Johnson's course on Russian and Soviet Social History and Peter Solomon's enthusiasm for legal culture sent me down the path that led to this book. Susan Solomon has always been supportive about work and about life in general; I treasure her intellect and her friendship. I have always known the intellectual and personal debt I owe to my supervisor, Lynne Viola. Upon re-reading her book *Peasant Rebels under Stalin* in preparation for teaching my own fourth-year seminar, it became clear to me just how much I owe to her ideas on colonization and the countryside specifically.

Candice Ward gave the manuscript a thorough going over and made it much cleaner as a result. Her warmth and encouragement will not be forgotten. I am eternally grateful to Richard Ratzlaff who understood immediately what I was trying to do in the manuscript and believed in the book from our first meeting. His unflagging support and enthusiasm made this process that much easier. Thanks also to Ruth Pincoe for the index and La Liga. Ian MacKenzie meticulously copy edited the manuscript and I am grateful for his keen eye and careful reading. Any mistakes that remain are my own.

I was lucky to be part of a strong and dedicated graduate cohort at University of Toronto. Olga Bakich, Kari Bronaugh, Blaine Chiasson, Dan Healey (brave fighter of mice and ceilings), Janet Hyer, Alison Meek (brave fighter of garlic presses), Eva Plach, Aldis Purs, Kathy Rasmussen, Rebecca Spagnolo, and Robert Wallwork continue to be excellent colleagues and even better friends. Kari and Janet did some serious home improvement work in 2009 for which I am eternally in their debt. And Janet performed a heroic proofread.

Dave, Deb, Gog, Aunt Grace, and Shane have been supportive, if often bewildered observers of this whole process. Dave read chapters, and the maps herein are Shane's work and expertise. I am grateful to my little brothers for sharing themselves, and now their own families, and their love. They mean more to me than I could ever say. For longer than anyone else, my parents have had to deal with me and my academic proclivities. Occasionally it would get too much and my father would yell, 'Why don't you just burn all of those damn books!' His anger at the source of my distress buoyed my spirits, despite the extreme solution he proposed. Without my parents' constant support, encouragement, and love, none of this would have been possible. My mum's love of damn books probably got me into this line of work in the first place. She has been a constant friend and companion and gave up many hours of time together so I could keep writing. Thank you to S. who arrived before it all began and never deserted my side. Finally, to Thomas, for many years of happiness, the last words here are his. On 5 October 2008 he came to the following conclusion: 'It's a bad idea to write about peasants. It's a bad idea to be a peasant.'

Parts of chapter 1 appeared as 'Riazanskaia derevnia,' in *Riazanskaia derevnia v 1929–1930 gg.: khronika golovokruzheniia*, ed. Lynne Viola, Sergei Zhuravlev, Andrei Mel'nik, and Tracy McDonald, xxii–xxxii (Moscow: Rosspen, 1998).

An earlier version of chapter 10 appeared as 'A Peasant Rebellion in Stalin's Russia,' *Journal of Social History* (Fall 2001): 125–46, and is reprinted by permission; 'A Peasant Rebellion in Stalin's Russia,' in *Contending with Stalinism: Soviet Power and Popular Resistance in the 1930s*, ed. Lynne Viola, 84–108 (Ithaca, NY: Cornell University Press, 2001); and was summarized in 'Otvet Riazanskogo krest'ianstva na nachalo kollektivizatsii,' in *Regional'naia istoriia v Rossiiskoi i zarubezhnoi istoriografii*, ed. A.A. Sevestianova et al., 42–7 (Riazan, 1999).

Parts of chapter 7 appeared as 'Soviet Bandit Tales: "The steam of the still and the lure of easy profit,"' *Canadian-American Slavic Studies* 35, nos. 2–3 (Summer–Fall 2001): 219–43.

Map 1 Riazan 1925. Adapted by Shane Bennett and Tracy McDonald from a Russian-language map found in Organizatsionnoe Biuro Tsentral'no-Promyshlennoi oblast, *Novaia volost' raion* (Moscow: Izd. Gosplana SSSR, 1925), 191.

FACE TO THE VILLAGE
The Riazan Countryside under Soviet Rule, 1921–1930

Introduction

> The most difficult is before us. The countryside is the most important and the most difficult. The countryside, there is the front which will present us with the most dangerous enemies of the Revolution: with the ignorant mass, with backward agricultural technology, and with the lack of organization of peasant labour. In the face of these fearsome enemies, our barricades, bank saboteurs, ministerial bureaucrats, and White Guard generals with all of their ridiculous regiments are not so grandiose.
>
> A.M. Bol'shakov, *The Countryside after October*

'It is high time to compel the entire range of our organizations to turn their face to the countryside,'[1] wrote Grigory Zinoviev on 30 July 1924. The slogan 'face to the countryside' (*litsom k derevne*) became a rallying cry dispatched from the Centre to scholars, the police, the courts, and to all manner of party and state organs to turn toward the villages and their inhabitants, who made up the vast majority of the population of the country. Zinoviev's call was made in the spirit of Lenin's emphasis on a link between the proletariat and the peasantry and the need to heal the wounds created by the bitter Civil War that had followed the October Revolution. Yet, from the very start, the relationship between town and countryside was fraught with tension and contradiction. It was never to be an equal partnership.[2]

Zinoviev's appeal itself was made in the context of fiscal anxiety, as his main concern was the prospect of a poor harvest (*neurozhai*). And the anxieties were not just fiscal, as he worried openly about the 'thousand paths' through which the peasant mood could influence the urban population. The answer to the problem was to create a solid party presence in the countryside, which, Zinoviev admitted, was still seriously lacking. Then the party/state could 'show the peasant that, in his year of misfortune, the worker-peasant state will do everything in its power to help.'[3]

Face to the Village embraces a variety of meanings. The most obvious is contained in Zinoviev's slogan and in the Centre's decision and need to pay attention to the countryside and its inhabitants. Facing the village for the Bolshevik regime meant to be cognizant of the challenges and problems of the countryside, to admit them, and to confront them with resolve. For the purposes of this book, the phrase also embodies a commitment to providing villagers with faces, names, and a testimony of their experiences.

Zinoviev's summons did not go unheeded. Party and state structures did turn to face the village, and they produced abundant material based on their observations. As L. Artimenkov wrote in the journal of the Commissariat of Justice, 'The question of the countryside stands as the order of the day everywhere. This question stands before the workers of justice, and especially before the workers on the ground, who come into the closest contact with the villages, contending face to face with the peasant.'[4] A contributor to the journal for the Commissariat of Internal Affairs (NKVD) insisted that it was rather the district police officer who was the key to connecting peasant and state.[5] Both the police and courts are of central concern in these pages because they were two of the most important parts of a complex state apparatus, along with the rural soviets, that were closest to Russia's rural inhabitants. Within two years, most of the organizations and individuals who turned to face the countryside did not like what they found there. In fact, the materials generated by the campaign alerted the regime to the extent to which the villages seemed to be peasant spaces far beyond the bounds of central control. The face-off between Bolshevik and local power shapes the overarching parameters of this book.

Why Riazan? Centre and Local

In order to capture sufficiently the level of detail required to explore the workings of power on the local level, this book adopts a close geographical focus on the villages of the central-Russian province of Riazan within the context of a set of broad thematic lenses. What is especially interesting about Riazan is that the province is literally Moscow's backyard. Typically when we think of the Centre and its periphery, we think in terms of a significant geographical distance; the city of Riazan is 200 kilometres southwest of the capital city, Moscow. Yet the province is considered a backwater and depicted historically as the embodiment of rural backwardness.

Despite the proximity of Riazan to Moscow, or perhaps because of it, the Riazan male and female peasant are seen as especially representative of the Russian villager. Both the masculine form (*Riazanskii muzhik*) and the even slightly more derogatory feminine form (*Riazanskaia baba*), and the very derogatory 'Riazan snout' (*Riazanskaia morda*) are used to refer to the archetypal negative image of the peasant or 'country hick' in contemporary speech. One of the most successful films of the 1920s, both at home and abroad, was Olga Preobrazhenskaia's 1927 film *Women of Riazan* (*Baby Riazanskie*). The film and its 'exotic' Riazan locales were themselves rapidly regarded as primitive along with Preobrazhenskaia because of her links to pre-Revolutionary film-making and the 'backward' themes of her film. The plot revolved around the concept of *snokhachestvo*, the desire of a father for his son's bride.

In Igor Savchenko's 1934 film *Accordion* (*Garmon'*), Savchenko himself played the villain whom the local girls referred to as the 'Riazan sorrow' (*Riazanskoe gore*) – which Denis Kozlov translated as Riazan pauper and appears as the epigraph of chapter 1 – in reference to his poverty after being de-kulakized. This film was 'shelved'; in other words, it was not banned outright but it was not shown either.[6] Because of all that Riazan represented it was an excellent mirror for Bolshevik fears and anxieties. And because of its proximity to Moscow, perceived deviance there was especially threatening. Thus, Riazan provides us both with a window onto the countryside, to the Centre's perceptions of that countryside, and to the Centre's hopes, dreams, and anxieties for its domains.

In his introduction to *Provincial Landscapes*, Donald Raleigh has written a passionate defence of regional or local history, arguing that these histories are vital and important.[7] A regional focus allows the researcher to narrow the work geographically, thereby permitting the historian to examine a wider range of phenomena. An emphasis on the local does not imply that the Centre is left out of the picture. Bolshevik power is always present throughout this work in the constantly shifting laws, resolutions, campaigns, decrees, announcements, pronouncements, criticisms, demands, dreams, and anxieties that emanated from the Centre. All too often the Centre's revolutionary dreams crashed on the shores of local realities, and the response on both sides was frustration and violence. A focus on Riazan allows for a close look at the mechanisms and processes of this frustration and violence. It is only by appreciating and investigating these local realities that we begin to approach a more complete understanding of the Soviet Union's complex history.

Riazan is a rich region for local study. The province was almost 100 per cent ethnically Russian, with a tiny Tartar population of about eleven thousand, or 0.6 per cent, in 1926.[8] In other words, the interesting but extremely complex variable of ethnic tension in the Soviet Union is not a relevant variable in this study. Located at the heart of European Russia, Riazan shares features of what is typically labelled the Central Industrial Region (CIR) and the Central Black Earth (CBE). The northern half of Riazan could not grow surplus grain, while the soil of the south was richer. Thus Riazan, within itself, captures one of the most important tensions that existed in the Soviet Union of the time – how to extract grain from the producers in order to provide grain to the non-producers. Moscow was far away, even when it appeared relatively close on a map; crude roads and an underdeveloped communications infrastructure made connections between the Centre and most village communities intermittent at best.

I have chosen to use the term *Centre* to represent the central structures of power, such as the Politburo, Orgburo, Central Committee, the various commissariats, and the endless flow of decrees, instructions, resolutions, and codes that originated within these organizations in Moscow. Much of the literature of the 1920s has been devoted to showing the complexity of this 'Centre.'[9] This work embraces that complexity to show what happens to legislation, constantly drafted and redrafted at the 'top,' as it confronted the realities of the local where communities largely managed themselves. The Centre could not possibly understand the varied conditions in every village from year to year – conditions that affected the harvest or the sowing and put pressure on the often fine line between success and subsistence or dearth. Villagers constantly made this argument in their letters and appeals to central power; they would present the situation in their village, or even in their particular household, as a way of explaining and justifying a course of action such as nonpayment of taxes or theft of wood.[10]

By focusing on the local, this book recovers the names and faces of as many historical actors as possible – individuals who are all too often left out of the historical record. We have a good sense of who the revolutionaries were that came to power in October 1917.[11] Yet we lack a clear sense of the majority of the population, people scattered in villages across the endless territory of the Soviet Union. Until recently, the Russian peasantry in the 1920s had been regarded as wanting simply to be left alone, uninterested in accommodating to the new regime.[12] *Face to the Village* maintains that peasants were interested in coming to a workable living arrangement with the Soviet regime in the mid-1920s. Many of the inhabitants of the villages who appear in these pages were active members of their communities in local struggles for power, resources, justice, and survival itself. The resulting portrait of both state and countryside revises our understanding of these crucial, formative years in the Soviet Union and is part of a growing body of scholarship that is rethinking and enriching our understanding of the complexities of the Russian and Soviet countryside. By concentrating on the daily encounters between peasants and local officials,[13] Corinne Gaudin, for example, shows that by the 1890s peasant communities were not closed off from the world around them. In *Face to the Village* local officials are *both* peasants and state servitors. They wear either identity, or both identities simultaneously, depending on what is asked of them and what they judge to be the most efficacious and appropriate behaviour in a particular context.[14] Peasants interested in politics had received training, in a sense, under both the old regime and the new.[15] Villagers learned how to interpret and interact with power in its multiple and multilayered manifestations.

Face to the Village is about the places and spaces of Riazan Province.[16] The 'place' of Riazan is taken here as the state-defined geographical province. The problem of defining 'place' is dramatically illustrated by the constantly shifting borders of the districts, and the constant redefining of the geographical entity itself when Riazan became an *okrug* within Moscow *oblast* for the initial push of collectivization.[17] The spaces of Riazan are even more abstract and contested. The rural soviet, for example, is such a space. It was understood in one way by Moscow, another way by the villagers who elected it, and yet another way by the officials who served in it. Is it a state space or a village space? Where does it begin and end? The soviets were far more than the shabby buildings they were able to occupy. What about the 'offices' of the forest wardens or the police?

Peasant Actors

There is much debate over the use and definition of the word *peasant*.[18] I have opted to use it for a number of reasons. Teodor Shanin has spent a great deal of energy convincingly wrestling with the notion of peasantry, defining *peasant* and defending the term itself as a useful analytic category.[19] The definition of *peasant* that has emerged from this debate fits the rural population of Riazan in the 1920s. Peasants are defined as small-scale agricultural producers who produce largely for their own consumption, using simple equipment and the labour of their families. They are regarded as politically and economically subordinate to the central state through the assessment and collection of taxes, which they are obliged to deliver, and through extremely limited access to state power at the highest levels.[20] In the 1920s peasants understood that the Revolution had promised them citizenship and they challenged policy that treated them like subjects. Still, the obligations of the subject were increasingly levied upon them as the twenties wore on, with little in return provided by the Centre both in rights and in goods and services.[21]

Like any other group of historical actors, peasants have complex characters, and each individual has multiple identities that he or she can choose to wear in a given moment. On one hand, when talking to an ethnographer, a villager might tell tales of wood, house, or water spirits. On the other hand, if that villager is cold, no wood spirit will keep her out of the forest. Peasants can be 'victims and agents, legal plaintiffs and outlaws, defenders and violators of private property, obstructionists and inventors, social protestors and social oppressors,'[22] as Cathy Frierson has argued. Throughout the pages of *Face to the Village*, peasants are enemies of Soviet power as well as allies, and the tables could turn overnight: a former ally could find himself an enemy between one decree and the next.[23] A 'bandit,' for example, who terrorized the village one day, might beat up a collective farm activist in early 1930 and make a political statement in the midst of the violence and chaos of collectivization.

I do not subscribe to a view of the unified, homogenous village. There were tensions of all kinds in the villages of this study. In moments of relative calm, such as the years of the mid-1920s, the village could be a fractured and contentious place. Those tensions did not disappear with collectivization, and the tensions that existed in the village may help explain those villagers who did side with the collectivizers.[24] David Hoffmann's *Peasant Metropolis* shows that the peasants who left the countryside and moved to the city after collectivization arrived with complex and variable identities and were able to accommodate and adapt to, as well as resist and change, their new surroundings.[25] Even if villages appeared to unite against collectivization, such unity was not necessarily permanent. The Soviet security forces made a point of rooting out and arresting 'instigators.' These men – and they usually were men – were arrested and often exiled, and their fate served as a powerful deterrent to those who stayed behind.[26] The story of how collectivization played out in the countryside in the decades that followed the initial charge is a fascinating subject for further research.

Peasants in the 1920s accepted the fact that they needed governance and they wanted a say in what kind of governance that would be. They challenged their role as subjects and had hopes of becoming citizens. Moreover, Bolshevik ideology had promised them such a say, even if Bolshevik actions gave them reason to doubt. Peasants were willing to enter state organizations, like the rural soviets, to engage the state or appeal to state offices over taxation issues, land use, matters of crime and order, as well as intra- and inter-village conflicts. But peasants wanted a *voice* in those state institutions; in the second half of the 1920s, some believed that they had such a voice. They had interests to defend and protect. Those in the village interested in politics worked in the rural soviets and believed that they would have a say in the new Russia. This conviction that they had a voice was one of the main reasons for the mighty clash between these very villagers and central policy during the years of collectivization. Thus the issues of negotiation, resistance, and accommodation are extremely complex and multilayered. There were local interests of the organized, criminal kind as well as of a kind that asked Soviet institutions to bring an end to lawlessness in the village. Those peasants who served in Soviet offices such as the police, the forest guard, and the rural soviets could aid and accommodate the regime, but they could also subvert it. At the lowest levels, the state and peasantry did not encounter one another; they were entangled. These entanglements comprise a major theme of my study through its focus on peasant intermediaries in a variety of situations, which in turn provides insight into the real environment in which people lived and in which the state, in all levels and complexities, had to operate.

This study adds to a literature that develops a more nuanced conception of identities and subjectivities and of the ways in which inhabitants of the Soviet Union interacted with the world around them.[27] The portrait of both state and countryside offered in this study revises our understanding of these crucial, formative years in the Soviet Union. *Face to the Village* conveys the previously unexplored and complex workings of local politics and the active role many villagers played in relations with power. It captures the informal practices of the way in which Russia functioned and, indeed, often continues to function.

The Anxiety of Building a Civilization

The Soviet regime was trapped in its founders' dualistic understanding of the 'state.' Yanni Kotsonis looks closely at this dualism embodied by Vladimir Lenin's conception of the state both as 'an instrument in the class struggle' *and* 'as a locus for the inclusion and transformation of all people.' This duality was further reflected in ideological understandings of the word *democratic*, which could mean 'elected' or merely 'staffed by the people.'[28] Thus, the Bolsheviks, unlike their tsarist predecessors, had an ideological commitment to a state that was built and staffed by the masses. That those masses could not be trusted proved one of the most anxiety-producing aspects of Bolshevik rule. The story of Bolshevik anxiety, then, has a profound role in this study.

The leaders of the Bolshevik Party were products of their experience as revolutionaries and products of the turn-of-the-century thought that gave birth to their movement. As early-twentieth-century revolutionaries and visionaries, they were committed to a complete overthrow of the old order: in their own words, the elimination of its poverty, barbarism, backwardness, slavishness, and exploitation. And nowhere was the old order more glaring and more present than in the 'dark' corners of the Russian village. Although there was great diversity in the thinking of the key Bolshevik leaders, they shared an intense faith in enlightenment and civilization, which could be brought into being through scientific progress and industrial development.[29]

Part of the creation of utopia is the construction of a legible world to govern. Legibility requires that the state simplify and homogenize the country as a whole. James Scott describes such state projects as 'high modernism.' The dreams of the modernists become those of a state constrained by economic and political realities and a willingness to use the violence and coercion aestheticized in modernism to realize revolutionary dreams.[30] In response to his critics, Scott pointed out that he 'devoted much space' in *Seeing like a State* to the 'messy encounter between tangled and ineffective state plans' and 'local forms of resistance' that satisfied no one.[31] *Face to the Village* is built on these messy encounters and daily routines, themselves testament to the complexity of 'state' and 'peasant' as one moves from the Centre to the local.

A recurring theme in these pages is the ambiguous and unenviable position of state servitors at the lowest levels – local judges, rural police officers, forest guards, or members of the village soviets. Central policy wrestled with the messiness of daily routines and local conditions, which in turn altered, diluted, or nullified many of the desires of the Centre. The policy of collectivization was in some ways the result of these constant alterations, dilutions, and frustrations. The vision of a collectivized Soviet Union embraced the grand, violent, and rapid thrust of modernism. This book makes no claims about the efficacy of that attempt; such a study would be a different and extremely interesting project entirely. But it is worth emphasizing that *violence* was an inherent part of the process. Peter Holquist argues that violence was an accepted and understood part of the Bolshevik arsenal, which was further honed by the brutalities that characterized colonial policies around the world and the carnage of the First World War.[32] The increasing ferocity and intensity of rhetoric and actions against perceived corruption, or against 'hooligans' and 'bandits,' were part of this broader process. Holquist goes so far as to make the provocative comment, 'Indeed, one can view de-kulakization as an all-encompassing, unionwide antibandit operation.'[33] Here Holquist makes explicit the connections among violence, hooliganism, banditry, and collectivization that are the connective threads that hold together the chapters in part three of the book. Amir Weiner also makes explicit the connection between the Bolshevik desire to remake or reforge the country and its population rooted in their conceptions of society as 'malleable' – a 'construct' that 'went hand in hand with a continuous purification campaign seeking to eliminate divisive and obstructing elements.'[34]

Individual Bolsheviks did balk at the violence of collectivization. M.N. Riutin described collectivization as 'a kindling of civil war against the broad masses of the countryside.'[35] I agree with Riutin, and others,[36] that collectivization represented a clash of two cultures broadly conceived. One was raised on the utopian, accelerated dreams of futurism, and modernist thought more broadly, and another was born and raised in the countryside. Neither group was homogenous within itself, and scholars have wrestled with the challenge of acknowledging difference *within* a group while still identifying the complex whole as a group. Local studies are one way to further such an agenda.[37] In the Soviet Union in the 1920s, the Centre had a vision of the ideal state. The problem was that the servitors of the state were themselves somewhat shy of exemplary. In the village, those who represented the state as its intermediaries became a battleground themselves as they were usually the first individuals blamed for any disappointment.

Very quickly after seizing power, the Bolsheviks realized that to remain in power meant the reconstruction of a state structure. A modern state needs to be systematized and standardized through a centrally determined and defined legal system, methods of taxation, policing, the control of food supply, and the formation of trained and loyal personnel to staff the new state structures according to a common understanding of the rules.[38] It is these particular needs that helped to determine the categories around which the chapters revolve in parts one and two of this book.

Leaning on Max Weber, Charles Tilly argues that building states 'entailed extracting the resources for their operation from several million rural communities.'[39] While Tilly is talking about an earlier century, the formula reflected Soviet reality on the eve of collectivization and merges well with Kotsonis's arguments about Lenin's ideas of the state that expected citizenly behaviour, on the one hand, and offered no protection for the individual, on the other.[40] In order to control resources, the Centre needed to find, map, and administer those resources and the territories in which they were located. The continual administrative change that Riazan underwent in the 1920s alone is but one testament to Moscow's frantic efforts to engage in precisely this kind of mapping and control.[41] Moreover, the economic debates that raged in the 1920s about *how* those resources were to be extracted from the peasantry suggest that policy escalated at a far more furious pace than the more 'mundane' centralization tactics typical of Tilly's model of state-building. Weber emphasized that it was 'essential' for the 'modern state to monopolize the use of force,' and the Bolsheviks shared this conviction.[42] The young Bolshevik regime in the 1920s also struggled to standardize, centralize, and monopolize the use of force in the village. The fact that villagers often seemed to apply their own rules as individuals, and sometimes in their roles as state servitors or intermediaries, was a source of very real anxiety for the Centre.

The Bolshevik regime faced the dilemmas of both a centralizing and modernizing – and, in some ways, colonial – state:[43] the commitment to enlightenment, coupled with the need to administer and extract resources from a largely unknown territory, with well-founded mistrust of the former administration and of the general population's goodwill. The dilemma was further complicated by the regime's commitment to socialism, by a high-modernist vision of the future, and devotion to building that future. Along with Marxist ideology, there was a commitment to a constituency – which included upwardly mobile workers; Soviet bureaucrats; traditionally disempowered peasants, who wanted the help of the new regime; disappointed Red Army soldiers; and true believers – which created, defined, and limited the world within which the young regime could work. This dual mission of administering and civilizing made the new Bolshevik regime very much like a colonial power. James Scott argues that the drive for 'uniformity and order alerts us to the fact that modern statecraft is largely a project of internal colonization, often glossed, as it is in imperial rhetoric, as a "civilizing mission." The builders of the modern nation-state do not merely describe, observe, and map;

they strive to shape a people and a landscape that will fit their techniques of observation.'[44] In fact, J.V. Stalin, among other contemporaries, was explicit about internal colonization. In July 1928, he said, 'Our country differs from capitalist countries, by the way, in that it cannot and must not engage in the plundering of colonies or in the plundering of other countries in general. Therefore this path is closed to us. But our country doesn't have loans from abroad either ... We are building the Dnieper Hydroelectric Station, which requires more than a hundred million. Do we have any loan here? No, we don't. All of this is being done in our country on the basis of internal accumulation. But where are the main sources of this accumulation? As I said, there are two such sources: first, the working class, which creates valuable output and moves industry forward; and the second, the peasantry.'[45]

Soviet internal colonizers also had a mission to improve this population through sovietization. *Face to the Village* explores the 'civilizing mission' as it evolved through the 1920s, both in its new socialist guise and in its carryovers from the pre-Revolutionary past.[46] In some ways the Soviet civilizing mission was a continuation of the tsarist project, but the information that flooded back to the Centre in the 1920s – about the autonomy of peasant culture and its jarring dissonance with modernist ideas of the 'perfect electric man' or the building of people's palaces on the ocean floor[47] – made the Soviet project a high-modernist one, with all of the violence such a commitment entails. As a writer for *Krest'ianskii iurist* asked in 1928, 'What did Lenin expect from the peasant activists under the leadership of the proletariat?' The role of the activist was to 'enlighten, organize, civilize [*vospitat'*], and discipline' the peasant masses.[48]

The Bolsheviks hoped that local officials could be the agents of this civilizing mission. Instead, the Centre, feeding on the local information it received – and in turn shaping what information was collected – became increasingly alarmed by the failure of its state representatives to be its missionaries. And, as Yuri Slezkine points out, 'Soviet purity begins at home.' Slezkine notes that state and party workers were the most closely monitored group precisely because they were supposed to be the 'leading vanguard' in all matters that were advanced and progressive. 'That was the point of all the purges and the reasons for many arrests and executions.'[49] The state was obsessed with the loyalty, or apparent lack thereof, of its representatives at the lower level, an obsession that captures poignantly the regime's sense of its own fragility as a state and a government. To succeed, the state would have to co-opt or destroy existing local systems.[50] Local elites and communities, of course, had an interest in 'withholding resources and knowledge from the Center.'[51] It is these relationships and the struggle over resources and loyalty that link the chapters in this book.

Bolshevik state-building collided with the local – especially peasant – hope for a say in local politics. Moreover, it clashed with both the reality of peasant self-government and the character of peasant customs, language, and traditions. Peasants were not averse to organization and local power (*vlast'*) as long as they could 'quarrel a bit' and 'smoke a bit' with it, as a prominent ethnographer of the period, M.Ia. Fenomenov observed. 'At this time the local peasant is accustomed to self-government (but more in the sense of independence), values highly the democratic side of the new order, namely, the absence of bosses: everywhere there are his people [*svoi*] with whom it is possible to quarrel a bit and to smoke a bit.'[52] By the end of the decade, however, power, as articulated by the Centre, was unwilling to do either. The pressure of high-modernist aspirations, the need for resources to quickly construct the industrialized state, and socialist ideology itself made such negotiations impossible. Moreover, peasant interests tended to be local and not national, a fact that in itself was problematic to the Centre.

The decision to collectivize the Soviet countryside at the end of the 1920s was an especially visceral, graphic, and violent attempt to implement a system of state simplifications that would homogenize and make more manageable desperately needed resources in the form of land, grain, and people. Collectivization was a brutal crescendo in what was a longer, ongoing civilizing mission to 'Sovietize' peasants and the spaces of the countryside, and to teach the inhabitants of the countryside how to speak the language of a new, modern, industrial country. The Centre needed to think in generalities and not local specifics. It needed universal laws, a consistent system of taxation, and shared understandings of criminality. Grasping the ways in which central and local conceptions of rules, law, and criminality collided in the Soviet Union in the 1920s is the key to understanding policy that originated in Moscow, the nature of its implementation or failure, and the subsequent development of the Soviet state.

Time

Bolsheviks had a profound sense of time forward, raised as they were on the culture of modernism and the dreams of progress that marked the early twentieth century. In *Dreamworld and Catastrophe*, Susan Buck-Morss argues that 'conceptions of temporality have political implications' and that 'time must be granted a greater complexity than former revolutionary narratives have allowed.'[53] She wrestles with the difference between understandings of time for the cultural avant-garde and for the party vanguard. She emphasizes the linear, constrained, Bolshevik concept of time that moved relentlessly forward in the course of progress and argues that Lenin was convinced that 'political movements could speed up the course of history.'[54] This accelerated sense of time collided with a peasant sense of time, tied as it was to the agrarian calendar and slowed down by the everyday realities of wooden ploughs and muddy roads.[55] Andrei Platonov, the most profound observer of the Russian countryside in the 1920s, captures this clash of peasant and revolutionary senses of time. No one better portrays the dissonance of world views represented by tradition, oral culture, and a peasant sense of wait-and-see, on one hand, with the ordered, recorded-in-our-files immediacy of the regime, on the other:

> The very last party, which had the very longest name, was behind the last door in the corridor. There sat only one somber man, while the rest had been excommunicated.
>
> 'What do you want!' he asked Zakhar Pavlovich.
>
> 'We want to join up together. How soon will the end of everything come?'
>
> 'Socialism, you mean?' The man didn't understand. 'In a year. Today we're only occupying the establishment.'
>
> 'Then write us down,' Zakhar Pavlovich rejoiced.
>
> The man gave each of them a packet of pamphlets and a sheet of paper half filled up with printing.
>
> 'Program, rules, resolutions, questionnaires,' he said. 'Fill them in and give two references for each of you.'
>
> Zakhar Pavlovich flinched at the presentiment of deception.
>
> 'It can't be done orally?'
>
> 'No. I can't sign you up in my memory, or the party will forget you.'
>
> 'But we'll show up.'
>
> 'Impossible. What'll I use to write out the membership cards? It's a clear business from the questionnaire, if the assembly confirms you.'
>
> Zakhar Pavlovich noticed that the man spoke clearly, sharply, and correctly, without the slightest trust. Probably this would be the smartest power, which would within the year either completely build the world, or else raise up such a fuss that even a child's heart would grow tired. 'You sign up to give it a try, Sash,' said Zakhar Pavlovich, 'and I'm going to wait a year.'

> 'We don't sign people up for trial periods,' the man refused. 'Either ours completely and forever, or else go knock on someone else's door.'[56]

Despite the fact that a sense of time was not shared, there *was* a shared desire for change. One side wanted the change immediately, at any price. The other wanted to negotiate, to experiment, but then to wait and check the results before proceeding. These differing experiences of time run beneath the surface of this book. There is a repeated clash between the justified hesitancy of peasants and the pressure for speed from the Centre. Throughout, 1926 is a turning point; the need and desire for speed on the part of the Centre intensified notably in 1926 and that increase is reflected in the tone and nature of central demands.

Power/*Vlast'*

Like the English word *power*, the loose Russian equivalent *vlast'* is an elusive word used in many contexts with many meanings. The Moscow-centred power referred to itself as *Vlast'*. The police and the courts were to defend *Sovetskaia vlast'*, or Soviet power. One could easily offend Soviet power. In fact, the only slander cases maintained in the Riazan archives were the ones against *Sovetskaia vlast'*, or against *vlast'* in general. These were cases against representatives of Soviet power at the lower levels – officials of the district executive committee, rural soviet chairman, the local police constable, or the people's court judge. For example, in January 1928, Vasilii Andreevich Pronskii of the village of Semkino in Riazan Uezd, was charged under Article 76 for slandering the members of the district executive committee. It seems that the executive committee was continually notifying his household that it had not paid its taxes. Pronskii arrived at the district office with a form from his own rural soviet, certifying that his father had indeed paid his taxes. The frustrated Pronskii told those present in the office, 'It is not my fault that here sit a bunch of fools' (*Ia ne vinovat, chto zdes' vse duraki sidiat*). When asked why he had slandered representatives of Soviet power, he claimed, in his own defence, that the comment was not directed at anyone specifically.[57]

The governance that existed in Riazan – and it did exist – was not the kind of power that Moscow envisioned. It was a local power, adapted to local conditions, that mediated between the villages and the Centre in a manner largely unacceptable to those who saw themselves as the knights of the modern. The ethnographer A.M. Bol'shakov realized the importance of defining the word *vlast'* as peasants used it. He wrote, 'It is necessary to say that under the term *vlast'* for the peasant comes all those in the district who have some kind of state position [*dolzhnost'*]: the members of the district executive committee, the executive committee clerks, the forest wardens, the doctor, etc. – one word covers all of the Soviet civil servants [*sluzhashchii*] in the district.'[58]

But peasants also referred to central power as *vlast'*. M.Ia. Fenomenov, a rival ethnographer, articulated the peasant view of central power: 'We are not averse to *vlast'*. We need *vlast'* ... Let *vlast'* organize who it wants, when it wants, just as long as it does not threaten, too much, the material interests of the peasant.'[59] Thus, I have elected to leave *vlast'* untranslated, in the hope that in context it will be closest to its original meaning.

The epigraph that begins this introduction was Bol'shakov's warning to his readers that the barricades may have come down, but the Revolution was not won. It is no accident that Bol'shakov followed his warning with a tale of how the chairman of a district executive committee 'steals land' from Soviet power and gives it to the peasants. He engineered this theft of state property by simply recording in his survey of the village that local villagers had less land under cultivation than was actually the case. Since peasants were taxed on the basis of the amount of land under the plough, the local leader effectively distributed a tax break to his constituency. The chairman then 'collects a fee for his good service in the form of moonshine and three eggs per household. He promises the peasants that they will therefore be taxed less; as a result, he collects a tax for himself.'[60] This district official understood local conditions and the economic situation in the villages under his jurisdiction. He judged that three eggs and some home brew were a manageable price to pay for a significant tax break in the near future. Villagers were accustomed to these kinds of arrangements; they were a part of everyday life. In the eyes of an insecure, modernizing regime, however, such negotiations were increasingly viewed as corruption and, once labelled as such, were criminalized and punished. A local leader who understood precisely how much his community could bear in tax pressures should not have the power to alter central demands on taxation.

Face to the Village focuses on the complexities of political life in the Russian countryside. It considers how power was exercised locally, how it was perceived from above, negotiated, contested, and subverted. One can still speak of the policies of the Centre, of its intentions toward the localities, its reinterpretation, and its alteration, but as one gets closer and closer to the village, the organs and representatives of the 'Centre' or 'state' become more and more muddled and overlapping and are inevitably drawn into the dynamics of village politics. In the same way, the identity of local inhabitants becomes more complex as they interact with and/or are asked to become representatives of the state. Thus our understandings of fundamental concepts such as 'state' and 'peasantry' are further refined; both become complex, multilayered, and entangled.[61]

By moving closer to the village, one can get a sense of how the local structures of power really worked. The picture that emerges is complex and sometimes contradictory, as patterns of power varied from village to village. However, some revealing patterns can be traced. Corrupt and abusive local officials did exist, but what frightened the regime just as much, and increasingly, as collectivization approached, were those local officials who *belonged* to part of an established, relatively independent, and often *functioning* village system of government. What contemporary observers were seeing was that state organs in the countryside, like the rural soviets, were quickly incorporated into local rule. This local rule may well have been dominated by the wealthier and more powerful peasants; sometimes local power did put a wager on the strong and did not protect the interests of the poor – a perfectly rational decision in the world of village economics. That such a power structure may have indeed existed does not translate into Marxist class struggle; or justify the development and application of the term *kulak* (the term that allegedly designated a wealthy peasant, but ultimately became the label for any peasant who opposed collectivization) and its punitive consequences; or legitimize the decision to collectivize, although it does help us understand why the decision was taken. The 'village nature' of individuals who were supposed to represent the state, such as police officers, judges, rural soviet members, and forest wardens, became increasingly alarming to the Centre through the decade that followed the Civil War. By tracing and explicating this sense of alarm, we gain a better understanding of both the Centre and the localities, as well as the urgency and violence that characterized the collectivization campaign, which began in earnest in the fall of 1929.

Organization

A number of questions animate the chapters of this book: How did Moscow deal with its ethnically Russian near-periphery? How did the Centre attempt to deal with all levels of that periphery from provincial to village structures, all of which, of course, had intricate lives of their own?

In turn, how did villagers deal with power at the village and the district level, right up to Moscow, both as its representatives and as its subjects? How did the shortage of resources determine behaviours in the countryside and shape reactions of the state? What can definitions of crime and deviance tell us about the Centre and the countryside? The patterns that emerge in these pages could be found in any aspect of Soviet state, society, and culture in the 1920s. I have chosen areas in which the patterns emerged most clearly to me and most directly touched peasant lives. Criminality was a fruitful area of inquiry precisely because Bolshevik anxiety often revealed itself in a fear of particular types of deviance like hooliganism or banditry.

Part one of *Face to the Village* is the setting for the actions of parts two and three. Chapter 1 is a background chapter that provides an overview of the 1920s and of the agricultural history of Riazan from 1861 to 1930. As institutional history is underdeveloped in the Soviet field, some groundwork needed to be done on at least some of the multitude of institutions that touched peasants' lives and sometimes recorded their voices. The chapters on the rural soviets, courts, and police are designed to provide the reader with a strong sense of the way the organizations that peasants dealt with regularly looked, operated, and could be experienced by Riazan's rural inhabitants in the 1920s.

I chose these three structures as 'points of contact' between peasant and state because they are the most important points of contact. 'Points of contact,' for the purposes of this study, are these three key spaces in which peasant and state met and became hopelessly entangled in the 1920s. In the multitude of sources that I consulted, the spaces and issues that shape this book were the ones that appeared most often. The struggle with backwardness – another prevalent theme in these pages – may lead a reader to wonder why the focus is not on reading huts or party cells. Throughout my research on the 1920s, I did not find that these organizations played a significant role in the countryside yet. They were symbols or indicators of the regime's desire to 'enlighten' its benighted peasant majority.[62] The Bolshevik Centre devoted far more emphasis and worry to state structures of control such as the police, the courts, and the rural soviets, and for that reason they are the focus of part one. The issues that themselves were played out in these spaces such as the dominant 'crimes' of the 1920s – like tax evasion and wood theft – or the dominant crime fears of the era – hooliganism, banditry, arson, and rebellion – thus became the foci of parts two and three of the book. This book is as concerned with the Centre's hopes, dreams, and anxieties in the period between the Civil War and collectivization as it is with peasant concerns and experiences of the period. The categories I have chosen are the most clear arenas to explore these divergent concerns, anxieties, hopes, and dreams.

In part two, the individual stories of the villagers come to the fore. The narrative of each chapter echoes the escalating tension of the 1920s in the countryside that culminates in the chaotic violence of collectivization. Chapter 5 deals with the development of the taxation system over time and its overlap with other means of extracting resources from the countryside, such as grain requisitioning and state bonds. Chapter 6 looks at the battle for resources through the struggle for control of the forests of Riazan. This chapter highlights once again the precarious position of those individuals regarded as supposed enforcers by the state, yet who remained deeply embedded in peasant life and culture by virtue of their background and often by their living arrangements.

Part three focuses on what violent crime and what state and peasant *perceptions* of violent crimes reveal about both sides in the 1920s. It is here in 'a struggle for souls' that the Centre's sense of its civilizing mission appears most clearly. The focus on crime is inspired, in part, by the ways in which historians have used criminality to access and explore society and culture. Geoffrey Pearson nicely articulates the contribution that an understanding of criminality brings to the study of societies: 'Every ideological tradition employs the existence of crime in a figurative or metaphorical sense to indict some aspect of the social order and to champion its own social causes.'[63] The modernizing Centre responded increasingly through the 1920s to local complications – often perceived of and then defined as crime and deviance – with simplifications. Moscow had to root out non-standard complexities in order to establish a firmer hold on the country.[64] Through a study of banditry, hooliganism, arson, and vigilante justice (*samosud*), I trace changing perceptions of the countryside at the central level, while simultaneously attempting to convey elements of everyday village life in Riazan in the 1920s. The Centre expressed an increasing fear of the backwardness, violence, and darkness of the countryside, as well as an escalating fear about the nature of its own administration at the lowest levels. It was one matter for Bolshevik visionaries to travel to Central Asia or to the borderlands and see 'backwardness,' and quite another to step outside their front door and find the darkness in their own heartland.[65]

Face to the Village ends with one of the darkest pages of Riazan's history, the Pitelino rebellion of early 1930. The final chapter provides an anatomy of the event, showing how the regime's fear fed on itself and played itself out at a fever pitch in the carnival of violence that was collectivization. The chapter is built of layers of narrative, beginning with the communications from the ground about the unrest, moving to a memoir of the 1950s by a party worker who participated in the events, to the fiction of Boris Mozhaev, who was a child in the villages at the time of the rebellion, and finally ending with present-day survivors. I conclude with the memories of those who lived through the rebellion – fragmented, troubled, and proud.

On Sources

Better, he said, to write a circular ordering the citizens to guard the old world without distinction, to keep their rubbish in case the revolution might perhaps have need of it, although it wouldn't be needed anyway, since the new world would be built of eternal materials which would never enter into a discardable condition.

Andrei Platonov, *Chevengur*[66]

James Scott once mentioned that his favourite footnote listed the contents of a tinker's sack.[67] The comment stayed with me. The historical works that most fascinated me as a student were the micro-histories of Natalie Davis, Carlo Ginsburg, or Leroy Ladurie, to name but a few.[68] They captured another world. I wanted my own students to have a much firmer grasp of rural Russia in the 1920s than was currently available to them. I wanted them to understand that central Russia's inhabitants did not own vast fields well stocked with cattle. I ask questions here about where the inhabitants of Riazan had to go to deal with the world in which they found themselves. What did the inside of rural soviets, police 'stations,' courts, or local prisons look like? These places with their particular smells and bitter winter cold were also constituent components of life in the village.[69] They were all part of how local life, politics, and power were experienced. I wanted to know what Riazan peasants had in their pockets. I found they had much-valued 'horse tickets.' Deciphering what the tickets meant, how they were obtained, and how they were lost revealed a great deal about local life in the 1920s.

This book is based on a decade of work in the central archives and libraries of Moscow and the provincial archives of Riazan. It was also inspired by a great deal of time spent living among and speaking with the inhabitants of that province. A range of scholars and concepts have motivated the themes, arguments, and interpretations of my study. Anthropologists' emphasis on ethnographic detail fuelled my desires to know the contents of the tinker's sack and inspired me to look for a 'multiplicity of complex conceptual structures, many of them superimposed upon or knotted into one another.'[70] And my acceptance of what were to me obvious and useful connections between anthropology and history were encouraged by a recent review article in which Douglas Rogers appeals for historians of Russia and the Soviet Union to embrace a multidisciplinary approach to historical study that is open to multiple methodologies and research questions but not slave to any one approach.[71]

'Combined underdevelopment,' to borrow a term from Laura Engelstein's play on Trotsky's notion of 'combined development,'[72] was the literal and ideological context of the 1920s. Engelstein argues that Russia is best understood as a 'superimposition of the three models of power chronologically separated (however imperfectly) in Foucault's scheme: the so-called juridical monarchy, the *Polizeistaat,* and the modern disciplinary regime.'[73] It was precisely this Russia, which had elements of all three models, that the Bolsheviks inherited. To this already complex circumstance, the Bolsheviks brought their own obsessions about revolution, loyalty, purity, capitalism, and culture.

Each type of source has its own unique advantages and disadvantages. Any student of a largely illiterate group must face the fact that sources are often refracted through the lens of a literate elite, state structures, and offices of the state.[74] In 'Reflections on the History of European State-Making,' Charles Tilly discusses the kinds of sources used for such a study. They range from direct reports to 'routine by-products of organizational work' and material that records interaction between state representatives and the population. The historian must cross-check the same occurrences from different angles and sources.[75] I employ these and many other types of documents and cross-check or triangulate them throughout this study of the Riazan countryside in the 1920s. I treated all of my sources as texts that needed to be interpreted in the context of their production – a methodological approach that Peter Sahlins describes in an interview with *Ab Imperio* as typical of 'most practicing historians' who 'still work in archives and now understand that they are working with texts in an important, literary sense, and that all of the aporia and explicit meanings of a text need to be studied as part of the way of making these texts speak to a particular intellectual problem that's being posed.'[76]

The sources used in this book include OGPU (*Ob"edinennoe gosudarstvennoe politicheskoe upravlenie* / Unified State Political Administration /

State Security) reports on the provincial and central level; documents of Narkomfin (*Narodnyi komissariat finansov* / People's Commissariat of Finance); documents of Narkomiust (*Narodnyi komissariat iustitsii* / People's Commissariat of Justice) at the Centre and in Riazan; party documents in Moscow and Riazan;[77] cases from the local courts and the provincial courts of Riazan; peasant letters, petitions, and complaints; reports of local officials; ethnographic work done on the peasants of the 1920s, statistical studies, congresses, and conferences; materials of the village correspondents; journals of the 1920s; and central and local newspapers. And the 'face to the countryside' campaign guaranteed a mountain of paper within each area. Each type of source presented its own challenges and rewards.

Legal cases were excellent sources, despite some shortcomings. Russian legal cases at the lower levels in the 1920s do not include verbatim transcripts of trials. This fact, however, does not render the sources unusable. Each case is preserved as a separate file. If the case is of a serious criminal nature and requires investigation, then the file includes the investigator's notes from his visits to the village and a summary of the case and sentencing written by the judge. In large-scale, sensational cases, especially in the Provincial Court, these notes and summaries could be detailed and spectacular. The problem here, however, is that I had wanted to focus less on the spectacular and more on the mundane. I wanted to hear how widows who distilled moonshine or homebrew (*samogon*) pleaded their case; how those who stole wood in the winter explained their actions. Unfortunately, these cases often took on the form of a mass gathering of the accused and individual fining, with little record of what was said in the courtroom. Still, I supplemented the legal cases with peasant letters, petitions, complaints, the reports of local officials, ethnographic studies, the rich journal literature of the 1920s, and central and regional newspapers. These sources in conjunction with the legal cases gave me a consistent sense of the issues that were most important both to the peasantry and to the regime through the 1920s.

Peasant letters, petitions, and complaints enable the researcher to hear the peasant voice, but they, too, present serious challenges for the historian. Sometimes the letters are written by a literate intermediary on behalf of an illiterate peasant. The letter-writers have a self-serving goal to present their case in a certain light for maximum state response to an individual's particular plea. In this respect, they fit into a long tradition of letter-writing as a form of appeal and may appear somewhat formulaic. There is a positive side to this formulaic quality; the letters are interesting as a genre. They reveal the degree to which peasants quickly mastered the vocabulary of the regime and they capture peasant interpretations of the ideology of the new Bolshevik state. Beyond being a mirror of discourse, these sources are a useful indication of real peasant concerns. Certain issues – taxes, wood, local government, crime – are raised repeatedly in letters, petitions, and complaints, and these repeated concerns have helped to determine the points of contact and the issues that shape this study's structure.[78] There was no shortage of letters from the countryside in the 1920s. Peasants flooded local and central offices with letters of complaint or explanations and with letters asking for information and advice. Letters were often written on tiny scraps of paper with pencil stubs. Once deciphered, they provide a colourful and diverse portrait of the Russian countryside.[79]

The popularity of secret police reports (*svodki*) has caused them to be objects of scrutiny, criticism, and attack as a source for the study of Soviet history.[80] Ehren Park and David Brandenberger decry the svodki as 'essentially written by policemen for policemen and therefore reflect little of the scholarly rigor that contemporary sociologists bring to a more systematic study of society.'[81] They cite Terry Martin's warnings about svodki at length, arguing that OGPU agents reporting on the countryside worked within the narrow frameworks of categories such as poor, middle, and wealthy peasants. They report 'unease and dissatisfaction within peasant communities with explicitly disloyal sentiments,' such as banditry or kulak sympathies, instead of more 'politically neutral motives' like 'the defense of community and tradition.'[82] While I agree that the svodki have their limitations, like any other source, and that they have to be used cautiously, that does not mean that the historian has to accept the *analysis* of the OGPU. In fact, repeatedly, the secret police reports can be used, and are used here, precisely to illustrate village culture, power, and motives.

Svodki, and local svodki in particular, are useful and rewarding sources. The Centre did not control the village, and it felt a strong need to do so. The material that came back to the Centre, and the way in which it was collected, presented, and read by Soviet bureaucrats dreaming of a modern, industrial state, created an intense portrait of local autonomy, criminality, corruption, chaos, and a dangerous mix of old and new. One has to think only of the way in which the security-police reports sent to key officials such as Molotov, Stalin, and Kosior were created. From what I have been able to piece together – based on reading reports from various levels – each provincial OGPU department received, from all of the uezds in the province, reports compiled from district reports. The district reports were very detailed. They included reports of rumours, recorded local prices for products as well as conversations about Trotsky, and reported the challenges of local sanitation. The local reports monitored agricultural conditions, described pests that threatened crops, and placed the behaviour of state officials in the context of local shortages and conditions. The most sensational elements from these reports were excerpted at the uezd level and sent on to the next level. At the provincial level, the most sensational reports from all of the uezds were sent on to the central office in Moscow. Here, the most sensational reports of outrageous behaviour and corruption from every province were collated and summarized to be sent on to high-ranking party officials. The central reports paint an unrelenting picture of rape, murder, banditry, arson, mayhem, and corruption by Soviet officials in every corner of the empire.

The secret police reports that I read in Riazan changed dramatically in 1926. Up to that year, the reports are much more like journals of observations on the countryside by the reporters, and they reflect the diverse and broad jurisdiction and the general concerns of policing. After 1926, however, the reports become much more standardized in their organization, language, and tone. The Centre sent instructions to the provincial level on particular themes that should be covered in local reports, among them banditry and the situation of the lower administration. This change suggests that a bureaucratic standardization was taking hold in the NKVD as it defined, established, and entrenched its power. The reports are as fascinating a source of information about the regime as they are about the peasantry. They carefully and compulsively record popular mood and rumour. Sarah Davies's work captures the reports' obsession with listening in on what was said by those beyond the Kremlin walls – in bread lines, on the shop floor, or at the cooperative.[83] The village, being the most remote of locales, was the most suspect of all. The kind of information collected in the provincial reports about the countryside tells us much about the regime's concerns at the local level.

The svodki that we find in the Russian State Archive of Socio-Political History (*Rossiiskii gosudarstvennyi arkhiv sotsial'no-politicheskoi istorii, RGASPI*) were compiled from reports sent in from all over the Soviet Union. There is a startling contrast between the documents of the Centre and those of the province; the central documents are much more sensational and spectacular. They concentrate on violence, corruption, and atrocity. It is fascinating to consider how and to what degree these reports, and their skewed portrait of the countryside, may have shaped central policy, as only the most alarming impression of the countryside entered the halls of power.

I also employed ethnographic studies and literature of the 1920s. Among these authors one finds some of the period's most talented and astute observers. From the ethnographic studies on the 1920s, the works of A.M. Bol'shakov and M.Ia. Fenomenov stand out. The two ethnographers conducted micro-studies in Tver and Novgorod and the surrounding area, respectively.[84] For the fiction of the 1920s, I turned most often to the work of Andrei Platonov. I found his pained observations often poignantly captured what was being repeated in the archival and ethnographic sources. Of course, in using the ethnographic studies and the fictional literature of the 1920s, one runs into the standard challenges of using elite sources to study the peasantry. Once again, such a challenge does not render the sources unusable. A careful, self-conscious reading draws much from these thoughtful, contemporary witnesses. In my final chapter, which explores the anatomy of a peasant rebellion in the eastern district of Pitelino, I draw on Boris Mozhaev's early glasnost novel, *Muzhiki i baby*. Mozhaev was a child witness to the violence in the region and the novel is the sense that he makes of it. His fiction is a vital and complex contribution to the layers of narrative at play in the chapter.

I have always been uneasy about the way statistical studies are embraced by certain scholars as a clean, unbiased type of source. A story told by Bol'shakov is a humbling reminder of their limitations:

> It is true that in the Centre there is the most varied statistical material. To what degree are these materials exact? In the Centre there are more than a few diagrams that are intended to draw the contemporary economy of the countryside, and, by the way, in various district executive committees of Tver Province (it is necessary to mention that it is not the only example), I heard the following:
>
> 'The Centre has already demanded much information from us. Questionnaire [*anketa*] after questionnaire. First these numbers and then others.'
>
> 'And you give them to them. If the state begins to build its politics on numbers, it will be the most truthful politics.'
>
> 'Forgive me, the district executive committee is overworked. Some information is not hard to give, so we give it. Other kinds of numbers it is necessary to collect and to collect knowledgeably, and we have no staff to spare.'
>
> 'Well you should seek them out.'

> 'It is impossible! And the deadline is established and there are threats of strict punishment. If you do not fill out the forms, then you end up in court for sabotage. In addition the inspector himself says, "If the numbers are not at your fingertips, make something up, off the ceiling [*s potolka*]."'
>
> 'What do you mean, "Make something up"?'
>
> 'It's very simple: Look at the ceiling, think a bit, and put down a number ...'
>
> 'That's no good.'
>
> 'We ourselves know it's not okay. Let them send to the district some kind of special statistician; he can collect information here – then it will be fine.'
>
> And so when I look at those beautiful diagrams, I remember this dialogue. I think, Who knows how much of this information is real and how much was taken 'from the ceiling'?[85]

In fact, a report on the results of the investigation of the rural soviets of Pitelino, conducted between 21 December 1929 and 12 February 1930, lodged the same complaint in the same terms. Apparently, many rural soviets and land societies had not sent back the requested reports on preparations for the upcoming spring sowing campaign, and those rural soviets who had sent reports were making up their numbers altogether 'off the ceiling.'[86] Still, statistics are used throughout this study, less for their precision than for the impression that they can supply the researcher and the reader on a particular matter. Statistics were kept on all manner of life in the 1920s, and they can be used in the careful triangulation of sources to provide additional information on administrative structures, the social composition of the state structure, the epidemic nature of wood theft, motivations for arson, a glimpse of local economic life, and as a window onto the kind of numbers upon which policy in turn was based.

Contemporary journals and newspapers fill out the details of the wider provincial and national context of the issues at hand and enrich the other sources employed in the study. In them, one repeatedly finds the concerns and hopes of the regime and of the times, especially in regard to the peasantry, and the need for order and enlightenment in the dark countryside. To a significant degree, I did let the sources determine my categories. I wanted to know what ethnographers, journalists, those who worked in the legal system, the police, and the state administration thought were the key criminal issues of the day. In turn, I determined what peasants considered the key issues of the 1920s. And if peasant and state concerns overlapped, as they often did, I tried to determine how each side viewed the particular matter. The combined sources reveal not only the points of contact between state and peasantry, but also the major points of conflict. They unveil the mid-1920s as a period of negotiation and illuminate the conditions in which the Bolshevik regime attempted to begin building socialism and all of the very tangible obstacles that particular utopian dream confronted.

The book ends with one of the most fascinating, and perhaps controversial, sources of all – the words of those who lived through and remember the events that played out in the fateful years in the Riazan countryside.

PART ONE

The Battle for Space: What Physical and Virtual Space Reveal about the Countryside

Chapter One

The Setting

'Orphan! Simpleton! Riazan pauper!'

Villain in *Accordion*

This chapter is a historical overview of the broad political and economic context surrounding agriculture and the Russian countryside in the years between the Civil War and collectivization. It is vital to have this historical framework in mind in order to fully grasp the significance of chronological developments as they are developed in the chapters that follow. The agricultural background of Riazan is aimed at the reader who wants to know more about the regional geography of the province, crops, markets, land, and livestock. It could be skipped over by the reader whose concerns lie elsewhere.

Moscow and the 1920s

Obviously the decisions reached in Moscow had a profound effect on the entire Soviet Union; in turn, events in the periphery shaped decisions made by the Centre. What occurred in Riazan took place in the context of the Russian Revolution and the formation of the Soviet Union. When the Bolsheviks lost the elections to the Constituent Assembly in 1918 and decided to evict the victors and lock the doors, the fledgling regime made the decision to defend its hold on power. What followed was a protracted and violent civil war that intensified an already profound mistrust of the territory the Bolsheviks had decided to make their own. This mistrust, more than anything else, coloured the way the Bolsheviks monitored and ultimately chose to rule the Soviet Union. The Civil War was indeed a 'formative experience.'[1] The bitter experiences of peasant resistance during and after the Civil War – as well as the experiences of the 'green' or peasant revolutions of the Civil War – convinced the state that peasant loyalty was suspect. The tenuous hold on power affected the way the Bolsheviks collected and processed information. There were extensive networks within each commissariat, the security services, the Party, and the Workers' and Peasants' Inspectorate (*Rabkrin*) that collected information about interactions with the village and their reports multiplied through the 1920s. This information was filtered on its way to the top, with the most sensational information remaining in the reports that reached the Centre and its leading Bolshevik decision makers.

The New Economic Policy (NEP) was introduced at the Tenth Party Congress in 1921, and it illustrated the regime's willingness to compromise ideologically in return for a continued hold on power. The policy was a 'retreat' from the harsh policies of grain requisitioning and violent attacks on the 'enemies' of the revolution that had characterized the years of civil war. Still, the Bolsheviks knew only too well that to be in power meant the governing and administering of a vast territory. Government and administration necessitated the construction of a state. A state required resources. The most crucial dilemma faced by the Bolsheviks rested in the need to construct a state, and the need to extract resources from the population through the standard methods of a state. Those methods returned more and more to violence and coercion by the end of the decade. And the NEP immediately faced challenges from all sides. Unemployment was high. The 'scissors crisis' hit in the summer and fall of 1923; the prices paid for grain were low and the prices demanded for manufactured goods were high. Peasants 'withdrew' from the market; Moscow responded by lowering the price of manufactured goods, reflecting, in part, an early soft line on the peasantry in the name of a peaceful link between town and country and concessions to market forces. The desire to heal the wounds of the Civil War was reflected in the policy decisions, legal recommendations and reforms, and the rhetoric of the early NEP regarding the village. In the debates surrounding the early economic crises of the NEP, Grigory Zinoviev called for a 'face to the countryside,' emphasizing the need to understand this largely unknown territory.

Still, in 1925, Nikolai Bukharin was confident enough in the generosity of the NEP to advise the peasantry of the country to 'enrich yourselves.' Lev Trotsky and Evgeny Preobrazhensky, among others soon to be labelled the 'Left Opposition,' argued that the peasantry, as the country's principle and most accessible resource, needed to be 'squeezed' so that more money could be diverted to the development of heavy industry. Initially, in 1925, Stalin sided with the Bukharin line, although he made sure to distance himself from any calls to 'enrich yourself' as misguided and un-Bolshevik. Harvests were good. The recovery of the economy to pre-war levels meant that the regime had to once again make a vital decision. Raising industrial production significantly would require substantial investment and a new economic line. The choices, broadly, were to continue working with the market or to place the development emphasis on heavy industry. The former path would mean encouraging peasants to enter the market even more and improving light industry to increase consumer goods. An emphasis on heavy industry would require marshalling all resources quickly. The path toward heavy industry began to take shape in resolutions of the Fourteenth Party Congress of December 1925. The emerging line called for 'socialism in one country,' which would require the victory of 'socialist economic forms,' rapid industrialization, and economic independence from the vagaries of the world market.[2] By the Fifteenth Party Conference, the Left Opposition was viciously attacked even though the attitudes of the conference suggested a shift toward the economic policies of the Left and industrialization. The pressure for the rapid transition to the socialist, industrialized future began to build. Peasants and peasant culture, perceived as traditional and backward, were seen as a powerful brake on such a future. As Anatolii Lunacharskii observed in 1926, there was a marked trend afoot of 'giving up on the peasant.'[3]

Through 1927, the NEP and the Bolshevik regime faced a multitude of crises. In order for revenue to be raised for industrial development, peasants needed to be persuaded, one way or another, to give up their grain. A shortage of goods for purchase meant peasants were becoming more reluctant to market their grain by 1927. Harvests were poor and peasants sold less to state agencies. In April, Chinese communists were slaughtered in Shanghai. In May, the British broke off relations with the Soviet regime, setting off rumours of imminent war. This war scare, as it is known in the historiography, led peasants to be even more cautious about parting with their harvest. Within the party itself, the idea of socialism in one country became more appealing in the face of the rapidly fading dream of international revolution. The language of the debates was saturated with concerns about the purity of revolutionary faith.[4] Blame for Soviet society's ills was increasingly assigned to groups, and then to individuals, and was increasingly pushed down the ranks of

Soviet society and officialdom where it was manifested in the violence of collectivization, only to percolate back up again in the purge violence of 1937 and 1938.

The Fifteenth Party Congress in December 1927 announced that the First Five-Year Plan would be built on the foundations of rapid industrialization and the collectivization of the peasantry. In January 1928, the Central Committee informed local party and state bodies that 'grain procurements ... represent the fortress that we must capture at any cost. And we will certainly capture it if we do the job in a bolshevik style, with bolshevik pressure.'[5] In these instructions, all of the sources that supposedly obstructed grain collection were identified: kulak speculators; middle peasants who considered holding back grain until prices got higher; and all of the lower officials who were too soft on them. The pressure to act was intensified by a 'grain procurement crisis.' With the terms of trade turning against them, peasants marketed less grain and instead sold other crops and more meat, for which prices were better. Bukharin advocated raising prices; Stalin personally led a delegation of officials and a police task force to the Urals and West Siberia where the grain harvest had been good. Markets were shut down and peasants were ordered to deliver grain or face punishment. Local officials were instructed to use Article 107 (on speculation) against the peasantry. If a peasant was caught with stored grain, he would be accused of speculation and punished accordingly. These tactics became known as the Urals-Siberian method and would be implemented nationwide by the fall of 1929. The compromises of the NEP were no more.

Through 1928, Stalin and his supporters moved further and further to the Left, and Bukharin came to occupy the position of a Right Oppositionist, as he called, in vain, for a return to less coercive action against the peasantry. Through 1928, and into 1929, peasants continued to try to negotiate in the old spirit of compromise – they made excuses based on local conditions as to why they could not meet grain quotas, they tried to play the market – but they were repeatedly rebuffed and thwarted in their attempts, in increasingly violent and punitive ways. The November Central Committee Plenum in 1929 made the decision to push for the 'wholesale' collectivization of the entire country. In December, Stalin called for the 'elimination of the kulaks as a class.' These central-level policies aimed to drag the rural inhabitants of the Soviet Union into the modern age.[6]

The Province

What follows is a historic overview of the province of Riazan that provides the setting – peasant work, diet, homes, markets, and landscape – in which the action of the remaining chapters takes place. The chapter traces the history of agriculture in Riazan from the Emancipation of 1861 to the collectivization of its countryside that began in 1929. It surveys the patterns of peasant unrest from the Emancipation through to the Revolution, and establishes the physical, geographic locale of Riazan itself.

Riazan is located in the heart of European Russia. In 1927 the province was 293 kilometres from north to south and 256 kilometres from east to west.[7] The province is cut in half by the Oka River and shares features of two of the four broad agricultural zones of European Russia: the Central Industrial Region, which was largely deficient in grain, and the Central Black Earth, largely grain producing. The fact that the northern districts in Riazan have much in common with the provinces of the Central Industrial Region, and the southern districts with the provinces of the Central Black Earth, makes Riazan an excellent choice for a regional study. Even if Riazan is considered part of the Central Industrial Region, it was the most agricultural of the provinces in the region.[8] Peasants made up more than 86 per cent of the population – some 1,847,535 up to the outbreak of the First World War.[9]

Emancipation to 1905

At the end of the eighteenth century, 45.9 per cent of all the province's land was under cultivation. By 1861, the cultivated area had grown to 56.4 per cent of all land, which placed Riazan Province sixth in European Russia for total land under cultivation. This growth was due largely to the ploughing of hayfields and pasture and to the clearing of forests. In the first half of the nineteenth century, 470,000 desiatinas[10] of forest were cleared. At the beginning and in the middle of the nineteenth century, rye, oats, and buckwheat made up about 90 per cent of all cultivation. The predominance of these particular crops remained right through to the eve of collectivization and well beyond. Rye occupied almost all winter fields, and the spring sowing was dominated first by oat and then by buckwheat cultivation. Wheat was planted mainly on the landlords' land rather than on peasant plots and largely in the southern parts of the province. The systematic cultivation of potatoes in Riazan began in the 1840s and developed slowly, representing only about 6 per cent of cultivation.

The use of advanced agricultural technology remained low through the nineteenth century and, in fact, beyond the Revolution, and the wooden plough (*sokha*) was everywhere present. The use of the more sophisticated plough (*plug*) was limited to only a few areas in the southernmost part of the province. Almost all harrows (*borony*) used on peasant land were wooden. The number of horses belonging to peasants grew in the nineteenth century, and by the middle of the century there were 35.1 horses per 100 people. The number of large livestock (*krupnye skoty*) per 100 inhabitants was only 21.4 by the middle of the century.[11] Riazan was a relatively impoverished province on the eve of the Great Reforms and right through to the years of collectivization. Mechanization and technological advancement in agriculture were minimal, crop diversification was in its early stages, and peasant households were largely subsistence oriented, dependent on horses and other large livestock, if they were lucky enough to own them, to work their land. Still, despite its reputation for poverty, Riazan compared favourably on the ownership of horses to neighbouring provinces such as Vladimir and Tver.[12]

The high numbers of serfs and landlords in Riazan before the Emancipation testifies to strong ties to agriculture and to the entrenchment of serf agriculture in the province. Riazan peasants struggled with this legacy up to the 1917 Revolution and through the Soviet period. On the eve of the Emancipation from serfdom in 1861, Riazan Province ranked third in European Russia for the number of landlords (in 1859 there were 5,595 with 5,046 estates), and fourth for number of serfs (395,180 in 1859). The patterns of serf labour reflected the north-south split so characteristic of Riazan. The province was an intermediate zone between the Northern Industrial Region, dominated by monetary payments (*obrok*) to the lords, and the Southern Agricultural Region, dominated by forced labour obligations (*barshchina*).[13]

The effects of the Emancipation settlement on the Riazan countryside were not unusual. Peasants were plagued by high redemption payments and the resulting indebtedness, land cut-offs (*otrezki*), land hunger, reduced or limited access to meadows and forests, and shortages of both livestock and machinery to work the land. According to local specialists, land shortages that plagued the southern part of the province were worse than in provinces typically associated with land hunger such as Tambov, Kursk, Orel, and Voronezh.[14] In the pre-reform period there were six to eight souls per household with 13.8 desiatinas of land. By the 1880s, the average household had 6.7 souls and only 3 desiatinas of land. Rent per desiatina in the 1860s was on average one to three rubles. In the 1870s, it had climbed to twelve rubles.[15] Peasants lost a significant amount of the land they held before the Emancipation to land cut-offs, which had been carried out by the former landlords. There was enormous variation among the districts, reflecting regional variation across the province. The southern districts suffered from the highest percentages of cut-offs, which reached as high as 28.3 per cent in Sapozhok Uezd, as compared to the average of 16.8 per cent for the province as a whole.[16]

Riazan peasants, like peasants across European Russia, struggled with the redemption payments established in the Emancipation settlement. High rates of indebtedness were recorded, again especially in the south. For example, in 1877, in Ranenburg Uezd, only 9.6 per cent of peasants who had been estate serfs and only 2.1 per cent of former state peasants had succeeded in paying their redemption payments.[17] Of course, this fact may testify as much to peasant unwillingness and avoidance of the payments as to their actual poverty. Through the 1870s and 1880s, Riazan peasants continued to struggle with the upheaval and the hardships that the Emancipation settlement had brought with it. To add to these challenges, cholera outbreaks and the famine of 1891 hit the province hard; the average yearly production of all grains was 24.7 puds per person between 1861 and 1870. Between 1890 and 1900 this total had dropped to 14.9 puds per person.[18] Through the second half of the nineteenth century, Riazan was characterized by high rates of outmigration for seasonal or temporary labour (*otkhodnichestvo*),[19] which once again highlights the differences between the northern and the southern uezds.

In 1870, the Ministry of the Interior noted that within Riazan, in the southern, more fertile uezds, most peasants were engaged in agriculture full time. In the less fertile northern areas, however, most peasants had to supplement their income through some kind of non-agricultural task. Outmigration was regarded largely as a supplement to agricultural earnings and was much more common in the northern uezds of the province, which were known for textiles, lace work, the production of fishing nets, and woodworking.[20] One of the effects of such a high rate of outmigration in the north, especially in Kasimov, Zaraisk, and Pronsk, was that women were often 'solely responsible for agricultural work.'[21] This fact may help to explain, in part, the key role played by women in the struggle against collectivization. The final chapter of this book focuses in detail on a peasant rebellion in Pitelino, where women played a significant role in protest and in preserving the memory of the events to the present day.

1905 to 1917

The tumultuous years of 1905–6 found some Riazan peasants engaged in violent protest against the state. On 19 April 1905, a land captain (*zemskii nachal'nik*) in Riazhsk Uezd commented that as a result of a large number of factory closings, many peasants were returning to their villages, bringing with them rumours of the seizure of the land of the manors and the coming of a universal land redistribution (*vseobshii peredel*).[22] Peasant protest in 1905 and 1906 had much in common with future peasant reactions to the state pressures of the Civil War and of collectivization. Peasants fought with the same weapons – rumours, illegal gatherings, marches under a flag or banner, proclamations, anonymous leaflets posted on telegraph poles and fences, petitions, arson, and uprisings.[23] In 1906 alone, there were 171 cases of arson on noble estates.[24] Peasants gathered in illegal communal meetings (*skhody*) and made specific demands to landlords regarding wages, rents, debts, or rights to forests and meadows. In some villages there were open demonstrations.

The most radical uezds in terms of peasant protest were those located south of the Oka: Dankov, Pronsk, Ranenburg, Riazhsk, Sapozhok, and Skopin. These were the uezds dominated by forced-labour obligations before the Emancipation and had battled the most with landlords over the size of land parcels, cut-offs, access to meadows and forests, and indebtedness. Ranenburg, located on the Tambov border, was especially volatile;[25] the first large-scale uprising (*krupnoe vystuplenie*) of the Riazan peasantry occurred there on 12 May 1906. The unrest began in the villages of Bratovka and Solova and spread to the neighbouring villages through the month of May. In June, the unrest spread to Dankov, Mikhailov, Pronsk, and Sapozhok uezds.[26] Peasant unrest intensified in November and December, rising to 82 reported incidents in these months alone, many of them involving large groups of peasants.[27] The first few months of 1906 were relatively quiet, but from May to August there were 42 uprisings, and in November and December alone there were 41 cases of unrest. The largest conflagration occurred in 1906. The disturbances began on May 20 and by June had spread to ten villages in the southern uezds of Dankov, Ranenburg, Riazhsk, and Sapozhok. From there they spread to Mikhailov and Riazan uezds. The turmoil peaked in 1906 with 214 reported cases of unrest compared to 59 in 1907. The protest in 1907 involved fewer participants and fewer villages. Peasants returned to more traditional and omnipresent passive resistance, such as the illegal cutting of trees and arson.[28] Reports of peasant unrest continued to the eve of the Revolution.[29] Thus, it is clear that Riazan was no stranger to peasant unrest, and we see a pattern emerging of which areas of the province were the most volatile. Interestingly, the above pattern reoccurs during the Civil War and in criminality through the 1920s but not during collectivization. Peasant protest against collectivization was more fierce in the northern districts of the province. The northern districts, which were much more dependent on the raising of livestock, especially cattle, protested collectivization more than their southern counterparts. Thus during collectivization it was the northern districts (*raiony*) of Pitelino and Tuma that were the most vociferous and violent. The reasons for this difference are twofold. One factor was the behaviour of the collectivization brigades in Pitelino and Tuma and the other was the importance of dairy and cattle and women's relationships to them in the north and northeast.

The period from the famine of 1891 to the 1917 revolutions was characterized by the tension between old and new, between tradition and change. Ironically, it was the famine that brought the city to the Riazan countryside. The famine forced many more young people to seek work in urban centres. When they returned home, they brought with them symbols of urban life, such as lamps, samovars, and accordions.[30] But while some peasants embraced the new, the majority continued to live according to custom and tradition. As Corinne Gaudin explains, while the commune membership was being eroded numerically, it was also being strengthened along traditional lines by those who remained within it.[31]

The peasants of Riazan did not respond as enthusiastically as those of other provinces to the Stolypin reforms (1906–11), and land relations continued to be determined mainly within the commune (*obshchina*).[32] The First World War meant the loss of working hands as the result of mobilization; 48 per cent of Riazan's able-bodied men served in the army. The chaos of mobilization, the requisitioning of livestock, and the resulting decline in harvests took their toll.[33] During the turmoil of the Civil War, already strong, traditional communes once again came to control most of the land held by peasants in the province. By 1917, the population of Riazan had grown to 2,738,000 inhabitants. Two million of them were illiterate. Peasants accounted for almost 2.5 million of the province's inhabitants, making up 543,914 households, with an additional 2,609 independent households. Twenty-five per cent, or 133,367 peasant households, did not own working livestock and 74,153 households did not have even a cow.[34] The average holding per household was four desiatinas and, on average, 2.9 desiatinas were under cultivation at any given time.[35] By December 1917, the situation in the province regarding grain reserves was critical.[36]

1917–1920

On the eve of the October Revolution, Riazan was still battling with the legacy of serfdom and the Emancipation settlement, as well as the turmoil wrought by the First World War. The province was plagued by shortages of grain, working hands, and livestock, a low level of technological development, high rates of outmigration, and rural unrest. Amidst a grain crisis in the winter of 1917, Riazan faced the chaos of the Civil War and the consequences of the Bolshevik victory for the peasant land question. The returns for the Constituent Assembly elections for Riazan are known to be 'substantially incomplete,' meaning that results for one or more districts are missing. In his study of the elections, Oliver Radkey singles out Riazan villages as having experienced significant intimidation from Bolshevik soldiers.[37] More recently, historians working with the election data show 427,364 votes for the Socialist Revolutionary Party and 272,153 for the Bolsheviks.[38] In January 1918 Soviet congresses were broken up and Bolshevik deputies beaten. Bolshevik control within Riazan was precarious, and through 1918 Socialist Revolutionaries and Bolsheviks struggled for political power within local administrative structures.[39]

The land question was indeed recognized by the new Bolshevik regime as the fundamental question for the peasantry – indicated by the fact that they adopted the land program of the pro-peasant Socialist Revolutionary Party[40] in its entirety – and Riazan Province was no exception. Between 21 and 24 March 1918, the Riazan Provincial Land Congress discussed how best to implement the decree on land. It was decided that all land – noble and peasant separator (as the Stolypin peasants were known) alike – that was not previously subject to division would be divided according to local custom in any given area. For some uezds, such as Skopin, this was simply recognition of a process already under way. Land was to be divided according to the number of people in a household, as well as traditional district norms. The new divisions met opposition, especially in the southern provinces, from the nobility and from some peasants. Obviously, the nobility did not want to give up the land that they believed was theirs, and those peasants who had amassed some land and developed a relatively prosperous household were also reluctant to submit to the new divisions. The ecological differences between north and south characterized the nature of disputes. The northern uezds, where livestock was especially vital for peasant subsistence, were especially plagued by disputes over meadows. The southern uezds were marked by disputes over forests because they were in such short supply. After the Revolution, as much as 98 per cent of the cultivated land in Riazan was under peasant control.[41]

Detailed records on patterns of communal land tenure have survived for Ranenburg Uezd and provide a spectacular window onto the complexity of the local. The records attest that even within one uezd there were four variants of land redivision. In one variant, land was divided according to the number of eaters twelve years and older living in the household. In the second, land was simply divided equally by family without regard for the number of members. According to the third recorded variant, the local land commune would hold all land beyond a set number of desiatinas that everyone was allotted in a common fund. Households could then rent from the fund according to the amount of land they were capable of working. Finally, the fourth variant stated that each household was allotted at least five desiatinas, plus a garden (*usad'ba*) around their household, and then the remaining land was to be divided among the available hands. It was further stipulated that an allotment could be taken back for 'laziness of the householders' (*v lenosti khoziaev*).

Ranenburg, however, was an exception within Riazan Province in its approach to land redivision. Among the twelve uezd congresses held in the spring and summer of 1918, which determined how land was to be redistributed, ten voted for redivision by number of souls, and two (Ranenburg and Mikhailov) voted for redistribution according to the strength of the household in its capacity to work the land (*rabochaia sila*). The historian Iu.V. Fulin makes a curious point in connection with the congress decisions. He points out that in several official works, the Commissariat of Agriculture mistakenly related to Riazan as if the whole province voted to divide land according to the strength of each household.[42] This categorization is interesting because this kind of division would be regarded by the central powers as a much less equitable way of dividing land and as a method more likely to support and foster economic differentiation because it would favour households with superior inventory and many working hands. These households, in turn it was further assumed, would become more wealthy than their less fortunate neighbours and deserve even more land in the next division. A province that favoured this kind of division would be regarded as more likely to become socially and economically stratified and could be seen by the Centre as more capitalist oriented than socialist. This misconception about Riazan might have influenced the Centre's policy toward the region in later years.

There is no doubt that land redivision was fraught with problems. Even if all households were given equal allotments, a family with fewer members or a shortage of agricultural inventory could not produce as much as a household with more working members or more working livestock. The Ranenburg documents reflect this awareness. Inequalities were bound to arise. Throughout the 1920s land was in constant dispute between districts, between households, and among the land commissions themselves.[43] The process of land redistribution illustrates the complexity of the land question for the peasantry and the deep roots of rules and laws regarding land division in local custom. Local land organs, courts, and peasants battled through the Civil War and the 1920s to reach an acceptable way of settling the land question. Collectivization attempted to sweep much of these negotiations away and, to many rural inhabitants, appeared a blatant attempt by the state to wrest control of their land, their livestock, and their livelihood from them once again.

Despite the critical situation regarding grain reserves and other shortages in December 1917, 532,000 puds of grain were procured in Riazan and shipped to Petrograd, Moscow, and the Red Army. In addition, 135,582 puds of milk products of various kinds, 2,407 puds of meat, 29,064 head of large livestock, and 1,289,00 puds of vegetables were procured and exported from Riazan Province.[44] Riazan experienced its own civil war as Bolshevik forces struggled to establish themselves in the province. During the Civil War there was widespread opposition to Bolshevik procurement and conscription policies. Rumours spread that the Bolsheviks had already lost power in Petrograd and Moscow, and there was a steady surge of peasant unrest through 1918.[45]

In November 1918, an uprising against the mobilization of men and horses in Kasimov quickly spread across the province, spilling over into the neighbouring province of Tambov. Peasants also rose up in the villages of Kashino, Pokrovskoe, and Sterozhovka in Sapozhok. Twenty-five soviet and party workers were killed. In the same month, a 'counter-revolutionary mutiny' shook Dankov, Pronsk, Ranenburg, Riazhsk, and Sapozhok. It is worth noting how closely the disruptive regions parallel those of the 1905 unrest. After an attempt in Pronsk villages to mobilize all men under fifty for the Red Army, rebellious villages joined forces, took over the railways and postal offices, and seized horses from soldiers sent in to help with the mobilizations. Cheka reinforcements were sent in from Riazan and Sasovo. At least three officials were killed in the unrest and the leaders of the 'counter-revolution' executed. Similar events occurred throughout the province in 1918, with significant losses on both sides.[46] In 1919, the first Riazan prison camp (*kontslager'*) was established under the direction of the Cheka in the former Kazan monastery, and another camp was established in Riazhsk later that year.[47] The battle for power continued with the chairman of the Riazan provincial Cheka asking permission to shoot the Menshevik and Socialist Revolutionary leaders of counter-revolution quickly.[48] Given the difficulties of establishing control in Riazan, as elsewhere, Moscow would not be secure in its inhabitants' loyalty as the country emerged from the years of Civil War.

The 1920s in Riazan

By 1920, Riazan was in disarray, having experienced poor harvests, hunger, and a significant drop in livestock since 1916. If the average harvest between 1903 and 1917 was between 40 and 56 puds per desiatina, in 1920 it had fallen to 29.4 puds. The number of livestock of all kinds had dropped from the 1916 level by as much as 53.5 per cent. The number of horses had declined by 75.7 per cent, cattle by 68.4 per cent, the number of sheep by 47.5 per cent, and the number of swine by 45.8 per cent.[49] In Mikhailov, peasants were feeding their livestock thatch from their roofs in an effort to keep them alive.[50] To add to these pressures in the villages, the province experienced de-urbanization. In 1920, the population of Riazan was 2.5 million, of which only 4 per cent lived in urban areas. The population of these urban areas was further depleted as urban dwellers returned to the countryside, hoping to avoid the hunger that plagued the cities. The number of urban workers in the province dropped from 33,000 to 22,829.[51] In the neighbouring province of Tambov, A.S. Antonov led tens of thousands of peasants in rebellion against Soviet power in the early 1920s. Known as the Tambovshchina or Antonovshchina, this struggle spilled over the Tambov border into its northern neighbour. At times Antonov took refuge in the Mozharsk forests of Riazan.[52]

Recovery was slow in the first half of the 1920s. The southern districts were gripped by poor harvests from 1920 to 1924. The total sown area had dropped far below the 1916 level of 1,414,00 desiatinas, but by 1923 the total had climbed to 1,213,000 desiatinas, and by 1924 to 1,297,000 desiatinas. Despite these impressive increases, Riazan had by no means recovered fully. There were reports of famine in Skopin in 1924.[53] In December 1924, the Provincial Executive Committee cut taxes by 17.1 per cent and the state sent 6 million puds of reserve grain to Riazan.[54] In 1925–6, the province received aid (*prodovol'stvennaia pomoshch'*) from the state to the tune of 2,641,000 rubles.[55] As late as 1926 the district executive committees were distributing flour to starving peasants across Riazhsk.[56] These southern, black-earth districts of Riazan Province, Riazhsk and Skopin, appear again and again through these pages as problem areas in matters of crime and perceived deviance.

It was not until 1926 that agriculture in the region began to approach the pre-1916 levels. Crop diversity returned and began to approach, and in some cases surpass, the pre-war levels in the cultivation of crops such as flax, hemp, and tobacco. Livestock resources slowly began to improve; the number of households without horses dropped from 46.5 per cent to 42.7 per cent, and the number of households without cows dropped from 32.4 per cent to 23.7 per cent.[57] The proliferation of markets across Riazan in 1926–7 reflected the growing diversification and the colourful bazaar life that was developing or returning to the province. In the course of a year, across the province of Riazan, there were 193 recorded markets, most of them spread out about the villages of each district.

Just a brief glimpse at the variety and proliferation of the markets testifies to the diversity of the NEP economy and its maintenance of the pre-Revolutionary market or fair atmosphere. The markets were held between June and November and sold an array of goods. They specialized to some degree, according to what each district produced. In Riazan District alone, there were fifty-eight different markets between June and November. Three of the fifty-eight were in the city of Riazan and sold sweets and pastries, toys, odds and ends, groceries, manufactured goods, agricultural implements, and cattle. The other fifty-five markets were spread out among the villages of the district, selling manufactured goods and groceries, white bread, apples, honey, crafts, and leather shoes. In Zaraisk District there were seventeen different markets, fourteen of which were selling cattle. Kasimov District had fourteen markets, most of them selling agricultural implements and crafts. Ranenburg District had sixteen markets, most of them specializing in milk products, as well as meat, eggs, cattle, livestock, wheels, sleighs, and carts. Riazhsk District had thirty-two markets, selling mostly livestock and manufactured goods. The Voznesensk market in the village of Sarai sold iron, dishes, shoes, bread, and wheat. The Sasovo District had twenty-eight markets with the most wide-ranging wares, including the Pitelino market, held in October in the village of Pitelino, which sold bread, cattle, seed, shovels, rakes, bast shoes, and hemp. The markets of Sasovo sold livestock, bread, vegetables, crafts, oats, wheels, carts, bast shoes, resin, tar, bast matting, knitted goods, and fruit.[58]

As colourful as the markets might have been, the peasant diet in Riazan was not so diverse.[59] As in the pre-Revolutionary period, rye continued to be the dominant crop on peasant fields, occupying 40 to 60 per cent of the sown area in each uezd, followed by oats, which occupied 8 to 30 per cent of sown area.[60]

Most peasants in Riazan lived in small wooden homes with thatched roofs. Each household consisted of a central living structure and a courtyard that might contain one or more outbuildings for livestock or storage. Villages tended to be organized along a single laneway with one row of homes on each side of the dirt road. This remains to the present day.

As late as 1929, more than 40 per cent of peasant households in the province were without a horse and over 20 per cent without even a cow. The vital importance of horses to the Riazan peasant is illustrated time and again throughout this book. In the late 1920s most of Riazan was still farmed on the old three-field system with wooden ploughs and sometimes without any draught power at all. The state of animal husbandry was described as 'primitive,' with the exception of the meadow region along the Oka. In other areas even manure use was 'spontaneous,' in that it was ploughed into the land wherever it fell.[61] The collective-farm system was in its earliest stages and Riazan hardly seemed ready for rapid and wholesale collectivization in a few short years.

The economic and statistical studies of the first half of the 1920s emphasize the regional diversity within Riazan and use these variations to make an explicit point about the complexity of measuring peasant wealth.[62] Any standard existing classifications used to measure peasant wealth could not be applied across the regions of Riazan, much less across the Soviet Union as a whole. The province itself was divided into four agricultural zones. The northern forested region was 44 per cent forest and the remaining land tended to be swampy. The northern region consisted of the uezds of Arkhangelsk, Murminsk, Spas-Klepiki, Tuma, and northern parts of Elat'ma, Erakhtur, Ermish, Kadom, Kasimov, Pitelino, Riazan, and Zaraisk. Grain grown here was for subsistence use, so the amount of land cultivated was small. Peasants depended on raising livestock, consequently livestock ownership was higher than the averages for the province as a whole. Therefore, if wealth were measured in arable land, most peasants of the region would be considered poor. On the contrary, if wealth were measured in livestock ownership, the peasants of the northern region would be considered much more wealthy. The Oka meadow region was suited for hay production, fishing, and raising cattle and consisted of parts of the uezds of Kuzmino, Izhevsk, Riazan, Rybnoe,

1 Village of Morozovo Borki Sapozhok, 1968 (photo archive of Evgeny Kashirin).

2 Recently abandoned village home in Shilovo, 2004 (photo by the author).

Sasovo, Zaraisk, Shilovo, and Spassk. The region supplied milk products to Moscow and contained almost all of the province's dairy cooperatives. Here again, the amount of arable land was quite small, but livestock holdings were more significant than in the south.

The Central Industrial Region, made up of parts of the uezds of Riazhsk, Sasovo, and Shilovo, was more diverse agriculturally, with cereal crops in the west, potatoes and hemp in the east, a horse-breeding micro-region, and small livestock raised to supplement household incomes. The fourth region, the southern agricultural region, was similar to the northern regions of the Central Black Earth region of the Soviet Union. This region contained most of Riazhsk and Ranenburg uezds and parts of Sasovo, Shatsk, and Skopin. Agriculture was most intensive in the south, dominated by rye, but also included oats and millet and some micro-regions of sugar beets, carrots, and hemp. The south, like the Central Black Earth generally, was much more densely populated than the north, with density at sixty-two to sixty-four people per square kilometre versus twenty-eight to twenty-nine people per square kilometre in the north.

When it came to trying to measure the 'wealth' of the Riazan peasantry so that the province's population could be divided into the requisite categories of landless (*batrak*), poor (*bedniak*), middle (*serednniak*), wealthy (*zazhitochnye*), and exploitative (*kulak*), the challenge was far from straightforward or simple. Peasants in the north had more livestock, but farmed much less land. Peasants in the central region of the province raised more fowl, especially those households with large families, but they were for personal use only. Bee-keeping helped to supplement modest incomes from agriculture. The commission trying to measure wealth in the province in 1927 and 1928 felt 'compelled' to 'conclude that there is no direct relationship between bee-keeping and being a kulak.'[63] Budget studies revealed that it was the size of a peasant family, and in particular the number of working adults, that was key to a family's wealth.[64]

Through the 1920s the collective-farm system was growing slowly in Riazan. In October 1924, there were 65 collective farms with 470 members; in 1925, 97 collective farms with 710 members; and in 1926, 105 collective farms with 950 members.[65] In 1926 still more than half of Riazan's peasant households ploughed the land with the wooden plough, 92 per cent harvested grains with a sickle or a scythe, and over 70 per cent threshed only with a flail (*tsepami*).[66] Over 40 per cent of all households rented livestock or equipment. Mechanization was slowly being introduced. There were 2 tractors working in the Riazan fields in 1924–5, 65 in 1925–6, 101 in 1927, and 106 in October 1928.[67] Comparatively, in the spring of 1928, there were 904 tractors at work in the fields of Tambov and 289 in the fields of Moscow region.[68] On the eve of collectivization, the Riazan party organization in the countryside was still weak. In July 1927, there were 210 party cells (*iacheek*) and twenty-four candidate groups totalling 3,239 people from a population of well over 2.5 million. At the beginning of 1928, the 1,588 rural soviets (*sel'sovety*) in Riazan were in a state of turmoil, undergoing a 'purge of anti-Soviet elements.'[69]

On the eve of collectivization in September 1929, Riazhsk Uezd had the highest percentage of voluntary collective farms, which occupied a mere 5.9 per cent of the total cultivated land, followed by Spassk at 3.7 per cent, Aleksandro-Nevskii at 2.4 per cent, and Spas-Klepiki at 2.2 per cent.[70] Peasant resistance to rising taxes and an increasingly insistent program of grain procurement escalated toward the end of the 1920s. By the fall of 1929, Riazan Province was still a grain-deficit region, in which a peasant population of over 2 million people worked their land with wooden ploughs and a limited supply of livestock. Peasants were wary of the Bolshevik regime in the wake of the Civil War, the unrest associated with the peasant revolution in neighbouring Tambov, and an increasingly harsh taxation system biased against them. It was to this physical and psychological environment that the policy of rapid, wholesale collectivization was introduced in the fall of 1929.

In January 1929, there were 218 collective farms in Riazan Province with 3,852 members, fewer than 2 per cent of the peasant population.[71] Yet by 20 February 1930, Pitelino was reported as completely collectivized, with the average for Riazan Okrug at 75.3 per cent collectivized.[72] After Stalin's famous 'dizzy with success' article of 2 March 1930, the percentage of collectivized households in Pitelino Raion fell to 6.[73] By the end of 1930, across the province, collectivization was at 45 per cent. Full collectivization was not achieved until 1935.[74] What these numbers tell us is that Riazan was one of the most contested battlegrounds of collectivization. It was so contested because it was Moscow's backyard and because the regional party first secretary, K.Ia. Bauman, who directed collectivization in the region, pushed Riazan especially hard to be a model and challenge to other districts. In fact, he explicitly pitted Riazan against Tula in early 1930 to enter into a contest of 'socialist emulation' for the highest percentage of collectivized households.[75] The numbers are close to those of areas that were known for especially violent confrontation such as the North Caucasus and the Central Black Earth.

What was Riazan like in the era of the NEP? How did the province's rural inhabitants interact with the Bolshevik regime? What did the regime look like in the village? Does understanding the countryside and the regime in the 1920s, in more detail, help us understand the violent confrontation that was collectivization? It is to these questions and issues, and more, that we now turn.

Note on Administrative Changes in Riazan, 1917–1937

The period between the Revolution and collectivization in Riazan was marked by constant administrative changes. No reader is expected to grasp all of them. They are tracked here to illustrate the extent and frequency of attempts to reorder the spaces of the province by central decree with the aim of improving administrative control. The complexity of the changes is itself a testament to the impetus felt in Moscow to order and systematize its domains.

In 1917, Riazan consisted of twelve uezds with a total of 248 districts (*volosti*). In 1919, Spas-Klepiki was formed of districts shorn from Egor'ev, Kasimov, and Riazan uezds. In May 1922, Egor'ev was included in the boundaries of Moscow Province. Elat'ma and Shatsk were taken from Tambov in January 1923. Six uezds (Dankov, Elat'ma, Mikhailov, Pronsk, Sapozhok, and Spas-Klepiki) were abolished from the fourteen that existed in February 1924. In August 1925, the districts (now totalling sixty-five) were consolidated within the eight remaining uezds (Kasimov, Ranenburg, Riazhsk, Riazan, Sasovo, Skopin, Spassk, and Zaraisk). On 14 May 1928, the Central Black Earth region was redefined to include Kursk, Orel, Voronezh, and Tambov. In June, the presidium of the VTsIK (*Vsesoiuznyi tsentral'nyi ispolnitel'nyi komitet*, the All-Union Central Executive Committee) declared that Ranenburg should also be part of the Central Black Earth provinces, minus Aleksandro-Nevskii District, which became part of Riazhsk Uezd.

The map changed drastically for the period leading up to and including collectivization. In January 1929, the VTsIK decreed the creation of Moscow Oblast, which would come into effect later in the year. The explicitly stated reasons for these administrative reorganizations was to consolidate areas with similar programs of development and to bring the periphery closer to the Centre for the latter's 'convenience' and to facilitate 'the Centre (Moscow)' in the implementation of directives and the resolution of conflicts. Here we see a physical mapping of the processes of state-building and centralization. Moscow Oblast was to include the former provinces of Moscow, Riazan, Tver, Tula, and part of Kaluga as regions (*okruga*). Riazan Okrug would be made up of Kasimov, Riazhsk, Sasovo, and Spassk in their entirety, and parts of Riazan, Skopin, and Zaraisk. The okrug was divided into twenty-seven raions: Aleksandro-Nevskii, Chuchkovo, Elat'ma, Erakhtur, Ermish, Iuzhno-Riazan, Izhevsk, Kadom, Kasimov, Klepiki, Korablino, Mikhailov, Pitelino, Pronsk, Riazhsk, Rybnoe, Sapozhok, Sarai, Sasovo, Severo-Riazan, Shatsk, Shilovo, Spassk, Starozhilovo, Tuma, Ukholovo, and Zakharovo. In June 1930, Severno-Riazan and Iuzhno-Riazan were consolidated into Riazan. The average raion contained about forty-three rural soviets, 124 villages, and about 14,000 households, and each raion was roughly twice the size of the former volosts.

On 23 June 1930, TsIK and SNK (*Sovet narodnykh komissarov*, or *Sovnarkom*, the Council of People's Commissars) of the USSR passed a resolution 'On the Liquidation of the Okrugs,' which was to take effect on 1 October 1930. It decided that after the okrugs were liquidated, the boundaries of rural soviets and raions would not change.[76] From 1930 to 1937, Riazan remained part of Moscow Oblast. On 2 March 1935, VTsIK issued another resolution 'on the new network of Moscow Oblast,' which established the 130 raions of Moscow Oblast; among these were 39 raions that would become Riazan Oblast in 1937. A TsIK Soviet Union of Socialist Republics (SSSR) resolution (*postanovlenie*) from 26 September 1937 divided Moscow Oblast into Moscow, Riazan, and Tula. Riazan was then made up of 39 raions taken from the former Moscow Oblast and 13 from Voronezh Oblast.[77] Riazan's borders continued to shift up to and beyond the Second World War. On the eve of the twenty-first century, Riazan comprised 25 raions, and the oblast had a population of 1,337,000.[78]

Chapter Two

The Police

The police officer is the mirror of Soviet power by which the population judges Soviet power.

Mikhail Kalinin[1]

One police officer in the countryside can befoul things so badly that ten members of the Central Committee would be hard pressed to put it right.

Mikhail Kalinin[2]

M. often repeated Khlebnikov's lines: 'What a great thing is a police station! The place where I have my rendezvous with the state.'

Nadezhda Mandelstam, *Hope against Hope*

Tsarist Legacy

The bones of a police force came into being in Russia only in the nineteenth century.[3] Like its future Soviet counterpart, the tsarist police force was understaffed and underpaid, and lacked rigorous or systematized training. Labour turnover was extremely high and pensions were negligible, if they existed at all.[4] A small number of officers patrolled large areas; it took an officer anywhere from three to five days to patrol the territory under his jurisdiction in Riazan before the Revolution. Toward the end of the nineteenth century, in the province, the ratio of police officers to inhabitants was roughly one officer to anywhere from twelve to fifteen thousand inhabitants.[5] In some rural areas, one officer could be responsible for close to two thousand square kilometres and as many as one hundred thousand people.[6] Tsarist-era police officers did the bidding of numerous other ministries. At least half of their time was spent serving as messengers among administrative offices or delivering summons and subpoenas, and perhaps most problematic of all, participating in the unpopular task of tax collecting. Imperial Chief of Police M.I. Trusevich complained in 1908 that the police force was 'the universal apparatus for fulfilling the task of every other branch of government.'[7]

As a result of the lack of personnel for the regular police force, policing in the countryside fell largely to elected peasant representatives. One representative, a tenner (*desiatskii*), was elected for every ten households with a supervisor, hundreder (*sotskii*), responsible for every ten elected men. According to Neil Weissman, these peasant officials were closely tied to their villages and such ties made them hesitant to report illegal behaviour to the official police.[8] These peasant representatives were supposed to make regular reports to the police on order and disorder in the village and to apprehend those who violated the law. Elected constables were instructed to deliver criminals to the proper authorities while keeping them safe from the reprisals of their victims. For this dangerous work, they received token salaries.[9] Tsarist police officers subsidized their meagre earnings by trading in moonshine or taking bribes and tried to compensate for personnel shortages through violence and threats against the rural population.[10] Of course, these excesses were precisely the kinds of situations peasants complained about. The records of police representatives who had closer ties to villagers and who accepted a reasonable bribe as fair exchange for a worthwhile return are harder to find. People tend to complain less about favours done for them and systems of patronage and bribery that actually function to their benefit. Peasants in the nineteenth century told ethnographers that they were often forced to take matters of serious crime into their own hands because the police failed to protect them.[11] The Bolshevik regime inherited the structures and challenges of the tsarist system in conjunction with the confusion and chaos produced by the Revolution and Civil War.[12]

Policing after 1917

After the fall of the tsarist regime in February, the Riazan Duma assumed power as provincial representatives of the Provisional Government. At the first meeting in the city Duma on 3 March, almost all of the delegates voted for a 'new revolutionary power' in the form of an Executive Committee of Public Organizations. Immediately, a local version of 'dual power' emerged as soldiers of local garrisons called for the creation of a city soviet that could give voice to the 'revolutionary will' of the people.[13] Initially, the soviet was dominated by Mensheviks and Socialist Revolutionaries. Many in the Committee of Public Organizations wanted to retain the pre-Revolutionary police force. Under pressure from the soldiers' garrisons, however, the tsarist governor, vice-governor, chief of police, and his deputy in charge of the criminal department, S.F. Baulin, and his staff were arrested on the night of 3 March.

Regular police were still in charge of protecting the city, but through March and April a 'people's militia' (*narodnaia militsia*), made up of soldiers and citizen volunteers, was created under the leadership of V.A. Anisimov. A Riazan circular of 12 March called for the resignation of former tsarist policemen and requested that they not meddle in the affairs of the new force. One hundred thousand prisoners were given amnesty; many were sent to the front and some 'politicals' joined the police. It seems that even the city of Riazan was not especially safe in April 1917; the assistant to the chief of police had his suitcase stolen at the train station. He lost all of his documents, 400 rubles, his revolver, and some personal property. In light of the pressing challenges surrounding effective policing, Anisimov requested that the former tsarist police official S.F. Baulin, as well as Baulin's assistants, be released to help investigate open cases and re-establish administrative order; they did their jobs well.

The new force was divided into 'active' paid officers and 'passive' unpaid volunteers. Anisimov attempted to liquidate the 'passive' section in May 1917, and he confiscated their bicycles. There were two reasons behind the attempted liquidation. Officially, when the passive militia conducted searches, items would go missing. Behind the scenes, a Bolshevik rival, G.K. Petrov, and his supporters were using the passive militia against Anisimov in an attempt to remove him from his position. An official court decision overruled Anisimov's decision to liquidate the passive militia.[14] Events in July further worried Anisimov as local police played a role in supporting the Bolshevik side. The existing police force could not maintain order through the summer and fall of 1917 in both the city and the countryside. Food supply lines broke down and both the Spassk and Dankov regions reported massive campaigns of wood theft.

By September 1917, a report to the Ministry of the Interior from Riazan stated, 'The situation in Riazan in the last few days is difficult and threatening. In Riazhsk, parts of Sapozhok, Mikhailov, Skopin, and Riazan uezds there is terror and pogroms ... The police are everywhere weak and lacking in numbers. The present organization is in no way prepared for this level of crime.'[15] September also saw the creation of the Red Guard by the Riazan soviet. Red Guard units appeared in several uezds across the province, and many members of the passive militia enrolled.[16] By December 1917, a new force was created under the leadership of Anisimov's rival, G.K. Petrov – nominally because S.F. Baulin and many others remained at their posts. The new force occupied the same buildings in Riazan as had Anisimov's former force. Anisimov himself was arrested; legend has it that he refused to turn over any of his policing materials to Petrov and told the men who came to arrest him 'to go off and gorge themselves on power.'[17] Petrov's reign was short-lived, however. In December 1917, he led half of the Riazan garrison and a host of volunteer police officers to fight on the Bolshevik side in the Civil War. Petrov died near Krasnovodsk in September 1918.

In the early months of 1918, Riazan was a scene of intense local struggle between Bolsheviks and Socialist Revolutionaries. Moscow intervened and established a Riazan section of the Cheka. The districts of the province were in complete disarray. Ad hoc security forces existed from region to region, each with a different name and under different auspices. Some still operated under old tsarist schedules and staff. On 29 May 1918, the Commissariat of Internal Affairs (NKVD) issued instructions that executive committees be established in all districts and within them an 'administrative department' (*administrativnyi otdel*), which would be in charge of sending weekly reports to the provincial NKVD and organizing the local Cheka, as well as the local police. The police were officially designated as 'an executive organ of worker-peasant central power in the localities, directly subordinate to the local soviets.'[18] An interesting series of contradictions entangled here would come back to haunt the young regime. The regular police were in a kind of dual subordination to the People's Commissariat of Internal Affairs, on one hand, and the state executive committees, on the other. Moreover, if the police were clearly an organ of central power *and* subordinate to the local soviets, the working assumption was that the local soviets were even more so organs of central power and the two would work in tandem as state representatives. The two often did work together, but not necessarily as the Centre envisioned.

The police were hierarchically structured with a provincial chief, uezd heads,[19] and below them senior and junior officers. Throughout the Civil War period, the police were, in theory, centralized and militarized, especially after the assassination of Mikhail Uritskii, head of the Petrograd Cheka, in August 1918. A Council of People's Commissars (*Sovnarkom/SNK*) decree of 3 April 1919 introduced major changes to the material and legal position of the police. The police force was to be supplied like the Red Army and subject to similar organization and strict military discipline. New uniforms with a crest consisting of red thread around a gold hammer and sickle were designed and made requisite wear. Officers had to be over twenty-one, literate, not disenfranchised, and not members of the former tsarist police. They were paid from the Centre and worked mostly in enforcing grain requisitioning and conscription, as well as rooting out deserters, with little time left over for day-to-day police duties. Moreover, despite promises to exempt half of the force from conscription, the police often lost their best officers to the front.[20] The police were expected to assist the Cheka in defeating any and all opposition to Bolshevik power. Across Riazan, such opposition usually took the form of peasant uprisings against grain requisitioning and resistance to the mobilizations of men and horses for the Red Army. The summer of 1918 saw uprisings in Egor'ev, Mikhailov, Riazhsk, Sapozhok, Spas-Klepiki, and Zaraisk. When the chief of police balked at allowing his men to participate in grain requisitioning – even calling on them to protect the population against the 'grain army,' which was taking everything from the peasants, including 'stockings, thread, shawls, right down to the last possessions of the poor' – he was reminded from above that, as an 'organ of Soviet power,' the force could not remain 'neutral.'[21]

In October 1918, the Criminal Investigation Department (*ugolovnyi rozysk*) was created to 'defend the revolutionary order,' and to contend with the complicated investigations of more violent crimes, especially banditry. The 'material technical basis of the Riazan provincial department of the criminal investigation department,' upon its creation, consisted of 'a horse, two telephones, and a Bertillon camera.'[22] The first chief of the provincial Criminal Investigation Department was the very same S.F. Baulin who had headed up the Tsarist Criminal Investigation Department and was released from prison to work for the Provisional Government in policing. By December, the department was subordinated to the Provincial Executive Committee under A.P. Melnikov. At the end of 1918, there was a total of 1,438 police officers in the province of Riazan. Melnikov testified, in a rather coded way, in his report to his NKVD superiors that his police force was not exactly what the Bolsheviks envisioned. He confessed that the 'cultural level' of his men was 'not very high,' and as a result they could not really be the 'true defenders of the Revolution' and of revolutionary values. Moreover, he admitted, there was a significant number of tsarist officers serving in the ranks, but he was doing his unflagging best to root them out.[23]

The Civil War hit the Riazan police hard. At home, officers were expected to fight against desertion and to struggle with desperate deserters hiding in the villages and forests. They were on the front line in the battle against diseases that raged through the province, which in turn exposed them constantly to highly contagious illnesses. To make matters even worse, police officers were at constant risk of being drafted to the Civil War fronts. From August 1918 to the end of the year, 52,592 men were drafted into the Red Army through twelve separate mobilizations in Riazan Province alone. In that process, half of the Riazan police force was drafted to fight on the side of the Bolsheviks. The civilian population met the conscription of their own sons with avoidance, desertion, and considerable protest. Riazan had the highest rate of desertion in the Russian Soviet Federated Socialist Republic (RSFSR).[24] By the end of the year, uprisings that began in Kasimov had spread across the province and police officers were working alongside members of the Cheka to quell unrest. Still, on 10 November 1918, district police chiefs were reminded to organize celebratory meetings on the creation of the Soviet police.

When the first meeting of the provincial chiefs of police was held on 11 and 12 November 1918, the top officers from Dankov, Kasimov, Mikhailov, Pronsk, Ranenburg, Sapozhok, Skopin, and Spassk could not attend because of serious peasant unrest in their uezds. A Commissariat of Internal Affairs resolution of 23 November exempted half of the police force from the draft because they were needed to control unrest at home. Police chiefs across Riazan sent curt responses to their superiors' reminders to celebrate the anniversary of the October Revolution. The chief from Spassk telegraphed, 'I am communicating that the holiday was not celebrated in light of the fact that all of the officers are in battle' (*nakhodilis' v boiu*). The chief of police in Mikhailov explained that there was no observance in his uezd because of 'near simultaneous kulak uprisings' in nineteen different districts.[25]

In 1919, outbreaks of typhus and Spanish flu battered the province, and police officers were responsible for introducing important hygiene and sanitation measures. In August, the southern district of Ranenburg experienced incursions from raids led by the Don Cossack leader Mamontov.[26] In areas where the Civil War touched Riazan, police officers were not only drafted into the Red Army, but officers who remained on the force were expected to fight alongside the Red Army and agents of the Cheka against Mamontov's forces. By 1920 the police had been divided into provincial, district, and city levels as well as separate rural, water, industry, and railway sections. Financial support for the whole

3. Members of Spas-Klepiki ChON (*chasti osobogo naznachenie*), ‘special section’ within the Cheka (photo archive of Evgeny Kashirin).

4. Members of Riazan ChON (*chasti osobogo naznachenie*), 'special section' within the Cheka (photo archive of Evgeny Kashirin).

5. Members of VOKhR (*voiska vnutrennei okhrany Respubliki*) troops for the defence of the Republic during the civil war in Skopin, Moscow, 1924 (photo archive of Evgeny Kashirin).

force was to come out of the general state budget through the accounts of the People's Commissariat of Internal Affairs. Police and Cheka personnel worked together closely in the period of the Civil War, and those years established a precedent for cooperation and unification of the regular police and the security police.[27]

Policing in the 1920s

The Riazan police emerged from the Civil War in a 'lamentable condition.'[28] They had lost many of their best officers to the front. Paperwork was in utter chaos and officers were short of food, clothing, and supplies. A 1920 report from the Riazhsk chief of police said that in his district most officers had no weapons at all and if a unit had a weapon, it was shared among all members. Melnikov reported, 'Foreign rifles are without bullets. There are few "Nagan" revolvers, and the "Smit-Vessony" and "Bul'dogy" have been endlessly repaired such that they no longer function.'[29] His entire force had twenty-five horses and they were so short of fodder that the animals were beginning to die of starvation. He added that if the region was not supplied with fodder soon, the officers would be forced to sell the horses to feed themselves. One-third of the force was illiterate and one-third had no uniforms.[30] The situation did not improve quickly. An impassioned report of August 1922 from the provincial department of the Riazan police spoke of the 'extremely burdensome material conditions' for the police of the province. There was no soap, no way to bathe or wash clothes, and electricity was 'a luxury only dreamed of.' Material conditions, the report emphasized, had to be improved for the police to perform their jobs because 'the condition of the workers of the police is shoeless, naked, hungry – the most desperate and hopeless, who could be classed in the category of the "forgotten."'[31]

Paul Hagenloh maintains that the rural police force in the 1920s looked and functioned much like their tsarist predecessors and sees the rural police as ineffective and incapable of systematic policing.[32] In some locales such a scenario was indeed the case. In a January 1923 report, for example, the Pronsk uezd police chief complained that the police felt cut off from the rural soviets.[33] In many other villages, however, local police become part of village power structures. My research suggests that the police and rural soviet officials, along with all manner of local officials, worked and socialized together and that such ties were even more worrying for the Centre than no ties at all. In fact, more often than not, police were part of the village, deeply embedded in the rural communi-

6. Riazan chekisty, early 1920s (photo archive of Evgeny Kashirin).

ties that they served. They shared the dangers of village life, the risks to health, the dearth of resources, and the shortages of food and livestock that were the everyday facts of life in the countryside.

On 10 June 1921, the People's Commissariat of Internal Affairs declared that the end of the Civil War meant the end of the military functions of the regular police force. The Soviet police were to be like the police force of any other nation. The police existed to preserve the public peace, to protect and assist the population, and to enforce laws and decrees. The ranks of the police swelled with demobilized Red Army soldiers after the Civil War such that the Central Committee had to pass a resolution on 2 April 1921 limiting the expansion of the force.

One obvious part of the state structure that came into contact with Riazan peasants over matters of crime and deviance was the local police. A chronic problem for the Bolshevik Centre in the first decade of its existence was extending a state presence to the village. Despite the extreme challenges for, and shortcomings of, the police in the 1920s, the district police – along with rural soviet officials – were the closest state representatives to the peasantry. However, their 'state' identity was complicated and often overshadowed by the fact that most police officers were peasants as well as officers. A survey conducted in the summer of 1925 showed that in Riazan Uezd 107 police officers were from the peasantry and only 5 were of worker origin; and these numbers pertain to the uezd that included the capital city of Riazan itself.[34] Even if the ranks of the police were filled in the period immediately following the Civil War with Red Army soldiers, the police faced constant labour turnover, which suggests that many demobilized soldiers did not stay in the force for long.

For a brief period from 1921 to 1923 the force was under the jurisdiction of a separate police administration (*Glavnoe upravlenie militsii* / main administration of the police). In April 1922, the Criminal Investigation Department was given independent status within the police administration and divided into an investigative section and a secret section. Many of the leading officers within the Criminal Investigation Department had worked for the provincial Cheka. The division meant that the regular police and the investigators competed with one another for scarce resources.[35] In October 1922, a resolution of Commissariat of People's Commissars and the All-Union Central Executive Committee transferred responsibility for the maintenance and financial support of the police to local budgets. As a result, the staff of the police were reduced by 30 per cent. District executive committees (*volispolkom*), already strapped for resources, were now responsible for maintaining and funding the district police (*volmilitsiia*). In late 1923, the short-lived separate police administration became a department of police within the People's Commissariat of Internal Affairs.[36] In November 1923, the Presidium of the Central Committee passed a resolution that reorganized the Main Political Administration (*Glavnoe politicheskoe upravlenie, GPU*) under the auspices of the NKVD, which had fulfilled the functions of state security after the abolition of the Cheka in 1922, into the United State Political Administration (*Ob"edinennoe gosudarstvennoe politicheskoe upravlenie, OGPU*) through the Council of People's Commissars.[37] The resolution meant that regular policing now fell to an 'administrative section' (*administrativnyi otdel*) within the Provincial Executive Committee (*gosudarstvennyi isponitel'nyi komitet, GIK*). The provincial administrative section had a secretariat, a subsection of regular police, a subsection of criminal investigation, and a department of prison inspection. The same structure was mirrored at the uezd and district level.

Officially, the duties of the police officer in the 1920s were rooted in the jurisdiction of the People's Commissariat of Internal Affairs (NKVD): to defend the revolutionary order, to defend the people and property of the Soviet state, to implement decrees and laws, to monitor and defend jails and prisons, to struggle with crime, to enforce sanitation regulations, to organize and oversee fire departments, and to insure that the postal service was safe and functioning. Such jurisdiction and responsibilities were in themselves already more than sufficiently broad. In reality, the Soviet police of the 1920s comprised, like their tsarist counterparts, the 'universal apparatus' that aided and serviced a host of other state organizations and commissariats. For the Commissariat of Agriculture (*Narkomzem*), police enforced decisions of the land committees. Officers were expected to assist the forest guards in trying to turn up individuals who were stealing wood or illegally using the forests for pasturing animals, gathering hay, extracting tar or potash and making charcoal, taking sand, coal, clay, peat moss, and moss in general. The police were asked to search for peasants who hunted or fished illegally. For the People's Commissariat of Military and Naval Matters (*Narkomvoenmor*), police participated in the counting and registering of horses. For the Commissariat of Finance (*Narkomfin*), the police assisted in tax collecting and accounting and running down peasants in arrears. For the State Insurance Agency (*Gosstrakh*), the police reported on all fires and on the investigation results regarding the causes of those fires. Police assisted the Commissariat of Internal Trade (*Narkomvneshtor*) in customs work. They assisted the Commissariat of Transport (*Narkomput*) in chasing after and fining travellers without train tickets. And finally, police assisted the Commissariat of Justice (*Narkomiust*) by enforcing decisions of the people's courts, escorting people to court, and extracting fines and court costs from individuals.[38] By the mid-1920s the workload for the police consisting of such extraneous duties comprised half of their total work. As one commentator noted in 1928, 'Almost every department [*vedomstvo*] has a strong tendency to use the police in the capacity of its own direct executive organ.'[39]

There were a number of accepted options for organizing officers responsible for policing the countryside, and all were in use in the 1920s. In one type of organization, all officers were located in the district centre, and the territory of the district was not divided into police districts; instead, police were sent to an area when they were needed there. In the second type of organization, the officers were located in the district centre, but the territory of the district was divided further into sub-districts with each officer responsible for his own section, which he toured periodically. In the third option, the chief remained in the district centre, as did police administration, but each officer was stationed in his own district in association with a rural soviet.[40] In general, the rural soviet was a kind of base for the officer in a district.

The district police were often physically located in the same space as the district executive committee, and the chief of the district police was directly subordinate to the chairman of the district executive committee. There was variation from place to place in the nature of police spaces across Riazan, and the situation improved gradually through the 1920s. In 1922 the Pronsk District Police, for example, found a peasant family living in the space that had been assigned to them. The family had made repairs to the building and both the police and the family appealed to the district executive committee to settle the matter.[41] In 1923 the Pronsk Uezd Police had accommodations, but complained that they had only two tiny stoves to heat four rooms such that the temperature inside hovered around five degrees and the rooms were full of smoke. The district police had no horses and the uezd police had only one, thus virtually all work had to be done on foot. The report complained that crimes took place more than thirty kilometres away and it took a week to get there so that criminals had a good deal of time to cover their tracks. Without horses, it was virtually impossible to fight illegal distilling, wood theft, or any manner of crime. Even if there was a rail link to an area, the walk from the station was long and arduous. Still, despite the harsh conditions, officers were working.[42]

Such conditions, naturally, took a toll on the health of officers. In a study of patients who passed through the central ambulatory unit in Moscow from April to September 1924, members of the regular police and the criminal investigation unit were well represented. In fact, they made up almost half of the patients that passed through the unit. Police officers suffered from extremely high rates of infectious disease, 'trauma,' and mental illness. In a more general study of police health, those who served in the countryside were, not surprisingly, at even higher risk of illness. The rate of illness among rural constables was 30 to 50 per cent, depending on how long they had served in the force. Of course, the longer one served the more likely one was to be sick. Typical illnesses were tuberculosis, rheumatism, respiratory illnesses in general, and nervous disorders.[43] The high rate of nervous disorders is visceral testament to the dangers and stresses of the job.

A decree of 27 March 1924 announced the creation of the position of village deputy (*sel'skii ispolnitel'*). The deputies were elected by the soviets from among all physically fit adults – men and women – and they were to serve a two-month term assisting the district police as their eyes and ears in the village. Village deputies were supposed to watch for criminal activity and report it to the police. They were to apprehend and hold prisoners and transport them to the district centre if possible. Deputies usually tried to avoid this rather terrifying task. Their job description was remarkably similar to that of the pre-Revolutionary elected police representatives. Like the village representatives of the pre-Revolutionary period, the Soviet-era village deputies feared jeopardizing their relations with their fellow villagers if they reported on them. Only 15 per cent of the peasants designated by the rural soviets as deputies ever turned up for duty. The overworked rural soviets resented the additional work of selecting and preparing deputies and considered the task a low priority, only rarely providing instructions and often selecting women, whom neither the district police nor the rural soviet itself took seriously. Often a designated individual would send a son, a younger brother, a mother, and even a grandparent as stand-in. For example, a sixty-five-year old man would arrive to replace his grandson, who, he claimed, was 'dying' or 'sick.' The district police became increasingly infuriated with the deputies, who would arrive with no instruction or training from the rural soviet, saying, 'The rural soviet did not explain,' or, 'I do not understand. We are dark people.' The regular police were further aggravated by repeated queries, entreaties, and observations on the part of deputies such as 'When will I be replaced?' 'I have no bread.' 'I thought it would be only one evening?'[44] Thus, the local Soviet police were intricately entangled with the local population and the rural soviets.

Within Riazan, the Provincial Executive Committee expressed concern in 1923 about the low 'cultural level' of the police force in the province. Indeed, literacy levels were not high.[45] In early 1925, the People's Commissariat of Justice noted in a circular that the police were often the only representatives of the legal system in the village, yet they did not know the law and were in desperate need of more training.[46] By mid-1925 there were eighteen schools in all of the RSFSR, training junior officers who served in the countryside, which produced about a thousand graduates per year. There were only three schools for mid-level police officers, which trained about seven hundred per year.[47]

Because salaries were paid by the district executive committees after 1922, wages now varied significantly, depending on the relative financial strength or weakness of a given district. Weaker districts, for example, either allocated token amounts of money for 'secret' work or refused to designate funds for such work altogether.[48] In January 1923, reports from the uezd stated that police had not received salaries. Existing funds

7. Lenin corner of Skopin militsia, 1925 (*Administrativnyi vestnik* 8 [Aug. 1925]: 79).

had to be spread among maintaining the house of arrest (*ardom*), feeding the prisoners, trying to acquire warm clothing, as well as repairing equipment and work spaces.[49] By the mid-1920s conditions in some places in Riazan were improving but only slightly. Officers in the village of Tuma, for example, housed themselves in a space that was 'in all ways' comfortable, clean, bright, and warm. The office was tidy and in the courtyard there was a stable and a barn for hay, with space to store material evidence, and a type of hut to hold prisoners. An internal report noted positively that the holding cell had a stove, but that since the roof was not sealed, it could not really heat the space.[50] The Spas-Klepiki police had a 'simple' space, comfortable but dirty, with a roof that needed whitewashing and walls that needed painting. They had two horses, which were well fed and properly stabled, with a sleigh and harness.[51] But the harness and sleigh were noteworthy, as most officers did not have harnesses or saddles. One officer was still responsible for thirteen to fourteen villages on his own and often on foot.[52] Reports on the conditions of local police operations by the mid-1920s made a special attempt to account for police horses – in other words, to find out if the horses were legally obtained and well fed and maintained. The Tuma police had a healthy horse, well fed, with a harness and sleigh.

The district police in the village of Solotche occupied one room in the buildings of the district executive committee. The space for detainees was dark and cold and made out of wood such that a prisoner could easily punch through the walls and escape. The storage space for material evidence was in disrepair and had no lock. There was no horse because the former chief of police had taken it with him when he left his post. Paperwork was in total disarray. Ordinary and secret matters were not divided into separate books, illustrating, according to the report, the degree to which the police had not internalized the need for ordinary versus 'secret' matters. There was no notebook for recording the village deputies or the dates of their service. One Riazan District unit had a space that acted as its offices, dormitory, and holding area for suspects combined. According to an internal report, the space needed massive repair or needed to be exchanged for better premises altogether. The storage space for material evidence was a barn in the courtyard with no shelves but it was orderly and always locked. At the time of the report, the material evidence included a Browning handgun, two pieces of pork fat, and nine playing cards. In terms of weaponry the unit had eleven cavalry swords, three rifles, and thirteen handguns. The rifles and swords were in a 'pyramid' in the chief's office while the handguns were divided among the fifteen officers in the unit. There was a serious shortage of bullets for the handguns. The unit had one horse but, at the moment of the report, she was old and pregnant and thus entirely unfit for service. The unit maintained good records, but investigations proceeded slowly. The officers pointed to general overwork and the condition of their horse by way of explanation.[53] Here again, it is worth noting the degree to which the local police lived like many others in the countryside. They struggled with all manner of shortages, especially of horses. They suffered from roofs and living spaces in ill repair and a lack of heat in the winter.

In April 1925, a central-level commentator for the Commissariat of Internal Affairs lamented that district officers were usually local peasants, with their own household and fields, who viewed the job as 'temporary earnings on the side' (*vremennyi pobochnyi zarabotok*). In addition, the negligible wages such officers received 'drew them easily into bribery and all manner of petty extortion.'[54] He also noted that criminal elements still existed on the force and he felt the need to remind officers that they needed to be 'polite and attentive, give advice and explain the law' rather than resort to threats and bullying. Crime, he added, needs to be dealt with 'quickly and calmly' and not with 'noise and yells.'[55] In December 1925, a law was passed forbidding the executive committees to pay police in 'premiums' because the practice was leading to corrupt behaviour. The premium system gave officers the right to collect fines at a rate set by the individual constable and provided a commission for each arrest made. Often premiums could amount to double the fixed wage.[56] In a central review, sent to the Politburo, of the salaries paid to members of the police in the provinces, it was estimated that the average wage for a village constable in 1926 was twenty to twenty-one rubles per month but that in some regions, monthly salaries were as low as thirteen rubles per month.[57] To provide some idea of the value of the ruble, ten eggs cost about thirty-three kopecks and a kilo of rye flour cost just over two rubles.[58] The estimated cost of outfitting a police constable – minus the cost of winter clothing which, if available at all, was usually inadequate to keep a man warm – was eighty-three rubles per year. In Riazan, local budgets for uniforms ranged from eighteen rubles and fifty kopecks to thirty-three rubles per officer per year.[59] When winter clothing did arrive, there were few sizes to choose from and usually no shoes or boots at all.[60] Paper shortages meant that reports and notes on questioning and interrogations, confessions, and testimony had to be taken on tiny scraps of paper, which made them telegraphic and truncated. Often there was not enough money in the budget to pay for telegrams or mailings, and correspondence had to be sent 'by chance' (*do sluchaia*) or 'if the occasion arose' (*s okaziei*), meaning if someone happened to be going near the addressee.[61]

In Riazan in 1926, there was on average one member of the police force for every eight to ten thousand people.[62] In 1929, People's Commissariat of Internal Affairs regulations stated that the ratio should be one criminal investigation officer to every five thousand people, but in Spas-Klepiki, for example, the ratio was still one to twenty-five thousand.[63] A village constable might have as many as fifteen to seventeen rural soviets in his district and be forced to walk as much as fifty kilometres in any direction from the district centre to get to some of these rural soviets.[64] There were constant complaints of the incredible waste of time spent fighting illegal distilling, delivering subpoenas, and attempting to enforce judicial decisions.[65] The district police and the Criminal Investigation Department had little access to telephones or to horses. A digression here into two particular arenas of conflict helps to explicate the position in which local policemen found themselves.

On Horses and Moonshine

Commentators for the journal of the People's Commissariat of Internal Affairs emphasized that village police had to have horses to end their daily absurd 'excursions' on foot. But they also realized the enormous cost of improving the police force. In the Leningrad region alone, to equip only the senior village officers with horses would have required the purchase of some seven hundred animals.[66] Horses had been requisitioned and lost in huge numbers in both the First World War and the Civil War. In 1921, the Riazan Provincial Executive Committee noted that there was a chronic shortage of horses among members of the force. Moreover, if a constable owned his own horse, he was reluctant to use it in police work because it was dangerous and tiring. Police work put such a strain on the horse that it was then impossible to use the horse on the land.[67] Such a concern is further evidence of the officers' literal connections to the land, the village, and peasant life. In most districts in Riazan, there was no transport whatsoever for police, and the province of Riazan was not anomalous. The situation was much the same in Kaluga, Novgorod, Samara, Smolensk, and Penza, to name but a few.[68]

As late as 1928, at a meeting of workers of the Criminal Investigation Department in Ranenburg, officers complained that they lacked sufficient funds and means to travel in the region and asked for free passage on the trains when conducting work and transporting prisoners.[69] Given how short the forces were on horses, it is not surprising that officers succumbed to the temptation to commandeer or confiscate peasant horses under false pretexts. The situation was so bad that a local Riazan paper felt the need to remind readers, in its column of legal advice to peasants, that no police constable had the right to requisition a horse under any circumstances.[70]

In a letter to *Krest'ianskaia gazeta*, one peasant related his harrowing tale of losing his horse to the police in Tula. The police told him that his papers were not in order and confiscated his horse, which they then proceeded to work to death before allowing him to come and pick her up. 'We sat in jail for five weeks and my horse was returned sixty-seven days after my arrest. In order to get the horse I travelled eight times on a rented horse and sleigh and paid forty puds of oats and thirty puds of grain and paid the police twenty-eight rubles and seventeen kopecks for the upkeep of my horse. When I got the horse back she had changed from a healthy peasant horse to a broken down nag [*kliacha*] with a damaged spine, and I had to load her onto the sleigh like a dead body and drag her home. I was advised not to pursue the matter because it would be expensive. I have already wasted so much, but decided I could not let the matter drop.'[71] This letter reveals much of the trials of day-to-day life in the countryside if something went wrong. First the vital relationship between peasant and horse is beautifully illuminated. Distances were significant, and without your own horse, one had to rent from someone in the village or walk. Moreover, one trip to 'negotiate' with power was never enough. Negotiation required repeated trips and endless patience at any level. Recourse and justice were next to impossible to pursue, much less receive. Peasants tried to use in their appeals the 'official transcript' of police as servitors of the state and people. When the police intimidated and brutalized peasants, those officials were indeed held up by villagers as state representatives who gave Soviet power a bad name. Such complaints fed into the Centre's frustration at their own inability to control, standardize, and discipline state power at the local levels.

In 1928, the People's Commissariat of Internal Affairs RSFSR requested that all district police provide an inventory of their horses that included the animal's name, size, colour, sex, age, and information on how the horse was obtained. The inventory was motivated by complaints about ill-gotten horses, and by the very real need to inventory horses in the event of future military engagement. After all, the inventory was called for on the heels of the war scare. The responses from Riazan are revealing again on a number of levels. By the fall of 1928, most district police had only one horse, a few had two, and the maximum was three in Tuma. It may be worth keeping in mind that Tuma was doing well in investigations of local police and resources *and* that Tuma in turn would be one of the most rebellious districts in protests against collectivization. That these two facts coincide supports the argument that well-organized and functioning local power believed it had the authority to resist the directives of the Centre.

Reading through the responses reporting the age, size, colour, and especially the names given to police horses – names such as Mal'chik (Boy), Bandit, Marus'ka, or Bystri (Quick) and Tamara from Spas-Klepiki, Laskovyi (Gentle) from Starozhilovo, or Tsyganka (Gypsy Girl) from Tuma – two details become apparent. Officers were attached to their horses *and* a significant number of the reports do not mention how the district police acquired the animals. In December 1928, for example, the Murminsk District Police were asked to provide the uezd police with all documents applying to the grey gelding Vas'ka, which had been exchanged at the uezd department for the bay by the name of Kolchak. The district police responded and admitted that they had no documents for Vas'ka.[72]

A significant number of reports stated that the force had one state-issued (*kazennaia*) horse and one that just 'wandered in' (*pri gul'naia*). Arkhangelsk District, for example, reported that they had two such horses. The report added that the state-issued horse was 'entirely unfit for work in the police as she is crooked and poorly fed' and that the horse that wandered in could be suitable for work, but she is seriously underfed. The horse had been with the police since May. 'Recently two citizens have pretended that she is their horse and the case has gone to court.'[73] One of the Tuma horses was also listed as a 'runaway.' A horse was a vital resource in the countryside – coveted, protected, stolen, and sought after by everyone. Horses will reappear throughout the pages of this book, especially in chapter 9, which devotes significant space to the place of horses in the countryside.

Horses were not the only grey area for local police of the 1920s. Local officers were accused of dealing in moonshine, speculation, and 'requisitioning fresh fish from local merchants.'[74] Internal reports of the Commissariat of Internal Affairs through the 1920s noted that for police officers 'trade in spirits' in tea shops was a principal means of supporting themselves.[75] In one Riazan example, Agafiia Zakhachova, from the village of Nikitinskoe, complained in a letter to the Pronsk Bureau of Justice that two other women in her village, Tatiana and Aleksandra Kochetkova, had stolen from her. She reported the theft to the rural soviet and insisted that police officers come to her village to search the Kochetkova home. Officers Maliuchin and Golovanov came on three separate occasions and she served them tea. On the fourth occasion she baked them a pie, cooked them some liver, and boiled some eggs. She then asked the officers to find her missing goods. At this point they explicitly asked for a bribe, which she refused to pay.[76]

One of the most common complaints against the police in the village was that they had a tendency to drink. Some 90 per cent of critical notes to the press about the police emphasized officers tolerance for, and indulgence in, moonshine.[77] In OGPU reports sent from Riazan to Moscow on the local situation, it was noted that in both the villages of the province and in the city of Riazan itself police officers participated in illegal distilling as a way of making extra money.[78] In such reports, the most common accusation was that local police did not take the battle against moonshine seriously and accepted bribes to look the other way.[79] One report claimed that the district chief of police knew exactly who distilled and sold moonshine but that he took no measures against them; because of his tacit agreement to look the other way, he always drank and ate well and even directed others to the source.[80] In his ethnographic study of Tver, A.M. Bol'shakov notes that the peasants complained, saying, 'We drink and they prosecute us, but power [*vlast'*] drinks – and nothing happens to it.' The police maintained special places in the village where they could go and imbibe, and Bol'shakov selected a short song (*chastushka*) made up at gatherings of young people in the countryside to illustrate the point:

And those who carry out the fight,	A te, kto s nei bor'bu vedut,
Drink with the same appetite –	Te tak zhe appetitno p'iut –
Her destroyers	Ee unichtozhiteli,
Are her users ...	Ee zhe potrebiteli ...[81]

Local policing was so thoroughly linked to the production of and struggle with illegal distilling that it is worth exploring the issue in some detail here. Moonshine (*samogon*) was part of village culture.[82] It also symbolized, for the Bolsheviks, rural excess, darkness, and backwardness. The campaign against drinking was one of the early nationwide Soviet campaigns in which the police on all levels were asked to participate.[83] The struggle with samogon was, in part, a holdover from the Civil War fight against the use of vital grain reserves for the production of alcohol; making a litre of samogon required more than five kilograms of grain and three-quarters of a cup of sugar, and a bottle sold for 15 to 140 rubles per bottle.[84] Article 140 of the Criminal Code signalled the beginning of a systematic struggle with illegal distilling of moonshine. By mid-1922, an individual or individuals caught brewing spirits illegally for profit faced a sentence of at least one year in prison and confiscation of property. By November an amendment to Article 140 stated that recidivists would receive a sentence of no less than three years of imprisonment and confiscation of property. Persons caught with a still who were brewing for personal use were to be fined 500 rubles or face up to six months of community service (*prinuditel'naia rabota*). Police officers could earn bonuses in the form of a percentage of fines levied for illegal brewing, which sparked wide-scale searches of homes by members of the force eager to supplement their meagre wages in one way or another.

Of course, news of police raids spread like wildfire across the village and most distillers had ample time to conceal themselves and their stills. Moreover, a prevalent complaint across the province was that 'local power,' namely, the rural soviets, also did their bit to conceal the producers of a local resource much in demand. The struggle against home brewing naturally intensified on the eve of holidays, and the local press participated actively in the campaign. Some villages became examples of the perils of illegal brewing and sources of ingenious ploys to hide the sale of moonshine. In the villages of Kanishchevo, Nedostoevo, and Semchino, for example, distillers painted bottles white, filled them with samogon, and sold the contents as milk.[85]

In 1923, two commissions working under the auspices of the Central Control Commission studied crime and imprisonment in Moscow city and province over a three-month period. The results of the study were written up and published by A. Solts and S. Fainblit. The first commission studied prisons and the second reviewed criminal cases already tried as well as cases awaiting trial. Several days after the commissions began work, the People's Commissariat of Justice issued circular no. 113, which underlined the need to engage in a 'decisive struggle with the preparation, storage and sale of samogon.' The commission was struck by the number of women convicted for illegal brewing; out of 1,086 convictions, 700 were women. Among these women were a significant number of 'poor peasants' (*bednota*), and more than half were widows. In 1924, 24 per cent of convictions in the courts of the RSFSR were for wood theft, and almost 30 per cent were for illegal brewing. The majority of the accused were sentenced harshly, even for a first offence. The commissions moved to give amnesty to individuals being held under Article 140 and to decriminalize brewing for personal use or on a small scale, thus dropping criminal conviction rates over the course of a year down to 9.4 per cent.[86] In 1924, voices at the Centre called for contextualization of justice and policing within local culture and local conditions. And although Fainblit was one such voice, his opinions and conclusions still reflect a general Bolshevik civilizing mission noted in his reference to the 'village idiocy' (*derevenskii idiotism*) that must be fought by the party, the state structures, and the courts.[87]

The struggle with samogon illustrates the clash between the Bolsheviks' civilizing mission and local culture. A provincial report on police work surrounding samogon complained that the force worked in a context of 'complete indifference to the struggle with samogon' from all levels of local power as well as private citizens.[88] Peasants defended their production and use of samogon in various ways. They argued that they needed the revenue to improve their farms. Villagers pointed out that in the city there was wine and beer; it was not a peasant's fault that he had no access to such luxuries and was forced to resort to samogon to celebrate the marriage of a son or daughter.[89] Moreover, peasants argued at village gatherings and rural soviet meetings that if Soviet power could simply see its way to reducing the price of vodka, peasants would not be forced to distil their own. In other words, 'Soviet power itself provides the way to the path of samogon production.'[90]

Drinking was part of both village and urban culture, and thus part of police culture as well.[91] Alcohol was currency in the village; it sealed agreements and cemented social relations. In Staroletovo, about thirty kilometres northwest of the city of Riazan, the chief of the district police, Kiriakin, was often treated to a drink by local distillers in the village of Churlikovo-Martynov in return for looking the other way on their moonshine business. In Ranenburg, in December 1923, Constable Vasilii Konkov celebrated his wedding; samogon was part of the festivities. One officer refused to drink; he was arrested by his colleagues and fired the next day.[92] An OGPU report of 1925 noted, with concern, that a Skopin merchant had invited all members of the district soviet and the entire district police force to his daughter's wedding celebrations, for which he had procured ten buckets (*vedra*) of samogon.[93] Holidays and celebrations were not complete without alcohol, and a legal observer such as V. Mokeev did not approve. He wrote, 'The extreme weakness of the cultural-enlightenment work, as before, legitimizes old customs – they celebrate drunken weddings, drunken funerals, and drunken holidays.'[94]

On *maslenitsa,* celebrated seven weeks before Orthodox Easter and akin to Shrovetide or Carnival, drinking was an integral part of the carnival events. The Riazhsk and Sapozhok state and party newspaper complained that in the village of Kreshcheno-Gai everyone staggered about drunk, while those selling samogon stumbled around peddling their wares.[95] One local newspaper lamented that in 1924 in the village of Serezevo in the Podvisolovo district of Riazhsk a citizen by the name of Riabokon' rented land to a fellow villager for twelve puds of rye and a bucket of moonshine per year, and Maksim Khoroshenchikov paid half a litre of samogon for the use of a neighbour's stud bull. The reporter was distressed that such customs should continue in the new revolutionary era, and, to make matters worse, he added, the chairman of the Iurakov rural soviet in Nikitin District had already been taken to court for brewing moonshine.[96]

Agents of the State Insurance Agency insured buildings and cattle in return for samogon and found in favour of those making claims in return for a bucket or two of moonshine.[97] In Tuma, the chairman of one rural soviet, Efim Khatin, refused to do anything unless presented with a bottle of samogon, according to a concerned citizen who could not lodge a complaint about her stolen property until she brought him a bottle.[98] In 1925, Cheremushkin, the chief of the Karino District Police in Zaraisk, together with Gruznov, a member of the district executive committee, arrived in the village of Letumovo and conducted a search. The two officials found the still of citizen V.D. Osipov, but instead of writing the incident up, the three fast friends drank three bottles of samogon together.[99] Finally, police officers themselves made extra money distilling and selling samogon.[100] Still, the force did work on the campaign, and in 1924 and 1925 combined, the Riazan police conducted 24,258 searches, issued 16,164 protocols against distillers, and confiscated 4,972 stills and 1,461 buckets[101] of samogon. In the RSFSR, as a whole, 135,000 stills were seized in 1924.[102]

From 1922 to 1924, in the spirit of healing the cracks between town and country, party and people, that had been created by the Civil War, educated observers and even members of the GPU/OGPU were inclined to see crimes such as wood theft and samogon production as rooted in need, custom, and backwardness. One GPU report of March 1924 noted that, as the result of 'lack of cultural strength,' 'a lack of education,' and the 'current economic situation,' peasants turned to the 'age-old tradition of producing samogon' in a 'serious attempt to improve their household economies.' The report claimed that almost all citizens, members of the rural soviets, and even members of the district soviets participated in moonshine production and sale to supplement their incomes.[103]

The defects of local power would become an obsession from the mid-1920s onward as local officials, including the police, came under harsher and harsher criticism for participating in local culture and crime rather than being exemplars and enforcers of a civilizing mission in the countryside. As one contributor to the NKVD journal *Administrativnyi vestnik* articulated in April 1925, the police officer was the closest representative of Soviet power to the peasantry, and as such, 'each constable, in the process of carrying out his duties, must not only be a good Soviet official, but also a good social activist and politically engaged person.'[104] By August 1925, the same journal carried an article about the 'dark stains' caused by police behaviour connected with drinking in the countryside. The author, Odinokov, had been reading local newspapers for his part in the 'face to the countryside' campaign. He reiterated that the police officer was often the closest representative of Soviet power in the village. And while the author noted the existence of honest officers who fought against illegal distilling, he then went on to cite numerous examples from local papers across the Soviet Union about the prevalence of connections among the police, local power, and samogon. From Voronezh came reports of an officer who confiscated samogon so he could share it with the chairmen of the rural soviet and the local Committee for Mutual Assistance. Local officers in Voronezh were said to engage in drunken brawls and to have drunken parties, complete with girls and dancing. In Lugansk an officer under the influence arrested a villager; when the villager argued back, the officer dragged him by the collar of his coat behind his horse to the district soviet, beat him with his revolver, and threatened to 'shoot him like a dog.'[105] This kind of extreme behaviour and abuse of power received far more attention in the local press and in the central-level journal of the NKVD than 'honest' or routine police work. A vicious circle developed in the mid-1920s whereby sensational material was generated by the 'face to the countryside' campaign, and that same material in turn played no small role in fuelling the fires of concern at the higher levels of the state and party hierarchy about the 'dark' countryside that surrounded them, of which local officials seemed all too much a part.

The documents generated by the 'face to the countryside' campaign in Riazan, at first glance, conjure up much the same picture. On a cold February day in 1925, for example, police constable Ivan Semenovich and his assistant, along with the chairman of the local rural soviet, arrived at the home of Afanas'ev Moskovskii, in the village of Vzvozovo, to conduct a search. According to an OGPU report, Moskovskii was able to talk the three men out of their original task. Instead, the four settled down to while away the rest of the evening (it was already 9 p.m.) with a bottle or two of samogon. At 2 a.m. the constables made their way back to their headquarters. As they sobered up, they realized that they were no longer in possession of their briefcase with all of their notes on weeks of criminal investigations. They returned to the village, searching everywhere along the route, to no avail. A month later, a good Samaritan threw the briefcase, anonymously, into the home (*izba*) of the rural soviet chairman.[106] The chief of the Parakhino District Police in Zaraisk Uezd, Aleshkin, went to the home of Timofei Lunin, in the village of Lanino. The two drank to such a point that Aleshkin lost his whistle and poured water into his holster. Another day, in a drunken state, he went to the village of Gudilovo and sang 'Christ has risen' for all to hear.[107]

Constable Pronin of Riazan Uezd went to the home of a local villager, Semkin, in the village of Nikol'skii-Gai, who was a known distiller of moonshine. Instead of conducting a search, constable Pronin began drinking with Semkin. After consuming a sufficient quantity of the green serpent, Pronin decided it was time to fill out a protocol against the distiller, but he was too drunk to do so. Higher authorities caught wind of the story because Semkin had regaled the chairman of the rural soviet and a whole group of citizens gathered at the local soviet with the tale.[108]

Listing such deportment of the Riazan police provokes an initial unsettling effect. The police force looks ridiculously ineffective, hopelessly incompetent, and utterly corrupt. Such lists made their way to important party members collated, in all their sensational glory, in the central-level secret police reports. When one takes a cautious step back, however, one can begin to consider not only how common such behaviour actually was, but also what such conduct reveals and means. The fact that it was noteworthy that a constable had lost his precious whistle and damaged his holster with water testifies to the literal shortage of police resources. In any interpretation of such police behaviour, the Bolshevik civilizing mission loses. Some of the behaviour was perfectly acceptable in a village context, such as securing a deal with moonshine or singing 'Christ has risen' when a bit inebriated. Yet actions that threatened, brutalized, or intimidated the peasantry did indeed discredit Soviet power. This kind of conduct could be used by the peasantry to criticize, at best, and mock, at worst, the Centre. Peasants could call the regime on its 'official transcript,' on state promises for honesty, order, and good government.[109] Of course there were many more villages in Riazan that did not produce such reports than did. Police conduct in those villages is difficult to assess. Drinking and familial connections were part of village life and likely part of most villages that functioned smoothly. One important thought to keep in mind is the view of the localities that was being transmitted to the Centre and confirmed not only in secret police reports, but in other ways, such as in central-level journals, through government agency investigations, and by ethnographers in the field. The typical view was that of a periphery grossly short of resources, largely beyond the Centre's control, and blatantly living a life of its own. The campaign against alcohol and the relationship of the police in the countryside with alcohol signals well the dissonance between policy and expectations from the Centre and realities on the ground.

The campaigns against illegal distilling slowed between 1924 and 1927. In 1926, the Criminal Code dropped articles against brewing at home for personal use.[110] The tactic was short lived as it was difficult to prove whether or not the alcohol produced was for sale or personal use.[111] In January 1928, a new decree stated that the brewing of samogon was once again to be prosecuted under the Criminal Code and to carry a fine of 100 rubles or community service of up to one month. The correlation between the renewed campaign in 1928, the tax squeeze, and intensifying grain requisitioning is not accidental. The campaign was one of several ways to raise revenue for the costly projects of the First Five-Year Plan – the Centre's program for rapid industrialization introduced in 1928. Peasants flooded the provincial soviet with petitions appealing the harsh fines levied on them for illegal distilling and offering excuses for the existence of their stills. V.G. Luzhkin of the village of Prilipki was fined thirty rubles. He claimed that he was a poor man and could not pay such a stiff fine. Moreover, he maintained, his still was not for making samogon, but rather for preparing *kvass*, a drink made from fermented black bread. P.F. Grishin of the village of Ol'khovets was fined fifty rubles and offered the same excuse as did I.M. Sekatorov of Pechatnik. The soviet rejected all of their appeals. V.I. Teterkin of Gemenok in Skopin claimed that since his starter was not actually working (it was not causing the proper fermentation), he should not be fined. Several trends emerge in the petitions. The soviet tended to lower fines if the accused pleaded poverty. This tendency was especially true for women accused of illegal distilling. The fewer outlandish excuses the petitioner offered, the more likely a decision was reached in his or her favour. Fines were often lowered if the complainants claimed that their farm was in danger of perishing if they were forced to pay the fine.[112]

Tracing the relationship between central demands on the police and illegal distilling serves as a useful case study for a periodization of the NEP, both in changing policies and motivations from the Centre and in highlighting the realities of life in the countryside. In the years immediately following the Civil War, one notes holdovers from the war mixed with idealism, a sympathetic attempt to explain rural deviance, and a commitment to healing the rift between the party and the people. In 1924, legal experts mocked strict rules and literal interpretations and shifted toward decriminalization of everyday crimes in an attempt to address the problems created by the mixed policies of the early twenties. At the same time, both party and state saw a need for more tangible information on the peasantry and called for all to turn to 'face the countryside.' The changes in turn produced confusion at the local level about shifting rules and interpretations that saw a mix of old and new and of custom with local variants of Soviet consciousness. Starting in 1925, the informational results of the 'face to the countryside' campaign were increasingly sensational, contributing to a panic about the perceived realities of rural life.

This rising panic in turn became entangled with tensions at the Centre manifested in the economic debates about the future of the NEP and Stalin's steady rise and consolidation of power. As early as 1926, evidence began to accumulate hinting that the NEP was being abandoned. Still, 1926 and 1927 were years of local experimentation, uncertainty, ad hoc decisions, trial and error, and a general lack of system in the countryside. By 1928, hard lines returned as fines increased, tax pressures intensified, and grain requisitioning made its presence felt. More and more emphasis and pressure were exerted on local state servitors to be loyal representatives of Soviet power. The issue had always been a concern, but as the decade came to a close such demands rose to a fever pitch, coinciding with central-level campaigns against corruption amplified with investigations of 'corruption' at all levels and within all institutions.

This pattern emerges clearly in the campaign against alcohol and concurrent expectations of the police. What also emerges in the sources is the way in which alcohol served as a social bond between the police and members of the village community. In early reports on the police, such drinking was indeed seen this way.[113] However, by the late 1920s, in reports on the functioning of the lower state structure, relations cemented by moonshine were usually cast in class terms; if an officer had a relationship to certain peasants based on moonshine, he was considered to be under the influence of 'kulak elements' in the village.[114] A report sent to the Politburo noted that 'such a situation [low wages] inevitably draws the workers of the militia into crime: bribe taking, extortion, and the embezzlement of those funds that they find in their hands.'[115] The report went on to note that the situation made the local constable vulnerable to 'kulak bosses,' who could afford to pay them off regularly, such that 'the village finds itself maintained entirely by the local kulaks.'[116]

The new hard line is expressed perfectly in a 1929 publication of the state medical press, D.N. Voronov's *On Samogon.* His short book, the first volume in a projected series called 'improving the health of the countryside,' begins, 'With quick steps we are returning to the dark [*mriachnyi*] drunken past.' The first connections made are between samogon and a rise in crime, in particular hooliganism, among young people. The state, he continues, sold 480 million litres of hard sprits per year and added to that in the villages a 'wide river of samogon pours forth – a drink much more evil than wine.'[117] Increasingly, those who distilled and sold moonshine were labelled 'kulaks,' and samogon became in the eyes of commentators a kulak weapon used to control and exploit the poor.[118] Moreover, 'village power' (*sel'skaia vlast'*) was regarded as indifferent to the struggle against samogon, at best, and, at worst, either made moonshine or protected those who did.[119] Here one of the tensions of central policy emerges in sharp relief. On the one hand, samogon was depicted as a weapon of the kulaks; on the other, it was an intrinsic part of local culture, local power. Thus local power looked 'kulak' too. For Voronov, the battle with alcohol was the most important crusade for the state and for Soviet society. In fact the panic escalates within the course of Voronov's book to a call for 'show trials' against distillers who are 'enemies of the people.'[120]

Conclusions

The same patterns are in evidence regarding the police more broadly. By 1927, there was a distinct change in tone in the discussion of the role and nature of the police in central commentary. For example, the idea of militarizing the police was raised once again. Individuals such as I.P. Kiselev, head of the police section within the Commissariat of Internal Affairs in Moscow, argued against militarization and instead proposed the continued professionalization of the police. Emphasis, he asserted, should be placed on improving salaries as well as living and working conditions for officers.[121] Despite Kiselev's efforts, the tone shifted in 1927 from one of concern about the shortcomings of the police to one of demands for self-criticism (*samokritika*) by police at the lower levels.[122] Blame for shortcomings in police work would increasingly fall on officers at the bottom. The internal critiques of the police were replete in 1927 with criticism of the general paltry condition of the informant network and called on the secret section to insure that 'every village, every factory, and every forest district' had at least one capable and reliable informant.[123] By 1928, there was a hint that the village deputies had been assigned a new role – to inform on the behaviour and functioning of the police[124] – and the year witnessed a large-scale campaign aimed at coaxing villagers, at the same time, to assist the police. Agents went out to villages and gave 'agitational speeches' to encourage the peasants to engage in the struggle against crime.

A decision of the second All-Russian Congress of Administrative Workers, in 1928, returned policing to the NKVD, rather than the soviets, in the form of three independent departments: administrative-surveillance, police, and criminal investigation. In connection with the beginning of a 'new stage of the class struggle,' the ranks of the police experienced a purge.[125] The Workers' and Peasants' Inspectorate investigated the local administrative structure in Riazan in 1928. Of the 4,387 workers investigated (all of the staff of the uezd and district administration section, as well as the staff of the rural soviets), 1,085 were deemed 'unsatisfactory.'[126] The purge was likely in part a preparation of the local administration for the launching of the First Five-Year Plan and a reflection of the continuing war against the Commissariat of Internal Affairs (RSFSR), which resulted in its liquidation in 1930.[127] Indeed, the Riazan press after October 1928 emphasized the need for the police to play a role in the 'front lines' of the new politics toward the countryside.[128]

In an effort to illustrate their loyalty and adaptability to changing politics, an article in the journal of the Commissariat of Internal Affairs, *Administrativnyi vestnik*, reminded readers that the police were not simply an organ of protection, but an 'armed organ' that worked tirelessly for the class line.[129] The ranks of the district chiefs were reduced by 30 per cent, and in some places, such as Riazhsk, by as much as 50 per cent. Next to the judicial apparatus, the police came second in the highest numbers of workers labelled as 'drunks' or 'former people' and purged. Through to the liquidation of the Commissariat of Internal Affairs in 1930, one can trace the increasing attempts to gain party control and influence over the police.[130] That changing tone matches general political changes at the Centre, including the consolidation of Stalin's power and the subsequent transition to the policies of rapid collectivization and industrialization associated with the period of the First Five-Year Plan that would tear apart many of the social structures and fabrics explored in this book. The fact those structures were rebuilt in the years that followed and the ways in which that fabric was stitched together again are crucial subjects for further research. Despite the problems of distance, overwork, and underpay, the police were still very much, and increasingly as the 1920s progressed, a part of the terrain of local politics and power.

8. Police parade in Riazan, 1929 (photo archive of Evgeny Kashirin).

Chapter Three

The Courts

Here in the countryside, where every word is devoured with excitement and interest, involuntarily you remember the wise thoughts of Comrade Kalinin that each judicial verdict is an act of political significance.

L.A.[1]

Many historians of the pre-Revolutionary countryside have focused on courts and legal records in their study of Russia's rural inhabitants.[2] This study also makes extensive use of legal cases. In fact, those cases appear in all of the other chapters. Therefore this chapter is designed to provide a sense of the structure and staffing of the courts and the Centre's concerns regarding the courts. Specific cases are employed elsewhere.

From the post-Emancipation legal reforms to the introduction of the District Congress of Land Captains and the Provincial Board for Appeals in 1889, district (*volost'*) courts were peasant institutions. They were autonomous and functioned with virtually no interference from the state.[3] The village gathering would elect a district assembly, which in turn chose a four-member court. In theory, each judge served for three years. Traditionally, the peasant district court is depicted as 'shielded from the world around it from its old autonomy of bribery and passivity.'[4] Stephen Frank outlines the significant role played by bribery in the form of money and alcohol, both before and after the reforms of 1889, as well as the sway over rulings of 'influential villagers,' kinship relations, friendships, and patronage.[5]

Jane Burbank challenges traditional views of the courts and of Russian peasants in *Russian Peasants Go to Court: Legal Culture in the Country-*

side, 1905–1917. It is worth drawing attention to the fact that Burbank's focus is on the district courts after 1905, meaning *after* both the late-nineteenth-century reforms and the experiences of the revolutions of 1905. Both of these events brought peasants into much closer contact with the state, and that contact might have served as a school of politics for many villagers.[6] Burbank maintains that peasants were 'not content with custom; they had to have the law.'[7] She confesses that in the course of her research, her findings led her to shed her views of the anarchic, collectivist peasant who was constantly resisting and was consistently hostile to the state.[8] Instead, she found individuals who, through their decision to use the law and the choices that they made about what to take to court, were 'inhabiting and strengthening legal culture in their polity.'[9] For Burbank, Russian peasants came to understand and respect legal culture between 1905 and 1917. Cathy Frierson engages with this argument and agrees that peasants gained knowledge of the law and used the courts when it served their interests in dispute resolution, but villagers were also selective in what they chose to learn and how they chose to make and interpret legal decisions, in the capacity of both plaintiffs and judges. Moreover, Frierson draws attention to the fact that respect for the district courts also coexisted with the use of vigilante justice when it came to dealing with crimes that seriously threatened the community.[10]

Burbank is critical of Stephen Frank for his focus on violent crimes and the role of customary law in judicial decisions in the village. And while some scholars may find the work of Stephen Frank and Jane Burbank diametrically opposed, I would argue that their works are not, in fact, mutually exclusive. Rather, their different foci help to shape the particular conclusions that they reach. Burbank looks at low-level cases in volost courts to argue that the courts were training grounds of civic change and consciousness. Frank looks at violent crime and official responses to it as a window onto a tsarist civilizing mission.[11] Corinne Gaudin and Frierson emphasize the conflictual and fractious side of peasant life in times of relative stability and, like Burbank, see such an emphasis as a useful corrective to tendencies to view peasant society as a collective, homogenous whole as it appears in times of crisis.[12] Gaudin argues that from the 1890s onward, the tsarist state increasingly came into contact with the countryside. The existing literature on the Russian countryside has 'restored agency to the peasant, but at the cost of marginalizing the state.'[13] Thus her interest lies in looking at daily encounters between peasants and officials in the village as 'sites of contact and exchange.'[14] Gareth Popkins also finds in his study of peasant appeals of volost court decisions between 1889 and 1917 that villagers were able to skilfully 'engage the power of the state in their self-interested struggles with each other.'[15] These recent works make an essential contribution to understanding the pre-Revolutionary countryside, and my findings build on and augment their arguments in a number of ways. I agree with Gaudin that we cannot marginalize the state, yet in the Soviet village I am not sure how to draw the line between peasants and state officials.

Peasants came into contact with the courts when they were ordered to appear for breaking the law, when dragged there by a fellow villager, or when they travelled there themselves to seek redress. Like the police and the rural soviets, the courts were a nexus for the clash between the utopian dreams of the Centre and the realities of the Russian countryside. The challenges of staffing the people's courts with 'reliable' and 'correct-thinking' servitors, along with the severe shortage of resources at the lower levels, made it impossible for the judges and the lay assessors (*zasedateli*) to fulfil the civilizing mission placed on their shoulders.[16] Instead, the legacy of the pre-Revolutionary past, as well as poverty, officials with ties to the countryside, and the nature of the information-gathering system, conspired to place the courts, in the 1920s, in the camp of the suspicious and unreliable. As Gaudin concludes in *Ruling Peasants*, 'There is indeed striking continuity between the late tsarist and Soviet periods: it is to be found in the governing elite's extraordinary anxiety that the wrong peasants still ruled the countryside.'[17]

The Bolsheviks formally abolished the existing justice system on the heels of the October Revolution. For the first year of the Revolution, local soviets at various levels controlled what existed of a lower court system. Often infractions in the village were dealt with by the village gathering (*skhod*), which decided on the accused's punishment. The matter might or might not have been sent to the district executive committee for approval.[18] As Gaudin points out, the tsarist government's reforms at the end of the nineteenth century were explicitly designed to penetrate the seemingly cohesive and autonomous village. For tsarist reformers, though, it made perfect sense to integrate peasants into a reformed judicial structure. The Soviet government was trapped in another dilemma. Local institutions were supposed to be a creation by and for the people; at the same time, they were to do the Centre's bidding in a loyal and modern way. The role played by bribery and patronage networks and the seemingly arbitrary nature of peasant justice, as it was perceived by the Centre, quickly drove the Bolshevik regime into the arms of a formal, legal system. Thus, as early as 1919, despite their initial hostility to a traditional, standardized legal system, high-ranking officials at the People's Commissariat of Justice began to move in precisely that direction. From 1919 to 1922, a two-tiered system existed, with the people's courts at the bottom and revolutionary tribunals at the higher level.[19] In October 1921, the new system was laid out in more detail. Serious cases such as banditry, murder, and armed robbery were to be tried at a higher provincial court (*gubsud*). The lowest level, or the people's courts (*narsudy*), would try minor criminal cases and could sentence the accused for up to two years in prison or to community work, or could levy fines of up to 300 rubles. The people's courts could hear civil cases or suits involving property valued up to 1,000 rubles. Any appeal of people's court decisions could be taken to the Provincial Court.[20] Circuit courts were introduced, which travelled to villages in an attempt to bring justice closer to the peasantry, a dominant concern for the Commissariat of Justice in the plans for the creation a new legal system.[21]

A key difference between the pre-Revolutionary system of justice in the countryside and the Bolshevik system was that many of the kinds of cases that were sent to the people's courts in the early 1920s would have been settled by other agencies in the pre-Revolutionary period. For example, illegal cutting of timber was dealt with by the forest service and such cases rarely went to court.[22] As the chairman of the Riazan Provincial Court pointed out in the early 1920s, in 1913 Riazan had 339 judicial and judicial-administrative organs, including 250 district courts, almost seven times more than the number of comparable offices in the province in 1924.[23] Complicated overlappings of jurisdiction continued as the old system and attempts to create a new one became hopelessly entangled. A student of ethnography captured the situation beautifully in an observation of a court session in 1924: 'The court sessions at which we were present very clearly reflect the contemporary life of the countryside. The old customs, the new order are interlaced in such a complicated and often contradictory knot that Solomon himself could not untangle it.'[24]

There were at least three variants of the people's court in the Soviet 1920s. In one, a judge (*narsud'ia*) could decide certain matters alone. In the second, a full-time 'professional' judge and two people's assessors ruled on cases. In this context it is important to remember that 'professional' did not mean legally trained, but simply that the judge's position was a full-time one. The third, which covered the most serious matters, involved a judge and six lay assessors. In 1922, it was established that people's court judges had to have two years of experience in 'responsible work,' which meant experience in a state or party position, or three years' prior experience as a people's court judge. From early days, the state tried to secure loyal servitors. Anyone who had lost his voting rights could not be a judge of any kind. Before 1922, local soviets could nominate judges; after 1922, judges were appointed by the provincial executive committees. Before 1922, anyone could be a people's assessor, but after 1922, lists of possible assessors were to be drawn up by a committee consisting of members of the district executive committee, the deputy provincial prosecutor, and a 'reliable' people's court judge. The lay assessors were to conform to quotas: 50 per cent were to be workers, 35 per cent peasants, and 15 per cent former Red Army soldiers.[25] These quotas were all well and good, in theory, but the reality in the lower courts looked quite different. How did the legal system really function at the lower levels? Who really were the judges and assessors in the people's courts? What challenges did the regime face in staffing and paying the employees of the legal system at the lowest levels? How did peasants experience this legal system? How did they regard it? How did they make use of it?

Each uezd in Riazan was divided into three or four judicial divisions (*raiony*). Each division had a judge, a people's investigator (*narsled*) assigned to it, and people's assessors. The judicial division served either the uezd centre alone or the uezd centre and a number of additional districts. A judicial division outside of the uezd centre served anywhere from four to ten districts. Each division, in turn, contained anywhere from 14,465 inhabitants (such as the first division of Ranenburg) to 99,483 inhabitants (as in the third division of Mikhailov).[26] Some of the courts were eighty to one hundred kilometres from the villages they served.[27] The people's courts dealt with a massive caseload. In December 1923 alone, 5,884 cases came before the courts of Riazan.[28] And like the district police, local court officials were grossly overworked and underpaid. Most judges in Dankov, for example, received less than half of their monthly salary, if they received any salary at all. In Sasovo in 1923, judicial workers received 10 per cent of their monthly salary.[29] The courts could hardly afford to hire any support staff, such as a secretary, a clerk to assist with paperwork, or a courier. In the second division of Spassk Uezd, for example, the judge received sixty-eight rubles and fifty kopecks per month; the secretary received forty-two rubles one month and thirty-five rubles the next; and the clerk (*kontorshchik*) received nineteen rubles and fifty-three kopecks. Since this court could not afford to employ a courier, summons, writs, and subpoenas had to be hand delivered through the district executive committees or the police.[30]

Within the province of Riazan, even within a single uezd, there was remarkable variation in the appearance and functioning of the people's courts. The physical condition of the courts was not optimal. Some of the courts were housed in ordinary peasant huts and the lucky ones in buildings taken over by the local executive committees. The people's court of the second division in Spassk, for example, was located in the village of Moslovo and housed in the same building as the district executive committee. The court was provided with two small rooms. In the office were two tables, three chairs, two stools, and a broken cupboard. During court sessions the tables and chairs were borrowed from the office and moved to the courtroom. There were no separate witness waiting rooms.

The court of the third division was located in the village of Shilovo and occupied three rooms in the building of the party club (*Partklub*) of the 'Shilovo organization of the Communist Party.' The rooms were put aside for the court by the local district executive committee and were often unavailable for court use, as they were also used by the club and for any necessary meetings or gatherings organized by the executive committee. Moreover, the entire building was in serious need of repair. The roof leaked in heavy rain, soaking any court documents left on the tables. There were no rooms set aside for private consultation or discussion, so witnesses all mingled together. As in Moslovo, the courtroom had no furniture of its own, so before court could be declared in session, furniture had to be gathered from the neighbouring rooms of other establishments that shared the building. The record book of court cases had been lost in the court's move from Izhevsk to Shilovo, and the court had to borrow assessors from neighbouring districts. The building was not equipped for the winter and could not function once the cold weather hit.[31] The winter sessions of a number of Riazan courts that had no firewood were moved to the homes of the judges.[32]

In Shatsk, the people's courts of the first and third divisions worked quite well. The rooms designated for the courts were clean and adequately furnished. The court received subscriptions to legal journals and had copies of the legal code. Cases were dealt with quickly and effectively, and the courts were on good working terms with other branches of the local administration. The court of the fourth division was located in a brick building belonging to the district executive committee, and the rooms allocated to the court were well lit and clean. The work and look of the second division, however, was another story altogether. The rooms of the court were dirty and untidy. Paperwork was piled up on all of the desks and not stored in the proper, secure fashion. The courts had a massive backlog of cases. The verdicts and sentencing were written up without providing motivations and, as a rule, kept as brief as possible. [33] These variations are not difficult to explain. If the court had personnel who cared about organization and cleanliness, they would do the best they could with the minimal resources at their disposal. In some places, individuals likely contributed personal resources to furnish and maintain a people's court.

The people's courts in Riazan faced constant shortages. Most Riazan courts could not afford to purchase a typewriter. They did not have the surplus revenue to subscribe to legal journals or newspapers and thus often could not follow the constant changes in the law and in the state's expectations of them. Most courtrooms had no electricity and no money for firewood for heating in the winter. They lacked the requisite portraits of Soviet leaders and there was a constant and acute paper shortage.[34] One judge in Mikhailov, it was ruefully reported, had to ask the accused for his cigarette paper in order to record the judgment of his case.[35] The patterns that emerge in a brief study of the lower-level justice system are remarkably similar to those that characterized the district police. The rate of labour turnover for justice officials, like those of the police, was extremely high. In Riazan in 1923, ninety-five judges were nominated to fifty-one positions, suggesting a rate of turnover for judges of nearly 100 per cent.[36]

In 1924, of the fifty-one serving judges, at the moment when a survey was taken, thirty-five were party members, six were candidates to the party, one was a member of the Komsomol, and nine were non-party members. Of these fifty-one judges, eight were workers, thirty-eight were peasants, and five were either local intelligentsia or in the strange 'miscellaneous' (*prochie*) category. Three of the judges had higher legal training, twenty-five of them had finished high school, and twenty-three had only a primary education.[37] Thus, the majority of judges were from the peasantry, with almost half of them having no more than a primary-school education. There were approximately five people's investigators per uezd.[38] The investigators were originally assigned to the courts and prepared the case against the accused. Like the police, they too questioned witnesses and conducted their own investigations. The investigators faced problems similar to those of their police comrades. They were responsible for an unreasonably large geographical area with limited access to transportation, and salaries were intermittent and small. When these investigators went out to investigate a crime, they had no place to stay. One investigator reflected that only criminals tried to befriend the police and the investigators anyway, but it was necessary to allow them to do so as they might become useful in the future.[39]

In the mid-twenties, there were 794 lay assessors in Riazan: 582 were peasants, 55 were workers, 150 were 'office workers' (from the difficult-to-define Russian term *sluzhashchie*), 73 were women, and 7 had been in the Red Army. Of the 794 lay assessors, only 5 had any kind of higher education and 508 had a primary-school education only. Eighteen assessors were completely illiterate, and 233 were semi-literate.[40] There seemed to be very little enthusiasm among peasants to be lay assessors. One report complained that peasants regarded the position of lay assessor as a 'compulsory duty.' The peasant assessors had a point; the position did not pay, and one usually had to walk at least fifteen kilometres to serve 'for nothing' because the court session would be cancelled due to the absence of the judge, a police officer, a witness, or the accused. Some assessors in Riazan even asked judges to sign petitions advocating that they be paid to serve. The frustrated author of the internal report that mentioned the request concluded that such attitudes were 'exclusively petty bourgeois' (*meshchanskoe*) and noted with some disapproval that villagers preferred to 'sit in their felt boots and gnaw on sunflower seeds, in their spare time, rather than serve in court.'[41] Still, the numbers do suggest that the lower courts were staffed predominantly by peasants. The judges were almost 75 per cent peasant and the lay assessors were at least 73 per cent peasant.

By 1926, the general situation within the courts had improved slightly, but only slightly, and certainly not at a revolutionary pace. A judge's salary, when he received it, was about eighty rubles per month, the secretary's just over fifty rubles per month, and the clerk's just over twenty-three rubles per month.[42] Widespread shortages of office supplies, legal literature, tables, chairs, and cupboards were still commonplace. In most legal offices and courtrooms, seating was limited to two or three benches. Paperwork was often stored in a haphazard fashion, incomplete, unnumbered, and unbound. Access to postal services was still limited, and the minuscule amount of money earmarked for office supplies and postal services seldom arrived from the district at all.[43] In Skopin, courts were still forty to fifty kilometres from most villages. Legal literature that was received there often remained unopened. At least one Skopin court shared a space with three other offices such that those office workers had to leave their desks during cross-examinations.[44]

Yet, despite all of these difficulties, peasants did use the courts to pursue their own interests, especially in cases of assault, slander, divorce, alimony, theft, or property damage. The use of the bureaus of judicial consultation that were set up to provide legal advice to peasants testifies to the amount of peasant concern and involvement with the law. In Moscow Province alone, in 1922–3, the seventy-four boards dealt with 85,000 peasant requests for legal advice. In 1924–5, they dealt with 333,000 requests.[45] In Riazan in 1928, there were forty-two bureaus for legal assistance and twenty-nine offices to assist with legal paperwork. Citizens complained that these numbers were far too few. In the first nine months of 1928, the bureaus alone received 10,695 letters requesting legal advice or assistance and 14,610 visitors. Of these visitors and letter writers, 82 per cent were peasants.[46] Through 1928 and 1929, the Provincial Executive Committee and representatives of the Provincial Court expressed grave concern about the increasing number of 'underground lawyers' who lacked legal training and, motivated by 'personal gain,' led 'citizens into pursuing hopeless causes, drawing up useless complaints and unnecessary petitions.'[47]

It was difficult for peasants to travel to the courts, yet travel they did. They might have to walk twenty-five to thirty kilometres to lodge a complaint and fill out the appropriate paperwork. Three weeks later or more they would be notified of a trial date. Often the parties involved did not return alone but would bring along at least three witnesses. Invariably, something would happen to cause the case to be rescheduled: one side might not appear, the judge or the assessors might not turn up, and the case might have to be rescheduled two or three times.[48] Of course, sometimes peasants gave up and settled the matter among themselves, but often they persisted, the important point being that peasants did take the courts seriously and used them to pursue particular kinds of cases. Riazan peasants saw the courts as worth consulting and worth having on their side in particular matters.

One frustrated observer in Skopin complained explicitly that the objectives of the state – the enforcement of the class line, the courts as an educational tool – clashed with the aims of the peasant litigants. He claimed that the two sides 'collided' (*stalkivalis'*) over cases that were motivated by the 'plague of malicious litigation that has already sunk its roots into the heart of the peasant population and begins to bear its bitter fruit.' He complained that more and more peasants were bringing cases to court involving 'trifles' such as chickens, wooden beams, or old buckets with holes in them. 'Very often the people's assessors, themselves peasants, shake their chagrined heads in bewilderment at the end of the session.' The author of the article regarded the way in which peasants used the courts to be rooted in their 'darkness' (*temnota*) and 'lack of political consciousness' (*malosoznatel'nost'*).[49]

Of course, peasant use of the system can be read another way. When peasants chose to go to court, they made the courts their own to some extent. They would use the courts if they could but they would also resort to vigilante justice in matters they believed the regime failed to resolve adequately, such as the punishment of horse thieves or arsonists. Villagers would take land matters and insult cases to court or to the land committees because these matters were tricky in the village itself and involved notions of honour and status, both of which might be boosted if an outside and official force came down on your side. People's court judges and assessors, in turn, were lenient with peasants, and especially with peasant officials such as police officers and rural soviet members who were involved in cases of vigilante justice. And local officials were frequently involved in attacks on horse thieves in particular. This leniency was extremely problematic for central officials on a host of levels. To educated state-builders in Moscow, vigilante justice was itself evidence of backwardness and of the darkness of the peasant population. Vigilante killings represented the inherent weaknesses of the justice and crime-prevention mechanisms of the state to protect the population and also to protect those suspected of wrongdoing. The tolerance of local court judges for community attacks on suspects meant that local court servitors did not share the sense of horror that central-level officialdom and the educated had toward such violent local solutions.[50] And while Burbank's warnings against concentrating on the violent peasant are well taken, the regime itself concentrated on such peasants through the second half of the 1920s. That focus in turn both prompted and justified increasingly violent attempts at centralizing and controlling the villages. Finally, the participation of local officials in vigilante justice showed to what degree these servitors were 'of the village' as opposed to being missionaries of the civilizing mission.

Much of the information on the functioning of the courts in the early 1920s comes from investigations conducted within the legal system itself, prompted by investigations launched by the Workers' and Peasants' Inspectorate. The 'face to the countryside' campaign directed its share of attention to the legal system in rural areas. On the recommendations of Rabkrin's 1924 studies of prisons and review of legal cases in Moscow, changes were made that tried to address the central problem of the clogging of both the prisons and the courts.[51]

This early study was done in the spirit of the NEP, with substantial tolerance for the legacy of the past and its influence on contemporary justice. Within two years, however, this liberal view would be seriously revised. In the mid-1920s, the Centre tried to address the situation by decriminalizing the kinds of crimes that were responsible for the overload – illegal brewing of samogon, illegal wood cutting, and mischief – but the courts simply filled up again with cases of assault and slander.[52] Moreover, the police and the rural soviets still had to deal with the decriminalized matters. The police had to run down wood thieves and the rural soviets had to administer fines on those caught and determine how to collect them. What is interesting about the early local reports from Riazan on the conduct of judicial officials is that the complaints and criticisms were relatively mild. The criticisms do reflect the Centre's conviction that these state representatives should be the standard-bearers of a civilizing mission, but the complaints are also embedded in a wider context provided by the reports, which *explained* the 'excesses' of justice officials. The authors of the reports made excuses for the behaviour of local officials, saying that they were impoverished and not properly trained for their positions.

By the time the reports on the state of the judicial system reached the Centre, however, they were concentrated reports of example after example of excess. A 1924 central-level report consists of highlights of the most extreme behaviour. It begins by stating that the lower levels of the justice system were 'clogged' with 'alien' and 'clearly anti-Soviet' elements, not to mention the 'unwavering drunkenness of the lower judicial apparat.' The report goes on to claim that 'the investigators, the people's court judges, and often the ranks of the procuracy take bribes, engage in "fattening themselves up" [*podkarmlivanie*] and "hobnobbery" [*iakshanie*] with the kulaks.'[53]

The central-level report uncovered the usual suspects when it came to class enemies who had been found working in the judicial structure, such as the son of an imperial senator or a former land captain. The report was even more concerned, however, with those who, in theory, should be loyal to Soviet power: 'The struggle for socialist legality in the countryside is difficult not simply because of hostility of anti-Soviet elements but from the "loyal ones" [*loial'nykh*] – those representatives of Soviet power who compromise themselves in the eyes of the population through "wild orgies" and arbitrary use of power.'[54] The report then proceeds to list one lurid example after another. The investigator of one district became drunk and, with revolver in hand, and together with the local constable, tried to rape the wife of the local doctor. A drunken company consisting of the local procurator, two regional tax inspectors, the accountant of the raion executive committee, and the chairman of the rural soviet, raped and beat two girls in a communal garden in front of local inhabitants. A people's court judge in Tula was reported to openly socialize with monks and to be 'strongly biased against those peasants loyal to Soviet power.' He supposedly accepted bribes regularly. In one case he accepted a sheep, a turkey, some pork, several pounds of butter, and several dozen eggs to decide in favour of one peasant in a quarrel over horses. Moreover, the report claimed, he had special agents who collected bribes for him in connection with his court cases. The secretary of the court played the main role in collecting and assessing bribes. The report claimed that the secretary had already been sentenced for taking bribes and for anti-Soviet agitation and that when peasants approached him with a case he would tell them, 'This matter will cost this much.'[55] Another judge supposedly put the cases of wealthy kulaks ahead of others and was accused of drinking moonshine during court proceedings. Regularly, claimants brought home brew along to help settle cases, and in a short space of time the judge had apparently 'built himself a new home on his extra income and set his farm in order.'[56] In Briansk, a peasant caught stealing wood allegedly got off by providing the judge with two mutton legs and two pails of moonshine.[57] The report goes on listing such events from district after district across the RSFSR.

Accusations of public drunkenness saturate the reports. A people's court judge in Orel was supposedly often drunk and consistently rude to anyone who approached him. He once locked two women in the bathroom for four hours for talking in court. A judge in Iaroslavl' went to court drunk, without his hat, and dragging his robe. The peasants, the report claimed, laughed at him openly, saying, 'There is our judge. He should judge himself first before he judges us; now the peasant who brews samogon has to go to jail, even though it may have been need that forced him to brew, and there you have our public servant [*obshchestvennyi rabotnik*] shamefully drinking. They write in the newspaper about public service and how it should be carried out. The peasant will not crawl himself from the darkness but [will be led] by the public servants.'[58] This particular peasant speech might have been an embellished creation based on the Rabkrin reporter's wishful thinking of a peasant's desire to be led from darkness by a public servant. It could also be a good example of peasant use of the official rhetoric of the state in a skilful and ironic way, which called the state on its own 'official transcript.'

When Rabkrin sent investigators back to the villages in 1925 and 1926 to report on local justice, the investigators probably went armed with the concentrated complaints of the central reports ringing in their ears.

Comrade Karnov is an excellent example of such an investigator. His experiences in Sasovo served from beginning to end to reinforce his convictions that local officialdom was inept at best and likely against Soviet power at worst. Comrade Pleshkin, as a representative of the Riazan Provincial Court, was supposed to meet and welcome Comrade Karnov when he arrived in Sasovo on 29 April 1925. Comrade Vatolin, a representative of the local cooperative, as well as the chairs of the rural soviet, the district soviet, and the lower-level party cells, were all supposed to form Karnov's team. Vatolin and Pleshkin begged off sick at every turn and managed to avoid making an appearance the entire time Karnov was in Sasovo. The first, second, and third of May were holidays and no government offices were open, so Karnov found himself waiting out the holidays in the district centre with nothing to do. Work officially began on 4 May. Only the representatives from the district and rural soviets and party cells appeared to assist him in his investigation. Karnov put in a request for reinforcements from the uezd, but no one was ever sent.[59]

In one judicial district in Sasovo, Karnov found that the decisions of the courts were so formulaic that if you read one, you had read them all. He found the cases characterized by the clichéd use of juridical language with words such as 'the one being incriminated' (*inkriminiruemy*) or other 'pompous phrases' like 'taking into account the absence of harm to the Republic; the case is thrown out' (*Prinimaia vo vnimanie otsutstvie vreda dlia Respubliki; delo proizodtsvom prekratit'*). Karnov pointed out that such language was not comprehensible to the layer of society using the courts nor sufficiently understood by the judges themselves. He went on to note, sardonically, 'Sometimes these wise words are in contradiction to the sentence itself. They are of no use in either the village or in the city. In the seventh district, without fail, every case used the verb *to incriminate* (*inkriminiruetsia*) in every conjugation and not always successfully. Most decisions do not make logical sense.'[60]

Karnov admitted that judges and assessors made attempts to rule 'by the class line' in all districts, but that these attempts were 'such failures that the results of such a line are rather doubtful.'[61] The investigator observed that fines levied by the courts were almost never collected because the district police who were charged to do it did not have the time to chase after delinquent peasants. Furthermore, if the police actually did go after a villager who owed a fine, the officer quickly appeared back at the court offices with a document from the rural soviet attesting to the inability of the individual to pay due to poverty. By law, the fine then had to be transformed into a term of community service. Since there was no local bureau to coordinate community service, it was not a viable punishment. Out of the fifty cases that Karnov reviewed in one local court, only two (a case involving horse theft and one involving bribery) carried any jail time. The rest of the guilty were fined or sentenced to community service, which, he emphasized, meant that they essentially went unpunished.[62]

The cases that most frustrated Karnov precisely illustrate the arguments made throughout this book. Karnov was beside himself about the cases that failed to punish state officials for acting like village officials in the interest of village functioning. A rural-soviet chairman, for example, who was caught lying about a family's wealth, went unpunished. Another chairman of a rural soviet was forgiven for holding back some of the money, given to him for a specific purpose by the district soviet, and using part of it to buy a storage cupboard for his soviet and dividing the rest between himself and his staff as salary. In the same fashion, the local court decided that another had taken funds not for personal gain but for the 'needs of the rural soviet.' Thus, he should not be found guilty of embezzling funds that he had used to pay the salaries of those who had not been paid, such as the guard and the director of the reading hut.[63] Here again, the situation can be read another way. On the one hand, peasant judges were trying, as best they could, to learn the tools of their new trade, which included an obscure new vocabulary. On the other hand, they continued to make rulings based on their own conscience and the perceived needs of local organizational structures, both formal and informal.

The reports on local justice officials likely have the same initial unsettling effect as those on the corruption of local police: the courts and their officials appeared corrupt, ridiculous, and far from civilized. Once again, distance and patience are needed to get beyond this first impression. High-ranking party members lacked the right kind of distance and certainly lacked patience by the end of the 1920s. Power did go to the heads of some local officials. Yet much of the reported corruption in the courts was simply the continuation of practices long associated with justice in the countryside. Deals were often sealed with samogon or a leg of mutton, which greased the wheels of village life and local politics. In February 1928, the Central Control Commission again investigated the lower judicial system to uncover all individuals whose 'honesty is in doubt' and who did not implement the correct class line in the courts.[64] As Moscow moved toward implementing the wholesale collectivization and rapid industrialization of the First Five-Year Plan, the need for reliable cadres and more effective functioning of the police and courts increased. Moreover, concerns over secrecy within law-enforcing hierarchies escalated. A secret circular of 28 April 1928, sent from the Commission on the Investigation of the Justice System in Riazan to all courts and justice officials there noted that it had come to the commission's attention that the courts and their officials failed to guarantee even a minimum of secrecy in cases and correspondence. In agreement with a Central Executive Committee SSSR resolution of May 1927, all secret correspondence had to be kept in a separate locked box and all cases had to be typed and stored in a different locked cupboard. At least one court officer replied to the circular, saying that he would like to comply, but could do so only if he was sent the funds to purchase a second locking cupboard.[65] Through 1928, the officials of courts of Riazan went through yet another purge, with the most common reason for dismissal being 'ties to alien elements.'[66]

The Centre tried to create a unified court system in a country that had long struggled with stretching the arm of the law into the countryside. In the pre-Revolutionary period, numerous institutions played a legal role at the village level, and, by 1928, Soviet legal theorists began to think along these lines as well. In February 1928, the Commissariat of Justice made a decision to organize 'conciliatory boards' (*primiritel'nye kamery*) through the rural soviets, first in Moscow Province and then in Leningrad. They were deemed successful enough for the commissariat to plan to extend the system. The aim was to redirect the petty cases that were plaguing the people's courts, such as disputes between neighbours, slander, minor property damage to crops from grazing animals, and similar cases to these conciliatory boards. The boards consisted of the chairman of the rural soviet and a governing board made up of members of the rural soviet and twelve others chosen at a village gathering by all those eligible to vote. The similarity to the pre-Revolutionary district courts is not a subtle one. The boards were to resolve matters quickly, within seven days, with no right of appeal.[67] The boards were renamed the 'village social courts' (*sel'skie obshchestvennye sudy*). They spread more rapidly than the People's Commissariat of Justice predicted and survived through the collectivization of the countryside.[68]

In many ways the legal system was again divided, in 1928, along the lines of the tsarist one. It was divided into a peasant part, which continued to rule more in keeping with custom and tradition, and an official part. This official part of the legal system was then mobilized for the war against the peasantry. Judges prosecuted peasants who withheld grain from the grain-procurement campaign as 'speculators.' Arson, assault, and murder directed at Soviet officials were harshly punished as political crimes. Judges who continued to give lenient sentences were accused of right deviation, and those who had ruled as peasants and for peasants were removed from the seats of official, Moscow-style, justice. The use of the death penalty increased. The justice system that had developed under the NEP gave way to a system of campaign justice from 1929 until as late as 1935. Legal officials participated in the brigades that swept into the villages to implement collectivization and played their 'legal' role in the prosecution of newly defined crimes such as killing livestock, authorizing the confiscation of peasant property, and sentencing peasants to exile. They also played a role in the prosecution of Soviet officials charged with 'excesses' in the exercise of their authority.[69]

A walk through the rooms of the lower courts of Riazan and a study of the information gathered on the legal system in the 1920s – and, most importantly, how that information was presented and interpreted – yield a number of conclusions. By 1928, enough sensational material on the dysfunction of lower courts and village justice had reached the halls of Moscow and mixed with central-level battles over the future of the Soviet Union. The legal system was reorganized in 1928 into a two-tiered system. On one level, peasants judged one another in village courts on the basis of custom. The other level was inspected and then cleansed so it would be more effective in the war on the countryside that was collectivization. Yet a look through the windows of the rural soviets will confirm that peasants were not opposed to negotiating over the creation and improvement of a legal system up to 1928. The people's courts of the early 1920s were plagued by shortages of resources, trained personnel, and suitable space. Peasants complained about the corruption of the courts, the long distances they had to travel, and the frequently bungled scheduling. Yet villagers continued to use the courts of the twenties. Moreover, certain kinds of 'corruption,' as viewed from the Centre, was merely part of judicial proceedings as they had always existed in peasant memory. Peasants used the courts where they deemed it appropriate to do so – to deal with personal insult cases and land disputes. They rejected the courts for areas in which official justice failed to protect them adequately. And people's court judges even took the failings of the justice system into consideration when ruling on cases of vigilante justice. Up to 1928, many people's court judges and assessors in the countryside were peasants, and they failed to behave and to pass judgments in keeping with the Centre's demand that they be a part of the civilizing mission. Instead, they accepted samogon and mutton in return for services rendered.

Chapter Four

The Rural Soviet

The headquarters of the village soviet are recognized immediately by the red flag floating above the door. As a matter of fact, the flag of our village has faded to a very sickly pink, which offers a butt for discreet jokes by some of the villagers. The house is brick with a tin roof, the residence of one of the rich villagers of the old days. Beside the soviet building is the village reading room with a sort of lean-to addition to the same building set aside for an emergency jail.

Karl Borders, *Village Life under the Soviets*

Origins and Responsibilities

As with the offices of the police and the courts, a system of government based on local soviets could not avoid overlap with the pre-Revolutionary forms of local administration. In the pre-Revolutionary period, the lowest level of village administration was the 'gathering' (*skhod*). The gathering was made up of male heads of each village household and together they chose a leader in the person of the local elder (*starosta*). After 1889, in an effort to monitor and control village politics, the individual selected to be the elder had to be confirmed by the local land captain. Land captains were state officials appointed from the local nobility and introduced into the districts in 1889. Corinne Gaudin characterizes them as the embodiment of tsarist paternal authority in the village.[1]

The village gathering also chose petitioners, assistants in police matters (tenners), and representatives to the district gathering. The gathering was responsible for road building and maintenance, grain reserves, fire defence, the public peace, detention of suspects for the police, and other village services. The elder was responsible for the assignment and collection of taxes and dues. These responsibilities would be echoed to the letter for the rural soviets. The gathering was depicted as chaotic on one hand, as one Riazan land captain put it, consisting of 'yells and noise and general incomprehension,' and, on the other hand, dominated by the village's rich and powerful.[2]

According to the Soviet Constitution of July 1918 the rural soviets were to be the lowest rung of the administrative structure. The entire population over eighteen could vote in elections to the soviet, with the exception of the clergy, members of the tsarist police force, and those who profited from hired labour. The size of the soviet depended on the size of the territory for which it was responsible and ranged from three to fifty members. Larger areas with more than a thousand inhabitants were supposed to elect an executive within the soviet of up to five members. One member of each soviet was required to attend a district assembly, which elected an executive committee for the district known as the *volostispolkom, volispolkom,* or VIK. Situated hierarchically between the rural soviet and the uezd soviets, the district soviets were to be responsive to the needs and goals of the village soviets. The administrative structure from the uezd, through the district, to the rural soviet was also responsible for implementing and enforcing legislation from above. Of course, the constitution had laid out the ideal of the political structure, but reality was very different. Few villages had soviets during the Civil War and continued instead the old practice of electing a representative of the commune often referred to by the old title of 'elder' (*starosta*). The term did not disappear in the twenties. Peasants still referred to local representatives, especially the chairman of the soviet, in this way, as well as using new names such as chairman or commissar. The duties of the early soviet overlapped with those of the commune and the soviets took on traditional commune duties in many cases. Village gatherings were called soviets in some places, meetings (*sobranie*) or gatherings (*skhody*) in others.[3]

The Centre placed high demands on and had high expectations of the rural soviets. These expectations were reflected in the endless stream of constantly amended instructions demarcating the soviets' functions, pouring down from the Centre. From the start the rural soviets had overlapping jurisdiction with just about every other branch of local administration, precisely because they were the physical presence of central power in the localities. The rural soviets were caught in the middle between the demands and dreams of the central government and the demands and dreams of a large peasant population, of which they were a part. The duties of the soviet were to fulfil the resolutions, instructions, laws, and orders from above while simultaneously protecting and serving the peasants in their jurisdiction. They were supposed to follow the class line and protect poor and landless peasants above all. The soviets were expected to maintain order in their districts and work closely with local police. They were expected to assess and collect taxes and to improve the economic and cultural levels of the locality with virtually no budget to speak of.[4]

From the beginning, the Centre was worried about losing its administration in the peasant sea and constantly repeated that the rural soviet was the highest organ of local power and the 'executive organ' of the village gathering. The functions of the rural soviet were remarkably similar to the earlier responsibilities of the gathering: to aid in the collection of taxes; to build, repair, and maintain roads and schools; to organize local fire protection, local water supply, medical aid and services, and sanitation; and to provide aid to orphans and the families of veterans and soldiers.[5] The soviets were explicitly obligated to 'protect the rights of the labouring population and implement the laws of the worker-peasant government, struggle against darkness, ignorance, rudeness, embezzlement, the taking of bribes, usury, conspiratorial dealings, and other violations of the law.'[6]

The central debate in the literature of the 1920s, and in the historical literature as well, focuses on the effectiveness of the rural soviets. The debate emerged out of a discussion of the continued strength and influence of the peasant land commune (*zemel'noe obshchestvo*) and the village gathering (*skhod*).[7] The consensus is that the rural soviet remained weak and subordinate to traditional village organization and that the real power in the village was the commune and the gathering. Technically, the meetings of the commune and the meetings of the gathering were separate in the legislation of the policymakers at the Centre. In theory, the meetings of the commune or land society involved the meeting of the members of the commune (the heads of each household), whereas the village gathering was a more diverse assembly of the village inhabitants. In actual fact, however, the two often overlapped in the village and there was little distinction between the two types of gathering. In these meetings many of the major decisions on village life were made.[8] Another tendency in the historical literature is to embrace and repeat, without processing, the contradictions of the sources themselves on the nature and relative power, or lack thereof, of the rural soviets.[9] Of course, the sources are confusing, and both peasant and official reports, as well as studies of the local soviets, complain of corruption, abuse of power, and drinking. The challenge is to make sense of the whole picture. Where does 'corruption' fit in and what does it mean?

The Centre, through the 1920s, was obsessed with the quality of the staffing and functioning of the administrative system of soviets. Once again the Bolsheviks were faced with a fundamental dilemma. On the one hand, the soviets were the fundamental building and organizational blocks of the Revolution with a claim to their own independence and sovereignty. On the other hand, the soviets were needed as the most basic rung of a state structure. To make matters even more tense, the soviets had been sources of opposition before; the slogan 'soviets without communists' epitomized such opposition during the Civil War.[10] The obsession with the role of the local soviets intensified with the 'face to the countryside'[11] campaign, which involved a 'revitalization' of the institution. E.H. Carr has traced the origins of the revitalization program to the October 1924 debates in the Central Committee. Kalinin, he notes, 'took exception to a reference to the rural district executive committees as "organs of local self-government," and propounded, for what must have been almost the last time, the classic doctrine of the sovereignty of the soviets ... But this was a lost cause or an excursion into Utopia. What TsIK was debating was not the theory of political power, but the practical problem of creating a system of local government.'[12]

In 1925, a contributor to *Vlast' sovetov,* the journal of the Central Executive Committee in Moscow, lamented that the rural soviet was still not a clear-cut organ of Soviet power because it consisted of a mix of old and new: 'On one hand [the rural soviet] is a petitioner [*khodok*] on the part of its electorate, and on the other hand, an executor of various tasks of the district executive committee.'[13] Like the staff of the police and the courts, the chairman and the secretary of the soviet, who performed the bulk of the work, were overworked and underpaid. M.I. Makeev from the village of Kikino in Riazhsk observed that the rural soviet sometimes served as the police, the people's court, the land committees, and the local vet. The chairman and the secretary worked twelve to fifteen hours per day, and during tax campaigns and at election time, they worked twenty-four hours per day. They received massive quantities of circulars, instructions, and requests from the district committees daily. And they earned between twelve and sixteen rubles per month with no holidays and no right to social insurance.[14] Despite this adversity, however, they continued to function and, perhaps because of it, they were inextricable from village government in general.

The Look of a Soviet

The physical appearance of the soviets captures the degree to which they were 'of the village.' They were housed in whatever building they could stake out as their own and were expanded and furnished with whatever happened to be available, as suggested in this chapter's epigraph.[15]

The ethnographer M. Golubykh also offers some sense of the physicality of the rural soviet. On the second day of his visit to the village of Beliaevka, Golubykh decided to go to the soviet to register. He asked several peasants along the road where the soviet was located and none of them knew. Finally, a villager figured out that he was looking for what they called the '*ispolkom*.' He found the soviet, or the *ispolkom*, in a two-story brick building next door to a public place of prayer. The rural soviet offices consisted of two large empty rooms with 'filthy floors and walls practically buried in political slogans and posters. There was a strong smell of harsh low-grade tobacco [*makhorka*] and cigars that had been made from rolled newspapers.' There Golubykh found two men, the chairman and a secretary of the village soviet, sitting at their desks 'swimming in paper.' The chairman, Petr Andreevich Kazakov, was a healthy, stocky man who had worked in a factory near Perm. He was a party member and did not own his own farm. He had been the chairman of the rural soviet in Beliaevka for three years and was capable of understanding the 'small matters' (*meloch'*) that made up peasant life. 'He was an energetic worker but too soft in those cases in which it is necessary to put pressure on the kulak. He lacks the disposition for displaying his own initiative.' The secretary had been the volost scribe for twelve years. He had been a member of the Communist Party for three years, but had left the ranks of the party as the result of poor health. He was literate and had an excellent relationship with the local peasants. Their wages were negligible. The chairman earned fifteen rubles per month while the secretary earned thirteen. Moreover, the chairman had to make a large number of unpaid trips to the district executive committee, located almost thirty kilometres away. In fact, transportation was a constant problem for the chairman, and he had to rely on local peasants to take him on business matters in his jurisdiction. The rural soviet was responsible for six thousand peasants and 480 households. The soviet was overworked and found it difficult to meet the district deadlines for tax collection.

Golubykh claims that the real decision-making body in the village was the commune, which met almost every Sunday to discuss and decide village matters. He notes, 'Thanks to the passivity of the rural soviet members within the gathering, decisions are made that are miraculous [*chudesa*] for our times.' For example, the gathering and the soviet had agreed that all of the local clergy could use the pastures of the former church lands for free and had been doing so for the last six years.[16] Golubykh paints a rather grim picture of the rural soviet, the lowest rung of Soviet government administration. There is, however, another possible reading. Despite the shortages, hardship, and adversity, the rural soviets kept going. They continued to be staffed, peasants took elections seriously, and the village community itself preserved the soviets far more than the state did in the 1920s. As a result, the rural soviets became part of peasant government and peasant advocacy and as such proved a serious challenge to the regime during the first collectivization drive of 1929–30 until the regime could reconfigure their ranks with more obedient servitors. What may be read as passivity in the face of the decisions of the gathering can also be read as agreement; in the face of the complexity of local life, the members of the rural soviet saw nothing wrong with engaging in a fair deal with the local clergy.

Elections

More than mere agreement, by the mid-1920s, the elections to the soviets suggested participation. In the countryside, the voter turnout for elections to the soviet increased each year. Turnout in 1923 was 22.3 per cent, 35 per cent in 1924 and 1925, and 47.7 per cent in 1926. If it was indeed the case that women did not tend to vote in soviet elections, then a turnout of almost 50 per cent is an extremely high figure for eligible voters indeed.[17] GPU reports from Riazan, reporting on the 1925 elections, expressed the concern that peasants saw the elections as a way of creating their own government (*praviltel'stvo*) and said as much. In Riazan Uezd, peasants were recorded as saying, 'We peasants need to propose our own [*svoi*] people.'[18] The report notes that 'since the announcements of elections to the soviets, the population has become noticeably more active.' The turnout to village gatherings was much higher, and, in some cases, everyone over eighteen showed up to the meetings. The dominant rumour, recorded by the GPU, was that the communists were getting weaker and would not be selected in these elections. Ivan Podlin was overheard telling fellow villagers in Krivopol'ska District in Ranenburg that now the peasants could choose who they wanted, and communists would not make the list. The GPU complained that the citizens of Orekhovo nominated the former rural soviet chairman again, even though he was related to samogon distillers, assisted fellow citizens in the stealing of wood, and carried out a struggle with the local Komsomol cell. In the village of Izhevskoe, Mikhail Grigorovich Zarshchikov, Vladimir Semenovich Gusev (who was the son of a priest), and Vasilii Ivanovich Bolgin were nominated for the position of rural soviet chair, despite the fact that all came from middle and wealthy households.[19] In the village of Mokroe, Riazan Uezd, the chairman of the rural soviet had allegedly been an SR and now called himself a Tolstoyan.[20] Letters to *Krest'ianskaia gazeta* made similar claims. One from a Sasovo village said that the mood of the village of Malyi Studenets was in general close to the mood of the 'kulak elements' and that it was 'very sad' (*ochen' zhal'*) that the son of the local priest would have won the position of chairman if he had been allowed to run.[21] A letter from Spassk said that a good communist who worked night and day had been elected to the rural soviet.[22]

The Centre's alarmed reading of the situation saw enemies of the class line and alien elements filling the ranks of the soviet. Here again, one might read the situation another way and argue that the individuals were elected precisely because they assisted in stealing wood, struggled with communist youth, had strong moral convictions, worked hard for the local peasants (communist or not), and came from strong households. The OGPU reported that it was the middle and wealthy peasants who were most interested in the elections to the soviets and that they actively supported their own candidates to represent and protect their interests. There were indignant reports of individuals securing their candidacy in the age-old tradition of supplying voters with alcohol.[23]

The 1926 elections proved just as complex at the local level. In the village of Uda, Sapazhok District, in Riazhsk, a village correspondent complained that the village had divided into groups, each promoting its own candidate for the rural soviet.[24] And in both the 1926 and 1927 elections, the wealthy still continued to be the most interested in the election process and in securing a position in the soviet.[25] The Centre's response to their frightened reading of the local situation was to attempt to control who had the right to vote. In the cities and towns of the RSFSR, 4.5 per cent of the population of voting age were denied the right to vote in 1926, and 6.8 per cent in 1927. In the countryside, 1.1 per cent of those of voting age lost their rights in 1926 and 3.3 percent in 1927, which was below official estimates of the size of the kulak population – an observation that further alarmed the Centre.[26] Pressure increased on the local electoral commissions (*izbiratel'naia komissiia / izbirkom*) to remove alien elements from the voting lists.

Nuances, complexities, and the loci of local power weighed in on who had the right to vote.[27] The electoral commission, which in essence compiled voting lists, became increasingly important as a result of the growing attention from the Centre on the elections and the voters themselves. In the rural soviet, the commission consisted of a chairman named by the district election commission from the soviet and a member chosen at a general meeting of those eligible to vote in the locality.[28] They too were of the village. A. Ivanov wrote every year on the elections to the rural soviet in the Moscow journal *Sovetskoe stroitel'stvo.* In 1927, he identified the principal problem in the elections as the lack of attention by election commissions to voting rights.[29] Kalinin reported that just before the 1927 elections he was flooded for the first time with complaints from people who had lost their voting rights. The fact that complaints came pouring into the Centre makes perfect sense, since the Centre had been putting increasing pressure on the election commissions to deal with the observed problems of the 1925 and 1926 elections. The fact that letter writers were increasingly upset by their loss of voting rights supports the notion that the elections were taken seriously at the local level.

One letter writer captured the sentiment nicely when he wrote, 'I am dreaming of the voter's card as if it was a magic talisman.' Of course having one's rights restored was also crucial in a host of other areas, including employment.[30] The central theme in the complaints seemed to be that the local commissions had local interests. They used their power to remove threats to those interests or applied the guidelines for who should be deprived of voting rights in local ways. In Riazan, for example, practically the entire teaching staff in some districts lost their voting rights.[31] Legal expert Naum Lagovier was scandalized by rulings he discovered in his review of decisions of the rural soviets across European Russia. And of course, on one hand, some of these rulings from the Centre would indeed have been alarming. On the other hand, the decisions are wonderful testimony to autonomous decision-making by the commissions. In one village, voting rights were denied to unmarried women on the grounds that they were nuns. In another village, one man lost his rights on the grounds that he was 'old.' Another man was struck from the list because he had been away working in Moscow. One woman lost her voting rights because her mother had fallen ill and she had hired a nanny to care for her children. One electoral commission did not want to remove a villager from the voters list because he 'gave machines to the poor.' A certain Abramov was not put on the list of the disenfranchised because he sent an official document saying that he was 'a desirable member of the community' (*zhelatel'nyi chlen obshchestva*) even though he had 224 desiatinas of land, a mill, and outbuildings. One rural soviet in Vladimir listened to a petition from three 'trader-kulaks' who argued that the self-taxation (*samooblozhenie*) levied on them was too high. The soviet reduced the amount for one by 53 per cent, another by 70 per cent, with an 80 per cent reduction for the third. The same soviet reviewed the matter of how to insure local shepherds; they decided to use some of the money collected from self-taxation that had been earmarked for the repair of bridges. Other soviets put self-taxation monies aside for the repair of church fences.[32]

In the village, the electoral commission and the community behaved in a traditional way, deciding for itself which voters were unnecessary in elections that they took seriously. Disenfranchising women was an easy choice to make. Traditionally, women were not taken seriously in the context of voting and village politics. Women had participated in the commune and gathering only if they were the sole representatives of their household. Peasant men said that women's heads would spin from the swearing and the tobacco smoke at meetings of the gathering, and that women had duties at home such as cooking and minding the children.[33] During the Civil War, the soviets had been 97.7 per cent male and the number of women members of the soviets did not rise much through the 1920s.[34] Of the women who did get involved, only 5 per cent were chairing their soviet.[35] When male members of the soviet were asked why so few women were members, they would respond with a quizzical, 'What do we need them for?' Women complained that not only were they not invited to meetings, but often they were thrown out of them.[36] There was constant concern from the Centre that not enough women were participating in elections or elected to rural soviets. However, when women did become involved, it was not always in a way Moscow envisioned.

In a guide to party activists working in the countryside, Agitprop warned that organizational work among peasant women (*baby*) would not take care of itself and that 'the self-organization of peasant women is sometimes more harmful than the absence of organization' because sometimes 'wealthy women' organized and used their votes to elect their own candidates. In Podol'sk, the guide continues, these wealthy women promoted a priest for election to the soviet 'and even when they failed in this attempt they disrupted and wrecked elections.'[37] Restoration of voting rights was also rooted in local complications. Peasants took advantage of the new decree that those citizens who had proved themselves loyal to the Revolution through labour could have their rights restored, and peasants based petitions on their own conceptions of who was a worthwhile citizen.[38] A look at who exactly was elected to the soviets further reinforces the argument that the soviets rapidly became conduits of village rule in the 1920s.

Staffing

E.H. Carr has dealt in detail with the notion of the revitalization of the soviets at the Centre and with the perceptions and reactions at the top levels of the Soviet government to election campaigns. Therefore, this aspect of the issue will not be repeated here.[39] What is of interest to the current study is the composition of the rural soviets during the 1920s. Who staffed them and how did this staff change, or not change, over time? The Commissariat of Internal Affairs kept detailed statistics on the social composition of the soviets. Tables in the Appendix provide a striking sense of the make-up of the lower administrative structures in Russia in the mid-1920s. Worthy of note is the degree to which the social composition of the rural soviets differed from that of district executive committees. At the district level, the state had been relatively successful in creating an administration that was almost half party members in general membership, and 80 to 90 per cent party members at the chairman level. The rural soviets were a different story altogether. The members and chairmen were overwhelmingly peasants and overwhelmingly non-party. In fact the chairmen were more likely to be peasants than the general membership as a whole. The pressure exerted by the Centre to have party members in positions of power does begin to show results by 1929, but, despite their claims to party membership, the chairmen were still overwhelmingly peasant.

Age breakdowns for a Riazan election in 1925 are also revealing. Of those elected, 55 per cent were between the ages of twenty-five and forty, and 27 per cent between forty and sixty. Only 17 per cent were under twenty-five.[40] Even a young rural soviet member who was twenty-five in 1925 was already seventeen when the Revolution of 1917 occurred. These were not 'new men.' The report compiled by the Provincial Executive Committee on the elections to the soviets in Riazan in 1926 reported peasants as saying that communists were 'still young' and should spend less time 'acting like hooligans' before they could be elected to the soviets.[41] In fact, this 1926 report on the elections to the soviets of that year contains insightful analysis. The author claims that although local Riazan newspapers are obsessed with stratification in the villages, the matter rarely comes up in the villages themselves. Perhaps, the author writes, the question of the kulak is not yet 'a real question for the Riazan countryside and the consciousness of the peasantry.'[42] The author goes on to elaborate, 'The idea of socialism ["in the countryside" is added in pen in the margin] is still weak, in spite of an increase in propaganda there. Bad experiences with collective agriculture in the cooperatives have led peasants to think about improving their lives on the path of independent farming and even with state assistance.'[43]

Shortages of skilled personnel had a similar impact within the soviet administrative structure as they did for the police, the courts, the forestry departments, and other land organs, just to name a few.[44] 'Former people' – those people associated with the tsarist regime – were sometimes elected to rural soviets. In Riazan, in 1928, a former landlord was elected as secretary to a rural soviet. When he was removed as a 'former person' (*byvshii chelovek*), the district executive committee hired him to supervise the paperwork of the taxation department, which made perfect sense, given the fact that he probably had the skills to do the job well. A former tsarist police officer had been removed as secretary of a district executive committee, only to be elected as secretary of a rural soviet.[45] The constant complaint against rural soviet chairmen was that they sided with the powerful in the village, or, as the reports claimed, with the 'kulaks,' and that they liked to drink. The chairman of the Ushakovo rural soviet, for example, was accused of being drunk constantly and siding with 'kulaks.'[46] Being 'of the village' provided yet another negative interpretation of rural soviet officials by those who subscribed to order and sobriety and a general civilizing mission. Village newspaper correspondents complained constantly that the chairmen of the soviets did not take the struggle with samogon seriously. In the village of Zhelovka in Skopin, the chairman of the rural soviet, A.E. Sh'ii, failed to deal with the green serpent because he himself 'loves to drink' and can 'warm up straight from the tap of the distillers.'[47] A member of the Kurbatovka rural soviet, S.M. Zhokin, went to a wedding and sang along with the accordion player. He imbibed a significant quantity of samogon and then proceeded to sing to the local clergy in a 'deep bass.' The next morning, apparently still feeling rather festive, he woke with a hangover and 'dressed up like a jester' to set off for work. 'He affixed to his behind a tail from bast, covered his face with soot, and in such a state walked down the village street. He skipped along accompanied by an accordion and wailed away in a wild voice.'[48]

The GPU reported similar occurrences among members of the rural soviets. The chairman and the secretary of the Khrapyshka rural soviet reportedly got drunk every day. They were often seen with black eyes because they got into brawls with one another in front of the other villagers. They would go drinking in the neighbouring villages and, as a result of their drunken antics in the village of Iurutovo, they had lost the soviet record books. The chairman of the soviet of the village of Ostroukhovo in Zaraisk, Kuznetsov, did not battle samogon, but instead drank in front of everyone. He was often to be found at the home of the distiller Andrianov, who lived next door. Moreover, the police met and drank at Andrianov's too. Constable A.I. Cheremushkin often got drunk and spent the night there. The bootmaker A.A. Chrikov made shoes for free for Kuznetsov because Kuznetsov promised to lower his taxes. At soviet meetings, Kuznetsov defended the wealthy peasants but never the poor.[49] Some chairmen were caught supplementing their salaries by collecting more money from peasants for taxes than they noted in the official records.[50] The apparent corruption of the rural soviet chairman does not contradict but rather supports the arguments made here: local power was exactly that – local. The chairman of the local soviet put his wager on the strong peasants because it was in the interests of the general success of the villages to do so. Drinking and brawling were part of local life and part of local culture.[51] Local officials socialized with one another and with other villagers. Finally, the eternally underpaid chairman offered, in return for services rendered, one source of revenue over which he had some control, tax reductions.

Real Functioning

In a major study of the relationship between the rural soviets and the communes, M. Rezunov noted with increasing frustration, 'The abnormality of the interrelationship of the elements of the village triangle – rural soviet [*sel'skii sovet*], commune [*zemel'noe obshchestvo*], and gathering [*sel'skii skhod*] – exists in all parts of the RSFSR.' It was common to find cases where the commune ratified protocols of the soviet or the gathering altered the soviets' protocols and resolutions.[52] Traditionally, in the Western literature, the rural soviets are often dismissed as insignificant. A closer look at the village suggests that there was such a 'triangle.' Peasants quickly made soviet organs their own – a fact that became increasingly clear and more threatening to the regime through the 1920s. The concern at the Centre was that the commune and the gathering dominated and controlled the soviet, and this claim is most often repeated in the secondary literature. But a more complex reading is in order, one that helps explain the resistance through the soviets to collectivization, discussed in the final chapter. The rural soviets became part of a village system of government. On the one hand, the soviet worked with the commune and gathering on the traditional responsibilities of village government. On the other hand, the soviet was the conduit for relations between the village and the state at the lowest level. The examples that follow show some of the ways in which the 'triangle' worked. There were village divisions and tensions; in some places, more wealthy peasants do appear to dominate. This fact, of course, does not justify the punitive consequences that were coming to the village at the end of the decade. Still, these facts may explain why some locals supported collectivization, at least at first.

In a 1924 letter to *Krest'ianskaia gazeta,* a peasant from Riazhsk complained that for two years the gathering had been meeting on the matter of land distribution, but no one could agree on anything. The author blamed the chairman of the soviet who, he claimed, had gathered a group of wealthy peasants around him and who together helped themselves to all of the cut-offs of land that they desired. The letter claimed that the chairman and secretary of the soviet, along with the chairman of the district committee, were in league with a group of rich peasants. When the rest of the village complained about the land allotments, the officials declared there would be no more meetings, to which 'they and their rich allies laughed and whistled and applauded, saying that what they wanted they took.'[53]

In 1925 K.M. Koldashov, a Riazan village correspondent[54] for *Krest'ianskaia gazeta,* wrote,

> In the village of Vysokoe, Skopin District, Skopin Uezd, Riazan Province, the rural soviet does not do a damn thing. All the bridges are in ruins. There is much stolen land [hidden from the commune] and the rural soviet takes no action toward changing the situation. In this village, every summer all of the poor peasants leave for peat cutting [*torforazrabotka*], but the kulaks remain. And at this very time the rural soviet calls a meeting of the citizens of the village to which only the kulaks show up [all of them have land hidden from the poor peasants], but the poor are engaged in seasonal work. When the poor return, there is another open meeting during which land is divided again. By these means the poor are given worthless land and some are even without land entirely. Every year the citizens of the village of Vysokoe all plough the fields, but this year the poor peasants have not ploughed because they are still waiting for the chairman of the rural soviet

to call a meeting at which land is assigned. Such a rural soviet must be dismissed and re-elected.[55]

This letter is also noteworthy for the degree to which its author understood what Soviet buttons to push and how best to push them.

In the local Skopin newspaper, Petr Mashnikov, chairman of the rural soviet, and his brother Fedor, who was the secretary, were denounced as 'kulaks' with strong alliances with other kulaks. Their denouncer claimed that they did not give tax exemptions to the poor and made up fictional invalids to receive extra oats, which they divided up among themselves to store and sell in the village later.[56] Other correspondents to the local Skopin paper claimed that the wealthy peasants controlled both the gathering and the rural soviet. One author, in fact, used the word *soviet* and *gathering* (*skhod*) interchangeably.[57]

A correspondent from the village of Petrovka, Andrei Fedorovich Morozov, writing under his nom de guerre Goremyka (victim of misfortune), wrote to *Krest'ianskaia gazeta,* 'At the time of the elections to the rural soviet in our village in Andreevska District, Riazan Uezd, the chairman of the soviet felt himself to be a dictator.' The author went on to complain that the chairman regularly funnelled state grain and other resources from the society of mutual assistance to his friends and relatives in the village and that all goods and services were delivered only to his 'companions in arms' (*soratniki*). He concluded that this favouritism should be a lesson to all not to elect a wealthy chairman. The correspondent asked that the name of his village not be included if his letter were printed.[58] Rural soviet chairmen were accused of conducting themselves like former village elders and filling the soviet with friends and relatives.[59]

In the summer of 1925, a large number of villages in Riazan were questioned about their financial situation. None of the villages was without its own expenses and its own private resources. The study found that rural soviets, in order to fulfil expectations placed on them both by higher authorities and by the village, 'engage in various clever tactics to hide themselves in the initiatives of groups of citizens.' The soviets would create a list of expenses and take them to a general gathering for approval for initiating self-taxation to cover them. The gathering voted on the resolution to collect self-taxation, and the majority carried the vote. The minority were pressured to conform and, if they tried to evade their assigned share, they were pressured morally or financially to contribute; they could be fined or could lose access to a communal resource. In the village of Novosel'ka, Kuz'mino District, Riazan Uezd, for example, some ten thousand rubles were collected through self-taxation to maintain bridges and ferries across the Oka and for the upkeep of a system of fire defence. The budget was formed and implemented by the soviet, but was monitored by a special financial committee elected at the gathering. The tax was graduated according to wealth, with the wealthy paying more, but no one was exempt. Anyone who was reluctant to pay was denied passage across the Oka.[60] Taxes were assessed and assigned in different ways, and varied from place to place and cause to cause. They could be assigned by household, by eater, by chimney, by amount of arable or sown land, or by work animal. Yuzuru Taniuchi describes one locality in which self-taxation was levied per household for fire protection, per person for shepherds, and per cow for the upkeep of the communal bull.[61] One could also pay for such services in samogon, as a Riazan reporter was distressed to discover.[62] On 21 June 1926, in the village of Pen'ki in Sasovo, the commune collected ten kopecks and a pud of rye from each villager. The collection was conducted over three days, and in the event of non-payment a peasant would lose access to meadow lands.[63]

In these ways the soviet, the gathering, and the commune worked together. Moscow was far away, and these institutions were the ones on the ground day in and day out. Their functioning varied from village to village and according to local power structures and local needs. They did not necessarily function fairly or ideally, but they did function. And as functioning institutions of local government they would have to be coerced, co-opted, or reforged if the Centre was to determine their ultimate workings. In a secret report of September 1926 to the Party Central Committee – with copies going specifically to Stalin, Molotov, Kosior, and Shvernik – the head of the Commissariat of Internal Affairs of the RSFSR, Alexander Beloborodov,[64] outlined his concerns about the situation in the rural soviets. He was worried about the power of traditional village structures, the commune, and the gathering, relative to the soviets. He wavered between the idea that the traditional structures completely dominated the soviets and the suggestion that the three entities worked together. In the latter case, he acknowledged that strengthening the soviets meant strengthening the commune and the gathering as well. The principal problem, as he saw it, was that while the state was trying to limit who could vote in elections to the soviets, all manner of peasants could participate in the commune and the gathering, creating the danger that 'kulaks and anti-Soviet elements' could play a 'leading role in the countryside.'[65]

On 14 March 1927, the Central Committee passed a resolution stating that only citizens eligible to vote in soviet elections could participate in the village gathering.[66] There was an attempt to prevent those deprived of voting rights from participating in the gathering, but there was little desire or method to enforce this aspect of the law in the village.[67] In a 1928 study, Rabkrin discovered that few rural soviets had even heard of the decree or of the new demands placed on them.[68] The same law insisted that all resolutions of the gathering had to be submitted to the rural soviets, which decided if the resolution was legal and expedient. If the members of the soviets thought that the resolution was not legal or expedient, they had to send it up to the district soviets for a final decision. Once again, the law could not be enforced. Rural soviets often agreed with unlawful resolutions. In one case, a commune resolved that owners whose pigs grazed in the fields of others would be fined. Not only did the soviet ratify the resolution, it added that unclaimed pigs would be given to the orphans' commission – a rather ingenious and kind gesture under most circumstances. In another case, a rural soviet chairman ratified a commune resolution giving the entire village permission to cut two cubic metres of wood per household from the state forest.[69] The gathering through the rural soviet in one village declared insurance for horses no longer mandatory because the cost was onerous.[70] Even in 1928, reports compiled by the Riazan Provincial Executive Committee noted that there was no real distinction made between the land communes and the rural soviets unless the commune did something 'illegal.' For example, the rural soviet intervened when a land commune threatened to withhold clover from peasants who refused to contribute funds to hire an 'underground lawyer' to defend the commune in a land conflict.[71] All of these decisions make perfect sense in the face of local needs and circumstances. But a modern state needs a monopoly on such decision making. Moreover, for the modern state, there needs to be process and system. As a result, such local initiatives appeared entirely inappropriate and ultimately threatening to Moscow.

Observers from the Centre argued that the weakness of the rural soviet was rooted in the lack of an independent budget. The soviets had to submit budgets to the district executive committees and basically depended on a trickle down from this already cash-poor organ. In fact, the commune had more legal access to local funds than the rural soviets because they could rent land and could collect self-taxation, which amounted basically to levies on the population for communal needs. There was a variegated array of mutual relations between communes and soviets, and even within a single district they could take many forms. Sometimes revenues from land societies were given over to the rural soviet budget altogether; in essence the two fused in form and function. Sometimes revenues were divided, and sometimes the two competed for revenue. Moreover, most of the soviets themselves engaged in self-taxation and kept two budgets: the official (*kazennyi*) budget, which was sent to the district committee, and their own (*svoi*) budget raised through self-taxation or donated by the commune.[72] Illegal fines and collections became a standard way of enhancing local budgets. District executive committees were accused of using their power in 'curious' ways by fining citizens for having cockroaches or bedbugs in their homes.[73] In August 1927 an All-Union decree was passed on 'self-taxation for local needs,' which allowed the rural soviets and the district executive committee to assess 'compulsory' self-taxation for a specific purpose, such as road or bridge repair. A general gathering would approve the tax, which could be paid in money or labour. As D.J. Male points out, 'The main effect on rural soviet budgets was probably to give a general impression (wrongly) that the rural soviet could now impose self-taxation.'[74] In effect, the state was simply giving some legislative strength to an existing practice.

Any attempt to describe the actual functioning of the rural soviets is extremely complex. The sources often produce sharp criticisms, whether they are peasant letters or official reports. One needs to read carefully between the lines to glean a sense of the actual processes at work in the rural soviets. What is important to remember is that peasants chose to maintain the soviets, even when administrative funding was withdrawn. In other words, despite the plethora of challenges that the staff and behaviour of the soviets represented, they were still worth preserving. In Riazan, in 1928, there was one rural soviet for every 1,553 people.[75] When Riazan underwent the amalgamation (*ukreplenie*)[76] of its districts in 1924, the Provincial Planning Commission (*Gubplan*) discovered that in the vast majority of villages – from which the rural soviets had been legally eliminated – the chairmen of the eliminated soviets in fact maintained their former responsibilities. Some of the new chairmen were referred to as village plenipotentiaries and others simply retained the title of chairman. These chairmen or plenipotentiaries were paid from the same budget as before – a local one raised from self-taxation – and chosen 'by the general gathering that considers their presence indispensable.'[77] Moreover, they were still being counted in the census as rural soviets within the old district and uezd organization. Peasants saw the soviets as necessary and did their best to maintain them. The commune and the gathering *chose* to maintain the soviets and the conduit between peasants and state when the state could not afford to do so.[78]

If one looks at a communal budget from 1926 to 1927 (table 3 on page 307), the list in itself is a wonderfully revealing itemization of what mattered in the village. Not surprisingly, land matters were of central concern. Beyond that, maintaining links to the outside world and to the state, on peasant terms, come a close second. The maintenance of the rural soviet, to which more was paid in wages than to commune members, and the maintenance of the postal system, both of which were the responsibility of the soviets, reflect the degree to which peasants were committed to supporting a dialogue with the outside world and with the regime. The evidence suggests that at least part of the peasantry was willing to work with the Soviet regime in the 1920s, on mutually negotiated terms. By 1929, however, the Centre no longer wanted to negotiate on such terms with such peasants.

The decision to endorse wholesale collectivization, taken at the November Plenum of the Central Committee of the party, introduced a new debate on the role and fate of the rural soviets. Increasingly, the soviets were seen as a brake on collectivization and a source of opposition.[79] Some claimed that once the collective farms were established, the soviets would be superfluous, as collective farm management could assume their functions.[80] Kalinin and Kaganovich came out against the idea of abolishing the soviets in January 1930 at the All-Union Conference on the Question of Soviet Construction. The rural soviets, they argued, were needed in the task of collectivization. To improve the work of the rural soviets and better guarantee their loyalty, more politically reliable workers were transferred from the okrug and district to them. City soviets were instructed to send brigades of their own members and activist workers to as many rural soviets as possible for temporary and permanent work. Activists were instructed to organize poor and middle peasants to approach the elections in the spirit of collectivization and the liquidation of the kulaks as a class.[81] Molotov called for immediate re-elections for the soviets that had failed to support collectivization. As many as half of all rural soviets underwent emergency re-elections in early 1930, and as many as 82 per cent of rural soviet chairmen were replaced.[82] Through the emergency elections and the brigades, the rural soviets were purged of members who opposed collectivization. Some of the rural soviet officials accused of corrupt behaviour were executed and some were imprisoned.[83] Ultimately, it was decided that the rural soviets should be preserved and the communes liquidated. In order to deal with the soviets' budget trouble, all of the communes' former sources of income would be turned over to the soviets. The communes were formerly abolished in 1930.[84]

The soviets operated in the village in the 1920s like a corner of the commune-gathering-soviet triangle. The soviets raised money in the same way as the traditional gathering and commune, through self-taxation and fining, and often worked with the gathering or the commune to do so. In some villages, there were taxes on dogs, fines for not registering a marriage with the state registry office, and fines for drinking.[85] Just as soviets and communes could enforce self-taxation, soviets also listened to petitions from local peasants about how onerous the self-taxation was, and soviets could and did reduce the tax for some petitioners. Some soviets set aside money to repair church property, just as the commune would have done in the past. With the push for collectivization and rapid industrialization, Moscow knew that the local soviets would have to be shored up to provide the necessary support base to collectivize the countryside. The elections of December 1928 and January 1929 saw rising tempers on all sides. The provincial department of the Commissariat of Internal Affairs and the Provincial Executive Committee issued stern directives on the active role the local police had to take in monitoring voting lists and elections and promoting candidates from the poor peasantry, and women, for positions in the rural soviets.[86]

Within the villages, some peasants opposed the new pressures. Aleksandr Markin, of the village of Medvezh'e in Starozhilovo, yelled at the chairman of the electoral committee, 'You come here all tow-haired, and you know nothing.' He was arrested under Article 58 for counter-revolutionary activity and handed over to the people's investigator. In December 1928, in the village of Shishkino in Rybnoe, the 'kulak brothers,' who gave their names as Sekretar and Miron Soldatov, spoke out against poor and female candidates. The brothers were arrested. On 12 January 1929 in the village of Kurbatov, Vasilii Alekseevich Geras'kin broke up electoral meetings by banging his cane on the floor and yelling, 'It is not necessary to advance candidates for us. We can choose our own.' He too was arrested under Article 58. On 16 January 1929, in the village of Zaralovo, a group of 'middle peasants,' Dimitrii Leont'evich Zhil'shchov, Ivan Ivanovich Shimakov, Efor Efimovich Shimakov, and Ivan Vasil'evich Tararashkin, broke up an electoral meeting and established their own candidates. They apparently shouted, 'There is no place for women in the soviets,' and pressured all female candidates to withdraw from the elections. The men campaigned in the village, repeating, 'Vote for us, and we will defend you.' And despite the fact that two of the men were in fact elected, they were all arrested and held under Article 58.[87]

In July 1929, the Moscow Oblast party committee sent instructions to the rural soviets on how to prepare for the collectivization drive. The rural soviets were to rent and furnish proper accommodations for themselves and to strengthen their material base by assuming control over all mills, smiths, and brick factories in their jurisdiction. The central directives attempted to disentangle local complexities by ordering that all lands and pastures, all enterprises, and all control over the forests of local significance, which were administered by the land communes, should be transferred to the rural soviets along with all income collected by the communes through self-taxation.[88] As usual, central-level directives were all well and good on paper, but reports from as late as June 1930 complained of rural soviets that did nothing in the struggle against the kulaks but were instead a means of 'kulak defence,' providing some three hundred certificates of poverty to individuals, many of whom had been denied voting rights themselves.[89]

A Soviet Review

In his 1929 letter to the okrug party committee, a party member, who failed to sign his letter, reported on his summer vacation. In July he had gone on leave to visit his mother in her Riazan village of Diatlovo. The letter writer claimed that he was very interested in the rural soviet, so he made his acquaintance with the chairman, a non-party middle peasant by the name of Grigorii Poliakov. 'My first conversation with him was on the agricultural tax and work with the poor peasantry. I emerged from the conversation thinking there is no work with the poor. The poor are kept down [*v zagone*] by the kulaks and various types of kulak supporters [*podkulachniki*].' In conversation with the local school teacher, the visiting communist found out that there was a shortage of schools in the area. There were only two small schools located a long way from the village, which were not big enough to provide space for all of the local young people. Not far from the village was a church with a wooden lodge and two empty additional rooms that the church could use for itself if their lodge were to be confiscated. The local soviet held a meeting to discuss the expropriation of the lodge from the church. But the 'kulaks,' led by Mikhail Chestokhvalov, began to organize against the confiscation of the lodge. According to the author, the poor dared not speak out at the meeting for fear that they would need assistance from the kulaks at some later date. Even the members of the soviet, fourteen people and the chairman, were against seizing the lodge. The author asks, 'What does the rural soviet do in the area of cultural work? Nothing. Here is a characteristic occurrence: Before I left the village on the 29th, the priest who had been in jail for five months was now going from door to door taking a census – asking how many members were in the family, how many were communists, how many were communist youth – with the objective of collecting eggs from believers.' The appalled visitor complained to the chairman of the soviet, but the chairman revealed his true colours at a subsequent meeting in which he said that the local children were going to hell because they were not being raised as Christians.

The letter writer was also outraged because the chairman of the soviet had not arranged meetings to discuss current events in China.[90] The visitor harangued the chairman of the soviet until he called such a meeting, at which the visiting communist volunteered to give a lecture on the international situation. The poor peasants, he reported, were ready with their pitchforks to take on the 'Chinese bandits.' But the 'kulaks' giggled in a corner, lamenting the sad fact that had now become apparent to them – they would no longer have Chinese tea in the village and instead they would soon be drinking 'Bolshevik hay.' The letter writer found tax irregularities in the village. There were kulaks, he reported, who made bricks and sold them, but paid no taxes. He was also horrified at the situation in the village regarding voting rights. A former merchant, for example, I.N. Sinel'shchikov, had owned and run his own store before the Revolution. After the Revolution, he worked in the cooperative as a shop assistant. He was caught stealing and the court ruled that he should be deprived of his voting rights. In 1929, he had been reinstated. Another peasant, Dmitrii Ivanovich Gudkov, a 'kulak' and a 'speculator' (*bar'shnik*), who continued to trade cattle and meat as he had before the Revolution, also recently had his voting rights restored.

When the visitor asked the chairman of the village soviet about collective farm construction and the measures he had taken to promote collective farming, the chairman explained that there was no nearby collective farm to which he could take local peasants to see how such a farm actually worked, so there was really little point in discussing the matter. The frustrated author concluded his letter with a synopsis of what he did on his summer vacation 'as a member of the party in the countryside': he gave a lecture on the international situation, promoted the seizure of the church lodge for the school, organized the buying of three sorting machines, and held two conversations on collective farm construction. He ended on a humble note of self-criticism, acknowledging that he had accomplished little. The problem, he explained, was that it was summer and the peasants were extremely busy in their fields. They agreed to speak with him only when the weather was unfit for fieldwork.[91]

One could easily read this letter in the terms and context in which it was written: a loyal party member goes to the village and finds it dominated by kulaks and rife with corruption and patronage. He finds the poor oppressed and cowed and the class and party line violated at every turn. The letter, however, yields a different interpretation. It can be read as a poignant illustration of local complications in the face of state simplifications of the realities of life. The chairman of the local soviet was a non-party middle peasant. He called meetings over matters of significance and importance in the village. He and his fourteen co-members of the soviet had a considered opinion on the matter. On the one hand, perhaps indeed strong peasants ran the soviet, just as the party feared; on the other hand, precisely such peasants were the ones interested in local politics. They had the most to protect, the most to gain, and the most to lose.[92] Moreover, they had the leisure time it took to get involved in local village politics.

If the local priest could succeed in collecting eggs from believers, what was it to the rural soviet? The chairman of the village soviet saw little value in lecturing peasants on the situation in China. The local 'kulaks' were, in this case, any peasant who laughed at the author. In actual fact, they were more likely a group of good-humoured peasants who made a harmless and funny – until politicized and classed – joke about the quality of Chinese tea versus the quality of the new Soviet varieties. Unfortunately, not only were Bolsheviks not vegetarians, they also lacked a sense of humour, especially when it came to themselves. The regime took itself very seriously. It was not to be laughed at, mocked, or slandered.

Conclusions

In this letter on the Diatlovo rural soviet, two of the regime's fears about the nature of the lowest level of the state structure emerge: who was elected to the local soviets and who voted in local elections? The 'face the countryside' of 1924–5 and the associated 'revitalization of the soviets' meant an upsurge of interest in the elections to the soviet and the crucial issue of who had or did not have the right to vote in them. As the soviets became increasingly important to the regime, expressed in a desire to empower them, they became increasingly important to politically minded peasants or, as one central commentator described them, 'peasants with an SR spirit' (*s eserovskim dukhom*). In even harsher terms such peasants were referred to as 'kulaks.' The same commentator went on to complain that the class categories developed at the Centre were ineffective in the countryside because the regime had not yet convinced the peasantry that it had set itself the task 'not of raising the number of poor peasants but diminishing them.'[93] Commenting on the results of the 1925 elections, a writer for the central journal *Vlast' sovetov* reported that the kulaks had proved their 'appetite' for participating in Soviet power, trying by all means to put 'their own [*svoi*] people' into positions of power in the rural soviets. He claimed that the wealthy and the middle peasants were forming a block against the poor.[94] Again, the situation was read in class terms, but it could just as easily be read as a rational, political village response. The soviets were an important aspect of local power, and the more successful elements in the village bonded together against poorer households, which weakened the village. Local complications are also evident in the matter of voting rights. In the eyes of the local electoral commission, or of local peasants in Diatlovo who petitioned on behalf of the men whose rights were reinstated, these men should, for whatever reason, be voting in soviet elections. And the potential reasons were many. Perhaps these men were knowledgeable and engaged in local politics. Perhaps the electoral commission was stacked with friends or family members, or infiltrated by other 'kulaks.' Or perhaps someone had drawn up a convincing petition that these men were now socially useful members of Soviet society.[95] When it came to collectivization, the chairman of the rural soviet gave an evasive answer to avoid an unpleasant topic and to protect the interests of landholders in his village.

The relatively recent availability of archival materials has allowed a closer observation of the local workings of the village soviet, a fact that makes it possible to see the role of the soviet in a new light. This reinterpretation suggests that rather than being weak and ineffectual, the soviets were simply another aspect of village government. They were regarded as useful by the peasants and often maintained by the peasants themselves rather than by state resources. In 1925, Kaganovich lamented that the peasants did not yet regard the soviets as 'their own' (*svoi*). However, if and when the peasants in fact regarded the soviets as 'their own,' the institution would no longer be acceptable to the state as a reliable executor of its will. The challenge here for the Centre was precisely the fact that peasants did want the soviets to be their own and regarded them as one of many parts of local government to which they could and did turn for redress.[96]

Peasant government was a system of management that was often corrupt and capricious, but in the resource-deficient 1920s, it was, for peasants, one that was worth working with nonetheless. The soviet was important to the peasantry as a platform in negotiations with the state over crucial issues – taxation in particular. The regime's attempts to strengthen the soviet at the expense of the commune simply meant that politically minded peasants became increasingly interested in the soviets themselves and how those soviets could work for them. The soviets did become stronger, but as a peasant institution rather than a state one. The use of 'peasantry' here does not preclude that there may have been divisions among the peasants within a particular village. As we have seen, different peasants used the soviets in different ways and for different ends. And as recent literature on the countryside has shown, in times of 'normalcy' when the village was not under siege, it could be a divided and fractious place.[97] When the Centre turned to 'face the countryside' in 1925, it was horrified at what it saw. As the regime tried to revitalize the soviets and weaken the commune, peasants interested in local government and village politics paid the soviets more attention. The soviets and the electoral commissions were of the village. This fact made the countryside appear even more alien and threatening to the Centre. Faced with the peasant nature of the rural soviet, the weakness and the peasant tenor of the police, and the people's courts, the Centre became increasingly obsessed with what were considered the signs of village deviance and corruption. Peasant officials who served in the offices of the state – a state that appeared increasingly alien to loyal party members in the Centre – were caught between the demands from above to play a significant role in the Bolshevik civilizing mission and the pressure from their communities, conscience, and sometimes self-interest to make reasoned decisions rooted in local circumstances and age-old practices.

Part one has focused on the struggle for space. Chapter 1 explored the mappable spaces of Riazan. Chapters 2, 3, and 4 looked into contested spaces of contact, power, and authority. These points of contact became more complex and more ambiguous at the lowest levels, where the judge, assessor, investigator, police officer, and rural soviet member were *both* of the village *and* state servitors. These officials were constantly harried and pressured from their constituents on one side and the demands on their position from above. All of them experienced increasing pressures to assist the Centre in its struggle for civilization, and as part two traces, in its equally pressing struggle for control over vital resources in the form of capital and wood.

PART TWO

The Battle for Resources: What Non-Violent Crime Reveals about the Countryside

Chapter Five

Taxation: Talking with the Taxman about Subsistence; or, Feeding the Proletarian Cat

Trotsky walks from wagon to wagon, on his side a red sack – please give, good people, to the proletarian cat.

Chastushka sung in the village of Krivopole, Ranenburg Uezd[1]

You shove
    a word
        into a line of poetry
but it just won't go –
    you push and it snaps.
Upon my honour,
        Citizen taxman,
words
    cost poets a pretty penny in cash
As we poets see it,
    a barrel
        the rhyme is,
a barrel of dynamite,
    the fuse is
        each line.
The line starts smoking,
    exploding the line is,
  and the stanza
    blows
        a city
            sky-high.

Mayakovsky, 'Talking with the Taxman about Poetry'

The peasant is like a lamb: Whoever needs wool fleeces her. The Tsar fleeced her, the followers of Denikin, and the comrades. And now it is necessary to feel sorry for her, otherwise the pelt will be taken too, and after that there will be no more wool to fleece.

Bol'shakov, *Derevnia posle Oktiabria*[2]

On 15 March 1925, Ivan Abramovich Guskov, a peasant subscriber to *Krest'ianskaia gazeta* from the village of Eliseev in Sasovo, wrote to the newspaper to 'describe the situation' of the peasants in his village. He wanted to explain village life from a 'material point of view,' focusing on the income and expenses for each household. He began his letter by assuring the editors at *Krest'ianskaia gazeta*, 'We have no kulaks in our village.' Instead, he emphasized, 'there are only middle peasants and a lot of poor peasants.' The village of Eliseev was located in the very northern corner of Sasovo, fifty kilometres from the city of Sasovo and six kilometrees from the district centre. The village had not had its own rural soviet since 1924, after the amalgamation (*ukrupnenie*) of the districts and soviets, when Eliseev was assigned to the Vlasovo rural soviet. The peasants of Eliseev asked the district and uezd executive committees for permission to have their own soviet, which they offered to support entirely with their own resources; but their proposal was refused. Guskov pointed out that not having a rural soviet of their own in the village created massive difficulties for the peasants in lost working time. In order to get any kind of official document, one could waste an entire day and sometimes even two days in travel to the closest soviet, five kilometres miles away, or to the district executive committee, six kilometres away.

For the peasants of Eliseev, their biggest concern in their relation to the political decision makers was the agricultural tax. They worked the three-field system. The first and the second field gave a bad harvest, even if the summer had been a good one, because the first field was too close to the forest. Moreover, the first sowing was often destroyed because of the fog from the forest. The second field was low. In spring it was possible to plough it only toward the end of May, when the peasants of the other villages 'already had green fields.' The problem was that the Eliseev field was one-third swamp and the soil was sandy. Guskov pointed out that for this field to give even a middling harvest, it required serious fertilization. Thus the peasants of the village had to keep a lot of cattle. Cattle required meadows, and since the village had few meadows of its own, the commune rented meadows for twenty to twenty-five puds of grain per desiatina. To make matters worse, the soil required a lot of preparation before the sowing. Guskov explained that it was clogged with weeds and that a successful spring sowing meant a painstaking weeding. And, he noted, 'No matter what we do, the weeds are victorious.' Guskov outlined the income and expenses of the Eliseev villagers. He emphasized that the entire income of a peasant household came from its field. There were no artisans and no outmigrants in the village and no other sources of income for the local peasants outside of agriculture. The state price paid for grain was seventy to eighty kopecks per pud, so to pay twenty to thirty rubles for the agricultural tax, one had to sell a huge amount of grain. The tax calculated for Eliseev in 1924–5 was 1,882 rubles. The village paid 1,826 rubles and four kopecks. Insurance dues were calculated at 225 rubles, thirty-six kopecks, and the villagers paid 214 rubles and fourteen kopecks. The total paid to the state was 2,140 rubles and twenty-eight kopecks. Moreover, the village had all of its own expenses: 100 rubles for the forest allotment, 20 rubles for forest grazing, and 264 rubles for general grazing. The school cost an additional 113 rubles. The village 'plenipotentiary,' most likely their unofficial rural soviet representative, earned a salary of 70 rubles. Sixty-five rubles were spent on the night watchmen for the communal fields and the rural soviet. It is unclear whether this watchman was for the new Vlasovo rural soviet or if Eliseev simply continued to run its own soviet anyway, as many villages in Riazan in the same position did.[3] Forty-five rubles went to unexpected commune expenses and 60 rubles to the support of communal livestock. These expenses were divided among the village's seventy households, a total of 412 eaters.

Beyond supporting local infrastructure, each family had to clothe its members and pay the tailor, the miller, and the blacksmith. After all of the expenses, the villagers had only a half of a pud of grain per eater left over. A number of families did not have enough seed grain for the spring sowing. Guskov wrote, 'Reading the newspaper on the slogan "face to the countryside" and thinking about how to implement it in real life, I think that the peasant lived through a difficult time and that he will construct his well-being in different conditions, and Soviet power will lead the peasant economy on the path of profitable economy. We can do this, but do not tax us so much – the poor get poorer.'

Guskov concluded his letter with his opinion on how the state should conduct its tax campaign in the following year. He argued that cattle should not be taxed at all; instead, the state should encourage cattle breeding. When assigning the tax, the assessors should take into account the quality of land and verify it on the spot through a local commission made up of peasants and 'representatives of power.' At the beginning of August, the commission must determine the harvest potential and working capacity of each household, taking into account the number of working hands. The collection of the tax should be divided into three fixed payment periods, announced well ahead of time because the changes of the payment periods this year meant several households were fined. The payment period was too short and the peasants learned of the change only two days before it was put into effect; thus, there was no way for them to raise the money for the tax. As a result, the poorer peasants had to sell their belongings and became even more impoverished.[4]

It would be easy to dismiss peasant complaints about taxes with the maxim that 'peasants always complain about taxes,' and that would be absolutely correct, because people do. Part of the definition of peasant includes the burden the agrarian toiler bears to the powers that bind him with duties and obligations. The Russian peasant of the 1920s was no exception. Yet Guskov's letter is interesting and revealing. It demonstrates that peasants were painfully aware of the language of the regime, of the regime's fears, and of its concerns. Guskov wanted his letter to be taken seriously, so his village had no kulaks, and the complicated variables of outmigrant and artisanal earnings were conveniently factored out of his portrait. The matter of the rural soviet was raised immediately; villagers wanted their own rural soviet and were willing to support it. They took the soviet seriously and saw it as a crucial link in negotiations with the new regime. These negotiations hinged upon the agricultural tax. Peasants needed to protect themselves and to make the state understand that taxes had to be kept within the bounds of the moral economy. Moreover, the state had to understand and be flexible in the face of local complications when assessing the agricultural tax. Sasovo is located in Riazan's northeast, and Eliseev in the most northern part of the uezd. In that region, soil was poor and villagers depended more on the raising of cattle than they did elsewhere. Thus, Guskov informed the state that the villagers raised cattle for fertilizer and out of the necessities of the local complications of farming, not out of a desire for capitalist gain. Therefore, he argued, peasants should pay less tax on cattle than in other regions.

Guskov factored in State Insurance payments as a kind of tax, a feeling that peasants across the country shared with him.[5] He provided a sharp, detailed picture of the subsistence-level existence of his village and the admirable way the village still managed to run itself. Most significantly, perhaps, Guskov captured the peasants' willingness in the mid-1920s to work with the regime. 'We can do this, but do not tax us too much.' Peasants in the mid-1920s agreed to engage in activities of the state and to interact with the state, but on mutually negotiated terms. The villagers of Eliseev, far from rejecting the Soviet state in 1925, expressed a desire to be more integrated. They petitioned the loss of their rural soviet and offered to support it entirely on their own.

Before the Great Reforms of Alexander II, the population of the Russian Empire was divided into taxpaying and non-taxpaying groups. One identifying marker of belonging to the common people, and not to the elite, was the fact that commoners paid taxes. The individual head tax was the main source of tax revenue, but indirect taxes on such essential items as alcohol and salt also fell most heavily on the shoulders of the peasant. Even after Alexander II abolished the head tax, revenue was still raised through taxes on tobacco, sugar, and alcohol and weighed heavily on the rural population. In 1885, 24.1 per cent of state tax revenue came from direct taxes and 66.7 per cent from indirect taxes. In 1913, direct taxes dropped to 12.9 per cent, while indirect taxes rose to 76.1 per cent.[6]

The desperate shortages and the need to supply the Red Army during the Civil War involved the replacement of a money economy with the forced grain and food requisitioning of War Communism. The economic pressures of the Civil War were crushing for the Russian peasantry. Pushed to the breaking point, peasants rebelled in their own 'green revolution.' Their protest was significant in the regime's shift to the New Economic Policy in 1921, when the grain requisitions were replaced by a tax in kind (*prodnalog*), which had its own challenges. The regime was still short of revenue, and the peasantry was forced to focus its energies almost exclusively on the products needed to fulfil the tax. The organizational pressures and transportation costs of collecting, storing, and transporting the goods posed massive logistical problems. The tax in kind was difficult for Riazan peasants; members of the state security forces complained in their reports that when local officials arrived in a village to take property inventories of households that had failed to pay their taxes, the families encouraged their children to cry and beg, making the officials feel guilty.[7]

After a transitional year in 1923, when the tax was a mix of a money tax and tax in kind, the unified agricultural tax (*edinnyi sel'skokhoziaistvennyi nalog*) was introduced to be paid in money alone. The tax was 'unified' because it was supposed to be the only tax that rural inhabitants had to pay, replacing a complex plethora of taxes.[8] Initially the peasant response was one of relief. When the transition to the unified tax was introduced, state security in Riazan reported that the peasant mood had lifted and that peasants in the region seemed to have hope and to anticipate a good harvest. There were virtually no complaints.[9] The first reports on the collection of the transition year 1923–4, from a mixed money and goods tax to the new unified agricultural tax, were cautiously optimistic on the local level. Despite the facts that the harvest had not been especially good, that poor households felt dependent on the wealthy to pull them through difficult times, and that peasants felt pressured financially, the numbers for collection of taxes for 1923–4 were better than they had been, with an average for the province of over 80 per cent collected.[10] In the first year of the unified agricultural tax, peasants were interested in the process and wanted to know when they would be taxed and how much. In areas where the harvest was good, peasants paid their taxes at a rate of 90 per cent or higher.[11] Thus, despite their tendency to contest and complain about taxes, peasants were ready to pay them within reason. In 1924, peasants were prepared to work with the new regime on reasonable terms. What did provoke peasant anger in these years were heavy fines for late payment of taxes. Farming was not an exact science, and the peasant farmer was at the whim of weather, the loss of livestock through theft or disease, fire, and natural disasters. The peasants were disposed to pay their taxes, but wanted tolerance and understanding of local complications in cases when they missed a deadline.[12] Moreover, in the early years, an order from Moscow would reach the local level on 20 February that all taxes were due on 15 February, and anyone who had defaulted was liable to fines and automatically assessed for both the tax and the penalty for late payment.[13] In December 1924, peasants in Ranenburg and other areas in Riazan Province refused to pay their taxes because they were extremely angry about such fines.[14]

In 1924, the Centre seemed keen to negotiate the issue of taxation with peasants, just as peasants, in the same time period, felt relatively confident about negotiating as well. A decree of 15 July 1924, for example, reduced taxes on livestock in response to peasant complaints. And the tone of the 1924 guide to taxation, written in the spirit of high NEP, was one of encouragement to peasants to improve their farms, enrich their soil, fertilize, and mechanize so that the 'necessary payment of taxes will feel much less.'[15]

What does become evident in the sources on the early years of the unified agricultural tax is that local complications made their way into the tax-assessment and tax-collecting system. The fact that peasants were grudgingly amenable to paying reasonable taxes did not stop them from discussing and complaining about them. In November 1924, Mikhail Petrovich Solonin of the village of Borganov, of the Alad'ino district in Sasovo, was charged under Article 83 of the Criminal Code for agitation against the tax. A local tax inspector (*finagent*) called for his arrest on the grounds that his agitation explained the poor showing of the village in its tax payments. The case went to the local people's court. At the trial, the chairman of the rural soviet testified that the village had indeed not paid their taxes in full. He went on to argue that this fact, however, was entirely due to their poverty and not a matter of any 'agitation' against the tax on Solonin's part. The village rallied around Solonin, sending to the court a petition with over forty signatures and at least another thirty crosses from illiterate villagers unable to sign their names in full. It seems that Solonin had indeed told his fellow villagers that there would be a reduction (*skidka*) in their obligation, but witness after witness testified that he never told them not to pay their taxes and that he never agitated against the tax. The Provincial Court found in Solonin's favour.[16] The case reveals the most basic level of local complication. The uezd and its inspector, desperate to collect taxes, searched for a reason why the peasants of the village of Borganov had not paid. The village, in turn, and its closest local official rallied around the scapegoat, and a tangle of investigation, paperwork, and ultimately a court case moved from the local to the provincial level, followed.

Still, despite the mild disputes of 1924, 1925 once again embraced a cautious optimism about the countryside and taxation in Riazan. The state security reports from the fall of 1925 on peasant mood and taxation note that heavy rains were affecting the harvests and were causing concern for Riazan peasants, and villagers expressed concern about taxes, but, in general, they felt that they were reasonable and that they would be able to pay.[17]

The People's Commissariat of Finance determined the total amount of taxes due in the country in a given year, based on the size and success of harvest. The commissariat then assigned a fixed amount to each province, based on an estimation of that province's yield. The Provincial Commissariat of Finance then further subdivided the assignments by uezd, based on how much the uezd was estimated to produce. Uezd officials then assigned an amount due from each district.[18] It was acknowledged that the Centre was unable to predict or completely understand local conditions, and provisions were made so that adjustments could be made locally, provided, of course, that the province met the tax obligation assigned by the Centre.[19] The district executive committees had a financial-taxation department, which worked closely with the uezd financial department. The district executive committee organized a tax commission for the district, checked the tax rolls created by the rural soviets, calculated the tax due, filled out the tax lists, received the payments for the district, participated in punishing those who failed to pay, and ensured that tax monies reached the uezd or province.

Each household was required to list the amount of ploughed land (*pashen*), the amount of sown land (*posev*) and hay fields (*senokos*), the number of horses and cows belonging to the household, and the non-agricultural income of the household for the year. The rural soviet then verified that the information was correct and called a gathering to inform the villagers of their assessments. One copy was sent to the district executive committee and another kept at the rural soviet. The district executive committee then converted all of the variables into the equivalents of ploughed land. These equivalents varied from place to place across the Soviet Union, depending on the worth of each item in that area. For example, in Samara a horse was the equivalent of 0.70 desiatina of ploughed land. A cow was worth 0.60 desiatina, and 2 desiatina of hay fields was considered the equivalent of 1 desiatina of ploughed field. The total was divided by the number of eaters in the family and then placed in a tax category accordingly. There were three payment periods. Thirty per cent was due by 1 November, 35 per cent by 1 January, and 35 per cent by 1 April. It was the responsibility of the chairman of the rural soviet to make sure payment was made on time. Payments could be made at the district executive committee, banks, or postal stations, and they could be made individually or collectively, the latter being more convenient for the village. The rural soviets were charged with familiarizing the population with the unified agricultural tax through the village gathering. They created a list of the inhabitants of the area under their jurisdiction and submitted the list to the district executive committee to be looked over as the foundation for the calculation of assessments for each household. Then the rural soviet was responsible for distributing the assessments to the taxpayers and keeping track of tax payments. Rural soviets were to explain the consequences of non-payment to the peasantry and struggle with 'under-payment.' Much time and resources of members of the rural soviets were devoted to tax collection, the principal demand on them from above. This role was important for the village as a whole because taxation was accepted as part of life and a process that needed to be constantly monitored, considered, and negotiated. Any input in the system was a valuable asset to the peasant.

Those entitled to reductions included impoverished households – those without working hands or cattle, or whose land holdings fell below viable norms. The families of Red Army soldiers, OGPU, the police, invalids, invalids from the Civil War or the First World War, students in party schools or workers' faculties, universities, medical or veterinary schools were all entitled to exemptions. Those households struck by natural calamities – such as fire, flood, loss of cattle due to disease or theft, the death or serious illness of a principal worker – could get the chairman of the rural soviet to verify their losses so they could receive exemptions. New settlers (*pereselentsy*) were exempt for three years. Collective farms and cooperatives were eligible for reductions or exemptions. Horses working for fire defence were exempt from taxation.[20]

Local complications once more challenged the simplicity of policy originating at the Centre. The rural soviet had incredible power to protect villagers of its choosing from taxation. There were frequent complaints that chairmen of the rural soviets misapplied reductions, passing them out liberally to friends and family and refusing them to invalids and the families of Red Army servicemen.[21] Some rural soviet chairmen made up 'fictional' invalids for their villages so that they would receive extra grain and oats, which they could divide among their friends or sell later.[22] Following tradition, rural soviet chairmen would levy fines for non-payment of taxes and pocket them. A bottle of moonshine could easily throw a local official from his original path of action. The chairman and secretary of the Griaznoe rural soviet in Riazhsk, for example, went to the home of a villager to inventory the property for confiscation because he had not paid taxes. Before the inventory began the rural soviet chairman, Mochnev, asked, 'Will there be samogon?' In lieu of an answer, a bottle of samogon and some comestibles appeared on the table; before long, the local officials were making deals with the villagers to hide land from tax obligations.[23] In the village of Iamskaia Sloboda in Kasimov, the brothers Ivan and Il'ia Zhivilov ran the local rural soviet. Il'ia prepared fraudulent receipts to send to the State Insurance Agency and to the uezd financial department. Ivan added extra eaters to each peasant household and decreased reports on the quantity of livestock each household owned.[24]

Local officials paid little attention to who was officially entitled to a tax reduction or exemption. Instead, they taxed the way they had always taxed, by household or by eater, assessing everyone in the same way. In 1925, Riazan peasants with sons in the Red Army wrote piteous letters about how their sacrifice for the motherland meant nothing to 'local hooligans.' A.F. Nesterov wrote to his son, 'You, my dear son [*synok*], serve in the defence of the motherland [*rodina*]. Now your parents are cut to the bone, but *Vlast'* is not responsible but rather the local hooligans.' Another father from Riazhsk wrote to his son, 'The families of Red Army men are being taxed harshly and if you do not pay in time they come and take an inventory of your property.' In another letter from Riazhsk, a father complained to his son in Voronezh that they had already come twice from the district to inventory his property. From the village of Putiatino in Sasovo Uezd, the parents of Nikolai Shadrov wrote to their son in Voronezh, 'Your certification did not help. They paid no attention in the calculation of the tax, which we had to pay in full.'[25]

Many poor peasants did not know about the exemptions for which they were eligible, and so paid the demands as set in the traditional manner by the rural soviet or the district executive committees. When a central-level legal commentator interviewed a poor woman who had paid a huge amount in taxes, she said that she had never even heard of the exemptions and that she had sold her wedding dress in order to pay. 'I was afraid. They told me I would have to sell my cow and that the children would have to go to an orphanage ... I am an illiterate woman. I do not know how to go to the district executive committee. I roll around in the dirt like a bug' (*Vorogaius' v griazi, kak zhuk*).[26] And one central-level report noted that some poor peasants who had been freed from the tax said they were 'ashamed' (*stydno*) that their neighbours paid taxes and they did not.[27] The rural soviets were to ensure that the appropriate villagers received tax exemptions and to note all households that had experienced a natural calamity. They were to punish those peasants who failed to pay their taxes and assist in the collection of all payments. Non-payment of taxes was punishable with an administrative fine for the first offence and with imprisonment or compulsory labour for no less than six months or a confiscation of property in whole or in part for repeated offences. Concealment of taxable property of any kind – sown land, orchards, cattle – was punishable with imprisonment for the ringleaders of no less than one year and the possibility of confiscation of property. Participants in such a process were punishable with imprisonment for no less than six months or a doubling of the original tax assessment.

At the end of each collection period and especially the final payment period, the district executive committee compiled a list of all who failed to pay their taxes for each village. The list was then sent to the relevant rural soviet, which was obliged to call a gathering and 'remind' peasants of their obligations. The chairman of the soviet or a representative from the district executive commitee then made an inventory of the taxable property of all peasants who failed to pay in full. The district financial department decided what property would be sold, and in what order, to meet the tax and fines. One member of the district executive committee was responsible for seizing property for sale. Detailed records had to be kept for the sale of goods, and no one who participated in the process was allowed to purchase these goods (i.e., no one from the soviet, the district executive committee, the police, or members of their families). In theory, only as much as was needed to pay taxes due (plus all late penalties) was sold and the rest of the property was returned. A peasant had seven days to appeal to the people's court if he felt his property had been sold incorrectly.[28] Of course, in practice the system was open to abuse and abused. In a 1924 circular prodding the people's courts to deal more swiftly with peasants guilty of not paying their taxes, it was noted that 'in practice it is common during the confiscation of property [from those found guilty of non-payment] for items to be listed for sale that include even the dresses worn by members of the family, small tools, etc. ... which is categorically forbidden by Article 38 of the Criminal Code.'[29]

Bol'shakov provides a wry account of the system of dealing with non-payment of taxes in practice. If a peasant did not pay his taxes, the rural soviet was required to 'begin a file' (*sostavit' akt*) on the household that had failed to pay. This piece of paper had to travel the ten kilometres or so to the district financial inspector. The financial inspector then had to write up the incident and send the paperwork another fifteen kilometres or so to the district controller. The controller had to send the paperwork to the uezd financial department, twenty-four kilometres away. The uezd inspector then imposed an administrative punishment for each peasant who had not paid. The financial inspectors then sent the paperwork to the police, ten kilometres away, for enforcement of the punishments. The police sent the paperwork back to the rural soviet, ten more kilometres. The soviet called in the peasant, who travelled ten kilometres on average, and gave him the paperwork. The peasant was then told to take the documents back to the district police headquarters (another ten kilometres), upon which he was requested to pay his taxes within three days. In 95 per cent of cases, those who failed to pay still could not and did not pay, and the process started again, this time ending up in court after the paperwork had travelled another fifty kilometres.[30]

On the local level, one can trace this paperwork nightmare. In August 1926, for example, the Provincial Executive Committee and the Riazhsk Uezd Executive Committee corresponded about the challenges of collecting taxes in the uezd. In particular, they singled out Sarai District and asked the district executive committee there why it was having so much trouble collecting taxes. The district executive committee forwarded a host of petitions from the peasants of the village of Dubrovka on their impoverished conditions, caused in large part by a particularly bad harvest. The Provincial Executive Committee wrote that the petitions were groundless and insisted that the peasants pay their taxes. The Riazhsk Uezd Executive Committee insisted that all healthy peasants pay up, but the peasants of Dubrovka continued to refuse to pay anything at all and instead sent a petition to the Central Committee.[31]

Peasants resented the Centre's shifting of payment dates and collection times as well as the fines for non-payment and were not hesitant to send their complaints to the highest offices in Moscow. Through 1925 in Riazan, the collection of taxes was hampered by the amalgamation of the districts, which occupied the workers of the district executive committees. Some of them were so overworked that they told peasants who actually arrived to pay their taxes to go away and pay as part of a collective at a later date. Local officials had to remind the Centre, which was pushing for collection figures, that until the set payment date was met, payment was entirely voluntary. Peasants naturally waited until the last minute to make payments and fall rains had made roads impassable.[32] Individual districts were hit hard by bad harvests and could not pay their taxes by more than half. In Borets District, Riazhsk Uezd, peasants were selling their last cows to pay the first half assessed on them, and, the OGPU noted, there was no hope of collecting the remainder; the resources simply were not there. Borets District had been hit harder than the surrounding districts. It is worth noting that in the reports of 1925 there was still sympathy for peasant explanations regarding non-payment.[33]

In 1926, tax policy turned sharply against the wealthier households with a much stronger emphasis on taxing subsidiary sources of income, such as bee-keeping, growing tobacco, raising grapes, or keeping chickens. Instead of being calculated in units of arable land, these products were assigned a monetary value.[34] Between 1923 and 1926, the tax was assessed on the basis of landholding. The government still relied on indirect taxes – on wine, tobacco, matches, alcohol, salt, tea, kerosene, beer, cigarettes, and sugar – and this reliance on indirect taxation meant that the exemptions for the poor from the agricultural tax were not as significant as the regime would have liked to suggest.[35] Taxes on the peasants in the 1920s were always high. In 1924–5 the agricultural tax was set at 326.2 million rubles, in 1925–6 it was 251.8 million rubles, 357.9 million rubles in 1926–7, and 354.2 million rubles in 1927–8.[36] In 1926–7 peasants paid 601.7 million rubles in indirect taxes.[37] The lower figure for 1925 captures a moment when the regime engaged in a short-lived indulgence of peasants who did not pay their taxes.[38] The relaxation was a temporary reflection of the mid-twenties reconciliation with the peasantry, but tax pressure returned in 1926 and increased in the years leading up to wholesale collectivization. Earnings outside of agriculture were taxed severely. Small livestock was taxed and all pigs over six months of age, as were sheep and goats that had lived through the winter.[39]

Through 1926, Riazan peasants increasingly voiced their concern that state taxes were 'beyond their strength' and would lead to the destruction of their households.[40] At the end of the year, pressure was on the provinces and passed down to the uezd to collect the tax in full. The Provincial Executive Committee decided once again to take serious measures against peasants who failed to pay their taxes and against local officials who failed to collect taxes or distributed the tax burden in their own local or peculiar manner. Specific criticisms made their way once again to the rural soviets. The chairmen of various village soviets, such as the soviet in Shost'e in Kasimov, agitated against the tax. The chairman of the soviet in the village of Karino in Zaraisk told the village that if they waited, they would all receive a reduction. The OGPU accused the chairman of the Dedinovo soviet in Zaraisk of being clearly 'indulgent' with peasants who failed to pay their taxes.[41] In 1926–7, the pressure intensified on the press to launch campaigns against those who did not pay their taxes and to impel peasants to pay up.[42] By the fall of 1927, entire villages were refusing as a collective to pay their taxes.[43] Adding to the burden of the agricultural tax, of course, was the increased pressure of grain requisitioning.[44] In Tuma, the price of grain had risen in spring and summer 1928 to as high as ten rubles per pud on the local market. Grain substitutes were once again appearing on the peasants' tables and petitions were pouring in for a reduction in the agricultural tax.[45]

In January 1928, the Central Committee of the party issued a secret directive on grain requisitioning, which complained about the 'intolerably slow' tempo of work of local organizations. It gave the local party organs one week to deliver grain and reminded party members that any excuses of any kind, any claims that holidays were in the way, would be 'considered a serious violation of party discipline.' Party organs were instructed to fulfil the directives on grain procurement, to fulfil all Central Committee instructions on 'removing accumulated money from the countryside,' to collect all outstanding dues for insurance and taxes, to take all measures to extend the campaign for the sale of State Insurance bonds, and, finally, to ensure that all local collections of self-taxation were filled.[46] In July 1928, Stalin himself explained the situation to the Central Committee:

> The situation in our country with regard to the peasantry in this case is the following: it pays the state not only ordinary taxes, direct and indirect, but it also pays relatively high prices for goods from industry – that is first of all – and it doesn't receive the full value of the prices of agricultural products – that is second of all. This is an additional tax on the peasantry in the interests of developing industry, which serves the whole country, including the peasantry. This is something like a 'tribute,' something like a surtax, which we are forced to take temporarily in order to sustain and further develop the current rate of industrial growth, to support industry for the whole country, to further improve the well-being of the countryside, and then to completely destroy this additional tax, these 'scissors' between the city and the countryside. This situation, needless to say, is unpleasant. But we would not be Bolsheviks if we papered over this fact and closed our eyes to the fact that, unfortunately, our industry and our country cannot manage without this additional tax on the peasantry for the moment.[47]

And peasants across the Soviet Union resisted. In the Far Eastern region there were 7,162 registered cases of peasant unrest in 1928, and 60.5 per cent of them were provoked by the tax campaign.[48] Households hid part of their harvest or livestock to avoid high tax assessments, and large fines were exacted from peasants who were caught. In Siberia, for example, 24,964 households were fined 1,141,951 rubles for hiding taxable inventory.[49]

With each passing year the pressure to collect taxes increased. In Riazan, in 1928, pressure was pushed down the ranks.[50] Instructions from the Centre to all lower levels emphasized repeatedly that state officials would be held *personally* responsible for the successes or failures of all collection campaigns.[51] Uezd executive committees and uezd financial departments called for disciplinary and judicial action against those who failed to assess and collect taxes. The district executive committees, in turn, blamed the rural soviets as the ones responsible in the failure to collect the agricultural tax for 1927–8.[52] Even in 1928, though, tax inspectors were *still* willing to verify that taxes were too onerous on some villages.[53] By the fall of 1928, special attention was focused on Kasimov, Riazan, Riazhsk, and Spassk uezds, where tempos of collection were considered critically low.[54]

The pressure on peasants to pay up was so intense in the late 1920s that the provinces over-fulfilled their tax quota. In 1928–9, for example, the sum for the unified agricultural tax was set at 400 million rubles; 465 million rubles were collected, with some peasant households paying five to six times more than they had the year before.[55]The pressure to pay more taxes dovetailed with other ways of raising even more revenue in the countryside, among them grain requisitioning, changes to the traditional process of self-taxation, and pressure to buy the state industrial bond (*zaem*). A 1926 official guide for rural soviet and district executive committee members who worked on taxation was still reminding local workers that there was only one legal tax, the unified agricultural tax. All other collections, such as self-taxation, were voluntary, and the rural soviet and the district executive committees were not allowed to make additional collections. The guide noted that often in the countryside special collections were taken for the upkeep of the rural soviet, the district executive committee, hospitals, and schools, but that this was incorrect (*nepravil'no*) and such expenses must come from district and rural soviet budgets. The guide reminded local officials that insurance was not a tax.[56]

By 1928, however, the Centre was trying to harness the resources that peasants had been contributing through self-taxation. The money was still to be collected by the gathering, but if the gathering was obstructive, the rural soviet could call another meeting to pass plans for self-taxation. The money was never supposed to be used for supporting the local state administration, but rather for building roads, hospitals, libraries, reading huts, red corners, kindergartens, daycare centres, orphanages, and veterinary stations.[57] There was widespread resistance to this new form of self-taxation.[58] It was not that peasants resented contributing to local infrastructure – they had already been doing so for years. They resented losing control over the self-taxation and the increasing encroachment of the Centre in the practice.[59] The pressure to buy the state industrial bond intensified and was yet another hated, and only theoretically voluntary,[60] attempt to raise revenues. Peasants complained that there was much 'unpleasantness' with the relevant authorities if they refused to buy the bonds, which they could not afford anyway.[61] By 1928, complaints were pouring into the Centre that the rural soviets and 'other public organizations' (*obshchestvennye organizatsii*) refused to support the state bonds.[62] Pressure intensified even more in 1929 to buy bonds through a complex entanglement of multiple jurisdictions. Local officials, police constables, insurance agents, and party members were called on to participate in the drive. In Riazan, state security reports complained that response to the third industrial state bond, set at six million rubles, was poor. Their reports protested that most local state officials were indifferent to the selling of the bonds. The reports noted that members of the rural soviet in particular were against the bonds. In most areas, local officials showed up in a village, announced the relevant protocol, 'and with this the matter ends.' Some Riazan villages refused as a collective unit to purchase the state bonds.

At an August plenum of the Iushta rural soviet in Shilovo, a member of the soviet gave a talk on the issue of the third industrial bond. No one spoke for or against the bonds. After a long silence, a resolution was adopted that each member of the rural soviet would sign on for no less than ten rubles. Of the twenty-five participants at the meeting, which included workers of the rural soviet, the cooperatives, and other local organizations, only three or four of those present signed up. One member of the rural soviet, Demidov, complained that he paid for the bond while the poor were simply given grain and suggested that the poor should have to buy bonds too. When he was told by a local communist that the poor 'in their poverty also help the state,' he replied, 'Well, let them help, and me, I am not going to sign up.'[63]

In the village of Shabaevo in Spas-Klepiki only three persons deprived of voting rights signed up for the bond for fifty-six rubles and two middle peasants for ten rubles. The state security report made a point of noting that the campaign to sign up for the bonds was being led by a member of the rural soviet by the name of Orlov, from the village of Shabaevo. The secretary of the Dubrovo party cell refused to work on selling the bonds, saying that he could never 'catch up' (*skhvatit'*) with the peasants during such an intensive farming period. Other rural soviet chairmen pointed out that if they forced peasants to sign up for the industrial bonds, it would put their lives in danger. In general, peasants reacted against the bonds and argued that the benefits would go only to the workers, and the peasants would receive nothing.[64]

There were also reports of excesses, violence, and considerable pressure to purchase the bonds in some regions, among which Pitelino stands out. In the village of Nesterevo, Pitelino District, constable Terekhin opened a file (*sostavil aktom*) on anyone who did not sign up. In the village of Sakolovo, the same constable drew up the threatening record twice on a peasant who refused to sign up. The next day the rumour flew about the village that 'if someone did not accept the obligation for the industrial bond, then the police would open a file on him.'[65] It made perfect sense in the context of the times that peasants were intimidated by the thought that their names would be written down and kept in police records. And they were right to be concerned, as their names often made it into the pages of the state security reports, especially the names of local officials who failed to represent the state adequately. It seems that the competition to sell the industrial bonds was fierce in Pitelino District. In the middle of an August night in 1929, the secretary of the Pitelino party cell, along with the chairman of the rural soviet, called on a local 'kulak,' the priest, and the church elder to purchase the state bond. They refused and were threatened with repression. In the village of Timirevo, the insurance agent E.A. Nesterkin sold A. Mukhina, of the village of Saverka, a bond while delivering insurance payments for the death of her husband. Likely there was some pressure on her to purchase the bond so that she would receive at least part of the insurance money owed to her. When the chairman of the soviet found out that she had bought the bond from Nesterkin, he came to Mukhina's house and asked, 'Why did you take the bond from Nesterkin and not from us? Now we will not certify you [provide proof you bought the bonds].'[66] The fact that Pitelino was singled out for excesses, when most areas were targeted for insufficient attention or downright opposition to the bonds, may help explain why the region erupted in rebellion in February 1930. In most places, resistance to the industrial bonds was strong. In August 1929, raion quotas in Riazan were filled on average by only 10 per cent. Members of the rural soviets were accused repeatedly of speaking out against the bonds and refusing to sign up for them themselves.[67]

One aim of the Centre's policy in the village was to destroy what it perceived as the grip of the wealthy on the village, the control of the wealthy of political, economic, and social power in the countryside. The hope was that poor and middle peasants would unite against the wealthy and become part of a Soviet organizational structure rather than a village one. In Riazan, at least, the policies of grain requisitioning and an ever-tightening tax grip probably instead united the middle and wealthy peasants against the poor. In April 1929, N. Chakulaev of Kasimov expressed the position of the middle peasant: '*Vlast'* runs only for the workers and satisfies their demands 100 per cent, and the middle peasant is destroyed, and the poor are pampered with privileges, and so the whole Republic is full of loafers. I will prove it with the facts. I myself went for grain to Pechaevo in Tambov Province, and there last year grain had been taken by a Red detachment, and therefore the peasants only planted on a third of their land. The peasants themselves told me that instead of thirty desiatinas they planted ten desiatinas.'[68]

In the village of Terekhovo in Spassk, peasants spoke against the poor:

'See, they help the poor, give them grain, loans, free them from the agricultural tax and self-taxation, and they don't strive to improve their farms, and they will forever sit on the neck of the state. And they give us middle peasants nothing, but they take from us taxes and self-taxation, and now it has come to selling our last animal so as not to die from hunger, or we crawl to the barn of the rural soviet for grain.'[69]

Even as late as the spring of 1929, peasants in Riazan believed that they could still assert themselves and negotiate in some fashion with *Vlast'*. In the village of Dedivovo in Zaraisk, a meeting was called so that grain could be distributed to the poor. The rest of the villagers came out against the distribution. One peasant warned, 'Now there is not a link [*smychka*] between the poor and the middle peasants, but a break [*razmychka*]. We will sell our cattle and become poor peasants. *Vlast'* pays all its attention to the poor and the lazy, and agriculture is not improved, it is ruined. If they do not give us grain, we will sell our cattle and become poor. If you do not give us grain, then we will take back our shares in the cooperative.'[70]

The threat to withdraw one's investment was a perfectly rational and reasoned response. Peasants did their best to resist the tax collections, the industrial bonds, and the grain requisitioning. As D'Ann Penner notes, the fact that peasants failed in their efforts to resist was more of a tribute to how seriously the regime took its task than it was a reflection on the peasants' ability to organize and struggle for some semblance of rights in the countryside.[71] The rural soviets, and especially their chairmen, played a key role in this resistance and in thwarting central policy.[72] Rural soviets resisted grain requisitioning by keeping grain 'on the road.' Peasants loaded up wagons and moved their grain around so it could not be inventoried in the villages, and the rural soviets helped them by issuing travelling papers.[73] They tried to reject grain quotas or stall on collection. In the summer of 1929, for example, the chairmen and the members of the rural soviet in the village of Vysokoe in Shatsk informed officials from the Credit Association (*Kreditnoe tovarishchestvo*) that they could not accept their numbers for grain requisitioning because the peasants would 'beat them' and 'tear them apart.' A member of the rural soviet, Gavril Ivanovich Kuznetsov, of the village of Samodrovka in Ukholovo, was overheard in a private conversation with citizens about grain requisitioning, saying, 'In my opinion, those peasants who take grain to the state are idiots. We need to store it in hell [*v preispodnoiuiu*] because they deceive us and we will be left without grain.'[74]

In the spring of 1929, in the village of Timoshkino, Shilovo District in Spassk, the rural soviet was charged with the distribution of flour to the poor. Instead, reserves went to P.I. Galochkin, who was a relative of one Silkin, chairman of the Committee of the Peasant Society of Mutual Assistance, as well as to P.S. Samin, 'even though he made boots and had a threshing machine from which he earned an additional seventy puds of grain.' Samin, the informer continued, 'had a land allotment, a brick house, a horse, a cow, a pig, and five sheep.' Silkin, who apparently also received a ration, had once owned sixty desiatinas of land, twenty desiatinas of meadow, forest, sheep, and cows. A certain I.A. Kharchikov received flour 'even though he has a brick house with an iron roof, a horse, a cow, a pig, three sheep, and two wooden homes that he rents out for four puds of grain.'[75] A. Fedin, chairman of a rural soviet in Skopin, told peasants that the only way to survive high taxes was to sell all of their property and move to Siberia.[76] These details, from a 1929 state security report, capture a number of local features, supporting the notion that rural soviets ran as patronage institutions. The details reveal the way in which a local informer highlighted those elements that would tag the recipients as 'kulaks' in all of their pathetic glory.

Even in late summer 1929, the rural soviets were doing their best to shield villagers from taxation. The chairman of the rural soviet, Ovchinkin, in Veraievo, Pitelino, lowered the obligation on families considered kulak. He was confronted by the chairman of the district executive committee, Aleshin, who demanded that he explain such a decision. Ovchinkin argued that the 'kulak' households had nothing else to take and did not engage in trade anyway.[77] This case is particularly interesting, as it relates to materials presented in detail in the epilogue. It is likely that this 'soft' rural soviet chairman was replaced by one who cooperated with the regime.[78] At any rate, the area was problematic, and, after the uprising of February 1930, Aleshin was removed from his post.

Conclusions

In his observations on the Soviet countryside in 1927, Quaker relief worker Karl Borders noted, 'The agricultural tax is the point at which village politics and economics meet, and where the peasant feels most keenly the hand of the powers that be.'[79] V.P. Danilov has asserted that in 'the system of interrelations of the state with the peasant milieu the most important place lies with tax obligations.'[80] N.A. Ivnitskii continued this line of argument in *Tianut s muzhika poslednie zhily*, where he argues that tax policy was both fiscal and social and one of the most important themes in the countryside, especially once the decision in favour of rapid, wholesale industrialization was taken in 1927 and 1928. He traces the increasingly punitive rise in taxes from 1927 to 1928. In the fall of 1927, the decision was made to exempt the poorest farmers from taxation. Thirty-five per cent of households were exempt and yet 1928 saw a 83 per cent increase in tax demands over 1927. Despite the constant tax increases, in September 1929 the Politburo expressed the need for better and higher returns and issued a call to intensify the struggle with those households that hid taxable resources with a focus on the 'kulak-capitalist elements.' Fines were to be utilized to their fullest as a form of punishment. Tax inspectors were to be freed from any work not connected to the agricultural campaign. Even after the collectivization of the countryside, both collective farmers and the few remaining independent farmers continued to be taxed.[81] In 1934, for example, there were still 13,657 complaints to Kalinin alone regarding the methods of tax assessment and collection in the countryside.[82]

Following the brutal policies of the Civil War, the Centre tried to introduce a system of taxation more tolerable for its rural inhabitants. The launch of the New Economic Policy meant that methods of raising revenue had to be more legitimate and more acceptable to the peasantry. Despite their wrangling and grumbling about taxation, peasants were willing to pay taxes within reasonable bounds. Even though they might try to avoid some part of the tax, they were not against contributing to the tax in principle. From 1921 to 1924, the peasantry watched the Bolshevik Centre with a mix of hope and trepidation, and with a strong degree of distrust, as they struggled to improve their farms. The years 1924 to 1926 were a brief period of optimism among the peasantry and of tolerance by the Centre. But peasant time and peasant negotiations move slowly; Revolutionary time does not. The Centre had little tolerance for peasant excuses and peasant negotiations over how old an animal should be, and in what region of the empire, before it should be subject to a tax or over what side earnings should be taxes and which should not. The pressure of the dream of the utopia of progress and development, the tensions within the party, perceived or real international pressures, and the fear of the powerful 'darkness' of the mass of the rural population pushed the regime forward. The peasantry was the regime's primary resource, and by 1927, debate turned decisively toward determining how best to exploit this resource. Peasants, and their representatives, continued to try to negotiate with the state as best they could. They persisted in attempting to explain local complications. But these local complications were drowned in the increasing pressures of the intricately connected policies of taxation, state bonds, grain requisitioning, and, ultimately, collectivization.

Yanni Kotsonis has written a careful and thoughtful work on the meaning of taxation, in particular the notion of a personal income tax, in post-Emancipation Russia and the early years of Soviet power. Kotsonis shows that progressive, liberal reformers, inspired by European models of taxation, saw the personal income tax as a mark of citizenship and citizen participation. Revenue from income tax was not a significant contribution to the general budget, therefore paying the tax was symbolic of breaking down the Old Regime/Estate social groupings and of the voluntary, universal acceptance of the duties and obligations of a citizen as part of a nation. But as Kotsonis points out, the taxation debates of the European states 'was premised on a duality that was absent from the Russian debates.'[83] This duality was the protection of the rights of the individual in exchange for citizen participation.

One major challenge for Russia was the lack of resources to enable the state to see its citizens. In 1898, Minister of Finance Sergei Witte conveyed to Nicholas II that in matters of taxation peasants were essentially invisible. Witte acknowledged that the state lacked the resources to see them any better.[84] As one contemporary economist pointed out, 'The absence of such a direct and personal relation with the population … produced a colonial regime's relations of "conqueror and conquered," with a truly alien government imposing obligations on an unknowable population.'[85] Because of this lack of visibility, village communes remained responsible for establishing individual tax assessments right up to the First World War.[86] Tax inspectors had 'few powers of enforcement'; laws permitting the seizure of peasant property were almost never utilized in the pre-war villages for fear of impoverishing peasant households.[87] But this situation would change drastically during the First World War and beyond; confiscation became the foundation of the war against the peasantry during the years of collectivization.

By 1916, the tsarist state at war was imposing 'merciless taxation' on its population, in a response common to all the nations at war. Kotsonis argues, however, that the other European nations had 'complex and evolved systems of information gathering that allowed the state to locate its population and make its claims with confidence. Such a state was "strong," thanks to this familiarity and its proximity to its population, not because it was crudely coercive. In the case of Russia, officials acted with the confidence but without the machinery to acquire the knowledge. The gap produced a fundamental tension in state policy: peasants would be taxed individually without any realistic way to assess them, thereby laying an individual claim on a group that could only be understood by collective generalization.'[88] Local discussions about tax collection reflected this dilemma. There were suggestions even from within the Commissariat of Finance to continue 'collective responsibility' for the peasantry, and more than one province made a distinction between peasants and persons.[89]

The members of the Provisional Government shared the conviction that good citizens would willingly support their state. When such expressions of citizenship failed to materialize in abundant voluntary tax returns, the subsequent disappointment in the quality of citizenship demonstrated by Russian peasants led to the conviction that they were simply too immature to recognize their duty as citizens. The forced requisitioning of grain was justified on precisely these grounds.[90]

The Soviet regime continued along the same lines. Tax inspectors were provided with Red Guards to compel peasants 'to honour their civic obligations.'[91] The 'tax in kind' levied on the peasantry in October 1918 was justified by the Commissariat of Finance on the grounds that taxation was the *right* of the citizen.[92] At this time, *kulak* was a term used loosely to refer to peasants who did not pay their taxes or showed other signs of 'withdrawing from the state.'[93] Violence against the peasants was thus justified as part of their instruction by and for the state of which they were an inseparable element.[94] 'Clearly the mass violence that followed under the Bolsheviks can be explained in terms of a traditional contempt for the peasantry in which the Bolsheviks shared. But the Bolsheviks were also driven by the opposite and simultaneous impulse: the heightened expectations of personal responsibility that this conception of government had produced.'[95]

Thus we see the peasantry of the 1920s caught in a vice between the demands of an idea of citizenship that offered no inalienable rights in return, on the one hand, yet retained all the expectations of citizenly behaviour, on the other. Policy toward the peasantry in all spheres reflected these heightened expectations, as did the violent response when such expectations were repeatedly frustrated by the police, the 'criminal,' the rural soviet chairman, the rural court judge, or the forest guard.

The following chapter explores another revealing conflict between Moscow and the countryside over a resource vital to all in the Soviet 1920s: wood. The clash between the needs and desires of the village regarding forest resources and the ideas and requirements of the state add another layer of complexity and meaning to the brutal simplifications that determined central policy toward the countryside.

Chapter Six

The Forest: Wood, Warmth, and Repair

Sasha crept up to his father's grave and lay down on his unfinished crypt. He was afraid to walk among the crosses, but near his father he slept as sweetly as he had before in the hut on the shore of the lake. Later, two muzhiks came to the cemetery and quietly began to break off crosses for firewood, but Sasha, carried off in his dreams, heard nothing.

Andrei Platonov, *Chevengur*

On 4 October 1923, M. Moskalev, a member of Riazan's forest guard,[1] sent a petition to the chief forester (*lesnichii*) of the Belomutsk Forest District (*lesnichestvo*). The chief forester sent the petition on to the provincial forest department. Moskalev, struggling to express himself in writing, complained that after every single court case in which monetary fines were levied against wood thieves he had caught, the thieves returned to break his windows. He requested permission to repair the damage and was very specific about what he had lost and what he needed to survive the approaching winter. On 25 December 1922 at 1 a.m., he writes, a horseshoe broke two panes of glass measuring 25 by 58 centimetres[2] each. The horseshoe landed on his table. On 8 April 1923, during the night, another pane of glass was broken, measuring 25 by 50 centimetres. On 15 September 1923, also in the night, while Moskalev was patrolling in the forest, three more panes of glass were broken with a brick. Two of the panes measured 25 by 50 centimetres and the third, 18 by 25. All of the losses together he valued at 2,200 rubles. Moskalev had no money to replace the glass and so requested five ends of dead wood, 21.5 centimetres in diameter with which to replace the windowpanes.[3]

In January 1924, the chief of the area's forest guard was still trying to get assistance for Moskalev.[4]

This petition from a barely literate forest guard takes us into a forest guard's hut and introduces the key themes of this chapter. First, the abject poverty of the Riazan countryside in the 1920s, in general, and of the forest guard, in particular, is palpable. Second, the guard was well aware that although he was surrounded by forest, he could not cut any, nor could he even utilize dead wood, without the proper permission from above. Third, Moskalev's case captures the personal danger that local officials faced daily, caught as they were between the demands and expectations of their community of fellow villagers and the demands and expectations of their employer, the Commissariat of Agriculture. Who was Moskalev in his role as forest guard and who were the people throwing horseshoes through his windows?

The forests of Riazan in the 1920s are another locus of peasant–state contact in the struggle over a key resource – in this case, wood. It is important to note that Riazan was not a forest-rich area of Russia by any stretch of the imagination and the dynamics found there represent those of an area where forest resources were in short supply. The dynamics are slightly different in areas rich in forest resources.[5] The villagers of Riazan were, and to a significant degree still are today, utterly dependent on wood to heat their homes, to construct new buildings, and to repair any existing structures.[6] The forest was essential: for the grazing of livestock; for building materials such as potash, tar, and pitch; and to supplement one's diet with berries, nuts, and mushrooms. Peasants needed thatch for roofs, wood to make and repair harrows and ploughs, and bast to make footwear.[7]

How did one obtain wood for warmth and repair? How did one maintain access to the forest for these other crucial supplementary needs? The simple answer: any way you could. The simple answer leads to a portrait of peasant–state relations in the 1920s surrounding a crucial resource for both peasant and state. The conflict over forest resources provides another prism for the Bolshevik dilemmas of the period. Moskalev was both a member of his community and an employee in the pay of the state. Like the chairman of the village soviet or a local judge, he walked that line and as such he was on the frontlines in the 1920s of the complex workings and failures of administering the countryside.

If we look closely at the (dys)functioning of the administration of forest resources, a familiar pattern emerges. There were honest attempts to try to develop a workable system, but ultimately the system failed in the context of the pressures of Revolutionary time, the tsarist legacy,

9. Tar ovens, 1908 (photo archive of Evgeny Kashirin).

the realities of poverty, general shortages, problems of distribution, and problems of administering a large agricultural country in the face of local communities that were often used to, and forced to, rely on their own resources and systems of organization. Such a claim does not imply that the village was 'closed.' It was not, but in order to function a village needed to be able, at times, to serve itself. When we come down into the villages and look at one small cross section of administrative challenges – in this case, the forest – we can factor the complexities we find there into an understanding of the pressures placed on the Centre in its attempts to administer and control the periphery. In 1925, Bukharin told peasants to 'enrich themselves.' In the mid-1920s, the reams of paper produced that tried to deal with difficulties of supplying wood and protecting forests reflect this earnestness and spirit of slower change. Yet the mounting challenges and the concurrent frustrations led to more radical ways of interpreting the problems and responding to them. The war scare of 1927 and the defeat of first the Left Opposition and then the Right Opposition prompted the central administration to search for

10. Wood in Gridino, 2004 (photo by the author).

radical solutions rooted in a growing sense of urgency and fuelled by frustration and distrust. One motor of distrust was the reports, generated from all commissariats and especially from the security services and Rabkrin, that local state servitors could not be depended upon to propel the Soviet Union into a bright future. At the same time, a study of these local employees – in this case, forest guards – brings to light the very real dangers, struggles, and tensions in the countryside. What we find, once again, are local complications that the Centre perceives as needing to be addressed through centralization and systemization.

The chapter begins by looking briefly at the place of wood and forests in historiographical context broadly and in the Western and Soviet contexts particularly. It then establishes the ideological dilemma for the young Soviet state posed by forests and wood thieves. Next, the tsarist legacy regarding forest legislation and forest management is laid out to convey the situation the Bolsheviks inherited and then revised, rewrote, or built upon in their own legislation and forest codes. As a result of the tangled undergrowth that is the issue of wood and forest use, I have separated the discussion thematically and covered the same chronology within each theme. I begin with the system introduced in the Forest Code of 1923 on how one legally obtained wood. I then look at the challenges faced by that 'system' in the real conditions of Riazan, which basically *created* wood thieves. Next, I turn to the definitions of wood theft and of forest-use violation. Here the Criminal Code and the Forest Code needed to speak to one another. The codes originate in the Centre and can be used as a measure of both the goals of the Centre and a response to real conditions. Finally, real conditions, the challenges of administering the countryside, and the escalating tension and sense of urgency of the late 1920s are brought into relief through a discussion of the forest guard. The forest guards emerge as negotiating the rural world either as insider or as outsider. Insiders accommodated the local inhabitants, making special deals and negotiating forest usage. Outsiders tried to enforce the law and were often punished for their troubles by the communities in which they worked. Often it was better to adapt to one's local conditions and become a negotiating insider, but such a choice of action made one an enemy in the eyes of one's employer. The razor-sharp edge of local officialdom was a tricky line to walk.

The Meaning of Wood in History

The conflict between a centralizing, modernizing state and its peasant population over forest resources is vital, age-old, and revealing. The study of this conflict has a long prestigious pedigree as a means of tracing the ways in which a centralizing state encroached on traditional customary rights.[8] Peter Linebaugh goes so far as to argue that both Marxism and modern criminology were born in Marx's indignant reactions (published in 1842) and the reactions of other, more conservative thinkers to the debates on the law on thefts of wood in the Rhine Provincial Assembly.[9] Marx made a characteristically wry comment that the new changes to the law would cause 'the right of human beings to give way to the right of young trees.'[10]

Scholars have recognized the crucial role of the forest and forest industry in both Russia and the Soviet Union. Jane Costlow has traced the increasing articulation of the need for a rational forest policy by concerned nineteenth-century intellectuals from a member of the St Petersburg Forest Institute, Alexander Rudzikii, to Anton Checkov, Ivan Turgenev, and Vladimir Korolenko.[11] A handful of studies look at forestry and ecology and examine timber as a key resource, the extraction of which was closely connected to forced labour and the gulag system.[12] The role of the forest and its importance for local populations are the least studied of an understudied area.[13] In 1976, John Keep threw down the gauntlet. He wrote, 'During 1917, and still more so in the ensuing years, Russia's woods and forests were the scene of a peculiar kind of guerrilla warfare that has yet to find its historian. The importance of the timber industry in the country's economic life, always great, was enhanced by the shortage of coal and oil. Wardens were employed to protect the forests against damage, theft or fires, but these guards could hardly be expected to put up effective resistance to massive assaults, especially when those responsible carried firearms and were backed by local sentiment.'[14]

For historians who lived and worked in the Soviet Union, however, the matter required that they embrace the contradictions of dialectics. In the context of the pre-Revolutionary period, wood theft was a form of political protest against the tsarist regime and against the private property of the nobility; the persecution of wood thieves was evidence of the exploitation of the toilers.[15] The forests provided a safe haven for the exploited in their desperate struggle against an oppressive system of rule. One enthusiastic observer of the 1920s recorded his romantic vision of the forests of old Russia, which 'provided a reliable protection for the oppressed peasants and the poor who had been united in their democratic societies for the struggle against the feudal lords. These societies were the first communist republics.'[16] The problem was, however, that these same forests provided shelter for the 'bandits' of the Civil War and beyond, and were thus less romantically regarded. A specific example from Riazan illustrates the shifting understandings of forests and those hiding in them. In 1923, a panicked dispatch from the offices of the Riazan provincial NKVD to the Riazan party committee and the Riazan provincial soviet noted that Riazan had received two heavily forested districts from Tambov to which there were no rail or water links. The dispatch warned that the forest sheltered individuals associated with Antonov, who had 'changed their colours from criminal to political' by attacking party workers. Three bandits and one agent had already died in shoot-outs.[17] Thus in a space of a few years the forest no longer sheltered democratic peasant communities. Noble savages had become a new kind of political bandit dedicated to the overthrow of the regime. Now the Bolshevik regime had to root out enemies hiding behind every tree. The regime had to discover how to satisfy peasant demands for access to a diminishing and limited resource. Someone had to begin to repair the conservation damage caused by the World War and the Civil War. Beyond these serious issues there was the even more pressing matter – how to simultaneously utilize the country's primary fuel resource to build the dream of the modernized, industrial nation. The Bolsheviks inherited a tsarist system that had fought some similar battles.

Tsarist Legacy

The dilemmas faced by the Bolshevik regime in the forests were not entirely new; the tsarist regime had struggled with forest violations explicitly since the reign of Peter the Great.[18] In the pre-Emancipation period peasants traditionally had the right to enter the state forests or the forests of the nobility to gather dead wood for heating, repairs, and fencing, and to obtain bast. While they were prohibited from cutting live trees, theft and destruction were a 'time-honored tradition.'[19] The Emancipation of the peasantry in 1861 saw weakened state and noble control over the forests, which had depended on serf labour for cutting and forest surveillance. In 1869, paid forest guards were introduced to fill the vacuum of landlord control left by the emancipation. Tensions led to a more defined set of regulations, and the law of 13 June 1873 provided peasants with forest access according to defined terms of use. Under Alexander III, in 1882, fines were introduced for forest violations, which increased for repeat offenders with a maximum fine of three times the value of the goods taken or damaged and a six-month jail sentence. The numbers are interesting to keep in mind, as they reappear in Soviet policies in the 1920s. The 1888 Statute on the Safeguarding of Forests (*Polozhenie o sberezhenii lesov*), widely considered the most important piece of pre-Revolutionary forest protection legislation, created 'forest protection committees.' The statute gave the state the right to designate any forest as protected and to take over any forest that was considered mismanaged. The pre-Revolutionary legislation represented a steady move toward state intervention and centralization. In 1894, with the creation of the Ministry of Agriculture and State Domains, forest matters fell under this new ministry's jurisdiction. On the eve of revolution, imperial forest protection, like its Soviet successor, was plagued by overlapping jurisdictions as enforcement of forest regulations fell to forest preservation committees, land captains, the forest guard, foresters, and the police.[20]

Peasants argued that the forests were God's and thus should be accessible to all. And while some educated observers of the nineteenth century lamented that peasants had no understanding of private property as a result of their dark, backward natures, Stephen Frank points out that peasants were quick to charge one another with wood theft if wood was taken from a personal supply. The commune took action against those who cut illegally in communal forests. Frank traces intensifying conflict in the post-Emancipation period as peasants took advantage of wood hunger to make a profit procuring and reselling wood. And he points out, nobles and priests found themselves customers for illegally obtained wood.[21] Once again the patterns identified by Frank carry over with remarkable similarity into the Soviet period, where individuals and state offices alike provided desperate customers for wood, no questions asked.

The years 1905 to 1917 saw the growth of an increasingly dynamic and passionate debate on forest conservation among educated forest specialists. Running through the debate were strong anti-capitalist sentiments against the private ownership of forests and a sense of the need for state ownership, control, and protection.[22] The pressures of the First World War intensified demands for timber for both the tsarist regime and the Provisional Government. Both regimes engaged in procurements and increasing state control of the forest economy.[23]

Underbrush of Law and Jurisdiction after 1917

The Bolsheviks continued intense procurement of forest resources to support their own war effort during the Civil War. The conflict allowed for a vacuum in the protection of the forests, and many conservationists of the 1920s looked back on the peasants in this period as rapacious marauders swarming over the forests and cutting as much as they could.[24] But for the peasantry, free forest access was a promise of the Revolution. Peasants believed, and indeed they were told, that the forests would be turned over to them after the October Revolution of 1917. So in the months following, they made use of the forests as if they were their own, but with a keen awareness that such a paradise might not be eternal. The period of the Civil War in Russia saw massive felling of trees as peasants heated their homes like never before, repaired their wooden houses and outbuildings at an alarming pace, stocked up for future needs, and grazed their livestock freely. Their hunch was correct. After the chaos of the Civil War and as the young Bolshevik regime took stock, the new power quickly understood that protecting forest resources was definitely in the state's interest. A new Forest Code was written and a system of forest wardens reintroduced.

In early 1918, the Commissariat of Agriculture began to try to dismantle the old forest-administration system as one of the symbols of the tsarist order. Forest sections or departments (*lesotdely*) were created within the provincial land administration departments (*gubzemotdely*), and forest protection was handed over to 'conscious citizens' through the soviets. And while there was some local hostility toward the old forest personnel, many remained at their posts and still served within the new forest administration.[25] Almost immediately the new state saw the need for a professional forest guard. The Law on Forests of 1918 repeated the maxim that the forests of the Russian Republic were a single public inheritance and could not be divided. In theory, the forests remained under the authority of a forest administration within the Commissariat of Agriculture. However, and never stated in the law, the Supreme Council of the People's Economy had jurisdiction over the procurement of wood for state and industrial needs with a forest section and a wood fuel section, which meant that it could, and did, engage in cutting for heating for industry without the input of the Commissariat of Agriculture. During the Civil War, the railways sometimes ran exclusively on wood fuel, and local committees were struck to find timber to supply the railroads. These committees were not responsible to either the Commissariat of Agriculture or the Supreme Council of the People's Economy but to the People's Commissariat of Transport, complete with their own Central Administration for Fuel and Forest Supplies. The Law on Forests theoretically gave citizens the rights to receive firewood, wood for construction and repair, fallen wood, and rights to secondary forest usage such as grazing livestock, haymaking, hunting, fishing, gathering mushrooms, nuts, and berries, and collecting rocks, peat, clay, or sand. Quotas on wood were established by local organs according to a central plan on wood availability in the country as a whole as well as the needs of the state for wood. The code was drawn up by conservationists with definite ideas about 'rational' forest use in the long term. A closer look at the law shows that local Soviet organs had control over fees and the terms of secondary usage. Moreover, implementing the new law was extremely difficult; local provincial land committees often disregarded the law altogether and divided and managed forests as they saw fit.[26]

The Forest Code of 1923 divided the 'single state fond' into 'forests of local significance' and 'forests of state significance.' The forests of local significance were reminiscent of the pre-Revolutionary peasant forests, from which peasants could obtain limited resources, provided they had the right paperwork. The forests of state significance were off-limits to peasant cutting entirely. In heavily forested areas, communes were assigned to forests of local significance. Some 15 million hectares were designated to be 'handed over' to the peasantry across the Republic. In under-forested areas, wood for warmth and repair was distributed from the forests of state significance through lumberyards or state-forest cooperatives. Individuals had to bring statements of need from their local soviets and proof of their status if they were entitled to free or discounted wood. The families of serving Red Army personnel and those freed from paying the agricultural tax were entitled to discounts of up to 70 per cent. Peasants struck by natural disasters such as fire or flood, new settlers, schools, and hospitals were all entitled to free wood. To cut wood in the forests of local significance, or to graze one's livestock there, one had to receive permission from the forest-area administration. Cutters and grazers had to be in possession of a 'wood-cutting ticket' or a 'grazing ticket.' According to the code, the forest users themselves were responsible for forest protection in forests of local significance. They were to protect the forests against theft, illegal grazing, fires, and pests and were bound to utilize the forest in accordance with the provincial forest plan drawn up by the offices of the Commissariat of Agriculture. Violators were subject to criminal prosecution, and forest use could be denied to villages that repeatedly violated the laws protecting the forests. Secondary forest uses could be paid or unpaid, depending on local circumstances, which sounds vague precisely because the law itself was vague on this matter. All secondary use had to avoid damage to new growth.[27] Riazan had both systems of distribution. The south tended to be well forested, while areas in the northwest were not. Even in the forested regions, the amount of wood that villagers were allowed to cut in a designated cutting area still did not meet demand. Most requests for wood and complaints about the system came from village communes through a representative, but some came from individuals.[28]

Despite the Forest Code and an endless stream of explanatory circulars, there was no real, systematized way to obtain wood. One forest administration office, for example, was open only on Mondays and Tuesdays. In order even to get near the office one would have to arrive on Saturday. People travelled up to fifty kilometres to find a hundred people already waiting, and the office would take only twenty. Villagers could find themselves standing 'under open skies' for four days without results. One could go several Saturdays in a row and still not receive an allotment of wood.[29] Thus one had to walk great distances and face significant obstacles to get the necessary paperwork to receive wood legally. Moreover, even if the rural soviets themselves followed proper procedure, wood ordered in September arrived in February.[30] Theft was usually a much better option if one wanted to avoid freezing. And in provinces such as Riazan and Tambov the amount of wood stolen was two to three times the amount allotted for cutting and distribution. And still in 1925, Rabkrin estimated that if one added together the amount of wood allotted and the amount of wood stolen, villagers were still getting less than half as much wood as they needed.[31]

The Mozharovo forests, located in Riazhsk in the southern portion of Riazan, illustrate the challenges for peasants and state in an under-forested area. The forests were surrounded to the east and west by regions without forests of their own. The forest-administration office served some forty-seven villages with a total of about ten thousand households. If the considered norm per household was half a cubic metre of building materials and two cubic metres of firewood, the demand for the total area would be about 25,000 cubic metres in total. The output of the forest was about 3,200 cubic metres; the administration could satisfy just over 20 per cent of the local population's need. Wood in the area was allocated by district committees made up of the chairmen of a district soviet and the cooperative, the chief forester, and a village representative. There were three such committees operating out of the district soviets of Borets, Sapozhok, and Sarai and serving the more than ten thousand households that needed wood to survive from the Mozharovo forests. In 1925–6, almost three thousand claims passed through the forest administration. The administration then used the list of claims to issue wood-cutting tickets 'through which several citizens or individuals' could claim wood, collect it, and take it away on horseback. In some cases, usually if the wood was from windfall or dead standing, it could be collected by individual tickets.[32] The point is that only a small percentage of the wood needed could be obtained through the complex and slow bureaucratic system. Thus, even if a household wanted to live by the rules and regulations, it could not. The Mozharovo forests were not an isolated example. In Zaraisk, to the northwest, one cutting area could meet about 10 per cent of demand and another could not even meet the needs of those entitled to free or discounted wood.[33]

Moreover, the wood had to be paid for with funds collected from the users, and there were constant problems with collection. The population interpreted the collection as a levy for the wood itself, saying, 'Before we paid for wood, now the forest is ours and again we have to pay for it.' Other villagers pointed out that that they had already paid the agricultural tax and did not see why more money was being asked of them. One rural soviet dealt with the problem by dividing the entire population of the village into tax-exempt categories. Everyone in the village was family of a soldier serving in the Red Army, a poor widow, or simply poor enough to be exempt from taxation. These astute classifications meant that the entire village was entitled to free wood.[34]

Distribution was another major issue, because once the wood reached the village it was usually the decision of the gathering that determined how it was distributed. Such decisions varied considerably from place to place and, not surprisingly, usually were determined according to tradition or custom rather than the 'class line.' In some cases wood was divided according to how many strips the household farmed, or by soul, or by land allotments. The Centre was alarmed at those with 'kulak leanings' who seemed to believe that if they grew the trees themselves they had the right to cut and sell the wood at will.[35] The Centre's reaction to this dilemma through the 1920s was to place more and more responsibility for wood distribution on the rural and district soviets and weaken the role of the village gathering.[36]

In 1927, the inspector of forests stated at an uezd conference on the struggle with wood theft that the main cause of wood theft in the area was the shortage of heating materials and wood for construction and repair. In February 1926, for example, the uezd soviet had requested 391,868 cubic metres for use by the population and received 13.5 per cent of the requested amount. The inspector reported that the population had been forced to cope with the shortage by burning almost their entire harvest of thatch and, in some places, all of their manure *in addition* to stealing wood. Moreover, selling stolen wood was a major supplement to the household budget for those who lived near a forested area. Villagers stole wood and then sold it twenty to thirty kilometres away, 'where they are unknown and officials likely turn a blind eye to them' since the local population was so desperate for wood. This 'lack of punishment' was, he thought, another major cause of the chronic wood theft in the area.[37]

Ethnographic studies of the 1920s note the central place of stolen wood in the Russian countryside. M.Ia. Fenomenov noted that everywhere he saw brand-new wood structures and stocked supplies of building materials that he was convinced came from the 'destructive plunder of the forests.'[38] In the mid-twenties, A.M. Bol'shakov discovered that a rural soviet provided a local woman with the documents to certify her poverty so that she could obtain wood. The documents attested that she had no cow, no horse, and that her izba was falling apart. But a check (*proverka*) established that she had a horse, a cow, a good number of pigs, and that her home was in fine condition.[39] B.G. Tan-Bogoraz and his students travelled around the villages of Leningrad region. He reflected on the meaning of the Revolution in the countryside:

> There was a moment when wood could be cut without punishment, and this temptation still exists. We travelled through fifty-one villages and in almost every one we saw newly raised izbas built with fresh-cut or reserve wood. And it was very doubtful that all of it was paid for. And in connection with this again springs up a whole host of peculiar situations and surprising cunning artfulness [*ukhishchrenie*]. We heard the following case: Four peasants carried wood on the sly from a state forest; they could not carry it away unnoticed so it was decided that it would be better to run ahead and cajole the forest 'agent.' Three of them, having grabbed some samogon, a tenth of eggs, and some ham, approached the agent, presented him with the bundle, and began a conversation with him. He decided to accept their 'hospitality' and say nothing, but he demanded that the peasants write up on a slip of paper that they had given him a bribe and that he was silent so that 'you don't go and then denounce me saying I took a bribe from you.' The paper was drawn up, the peasants signed it, and set out to find two more friends for their signatures. And after some time they were all in court on charges of bribery. Each received a term of one year in jail.[40]

The peasants might have told the professor and his students a local myth that illustrated how the system worked against them. Still, true or not, the tale highlights some of the main issues of the struggle over local forest resources. First, rural soviets colluded with members of their constituency to secure resources. Second, during the unruly years of revolution and Civil War, peasants took the opportunity to repair their wooden structures and to stock up for a rainy day. Third, guards were hungry and could easily be bribed. Finally, bribery was a significant part of the working of the local system.

Crime and Punishment

What exactly constituted wood theft and forest violation? According to the instructions of the Commissariats of Justice and Agriculture, violation consisted of any of the following: taking damp or dead wood from a place not indicated on your wood-cutting ticket; cutting wood in an area not designated on your ticket; taking wind-fallen trees or branches; changing the stamps on allotted wood; taking wood burned by fire; extraction of tar and potash, collection of hay, and the organization of beehives without permission; pasturing livestock without a ticket; building shelters or storage structures of any kind in the forests; constructing roads or portage; using the forests contrary to the forest plan; and failure to observe proper care in regard to forest fires.[41] Wood theft fell under Article 99 of the Criminal Code. Before 1924, Article 99 stated that those who violated the laws of forest protection, in any of the ways outlined above, faced imprisonment or community service for up to one year, with confiscation of the illegal spoils, as well as the instruments used to obtain them, or a fine of fifty rubles.[42]

Soon the courts were full of an embarrassing pre-Revolutionary 'crime of need.' A 1924 investigation of the legal system found places of detention full of peasants sentenced for wood theft. In the associated debate, advocates of decriminalization pointed out that wood theft cases not only clogged the courts, representing as much as one-third of all local cases, but also prevented them from dealing with 'more serious crimes.' In a review of the Moscow courts, a contributor to the journal *Proletarskii sud*, who was in favour of decriminalizing wood theft, provided examples of cases to make his point. In Zvenigorod, for example, an old man was caught stealing less than a foot of damp wood. When the judge asked him if he recognized his guilt, the elderly peasant answered that he knew that he was guilty, but the stick that held his wife's oven open had broken so he went into the forest and cut another one. The author asks, 'What should the judge do? If he does not recognize the act as a crime, then every peasant will go to the forest and cut himself a small piece of wood. And if the village has 150 peasants, then we already need a multiplication table.' The indignant legal observer went on to explain that the old man pleaded that he was sixty-five years old and had never been convicted of anything. He was fined twenty-five kopecks. In spring, the author continued, peasants needed to build fences so that cattle would not trample newly planted crops; they needed wood to build them. In winter, roofs would cave in under the weight of the snow and peasants had to go to the forests to get wood to repair them. 'Again the forest guard stumbles upon them or a neighbour tells the guard who is at a local drinking hole' about the thefts, and again the peasant goes to court.[43]

In March 1923, Sergei Vasil'evich Lipaev appealed to the Provincial Court on behalf of fifty-five others because the people's court had fined all of the accused seventy-five rubles each for wood theft in Elat'ma. Each of the accused included the personal circumstances that explained why he or she had, or in some cases could not have, committed the crime. One of the accused, for example, claimed he was serving in the ranks of the Red Army at the time and was not in the area. Another said he was covered by an amnesty and had already been excused. The Provincial Court upheld the guilty verdict of the lower court but excused all of the individuals from the fine on the grounds of the amnesty granted by the fifth anniversary of the October Revolution.[44]

The cases are instructive; the extent of peasant need for wood was very real and the limitations of the law obvious. The legal investigators of 1924 recommended that petty cases of wood theft be decriminalized and handed over to local bodies to deal with administratively.[45] Changes to the law were introduced. Damages up to fifteen rubles in value were dealt with by administrative fine through the district soviets, at fines of no more than three times the value of the stolen wood. Damages or theft valued at more than fifteen rubles, or exploitation of the forest 'as a means of livelihood,' were dealt with by the courts. The accused could be punished with imprisonment of up to one year or a fine of up to 100 rubles.[46]

Contributors to the Commissariat of Justice's weekly journal worried that the new law was too flexible to take into account a peasant's class status. A poor peasant, they argued, might steal fifteen rubles and twenty kopecks' worth of wood to 'repair his ramshackle izba' and have to liquidate all of his assets just to pay the court fine. In contrast, they pointed out, a wealthy peasant who stole just under fifteen rubles' worth of wood would be safe. Moreover, fines collected by the district soviets were being misappropriated.[47] The prolific legal specialist Naum Lagovier noted the same problem. Overworked district soviets would continue the old court practice of fining groups of thieves lump sums without regard for the financial situation of each transgressor. People's courts behaved exactly the same way.[48]

Branches of the state involved tried to clear up where money from fines should go. The Commissariats of Justice, Finance, Agriculture, and Internal Affairs issued a joint resolution in June 1925 that made matters even more confusing. Part of the fine was to go back to the forest users and part to the general state treasury.[49] More clarification was given in April 1926. Thirty per cent of the fines collected were to go back to the forest guard and the police (already a challenge, since the guard was under Commissariat of Agriculture jurisdiction), 40 per cent into the state treasury, and 30 per cent into the district budget.[50] The problem was that the district soviets often put the entire amount collected into their budget to pay their own salaries or those of the police.[51] There was also a very good chance that whoever caught the wood thief, be it the forest guard or the police, would collect a fine on the spot and consider it wages.[52] There were reports of the police refusing to deliver fines collected to the district soviet because they had not received their cut in the past.[53] Many district soviets just let the cases pile up. One soviet had not reviewed its wood theft cases for two years. Even when fines were levied, collection proved itself the next challenge. In one district 3,035 rubles were levied in fines, but only 846 rubles were actually collected.[54] For 1926–7 across the province of Riazan, 13,664 cases of forest violations were sent to the district soviets and of these 7,234 were heard. Of the 2,922 sent to the people's court only 693 were dealt with. Fines were levied totalling 610,862 rubles, but only 73,784 rubles were collected.[55] In an attempt to pressure the soviets to process the cases more quickly, the Commissariats of Agriculture and Justice issued joint instructions on 21 March 1927; all cases had to be processed within one month of the crime being committed or be declared invalid. As a result, the overworked local authorities just let even more cases expire without punishment.[56]

A new provision on the forests of local significance appeared on 30 December 1927. This decree preserved the earlier one, but added much more detail on the role of the rural and district soviets. The addendums attempted to combat the ways in which the commune and the gathering improvised how they distributed wood.[57] More changes were adopted to Article 85 (wood theft fell under Article 85 and not 99 in the later addition of the Criminal Code) in January 1928. Courts dealt with cases only if the value of stolen or damaged materials was over 100 rubles. The new penalty was community service for up to six months or a fine of no more than three times the value of the material if it could not be recovered. If the theft was systematic or the material taken was earmarked for industrial use and worth over 100 rubles, the theft carried a penalty of loss of freedom for up to one year.

The rural soviets were to deal with cases involving wood of up to three rubles in value. They could levy fines as high as six rubles, and if the individual could not pay the fine, the soviet could sentence him to community service of up to one week. The district soviets or the chief of police would deal with thefts or damages worth up to twenty-five rubles. Those thefts carried fines of up to fifty rubles or community service for up to two weeks. If the officials of the rural or district soviets or the police believed that the accused could afford the fine, but just did not want to pay, they could confiscate property and make an arrest, provided their decision was ratified by the uezd. For cases involving damages between twenty-five and one hundred rubles, uezd officials could levy fines of up to two hundred rubles or sentence an offender to community service for up to one month. All cases had to be dealt with within three months of the day the material was stolen or the case would be considered closed.[58] The practical impact of the changes was further chaos. Virtually everyone who was accused of wood theft would appeal his or her case up to the next administrative level.[59] By the time the case was reviewed and returned, the three-month period was likely over, and so in turn created the impression, not altogether mistaken, that one could easily get away with wood theft.[60]

Jurisdictions continued to be muddy, confused, and overlapping through the 1920s. The Commissariat of Agriculture had administrative control of the forests but still had to make agreements with other organs such as the Supreme Council of the People's Economy, and the People's Commissariat of Transportation, all of which had to be ratified by the Council of Labour and Defence (STO). On the ground, life was just as complicated, with foresters and their administration, the forest guard, the police, rural soviet members, and members of the district soviets all having equal rights in apprehending and punishing violations of the Forest Code.[61]

The Forest Guard

The individuals who shouldered the burden and often the blame regarding forest violations were the forest guard. Like other state servitors at the lowest level, they walked a razor's edge between responsibilities to the communities they served and obligations to serve state interests. It was unclear how one became a forest guard in the 1920s and where one's wages came from. Practices varied from place to place. In some places there was bidding, with the job going to the individual willing to take the lowest pay. In others, guards were paid 'in kind,' which usually meant the right to graze livestock in the forest free of charge. Elsewhere, villagers took turns being guards and were paid by the commune.[62] In others, forest guards were hired by the forest administration and assigned to an area. This last method was the most difficult for a guard. As an outsider, he was the target of a local community's wrath if he refused to come to personal agreements on wood with the surrounding villages. If he did come to such agreements, the deals likely made him an insider. In some places in Riazan, salaries for the forest guard were as low as three rubles per month as late as 1928. Such wages were but a tiny supplement to the household income, unless of course one worked creatively at one's job.[63] Accommodating the desperate need for wood on the part of the villagers who lived around you was the safest and most profitable course of action for a forest guard.

There was a constant tension among the local police, the forest guard, and the courts. The forest guard repeatedly asked for help. Representatives of the police told the forest guard that they were already overcommitted and that the forest guard should work harder to fight forest violations. A meeting of the uezd police in Ranenburg resolved that forest guards should take all measures to keep track of anyone going in and out of the forest, especially at night. There was no elaboration on how exactly they were supposed to attain this utopian feat.[64] Forest guards argued that while they did their job and apprehended wood thieves, the courts failed to do their job and prosecute them.[65] The courts claimed that as a result of illiteracy, forest guards consistently filled out the protocols incoherently and the court was forced to throw the cases out.[66] In some areas of Riazan, the forest area administration offices and the district soviets were so far apart that the police were the only connection for the exchange of any and all information, yet the police refused to act a courier service. The forest administration asked the forest department to compel the police to deliver the correspondence.[67] In other cases the police did nothing but forward correspondence and made no attempt to stop forest violations.[68] By January 1928, the police of Riazan Uezd had notified the provincial soviet that, as a result of the pressure of other campaigns, they could not participate in the struggle against wood theft.[69]

Realities on the Ground

The system was plagued by all manner of troubles. Many members of the forest guard had been guards before the Revolution. Wood that had been cut already was a shambles. Telegraph poles at one cutting area were improperly cut and rotting. The remaining wood supply was waiting for full payment from communes, rotting, slowly being pilfered, and lacking official stamps. Legally allotted wood and the stumps left behind were supposed to be stamped to indicate that it had been cut under a properly issued wood-cutting ticket. The stumps of stolen trees were to be stamped in another way so that the administration could keep proper records on how much was stolen. A wood-cutting ticket itself was technically obtained from the forestry department on the basis of documents from the district or rural soviet about the needs of the citizen. There was much confusion over the tickets. Records indicated ticket numbers but not the amount of wood allotted to each ticket, leaving a significant grey area for improvisation. One forester ran a scam in which he filled out three copies of each wood-cutting ticket, allotting one for himself, one for the guard, and one for the citizen who requested the ticket. Wood was cut on each ticket. Another guard filed claims for forest fires that had not actually occurred and then allowed, for a fee, cutting in those areas.[70] Grazing tickets were equally complicated and subject to manipulation. Forest guards used their right to pasture ten heads of livestock for free by taking bribes from locals to include their cattle among them.[71]

The confusion was not only local and sometimes made its way to Moscow itself. The Council of Labour and Defence decreed in January 1923 that the tickets had to be issued for all wood cut everywhere at all times. However, wood was issued even to the Moscow-Kursk railway line without the proper tickets. Not even this massive request for wood – a request of national significance – was recorded in a chaotic accounting system in which records were hardly kept, much less balanced.[72] There was no way of keeping accurate records on theft save for the 'protocols' issued by the forest guard. However, there was a serious shortage of blank protocol books. In their own defence the forest guard pointed out that they were responsible for massive areas, were in constant danger, lacked the arms that they were entitled to, and lived in fear of reprisals from the community. Moreover, the actual process of writing up protocols against wood thieves was a ridiculous one. If the guard held the thief, he would have to drag him back to the forest administration office or even further to the police, often some twenty kilometres or more away.[73] If he let the thief go, he waited until the guard was out of sight and went right back to what he was doing. A 1926 Rabkrin report made the same point: 'It is natural, owing to such a difficult situation in which the forest guard finds itself, that wood theft in several areas had come to be considered absolutely commonplace, and ultimately a right of citizenship, on the level with other branches of non-agricultural activities of the local population. The struggle that is conducted in the forest areas against wood thieves could be called "the game of protocols" because as soon as the wood thief gets his protocol written up, he turns around and goes back again to the forest.'[74]

A Smolensk guard had a rather graphic means of showing his frustration with the system. Local peasants complained that when he caught them with stolen firewood, he used the time in which he was supposed to be writing up his protocol to chop their sleighs into tiny pieces.[75]

The forest guards who tried to do their job as prescribed had their work cut out for them. In desperation, they confiscated saws and axes, in an act that was actually illegal, given that peasants needed these vital tools to survive.[76] Some districts took matters into their own hands and passed supplementary decrees to aid in the local struggle against wood theft. In December 1926, the Riazhsk soviet resolved that 'with the aim of protecting both the state forests and the forests of local significance from wood theft and to stop the never-ending destruction of the forests – all citizens are forbidden from entering the roads through the forests with any tool that could be used for wood cutting, such as axes, two-handed saws, and saws – whether or not the citizens have cut wood with them – all such tools are subject to confiscation.'[77]

Those engaged in forest violations would often just give the forest guard a fictitious name and disappear into the villages. The forest guard simply had no time or energy to walk the twenty kilometres or so to the village in order to verify a name. In February 1928, the chief of the provincial security department asked again if the forest guard could at least confiscate axes and saws until the thief was forced to give his real name to get them back.[78] The Commissariat of Justice responded with a reminder that axes and saws could be confiscated only if there was proof that they had been used to cut wood.[79]

Pressure on the overworked rural and district soviets and the forest guards to eradicate wood theft continued to increase as representatives of each group were threatened with criminal charges of negligence if they failed to protect the forest.[80] One repeated theme in this work is the precarious position of state employees at the lowest levels. Repeatedly, one gains access to the world of the villages through those individuals caught between the demands of their employer, the state in one of its numerous guises, and the communities they served. Forest guards were no exception. They were peasants themselves and were either members of the communities that they served or were sent to work in an area in which they were isolated and vulnerable.

The Forest Code of 1923 meant increased pressure on the forest guard to enforce new legislation on forest use. The forest guard found themselves caught in the vice of state demands on one side and pressure from the communities they served on the other. The 'housing crisis' in the forest complicated matters. Because there were no barracks, or barracks belonging to a given forest district were in such poor repair, guards lived among villagers desperate for wood.[81] In October 1923, the Riazan forest department reported that in one month alone three separate homes were burned to the ground for housing members of the forest guard. The forest department requested funds to build permanent accommodations for the forest guard and their families within the grounds of the forest area they served. From the tone and content of the letter, the author understood that no funds could be provided, and thus he also asked for permission to acquire wood so the guard could build the housing themselves.[82] Within a year, however, a crime would rock the province and the country that highlighted the dangers for guards and families living in remote forest areas in Riazan.

Anyone who could make a bit of extra money from wood did so. Villagers traded in stolen as well as legally obtained wood. The district soviets paid their salaries with fines, the police supplemented theirs. The forest districts sold confiscated wood, in a practice which was strictly prohibited.[83] In Riazan, the fact that forest guards were participating in or facilitating theft was long known before and after the Revolution; guards were paid poorly, and bribery, nepotism, looking the other way, and spending time farming one's own allotment to feed a family were the order of the day.[84] In March 1924, two articles on the forest appeared in a Riazan provincial party newspaper. The articles were entitled 'Destruction of the Forest' and 'The Last of the Forest Is Being Stolen while the Forest Guard Sleeps.' The provincial Rabkrin office immediately sent a note to the provincial administrative office of the Commissariat of Agriculture wanting to know what was being done to protect the forests from 'the plunder of the forest guard.'[85] The Commissariat of Agriculture turned the matter over to the forest department, which then asked the newspaper to send their sources for the articles. The articles, it turned out, were based on two short denunciatory letters. The first letter, signed by Proezzhii or a 'passer-by,' reported that in the Fedorovka District of Spassk Uezd 'systematic wood theft could be observed.' Each night the villagers of Fedorovka and Novinskaia Sloboda took up to 200 cartloads of wood from the forest. Passer-by noted that there were several forest guards, but instead of guarding the forest, 'they steal more than anyone else. For example, not long ago the guard Arbuzov came to our forest area. He arrived poor and now he is bourgeois [*burzhui*]; he has three cows, a horse, and a barn full of grain. He acquired all of this, of course, on the forest.'[86] The newspaper article had borrowed its headline from the second letter from the village of Iagonovo, Dankov Uezd, signed by Proiaev 'the revealer,' who wrote, 'Not far from our village is located a huge forest (of the former pomeshchik Khomikov). The peasants pitilessly rob it. It is hard to imagine, but the forest in the last little while has been reduced to half. The forest guards are negligent of their duties. The forest is plundered behind their backs, and it is as if they cannot see. If this is going to continue much longer, then all that will remain are stumps.'[87] The forest department tried to put an end to the matter quickly in its correspondence to Rabkrin, saying that there was no way to check the facts because no particular citizens were mentioned.[88] But the 1924 Rabkrin investigation of wood theft and the forest guard was already under way.

The materials collected from the forest districts in 1924 provide a vivid picture of the challenges on the ground. When asked to explain the massive theft of wood from his forest district in Dankov, the forest guard Grigorii Bogoslovskii stated, 'The wood theft occurred mostly in 1924. I try to protect the forest, but it is difficult to protect all of it because my section is surrounded by villages on all sides. As for the citizens, they have little wood for heating, so they all take to the forest. Men, women, adolescents all go to the forest with rope and hand-pulled sleds. When they see me, they scatter and they hide and watch until I leave the forest again. I conduct searches [in the villages], but I rarely find anything because typically the citizens steal one day's worth of firewood. There is theft at night, but at night it is dangerous for me in the forest because I am not armed, and I was already beaten in 1923.'[89] Bogoslovskii was dismissed for his troubles by a commission associated with the review.

Some members of the forest guard who were dismissed fought back.

On 18 June 1924, Andrei Anisimovich Ivantsov, Prokhor Grigor'evich Efimov, and Makar Egorovich Zemskov from the Petrovskoe forest district in Shatsk wrote a well-informed, articulate, and ideologically astute letter, appealing their dismissal. The wording and content of the letter suggest that these men were willing to engage with the state structures that they encountered, using terms and language that the regime itself produced and understood. They were familiar with central-level resolutions and appealed to the laws of the land, which, they pointed out, stood above not only them but state authority as well.[90] The letter began by stating that the reasons for their dismissal 'remain a mystery' to them as they had never been charged with a crime or censored administratively by their superiors. They referred to a Central Committee resolution of 5 August 1921, which stated that all organs of Soviet power must behave within the laws of the Republic; the letter argued that firing them violated the interests of the toilers and thus, by extension, the laws of the Republic. The three men wrote that they were peasants by their social situation and had never exploited hired labour: 'We are selfless and honest and none of this was taken into consideration by the commission and we ourselves were not allowed to present our social and property position. In our political orientation we are entirely loyal, not just as servitors [*sluzhashchie*] but, in general, as rank and file peasants. Through the years of Soviet power we have never participated in any kind of active opposition against the established order, never even been under suspicion for undermining faith in power [*vlast'*] or for discrediting it in an improper or criminal way. Therefore we have to think that the commission, while reviewing the ranks, failed to understand our political physiognomy.' The men asked to be returned to their full duties, as the commission could not prove any impropriety on their part. They concluded their letter by pointing out that they lived under a double threat from the authorities, on the one hand, and from those they sent to court for wood theft, on the other. 'I, Ivantsov, had my horse stolen by someone who sought revenge against me for doing my job. No less serious are the threats to our life from those we collide with while they are stealing wood. All of this testifies to the danger that permeates our position.'[91] Their position was indeed dangerous. If they happened upon peasants desperate for wood, there could be a conflict. If a forest guard was true to his duties and prosecuted wood thieves, he could find himself burned out and homeless. There were even more deadly threats in the forest; guards were sometimes beaten and left tied up waiting for someone to happen upon them.[92] The forests did provide hiding places for very real organized gangs of criminals who robbed peasants on the road. Forest guards were in serious danger is they stumbled upon these men. Moreover, the forest guards sometimes had guns, which were attractive bounty for the gangs.

The dangers of living within the forest were brought home in the summer of 1924. Mysterious things had occurred in the forest area of Kudom, in late 1923, with the disappearance of forest guard Sergei Parashukov and his wife. In late January 1924, the body of forest guard Nikolai Mochalkin was found in the forest, and in mid-February the forest guard Martykhin was found with his skull crushed. But nothing compared to the scene that awaited the shepherd Sorokin, who returned to the compound with the livestock of the forest administration workers on a July evening in the summer of 1924. He was met by an unusual silence and the doors locked from the inside. Sensing something was seriously amiss, he ran to the adjacent lumberyards and gathered a group of workers to enter the compound with him. They found the chief forester murdered in his bed. Sorokin found his own wife and daughter murdered in their rooms and sixteen more victims in the locked barn. The victims themselves provide a rare look at daily life in the forest community. Here life and work were inextricably linked, for among the victims were adults and children of all ages and all manner of relationships both to the work of the forest and to one another. The victims included secretarial staff and their wives, siblings, an aunt, a nursemaid, and children, a forest guard, a former forest guard, two villagers, and the wife of a worker at the lumberyard and her three children. The compound of the forest administration was a communal gathering place of sorts.

The details of the investigation itself are also revealing. The poverty of the forest administration and guard is striking. The bandits got away with four rifles, 140 bullets, and 937 rubles. We know that the rifles were made in 1870 because the police asked the forest department the value of the rifles and bullets so they could factor that cost into the fines against the perpetrators. The murders were committed by a bandit gang living in the forest and the police were able to track all but one of the gang members down in relatively short order. Their trial was held in December 1924, and all were sentenced to death.[93] The Kudom massacre was not an everyday occurrence, certainly not typical, and is still remembered and spoken of with horror in Riazan today. An especially vicious group was hiding near the forest administration offices (*lesnichestvo*), and its members engaged in an unusual and atypical act of violence and cruelty by going on a brutal killing spree. The existence of forest patrols likely threatened the gang's hiding place, but there were many ways to intimidate or to work with the forestry department, and resorting to a massacre was not customary. What the massacre did do, however, was present the forest guard with a temporary window of opportunity; they could use the Kudom massacre to illustrate the dangers of their jobs and thus as leverage in appeals for more resources.

Immediately, requests began to pour in from members of the forest guard for revolvers or at least rifles so they could defend themselves.[94] The case brought the horrendous conditions of the forest guard to the fore, initiating a short-lived sympathy for their plight. In August 1924, *Bednota* reported that the average salary for a forest guard was just under four rubles per month, which was not even 30 per cent of the pre-Revolutionary wage. 'The price of bread rises, no uniforms are issued, and boots wear out. And here the forest guard's soul becomes twisted and instead of honestly defending the forest, he becomes, against his will, the destroyer of the forest.'[95] A member of the guard had two options: leave employment as soon as humanly possible (and many took the option, as labour turnover was more than 100 per cent annually) or supplement his income through his position.[96] But sympathy for the dangerous life of the forest guard was soon replaced by a concern over the wasting of bullets. On 12 January 1925 a circular reminded forest guards that they were required to account for all shots fired. Bullets, they were told, cost ten rubles each, and any guard who was caught firing his weapon without an explanation, more than twice, would be charged officially with embezzlement.[97] A continuous flood of circulars demanded strict record-keeping of the number of weapons and bullets a forest area had and on all reported losses or thefts of weapons. Detailed information was required on the forest guard who claimed the loss.[98] A 31 March circular complained that no one was taking the early circulars seriously and paperwork was partial and haphazard.[99] Such messiness could be read in at least two but not necessarily mutually exclusive ways – as examples of the bureaucratic chaos of the lower levels in the 1920s or as evidence that the forest administration had much more important matters to deal with first. The police wasted no time in taking advantage of the situation. They confiscated weapons from the forest guards or the forest administration on suspicion of illegal use and redistributed the seized weapons to their own officers or to other agencies. Such action was strictly forbidden, as it reduced the total stock of the Commissariat of Agriculture.[100]

With the memory of the Kudom massacre fresh in their minds, frightened forest guards at the Berezovo forest district failed to fight

11. Kudom storyboard (photo archive of Evgeny Kashirin).

back when their meeting was raided by six bandits. The forest department's report on the incident is replete with critical asides about the guards' failure to resist. According to the report, bandits burst into a meeting of about twenty people shortly before 5 p.m. on 21 February 1925. Everyone was told to lie on the floor, and they 'did without questioning.' The bandits then asked who had a weapon. When the chief forester Alpatikov moved to hand over his gun, he was shot twice and killed. Everyone continued to lie on the floor 'without even the slightest attempt at resistance' while the bandits searched them 'unimpeded.' The bandit haul consisted of two rifles, fifty-eight bullets, a revolver, 638.62 rubles in state funds, 120 rubles belonging to the office, and a clock. The report claims that the entire staff panicked and 'lost their heads.' Their weapons, apparently, were standing in corners or leaning against the walls and such 'carelessness on the part of the forest guard emboldens the bandits.' The forest guard, the report concluded, must realize they are 'soldiers' who should 'never put down their rifles' in order to protect the forests, themselves, and their co-workers.[101] Given the conditions they worked in and the token salaries they received, such a demand was not only unreasonable, it was impossible.

Being the overseers of such a scarce and much-needed resource, located in remote and concealed areas, underpaid, frightened, and impoverished, forest guards had compelling incentives to engage in extralegal dealings involving wood and grazing rights. Forest guards supplemented their meagre wages in a host of ways. Wood was released without the proper paperwork, stamps, or accounting, leaving considerable leeway for guards to improvise.[102] They rented out grazing areas in the forest privately. They accepted contributions of samogon, money, food, and goods and in return allowed villagers the customary right to collect windfallen trees and branches. They helped their families and friends acquire wood for heating, building, and repair.[103] A legal consultant in Sapozhok, Riazan, in July 1924 reviewed the case of the patroller Zhivikhin, who permitted 'massive theft of new-growth' in exchange for grain from the citizens of the village Novyi Khutor. Zhivikhin said that he had never accepted a bribe, but that perhaps the citizens of Novyi Khutor had given him forty puds of rye 'for his troubles' (*za khlopoty ego*). The consultant recommended that Zhivikhin be tried under Article 114 of the Criminal Code for bribery.[104]

Boris Mozhaev's *Muzhiki i baby* captures the situation of the forest guard beautifully. The patroller Sen'ka Knut assisted the horse thief Ivan Zhadov and his gang, who hid out in the isolated Sen'ki corridor on the border of the Ermilovo forest. Sen'ka turned a blind eye to their activities and sometimes sold stolen horses and goods for them. He refused payment in money, which he regarded as the root of sin, but accepted the odd spiritual reward in the form of an occasional drink and something to eat. His superior, the senior forester, never participated in Zhadov's crimes but did accept a steady flow of small gifts and sometimes asked Sen'ka to skin a lamb 'for the ladies.'[105] Patrollers and foresters worked together, toured together, and protected each other. Two peasants of the village of Naumovo in Spas-Klepiki protested that the forester of their forest area, I.K. Tiabin, treated wood allotments as if they were his personal property. Moreover, they claimed, he stole wood and gathered brushwood himself and sold it. They complained during the Rabkrin investigation, but Tiabin was not punished because the patroller of the same area swore that the forester was a good person, and the forest administration refused to forward the peasants' complaints to the investigators.[106]

From February to May 1924, the Riazan forest department participated in an overview of the forest guard. Out of the 1,610 people investigated, 577 were dismissed. Of them, 410 were dismissed for 'political crimes' and 167 for being 'kulak elements.' A purge review committee reinstated 49 of them. In December 1924, the forest guard in Riazan consisted of 254 patrollers and 1,063 foresters.[107] The review of the provincial forest brings into sharp relief the situation in the forest in regard to both the forest guard and those who procured wood, with or without their help. The review lamented the population's attitude toward the forests of local significance, noting a 'desire' to receive them with no controls at all. Peasants, the reviewers noted, had 'tendencies' toward 'too diffuse interpretations of their own interests in the legal use of the forests of local significance.' In addition, there was some concern over losing free rights of pasture since such use was a crucial aspect of the peasant economy.[108]

The published central summary of the countrywide Rabkrin study complained that even though each community needed to sign an agreement on how they would use the forests of local significance, villages took forest use as a 'general right,' which led to wood theft in the eyes of the state. There was widespread doubt and confusion surrounding rights to haymaking and pasturing. New villages were assigned areas that overlapped with pre-Revolutionary areas of pasture for other villages, and conflicts resulted in petition after petition to the land organs. The Rabkrin study concluded that making decisions about forest use, among users and among class groupings within a given commune, was extremely complex. The study concluded that 'the peasantry itself cannot correct this situation without help from the state. Thus both central and local organs must take the lead in the matter of working out the form and right of using the forests of local significance.'[109] Such analysis foreshadowed, and indeed likely helped to shape, the escalating shift toward extreme centralization of decisions made on how to deal with the countryside.[110]

Response from Above

A familiar pattern emerges in a study of the forest guard. In the early NEP years the harsh remnants of Civil War policies were reassessed in a way more sympathetic to the peasantry. In the 1924 review of the judicial system it came to light that the prisons were embarrassingly full of peasants who had committed a crime of need; wood theft was decriminalized in October 1924, along with a general amnesty to celebrate the seventh anniversary of the great October Revolution.[111] In 1924 the 'face to the countryside' campaign began and the horrifying news of corruption, lawlessness, illiteracy, lack of political consciousness, and general autonomy in the periphery began to flood the Centre. The years 1926 and 1927 were marked by a panic about crime, hooliganism, banditry, forest destruction, and a host of other 'threats' to the fledgling Republic and a return to pressure for harsh measures from the Centre to contain and eradicate such threats.

In 1927, the provincial forest department was already complaining that the punishments laid out in the Criminal Code were not 'sufficiently repressive' and thus did not 'produce results.' The majority of Riazan's rural inhabitants were too poor to be assessed monetary fines and so were assessed community service. But the entire infrastructure for performing community service was absent in the province, so wood thieves went unpunished and became emboldened. This letter to the provincial soviet concluded with a request to appeal to the Central Committee to strengthen the punishments of wood thieves in Article 85 of the Criminal Code, including up to six months in prison.[112] A March 1928 article in the Riazan party paper reported frantic statistics on wood theft provided by the provincial inspector of forests, Makukhin. The article claimed that in 1924–5, there were 11,046 registered cases of forest violations in the province of Riazan valued at 64,969 rubles. In 1926–7, that number almost doubled to 21,122 cases, valued at 218,559 rubles. For at least half of the cases there were no suspects and the number of unresolved cases was well over 50 per cent.[113] The 1928 meetings on the struggle with crime in Riazan – attended by the procurator, his assistants, the chairman of the Provincial Court, representatives from Rabkrin and from the provincial security department, the police, and the inspectors of the forest – reflect the turn to harsher policies. There were calls for the militarization of the forest guard and the need to merge them with the police or the NKVD.[114] There were repeated calls for a disciplined, literate staff that knew their duties and responsibilities and were under strict supervision and control.[115]

Once again in 1928, Rabkrin investigators spread out to the forest areas of Riazan to conduct another investigation. Members of the forest guard were dismissed for being 'alien elements,' stealing wood, being absent from their posts, drinking, 'protectionism,' having connections to bandits, harbouring criminals, beating peasants, and taking bribes. A lengthy report complained that members of the forest guard who were denounced by some locals and taken to court for such crimes always had villagers and members of the rural soviets who would provide character witness for them, swearing that they were honest men and had never affronted the local peasantry.

The administrators of the districts, the chief foresters, and their assistants were accused of being the 'sons of kulaks'; improving their own homesteads with state wood and stockpiling firewood; being rude to the forest guard; being rude to peasants; having ties to kulaks, religious individuals, and 'former people'; favouring the wealthy with grants of wood and pasture; being 'self-possessed and clever'; and finding positions in the administration for relatives. The chief forester of the Lesynovo forest region, for example, was accused of engaging in hooliganism, debauched acts with women of ill-repute, drinking with other local officials, and cursing in the company of women and children of good reputation. Moreover, he constantly complained how low his wages were in comparison to his earnings of the pre-Revolutionary period. He spoke ill of Soviet power, saying that he would go to America or 'some other bourgeois country' if Soviet power continued to harass him. The inspector of forests for Sasovo was written up as a 'lickspittle' (*podkhal'*) and a former officer who ran off to fight on the side of the Whites and returned after the Civil War and answered the call for specialists.[116]

The Rabkrin review of Riazan that resulted noted that the population and the rural soviets made their own decisions about how to use the forests and other local resources according to the ideas of individuals and groups in their midst or the decisions of the village gathering. One commune passed protocol 39 on 17 March 1928, which stated, 'Be it noted that the theft of wood in 1926 and 1927 took place for lack of consciousness of the citizens of the village, and their poverty, in that the grain they had lasted only until January and after that the majority of the citizens of the village lived on money they made from the sale of stolen wood.'[117]

Wages for the forest guard remained so low that the job was still regarded as a meagre supplement to the household budget. Most forest guards were still insufficiently literate to fill out protocols accurately or to master their rights and responsibilities.[118] In every area investigated in Riazan, no guards had temporary shelter from the rain. Turnover was extremely high, with the average length of service at about six months. Guards were still responsible for large areas that they had to patrol on foot as the result of a shortage of horses and the financial resources to acquire them. About 19 per cent of the guard were armed by the forest administration, while 15 per cent had their own weapons. There were official reminders in 1928 that under no circumstances were members of the forest guard to be given revolvers, only rifles. The rifles they did have were made in the 1870s and weighed about thirteen pounds. Many, however, had no weapons, no special clothing, no horses, little instruction, and virtually no guidelines for their work. The guard still had no books of blanks for writing up protocols. In some places the commune continued to elect and pay the guard.[119] Offices in the forest district still lacked basic furniture and such crucial details as fireproof boxes for money and documents.[120]

So the criticisms of the forestry workers became more and more shrill, but conditions were barely improving. Meanwhile, the bazaars did a roaring business in stolen wood, and the demand was not just from villagers but from factories, various other enterprises, and state offices as well.[121] The pressure from the population on the forest guard also increased, as did the guards' frustration at the fact that they could not do their job even if they wanted to. Again in Riazan in 1928, wood thieves were burning homes and haystacks of those who rented to members of the forest guard. For example, one member of the guard rented a place to sleep from Ivan Vladimirovich Grishakov in the village of Ploskoe in Sapozhok. Grishakov's horse, which was stabled in the barn, had its tail cut off and cut into little pieces. The uezd soviet and the land administration offices recognized that the guard was put in the position of either siding with the thieves or becoming homeless along with his family. Moreover, villagers near the forest were refusing, naturally, to rent to members of the forest guard. The guards then had to look for accommodation further and further from their posts. There were armed attacks on forest guards, even in daylight, and guards were forced to fire back in self-defence. Apprehended thieves were resisting and beating members of the forest guard. In turn the guards asked to be released from service because they could not endure the conditions of the job – specifically, the absence of any kind of shelters, the lack of arms, and the shortage of bullets, especially since the thieves themselves were better armed. The forest administration began to ask for harsher measures against wood thieves involved in violent resistance to the guard and asked the police to search the villages around the forest district to find and seize weapons. Foresters began to echo calls for show trials of wood thieves who injured members of the guard.

The rural soviets sometimes engaged in wood theft themselves and often protected their own, ignoring the protocols written up by the forest guard. In the village of Verki, one villager had already been caught stealing wood eleven times in five or six months and had a house built entirely of stolen wood; the local soviet looked the other way. Apparently twenty-six of the sixty homes in Verki were built with stolen wood.[122] Some soviets tried to defend themselves against accusations that they did not take wood theft seriously. A Sapozhok soviet had made thirty-nine charges of three rubles each but had failed to collect so much as a 'single kopek.' The chair pointed out that the election campaign had dragged on for a month and a half, and the soviet had been engaged in shock work in the collection of the agricultural tax as well as the sowing campaign.[123]

Access to wood and distribution had also changed little.[124] In some areas in Riazan both firewood and wood for repair was distributed by household and in some places 'even by eater,' or by soul. Wood continued to be distributed by the commune or the gathering with no attention to state-defined preferences. Each household received between two and ten pieces of wood for repairs, which often went for firewood too.[125] According the Rabkrin investigation, all of Riazan was experiencing 'wood hunger' in 1928. The report complained, 'In the majority of cases, forests are regarded as the property of the commune and not the state. Wood that is taken from the forest district does not have the required accounting and is not stamped. The absence of an inventory of released wood and of any existing order to distribution allows the forest guard to do whatever they want with impunity. Control is virtually impossible.'[126]

As the country moved toward wholesale collectivization, the tenor of the discussion in Riazan about wood theft changed also. Increasingly, members of the rural soviets were targeted for their lack of consciousness, exhibited in their protection of their constituency, rather than their devoted service to the state. In 1929, the uezd commission for the verification of the forest administrative structure felt obliged to emphasize the 'disgraceful attitude of the rural soviets toward the forest economy in general, and toward forest destruction in particular.' Rural soviets were providing certificates of need to anyone who asked for them. When the chairmen were confronted and questioned about such actions, they replied, 'They are all needy.' In some cases the rural soviets supplied wealthier peasants, arguing that they had the means (carts and sleighs) to move the wood. The report claimed that the rural soviets played no small role in the ruin of the forests and often enabled wood thieves. For example, the chairman of the Ishchered' soviet, Galkin, not only refused to help the forest guard Karpunin, but instead seized his protocols and his protocol book. In the village of Vorottsy, the chairman and his brother (who happened to be secretary of the soviet and a member of the Komsomol) 'actively intervened on the side of a wood thief against the forest guard.' The report summarized the situation with a flash of insight: 'Maybe these things happen because they [the representatives of *vlast'*] are citizens as well as low-level personnel. And maybe because they are afraid of the red rooster [a common term for arson].' The world of the forest was too 'closed' and too many were considered 'insiders.' The secret report observed that the forest structure was so remote from central control that it had been dubbed an 'autonomous republic.'[127]

In the midst of Riazan's wood crisis, reports began to appear in 1929 complaining of the shortage of experienced workers in the province to cut wood of export quality.[128] The talk of wood hunger and shortages in Riazan disappeared and was replaced by the talk of a fuel crisis in Moscow, and of the need to requisition wood from Riazan. Not that Riazan particularly delivered at first, since only 25,000 of the 230,000 cubic metres of wood requisitioned within Riazan, for the city of Moscow, was collected in 1929–30. One of the main problems was transportation. The Moscow soviet informed its okrugs in September 1929 that they needed to conduct an explanatory campaign among their peasants on the need to strengthen wheeled transport. 'In those districts where an explanatory campaign does not provide results, authorize rural and district soviets to organize the carting out of wood by way of a compulsory contribution among peasant households, secured by living and non-living inventory.' In other words, cart wood or face confiscation of your property. The forests of local significance were to be tapped for construction of buildings needed on the new collective farms. Moreover, those living on collective farms were to receive allocations of wood ahead of those who had not yet joined. Those who had been deprived of their voting rights were not entitled to wood allotments at all by 1930.[129] Given the scarcity of the resource, this motivation likely proved a powerful impetus for peasants to enter the collective farms over time. Perhaps it is no coincidence that a seventy-six-year-old woman in Kadom who was interviewed by an ethnographer in 1992 boldly stated that on 'the collective farms forest demons became communists, while the good people were exiled.'[130]

Conclusions

It is no accident that the forest is such a suitable location for a study of local communities and of the clash between the realities on the ground and the modernizing dreams of the Centre. In her introduction to a special issue of the *Slavic Review* devoted to nature as both proxy and actor, Zsuzsa Gille reminds us, 'There is still, and there will always be, another layer of political action: often local, often hidden in the nitty-gritty of the everyday materiality of nature and human bodies, but consequential nevertheless.'[131] Moreover, as Jane Costlow wonderfully articulates, the forest is an exceptional symbol of the 'gothic,' of that primordial threat to the modern. The forest is a space in which the 'order of modernity is always threatening to slip back into an anarchic and violent past, in which passions – rather than reason – rule the day.'[132] And there was no better example of such fears than the massacre at Kudom.

Tracing the discussion surrounding forest violations and the corruption of the forest guard – in newspapers and journals, ethnographic studies of the 1920s, the archival records of the Commissariat of Agriculture and its forest departments, the records of district and provincial executive committees, and the materials collected by Rabkrin – provides a fascinating mirror of the discourse of the NEP itself. With the introduction and attempt to enforce the Forest Code of 1923, reports of the challenges on the ground began to stream into the provincial office of the Commissariat of Agriculture and its forest department from the forest-area administration. These reports provide a hint of who stole wood and why, as well as a sense of the varied responses of the forest guard to their position. It was not always easy to grasp a portrait of the typical wood thief. Both the soviets and the people's courts tended to group wood-theft cases together and fine individuals en masse; thus it is almost impossible for the researcher to hear individual voices in the trial records. Often everyone was fined the same amount by the people's courts and then individuals appealed to the Provincial Court on the grounds that the class line was violated. Looking at the individuals charged and engaged in appeals from the early twenties through to the late twenties, one sees that the majority of wood thieves tended to be men, and that is understandable, given the strength needed to cut and haul the wood. The ages of the accused varied from eighteen to fifty-seven, and the men tended to steal wood to repair their homes and outbuildings, or for firewood.[133] Women were more likely to be the recipients of illegally obtained wood.[134] Wood theft was also often committed by entire villages and usually motivated by need, and this motivation remained constant through the 1920s.[135]

In 1924 the party, the commissariats, and their newspapers turned to face the countryside; there they found and reported on all manner of irregularities. Picking up on the campaign cue, Rabkrin began to look into the matter at hand. In the area of forest administration, the initial Rabkrin and Commissariat of Agriculture investigations of 1924–5 involved widespread dismissals, but also considerable sympathy for the conditions in which forest workers and the local population found themselves. As the tenor of the times changed, the findings and the purging of local officials in 1927–8 took a harsher turn, providing insight into the mood that governed the decisions to introduce the first five-year plan in 1928 and to call for rapid industrialization of the country alongside collectivization of the peasantry.

This examination of Riazan's forests brings the reader as close as possible to the individuals (villagers, forest guards, rural soviet members) within the context of social, economic, and political (dis)organization. An examination of the conflicts over forest resources illustrates the escalating impact, on all parties involved, of the massive gap between central regulations, in their attempts to systematize and simplify, and the complications of local realities. Local realities were oriented to surviving in difficult conditions, in an economy of shortages, and utilizing every means possible – barter, exchange, tradition, the gathering, the rural soviet, certificates of need, wood-cutting tickets, appeals – to secure wood, warmth, and repair. The conflict over forest resources captures the chaos and complexity of only one of thousands of elements that constituted the running of a state. The demands and the work heaped upon the rural and district soviets are undeniable. The members of the rural soviets and other local representatives of power – forest guards, police, people's court judges – were trapped between the pressures from above and from below. In the period under examination here, the pressures from below were stronger. The Centre needed a way to alter that equation.

The study of the trees reveals a customary system of barter and exchange, dubbed bribery by the Criminal Code, and the traditional decisions of the gathering. The Centre's representatives in the 1920s tended to work for themselves first and then for the villagers they served. Rural soviets issued certificates of need to all they deemed worthy on their own terms. Forest guards worked up their own systems of wood supply and pasturing along with the local inhabitants. The existence of these seemingly 'autonomous republics' was not acceptable to the Centre.

Finally, a close study of the forest provides further insight into the workings of the NEP: the overlapping jurisdictions, the crucial role played by Rabkrin, the responses of the Commissariat of Agriculture. One can see the shift from a softer line, which emphasized poverty and need, to a harder line emphasizing discipline and control. When the Centre faced the countryside it received a flood of reports of chaos, lawlessness, tradition, lack of consciousness, and the absence of surveillance and systematization. Local officials, as the most visible to the state and thus the most vulnerable, came under increasing scrutiny and criticism. An exploration of the conflict over forest resources brings us closer to understanding the local complications that drove the Centre toward the grand simplification of collectivization.

The story of forest resources also captures the elements of the harsh new realities that were introduced in 1928 and 1929. Wood, like grain, despite shortages, was simply requisitioned. The need for wood did not go away; villagers continued to struggle with the cold, and through the 1930s they took ever-increasing risks to stay warm. The theft of wood was covered under the law on the theft of socialist property of 7 August 1932, which made stealing wood a crime against the state. As Andrei Stepanovich Arzhilovskii wrote in his diary on 2 February 1937, 'I stole two long poles for firewood from someone who had already stolen them for himself. And I got to thinking … to commit a criminal offence (theft of socialist property, for even though it is just rubbish, still every scrap is government property). Just to get warm, you have to take risks every single day, wear yourself out. So it is now and so it will be, from now to the end of time.'[136]

PART THREE

The Battle for Souls:

What Violent Crime Reveals about the Countryside

Chapter Seven

Bandit Tales: The Steam of the Still and the Lure of Easy Profit

I am dying for communism.

V.T. Shchelokov[1]

In the early morning hours of 6 November 1927, the body of a rural newspaper correspondent (*sel'kor*), V.T. Shchelokov, was discovered in a Moscow apartment. Shchelokov had helped himself to a considerable quantity of strychnine and added a tragic crescendo to the 'case of the Riazhsk bandits,' as the case had become known in the local Riazan press and the national press. His suicide note read, 'I am dying for communism' (*Umiraiu za kommunizm*). The case was featured in the national peasant newspapers of *Bednota* and *Krest'ianskaia gazeta* as a (im)morality tale of the corruption and violence deeply embedded in village power structures. The story captured perfectly the Centre's fears about the village as a space devoid of civilized rule of law, beyond state control, in which state institutions that were supposed to be civilizing had been themselves infiltrated, corrupted, and defiled. A valiant communist martyr gave his life for the communist ideal in a struggle against forces that did their best to undermine the promises of the great socialist future.[2]

The martyr-hero Shchelokov had been waging an all-out war with the bandit gang of Popov and Gavrilov for years. Eventually his tortured imagination 'painted enemies all around him,' until, in a Moscow apartment belonging to relatives and safe from the threats to his life in his native village in Riazan, he took his life.[3] It is rather a melodramatic story, yet, beyond the melodrama, the details of the case of the Riazhsk bandits provides a rare close gaze into a village of the 1920s. This chapter begins by laying out those details to draw the portrait of power in the village that emerges. It then looks at the meaning of the portrait for the Centre. It moves on to wrestle with the tangled notions of 'banditry' and 'bandits' in the legal codes and in the historical literature before moving to the faces of banditry in the Riazan countryside through the 1920s and what their stories can tell us about the bandits as well as the countryside and its inhabitants. It is not so much an exposure of 'banditry' as an exploration of what 'bandits' and 'banditry' reveal of the situation that the Centre and rural population found themselves in through the 1920s. Finally, the chapter looks at the changing face of banditry during the first collectivization drive.

Borets

Village correspondent Shchelokov lived in the village of Borets, which was located in Riazhsk Uezd, in the southern section of Riazan Province. Before the Revolution, Borets was 'specially handled' (*osobenno orudovan*) by a village constable (*uriadnik*) by the name of Malinin. Malinin had three sons, Aleksei, Ivan, and Mikhail, and two daughters, Anna and Antonia. It seems that the Malinin clan remained very powerful in the village of Borets after the October Revolution. Aleksei Malinin worked for the Criminal Investigation Department (*Ugolovnyi rozysk*), and his brother Ivan was chairman of the local rural soviet. As his daughters came of age in revolutionary Russia, Malinin senior strengthened his position in a traditional village way, through marriage ties. His daughter Antonia married a certain M.S. Gavrilov, who was a party member and a member of the Riazhsk Uezd Executive Committee (*uezdispolkom*). Anna married T.E. Popov, the criminal mastermind of a well-organized local bandit operation. Already sentenced to death in 1917 for his criminal activities, Popov was saved by an amnesty only to be rearrested in 1922 and released once more. In 1923, Popov murdered at least two witnesses to his bandit activities. One of the victims, Stepan Sitnikov, had witnessed Popov stealing a horse from a fellow villager. In the other case, Popov commanded the wife of his victim to give him the murdered man's identity papers so that he could use the victim's identity for himself or profit by selling his documents. There was always a hot market for documents in the criminal underworld and even in the countryside at large.

Popov, Gavrilov, and the Malinins engaged in and covered up a host of local crimes ranging from theft to arson, robbery, and murder.[4] Moreover, Popov had an alternate career. He worked for the local state security, the OGPU. He had offered his services at first to the criminal investigation department of the local police and then to the uezd representative of the OGPU as an undercover worker (*sekretnyi sotrudnik*) in the local struggle against banditry. Always strapped for cadres, the OGPU accepted his services. Thus, Popov became the official OGPU representative in the district. As such he had regular visits from the local head of police and from local officers. And Popov, ever hospitable, even had the chairman of the district executive committee live in his apartment for a time.[5]

Unfortunately for him, village correspondent Shchelokov overheard a conversation behind one of the village threshing barns in which the hidden interlocutors were plotting a murder. The correspondent immediately reported the conversation to the office of the district executive committee. The office called in the local police, who surrounded the threshing barn; a shoot-out ensued. Popov emerged from behind the barn with his hands up and informed the officers that he was working undercover for the OGPU and that the interference of the police had just ruined everything.[6] The police accepted his version of events and retreated. Meanwhile, Popov's partner in crime, Gavrilov, used his position as a member of the uezd executive committee to hound and badger Shchelokov relentlessly and through administrative channels. Gavrilov, for example, blocked all of Shchelokov's attempts to attend special classes that would provide him the necessary training for a civil-service position. In addition, Gavrilov further used his position to protect the members of the wider bandit group from punishment.[7] According to the newspaper *Bednota*, 'As a result of all this torment, sel'kor Shchelokov became mentally ill.'[8] Shchelokov's illness was further compounded by threatening visits to his home by Popov.[9]

From as early as February 1925, two and a half years before, Shchelokov had been flooding the Moscow-based newspaper *Krest'ianskaia gazeta* with letters about the Popov gang's activities in Riazhsk. In a February letter, for example, Shchelokov expressed his outrage over the fact that Gavrilov had received an illegal allotment (*nadel*) of land for his family by exerting considerable and threatening pressure on the local village gathering (*skhod*), which had the power to decide such matters. And in this particular letter, Shchelokov linked Gavrilov with Popov's band. The letter was forwarded by *Krest'ianskaia gazeta* to the Riazan provincial OGPU for investigation. A case was brought before the Provincial Court but was quickly dismissed. Shchelokov continued to write incessantly to *Krest'ianskaia gazeta*, and his letters, in turn, created the necessary pressure to reopen the case.[10] These early letters were among the few that got through to Moscow; apparently the newspaper had not received hundreds of Shchelokov's letters. Members of the Popov gang were able to use their positions to block the letters before they left the uezd.[11] According to local secret police reports, the Popov gang was finally caught in the act of a bandit crime and arrested near the village of Aleksandrovka in the northeastern corner of Riazhsk Uezd. The band had committed armed robbery of a postal station, stealing over 3,500 rubles. At least seven members of the group, male and female, were apprehended on site and a detailed investigation began, leading to the arrest of twenty-one other band members.[12]

The trial of the Riazhsk bandits began on 5 September 1927, at noon, in the uezd centre of Riazhsk at a special session of the Moscow, rather than the Riazan, Provincial Court. Packed as it was with peasants from across the uezd, the help of the police was required to force the courtroom doors closed to keep out those milling in the corridors and stairwells. Twenty-eight people were tried on charges of banditry, with over forty witnesses providing testimony against them.[13] Well over half of the members of the bandit group came from Arzamtsev, Malikov, Malinin, and Abramov families and were related to one another through kinship or marriage.[14] One of the clerks of the Provincial Court had to be dismissed when it was discovered that she had been taking information about the investigation to the families of the accused and to the prisoners themselves.[15] At the trial, running from 5 to 17 September 1927, witness after witness testified that the villages of Riazhsk had lived in constant fear of the gang and were terrified to report on their activities because so many of the band members were highly placed within the local administration, from the village to the uezd. The rural soviet chairman of the village of Sysaia, Fedor Petin, and his wife were murdered when members of the gang ran out of snacks (*zakuski*) at a late-night drinking fest and barged into their home demanding moonshine and food.[16] The gang repeatedly threatened the region's inhabitants and stole from them without mercy. Members of the band then insisted that local residents buy back their own stolen materials.[17] Peasants constantly reported the thefts to the local police, to the constable Alenkin, and to the former head of the district police, Litvinov. But because these men were in league with the band, nothing was done about the crimes.

Malinin's extended family was called on to testify. They were all members of elected local office, in both the party and the state administrative structure; Antonia Malinina-Gavrilova, for example, led the uezd committee of the Communist Party's women's department (*zhenotdel*).[18] All were found guilty, and penalties for the twenty-eight bandits ranged from exile from the province, to imprisonment (with terms ranging from three to ten years), to the death penalty for Popov, Mordvinov, Arzamashchev, Malinin, and Litvinov.[19] As the prosecutor pointed out, Popov, Gavrilov, and Ivan Malinin had all worked for the GPU, and since its founder, comrade Dzerzhinskii, had demanded 'crystal purity' in its work, they deserved to be harshly punished.[20] Apparently, bandit activity did not cease in Borets, and the mantle was taken over by a new leader, Stepan Petrovich Kuz'min. Kuz'min allegedly said to local peasants, 'Just as Ilya came down from the sky on his chariot, placing Elisei on earth, so Popov-Aleksinskii, now in paradise, bequeathed to me, Kuz'min, his path.'[21]

The story that emerged, then, is of an endless cycle of violence and abuse in the villages, with every state institution taken over and corrupted by extended kinship networks that protected one another and worked the system to their advantage. The prosecutor called for the need to purify these power structures in a language and tone that echoed the turning point of 1927, with its trials of engineers in Shakhty, its expulsion of Trotsky, its escalating fear of crime, and the rapid shift toward radical and all-encompassing solutions such as industrialization and collectivization. Nothing short of tearing down and rebuilding the rural world would root out the rot that had taken hold in places like Borets. And who could know how many villages like Borets dotted the Soviet landscape? Thus, on a grand scale the case led to the conclusion that only state simplifications could heal the disease of local complexities.

Beyond Riazhsk

If we step back from the case of the Riazhsk bandits, a number of complexities are revealed that implicate the decisions of the Centre as well. We see the potential problems created for the population by the justice administration's amnesties of the period.[22] Popov was twice released from custody and returned to the area. Peasants complained constantly about the danger to the village communities from bandits, hooligans, arsonists, and horse thieves who were granted early release and usually returned home to begin their old activities anew. The case highlights the kinds of crimes that threatened the village, such as horse theft, and crimes that undermined the regime, such as the traffic in illegal documents. It draws attention to a frequent object of bandit attack, the local postal system. But most importantly, the case provides insight into the intimate and often incestuous workings of village power. The case suggests that power, in this case abusive power, was situated firmly in marriage and kinship networks. And it challenges any notion of an innocent, united village. The observer notes how a former tsarist constable continued to consolidate and augment the status and influence of his family after the Revolution by marrying his daughters to powerful men. In turn, his sons found themselves powerful positions in the fledgling state's administrative structure, further promoting the extended family's power.[23] Moreover, the case suggests that local family circles of the village rooted in kinship ties – which the OGPU frequently complained about in their reports – were a very real phenomenon.[24] One sees the mechanisms of village control in the form of threats and intimidation by one member of the village community against another and just how effective they could be. Still, it is very important to note that such family circles did not *have* to be corrupt, criminal organizations to be effective, powerful forces. Many villages had power structures in which its members constituted a kind of village intelligentsia whose members were related by marriage and kinship ties. Many worked to defend village interests as a whole rather than to fleece and intimidate their constituencies. But they would still be threatening to the Centre, and it was precisely these structures that ultimately put up the best defence against Moscow's changing, punitive policies at the end of the decade.

There is an interesting gender dimension to the Riazhsk case, as women played a role in many aspects of the band's activities. Women were arrested at the scene of the crime that was the band's final undoing, suggesting that they participated in the group's violent activities. Women associated with the band also placed themselves in positions of power within the state apparatus. Finally, women were integral to the family and kinship ties that held the band together. A secret police report of October 1928 supports this notion in reference to events in another village in 1928. In a report of a conversation overheard among peasants of the village of Derevensk, Izhevsk District, Spassk Uezd, local peasant V.E. Zaitsev remarked, 'Soviet power in the village of Derevensk does a good job. But it is possible for it to be mistaken, like they can prosecute the innocent. For example, Pliakin, Andrei Ivanovich was not guilty, but instead Anna Svitskaia was guilty. She was the one who let the bandits into her home. All the young people come to see her and she leads them. The authorities don't approach her because she has connections with the police. She is responsible for twelve thefts, and nothing has been done. She is protected because she is related to the former head of the police, F.F. Gorshkov. In court she gave false testimony against Pliakin because he refused to marry her. She knows all the bandits' business.'[25]

It is fascinating to trace the roles that Anna Svitskaia was alleged to play in her village. She provided a place for the 'bandits,' or perhaps merely the rambunctious village youth, to meet. Because members of the village's criminal element met in her home, she was privy to their plans and discussions and participated in such activities herself. Moreover, her kinship connections and friendships protected her and her guests from the local arm of the law. Finally, there is a suggestion that local and private conflicts made their way into the courts even if Zaitsev himself was slandering Svitskaia.

One of the most significant and revealing aspects of the Riazhsk bandit case is the degree to which it fascinated the local and national press. The case was so alluring because it read like a dime-store novel but more importantly because it reflected, enhanced, and promoted the regime's fears about the countryside, that the countryside was anything but securely in Bolshevik control, and that the state at the lowest level was corrupt and alien, a part of an old world that operated by its own rules and outside the new culture. Rampant banditry that provoked the suicide of honest communists did not bode well for the desired image of a modern socialist state. Even more threatening was the sense that a new world was developing locally, which absorbed and subverted the organs of Soviet power for its own needs. In a way it emphasized that the administrative structure was fighting a part of itself as members of its local government used their positions for their own ends rather than in service to the Centre. As with the study of other types of crime, a closer examination of banditry cases reveals the nature of the relationship of peasant and state and provides a means to reconstruct aspects of life in the village of the 1920s. Bandit cases and the discussion of banditry in the press, legal journals, peasant letters, and secret police reports provide yet another lens through which to examine the Riazan countryside and ways in which that countryside was received and portrayed over the course of the decade.

Defining Banditry

Banditry was a constant concern for both state and peasantry. The issue was very much alive in tsarist times as well.[26] At times of violent upheaval such as the civil war period and the years of collectivization, 'bandits' could become 'partisans' when they attacked state and party individuals and institutions in an explicit anti-regime statement. Erik Landis explores the distinction between 'partisans' and 'bandits' in his study of the Antonov movement; Alexander Antonov led an anti-Bolshevik movement in Tambov at the end of the civil war. By the end of 1920, Antonov and his followers had managed to eliminate some 40 per cent of the Tambov Cheka and to kill as many as 800 of the province's state and party personnel.[27] On 18 February 1920, Antonov wrote a letter to the local police chiding them for labelling him and his followers common criminal 'bandits.' He pointed out that, in fact, his people were liquidating real criminal bandit gangs that looted and tormented the population and he offered to deliver upon request any such a gang to the police. Antonov insisted that his band protected the people of the region and fought exploitative Soviet power in their name, so they were honourable partisans and not common bandits.[28] Landis traces a process whereby the Centre was able to win a victory over Antonov by destroying his ability to retain the support of the local population, thereby rendering him at the time of his capture and execution, in June 1922, an isolated bandit once more.

In Riazan in the 1920s, the reports of the OGPU themselves distinguished between 'political' and 'non-political' banditry. Banditry that was directed at the state, state representatives, and state institutions was considered 'political' banditry, while attacks on ordinary citizens were regarded as 'simple' banditry. By January 1924, OGPU reports explained that there were no cases of 'political banditry' in Riazan, but there were many cases of armed robbery across the province.[29] 'Political' banditry would return with a vengeance at the end of the decade. An identifiable pattern emerges in Riazan through the years 1921 to 1930. 'Political' banditry in the form of attacks on Bolshevik representatives had, of course, been a serious problem for the regime during the civil war. By the early 1920s, however, the situation had calmed considerably.

In the early years of the NEP and its concurrent policies and attitudes geared toward repairing relations between the regime and the population, legal contributors could once more point to social causes as the reasons for crime. One contributor to the legal journal *Proletarskii sud* argued that banditry arose out of the need created by the civil war and famine and that such cases had already dropped by 60 per cent in the first six months of 1922.[30] Thus, if poverty and want were addressed, banditry would disappear. Given the pace of revolutionary time and expectations, it is no surprise, though, that by 1927 the problem of 'political banditry' began to escalate again, largely as a result of the increasing pressures on the peasantry from aggressive taxation and the beginning of renewed, forced grain requisitioning. And while the causes were still economic, the explanation for 'bandit' activity could no longer be.

The appearance of political bandits dovetails nicely with Eric Hobsbawm's theory of 'social banditry.' For Hobsbawm, social bandits are individuals who are *not* regarded as criminals by their community but only as such by the state or local rulers.[31] Moreover, social banditry becomes 'epidemic rather than endemic when a peasant society that knows of no better means of self-defense is in a condition of abnormal tension and disruption.'[32] Both the civil war and the period of collectivization were such times; thus the social-bandit phenomenon presented itself in the upsurge of 'political' banditry during these years. In the relative calm of the mid-1920s, banditry was much more likely to be perceived as a threat to peasant communities by peasant communities.

In Riazan of the 1920s the 'bandits' identified as such by the law, press, and police reports cannot be identified easily as Hobsbawm's social bandits.[33] They may have become social bandits when the disruption of collectivization swelled their numbers, but in our context the 'social bandit' label is much more appropriate for the tax evader or the wood thief or the brewer of samogon. Still, the Riazan bandits of the 1920s did attack the postal service and other state organizations as well as state representatives. It is difficult to ascertain the degree to which these individuals were targeted *because* they were state representatives and the degree to which they were targets simply because they were likely to be carrying money. What is important for this chapter's exploration of common bandits in the 1920s are the ways in which they were part of the everyday workings of the villages as well.

The remainder of this chapter focuses mainly on the most common type of 'bandits' in the 1920s, which were the criminal kind defined as such in the criminal codes. Several types of 'bandit' emerged in the course of study. The Riazhsk bandits represent the highly organized and established bandit operation deeply embedded in the official institutions of local power. The relationship between a group such as the Riazhsk bandits and the peasantry is a complicated one. Popov and Gavrilov's gang most closely resemble the Mafiosi described by Anton Blok in his study of a Sicilian village.[34] They differ in important ways too; rather than simply having ties to official power, often they *were* power in the village. Their undoing actually came about when they attacked a postal station and threatened the state directly. There are no grounds upon which to romanticize them as pro-peasant in any way; they terrorized local villagers but were tolerated as long as those villagers had no way of fighting them internally.

The Multiple Masks of Banditry

There were several other types of bandits. Many bandit groups were basically local petty-theft operations and were accepted by the peasantry as a part of life in the under-policed countryside. There were bandits who were marginals and outcasts – the highwaymen who lived in the forests, attacked travellers, and stole horses. They targeted state officials and local peasants indiscriminately. In the case of horse thieves, peasants would subject them to vigilante justice if they captured them, especially if the thief was not established and protected in the way a group such as the Riazhsk bandits was.[35] Finally, there were social bandits in the Riazan countryside, who emerged when the pressure of the centralizing state encroached on the village through collectivization. The bandit raids by these groups were much more violent than the activities that characterized the 1920s. These bandit activities were directed clearly at state targets and such bandits were often protected by the peasant community.

The legal materials and court cases, secret police reports, newspaper articles, and peasant letters concerned with the issue of banditry permit the researcher to explore a host of issues about the villages of Riazan in the 1920s. One can determine what kind of individual was drawn to the bandit life, who was likely to be a victim of a bandit attack, how safe the villages were, what peasant attitudes were toward bandits, the impact of bandits on local politics, and what kinds of items bandits took and how peasants reacted to their losses, which, in turn, indicates what was valued in the 1920s countryside.[36] Two important questions stand out. Do these findings strengthen those based on the Riazhsk case outlined above, and how did collectivization change the face of banditry?

A quick look at the activities of four Riazan bandit gangs provides a sense of how bandit operations functioned and the kinds of activities in which they engaged. In 1928, one district in Kasimov Uezd, Riazan Province, was plagued by three different bandit groups. The first operated out of the village of Dubnos, the second in the village of Kuzemkino, and the third from the village of Narmushad. The Dubnos band was led by Poliakov and Shashkin. According to an OGPU report, the head of the local Komsomol cell, Ivan Bychkov, was constantly under threat from the gang, because the group resented his attempts to reveal their activities to the authorities. In July of the same year, in order to punish Bychkov, members of the band stole a pig from his property. In mid-August Poliakov and Shashkin took shots at Bychkov, who managed to escape unharmed. The OGPU report maintained that the band terrorized the local population; the same page of the report, however, claimed that the 'wealthy bosses of the village' (*zazhitochnaia verkhushka derevni*) protected the band and tried by 'all measures to throw Bychkov off the path.'[37]

There is strong evidence that local bandit organizations were involved in local politics in both the literal and metaphoric sense. Of course, they were part of village politics, as they were a constant force to be reckoned with and negotiated with, but they were also often well connected to the powerful or were highly placed themselves in local administration. It is also interesting to note to what degree the band's attempts at muzzling or intimidating Bychkov were relatively peaceable, aimed at perhaps attempting some kind of accommodation; they began by stealing a pig from his yard as a warning and then escalated to scaring him with potshots.

The Kuzemkino band robbed the post office between the villages of Kuzemkino and Shost'e, and they conducted frequent raids on citizens travelling through the area. On 17 August 1924, for example, they waylaid a member of the Erakhtur District Executive Committee, A.P. Tumasov, on the road, but he was able to escape. Local officials were particularly vulnerable to attack, in part because they were representatives of authority, and, as such, were a direct threat to the bandit groups, but also for the practical reason that local officials were often travelling the local countryside extensively, and on foot, in the course of their duties. The Narmushad band conducted much the same kind of activities as the group in Kuzemkino. In addition, the group earned fifteen to twenty rubles per night controlling local river traffic across the Oka. It seems no local could cross the river without paying a small fee of passage. Judging by the amount of nightly earnings, the band charged only what the market could bear. On the night of 20 August, the band conducted a raid on the Erakhtur District Executive Committee, seizing goods belonging to the district police, including one rifle, two revolvers, eighty cartridges, two soldier's shirts, two hats, one overcoat, a rubber stamp, and, from the military section, 400 sets of military registration papers for horses. The list reveals just how short on resources the district police itself was and, more importantly, that registration papers for horses were exceptionally valuable in the countryside, for they would enable the group to engage in highly successful horse thievery.

A fourth band worked out of the village of Sanskoe in Shilovo under the leadership of Ivan Paushkin. Paushkin's uncle, I.F. Pekin, had been a village elder (*starshina*) before the Revolution. And it was under his uncle's protection that Paushkin gathered a group of 'hooligans' around him and earned his nickname, 'petty thief' (*zhulik*). According to the OGPU report on the bandit group,[38] Paushkin became a full-time bandit after the Revolution. He took a job as an inspector of stolen property and then resold the property in the village. In 1925, a local police constable, Ivan Danilov, uncovered plans by the local bandit group to conduct a robbery. Afraid that Danilov would expose the band, Paushkin and another member of the group, Mishkin, went to Danilov's home, called him to the window, and shot and killed him. Paushkin and Mishkin were caught and received sentences of eight and six years' imprisonment, respectively. Paushkin, however, received special leave from prison almost every month, during which he would return to the village, and within one and a half years, he was freed altogether. Upon returning home, in 1927, Paushkin and his band waged war on local party and soviet officials. The band threatened the chair of the local rural soviet and taunted members of the local Komsomol. Paushkin beat up those members who staged a 'Komsomol Easter.' Moreover, Paushkin was in charge of the village self-taxation (*samooblozhenie*). He assessed the taxes in a way that redressed the imbalance of new state taxes against the wealthier peasants. Paushkin's band stole from the local cooperatives across Spassk and Riazan uezds and resold the goods at local markets and bazaars.[39]

The portrait of banditry that emerges from these four cases is instructive. Bandit groups tended to be small and involved mainly in small-time organized crime and the occasional raid on cooperatives and the postal service. The itemized list of goods taken in bandit raids lays bare the abject poverty in real material terms of the local state offices and police. Bandits both overlapped with, and struggled against, local government and local power in the village. Often bands were protected by highly placed and wealthy villagers, who in turn were protected by the band itself. There are further suggestions that there were ties of kinship among bandits and between bandits and their protectors who were in positions of authority within the village. What is worth emphasizing is that, in some ways, the bandits were insiders to the village. They were usually from the village and known there since childhood, and that may help to explain why clashes with local officials were not more violent. The Narmushad band, for example, knew well the peasants who crossed the Oka and could assess how much they could pay on a sliding scale, and they organized their river-crossing business accordingly.

Moreover, bandits in the countryside could hold state positions and, notably, positions associated with the police. Paushkin, for example, a known 'hooligan,' had a job as inspector of stolen property. Furthermore, he had a position of responsibility in the village, assessing the self-taxation. Even more interesting in his case is that after 1927, when the situation in the countryside was moving rapidly toward the conditions of 'abnormal tension and disruption,' Paushkin's activities began to resemble those of a social bandit as he thwarted discriminatory state policies that were putting pressure on the village.

Who were likely to become bandits? The secret police reports provide an impressionistic portrait of the bandit of the 1920s as a displaced young man, often with a criminal record usually involving hooliganism. In a report of June 1924, for example, the Riazan OGPU complained that violent crime was escalating in the region. In May alone, over 4,500 criminal offences were registered in Riazan Province. Across the province, there were daily reports of raids, robberies, and in some rare cases murders conducted by groups of bandits. There was also an increasing number of unarmed attacks, the majority of which were directed against women, who would be forced to turn over anything of value to their assailants. The same report lamented that the freeing of over three hundred prisoners in an attempt to address overcrowding in Soviet prisons (*razgruzka domov zakliucheniia*) increased the number of lumpenproletariat in the province. These individuals were 'not shy' to hang about in local market places and railway stations, where they slept at night and begged for money and food. It seems the prisoners were released without money that would have enabled them to get out of the city. Dogged by the police in the city of Riazan, the former inmates disappeared into the neighbouring villages, where they engaged in 'light work' (*legkago* [*sic*] *truda*) – the report's ironic way of saying crime – to survive. The OGPU report lamented that the example of these men was followed and idealized by a part of the village youth who were charmed by the 'steam of the still' and the 'lure of easy profit.'[40]

A 1927 review of banditry cases that passed through the Supreme Court of the RSFSR during the previous year (still using the earlier code's articles on assault [*razboi napadenie*] [184] and banditry/group crime [76]), confirms the profile of who were likely to be bandits. Of those charged under Article 184, over 88 per cent were charged with group attacks. It is worth noting that Article 184 was indeed applied to group assault in practice rather than trying such cases under Article 76 for banditry. Almost three-quarters of all the attacks took place in the countryside. And of those convicted under Article 184, almost 90 per cent were either peasants or 'miscellaneous,' where the miscellaneous were mostly 'de-classed elements.' And of those convicted under Article 76, over 91 per cent were from these two categories. The recidivism rate was fairly high for banditry crimes, almost 37 per cent under Article 184 and just over 25 per cent for Article 76. Seventy-nine per cent of those charged under Article 184 were under thirty, and commentators in the 1920s were increasingly alarmed at the massive percentage of youth involved in group assault cases.[41] To summarize the profile that emerges, bandits, not surprisingly, tended to be male and young, younger than thirty if they were simply involved in a group assault or robbery and perhaps older if they were members of an established gang that systematically robbed travellers or the postal service. Peasant complaints about bandits and the available statistical evidence suggest that many guilty of banditry had been convicted already and released under one amnesty or another and subsequently returned to terrorize the village.

The Victims

Where was banditry most likely to occur? Who were the victims of banditry? What was taken, and what can the answers to these questions reveal about the countryside in the 1920s? In rural areas, robbery by bandits occurred usually along the roads between villages or between villages and nearby towns. Since so much travel was done on foot, or at best in a slow-moving horse and cart, and sometimes alone or in a small family group, rural travellers were especially vulnerable. The bandits, usually armed, would seize horses, carts, and their contents.[42] Women alone on the road were doubly vulnerable. For example, on the night of 23 September 1924, Praskovaia Gluzhaeva was attacked by six men who intended to rob her. In the scuffle, Gluzhaeva was killed.[43] In June 1925, a woman was found raped and murdered about two kilometres into the forest near the village of Dedinovo. The forest in this area was so dangerous that the inhabitants of Lukhovich and Lovets districts in Zaraisk Uezd, and especially those of the village of Dedinovo, found it almost impossible to travel the road that ran through it. Any travelling along the roads in the area had to be arranged and conducted in a large group.[44]

Roads surrounded by heavy forest were the most dangerous, as bandits both lived in and used the cover of the forest to lie in wait for passers-by. In 1923, members of the Antipov gang were apprehended in the forest near the town of Elat'ma.[45] OGPU representatives in Sasovo complained bitterly about the Merdush' forest, which extended through much of the uezd and neighbouring uezds and sheltered a large bandit group operating in the area. The group was able to hide easily and to travel all over the region under cover of the forest. In Sasovo Uezd alone, the band was known to have committed seven robberies of peasants coming and going in the uezd, and, by the middle of May, there were twelve more reports from peasants that the band would simply stop them on the road and take what they needed.[46] Those who worked in the forests as state officials (*lesniki*) were at high risk from bandit attack. On 21 May 1925, an assistant forest officer in a Kadom forest was attacked by four men who took 180 rubles, his revolver, and his hunting rifle.[47]

Storage sheds and barns were obvious targets for bandit groups and petty thieves alike, who would steal livestock, grain, and tools for their own use or for resale.[48] State cooperatives were also major targets for bandit raids. On the night of 5 January 1925, robbers came through the ceiling of the state cooperative in the village of Vysokoe, Borets District; it was robbed of 1,000 rubles worth of goods.[49] The state alcohol kiosk (*tsentrospirt lavka*) was another target, for obvious reasons.[50] Postal workers and postal-telegraph offices were frequent targets because they often carried money.[51] A quick look at the targets of banditry illustrates the degree to which the state could not protect itself, its organizations, or its representatives, much less its citizens in the countryside of the 1920s. Investigation of banditry cases, as with many other crimes, often took place months after the crime was committed, and the investigations themselves were often sloppy, careless, and ham-fisted. Moreover, bandit gangs were often spread over such a wide area that the investigative organs could not pin them down.[52]

What were bandits likely to take from their victims? Just about anything they could. They sometimes targeted peasants who had come into significant gain in some way. For example, on the night of 30 September 1924, five armed men descended on the home of Maksim Markin.[53] It seems that Markin had returned from a position in the Red Army from which he had been collecting bribes, and the bandits believed they would find valuable property in his home.

Peasants travelling along the roads were at risk of losing their horses in what were often violent stand-offs over such valued property.[54] The animals were, of course, a major target for bandits, and not just the horses themselves but the paper indicating their ownership and registration (*uchetnaia konskaia kartochka*), a priceless item in the villages of the 1920s.[55] On 2 January 1925, Vasilii Burtsev and his son Gavril' were travelling from Spassk Uezd near the village of Kal'noe, Troitsa District, when their path was blocked by five men, who took a sheepskin coat and a caftan. In the caftan was Burtsev's horse ticket, which he considered his major loss. From the men's sleigh the bandits took six sacks of rye and oats. The Burtsevs were told that if they reported the matter, they would be murdered.[56]

Peasant Attitudes toward Banditry

Banditry was a familiar part of everyday life in the countryside and common enough for peasants to believe that they could hide small, yet shameful, errors in judgment from their families under the mask of banditry. The existence of bandits and the threat of banditry on the roads could be a useful phenomenon utilized with surprising frequency by the peasants of Riazan Province. In May 1930, an OGPU report expressed alarm at the rising number of 'simulant' cases in the okrug – those in which peasants claimed they had been robbed when, in fact, no robbery had taken place, or those in which fires were set for insurance purposes.[57] A few examples provide the flavour of the crime. In the summer of 1930 alone there were at least four cases of peasants reporting that they had been robbed by bandits when, in fact, they had not been robbed at all. Grigorii Chizhov, a shop assistant at a Shilovo cooperative, claimed that at 7 p.m. on 23 July 1930, on the road between the villages of Naslednich'e and Sereevka, two unknown men armed with revolvers robbed him of 1,300 rubles of the cooperative's money, as well as his jacket, his trousers, and his shirt, leaving him in his underwear. The investigation by the OGPU established that there was no robbery and Chizhov made the whole thing up. The 'simulant,' Chizhov, was arrested and imprisoned.[58]

On 26 August 1930, Ivan Kurdin of Sapozhok claimed that a band stopped him in the road and stole fifty-eight rubles from him. Further questioning by the OGPU revealed that Kurdin, indeed, had fifty-eight rubles on his person when he set out for the Mozharovo forestry station. On route, however, Kurdin stopped to have a drink. Kurdin could not remember if he had spent all fifty-eight rubles on drink or if he had somehow lost it while drinking. In order to hide the actual means by which he had lost the money from his family, Kurdin reported the bandit raid.[59]

Peasants in Riazan talked about banditry among themselves. The general attitude of the rural population was that banditry was widespread because of the 'soft' punitive measures of the justice organs and the frequent amnesties of criminals who simply returned to a life of crime upon their release.[60] As usual, peasants felt that the state did not and could not do enough to assist and protect them.[61] These attitudes can be gleaned from police reports, peasant letters, and police investigation notes. A comment by B. Artapkin, citizen of the village of Degtianoe, Izhevsk District, Spassk Uezd, is particularly revealing. Artapkin used the state's inability to combat banditry as a kind of excuse for non-payment of taxes. Artapkin lamented, 'In the current time peasants do not pay attention to taxes and other obligations, because of the growth of banditry here. The peasants do not have the strength to cope with them [bandits], and the authorities [*vlast'*] do not accept the responsibility to battle banditry, even when they know all about it. Bands [*shaikas*] lie in wait for every peasant when he is absent, or even during dinner there are attempts to take his property or grain or clothes.'[62]

Peasant frustration with light sentencing and frequent amnesties made it more likely that local inhabitants would take matters into their own hands and resort to vigilante justice. Peasants frequently complained in letters to *Krest'ianskaia gazeta* about the bandit problem.[63] One pointedly criticized the police for not permitting peasants to take matters into their own hands, complaining that an officer had stopped a peasant from throwing a known bandit under the wheels of a train. He lamented that bandits steal and murder and are sentenced to a year and then they are 'back to their old ways.'[64]

Collectivization and Banditry

The drive for wholesale collectivization began in the fall of 1929, and the subsequent years of intense pressure to push peasants onto collective farms changed the mask of banditry as new bandit gangs developed and the ranks of existing gangs incorporated desperate runaways. Peasant sympathies shifted in support of those now labelled 'bandits,' who raided collective and state farms and destroyed state property. Moreover, when ordinary citizens were robbed, on average they had a lot less to take than in the years before collectivization. In November 1929, for example, in a number of robberies on the roads in Sarai and Spas-Klepiki, a chairman of a rural soviet was robbed of thirty-six rubles; a group of peasants returning from a grain-delivery station lost ten rubles each; and two Komsomol members returning from a state farm in Chuchkovo District were relieved of three pairs of underwear and some hand-rolled cigarettes.[65]

Recent work on peasant insurgency continues to support Hobsbawm's original thesis that social or political banditry occurs most in times of great stress on the peasant community.[66] 'During this so-called "twilight phase," a "switching of codes" takes place among the peasantry, a cognitive rite of passage that transforms bandits or criminals into insurgents.'[67] This 'switching of codes' occurred in Riazan. Banditry in Riazan and across the Soviet Union became much more directed at political targets – at state officials and state organizations.[68] Banditry became more desperate and more violent as the groups were augmented by frightened and radicalized peasants who had been persecuted in the villages during the collectivization push and were on the run from de-kulakization and forced exile. While the studies that examine banditry during collectivization focus almost exclusively on the problem in Siberia, where banditry was most pervasive, in areas not far from Moscow state authorities were battling 'bandits' too. Rumours swirled in Sasovo Uezd that there was a band of at least fifty strong in the forests of Staro-Berezovo, made up of kulaks who had fled from the wagons taking them into exile. In July 'bandits' were coming into the villages for milk, and no one notified the authorities.[69] On the night of 20 August, three bandits arrived at the cabin of the Berezovo forest warden, Petr Shubarikov. The men appeared armed with revolvers, grenades, and raw meat, which they ordered Shubarikov's wife to prepare; they warned the couple not to tell anyone on threat of revenge. Two to three days later, the same bandits arrived with seven geese, which they asked Mrs Shubarikov to prepare for them.[70] In Spas-Klepiki District, a band of about twenty-five people who had escaped from deportation points and trains were living in the forests near the village of Bel'skoe; some of them approached peasants working in the fields and demanded food, which they took back to hiding spots in the forest.[71]

Grain-delivery points (*ssypnye punkty*) became principal targets of bandit attacks. On the night of 7 October, for example, twelve kilometres southwest of the village of Sarai, a band of eight to ten people with rifles and revolvers robbed a grain-delivery point, escaping with 11,000 rubles, but not without the deaths of a cashier and an accountant and the wounding of a guard.[72] Cooperatives were still targets of bandit attacks, but now the emphasis had shifted. Earlier the aim of the attack had been robbery; now the attacks turned deadly. In the village of Akhulev, in Tuma, at 3 a.m. on 9 March 1930, there was an armed raid on the local cooperative. Bandits, who had been hiding from the authorities in Kasimov, opened fire on the cooperative, but nothing was stolen.[73] Collective farms were targeted; in Kolomna, bandits tried to rob the Gol'dino collective farm of horses.[74]

Cases of hooliganism overlapped with banditry in the period of the first collectivization drive; it was not uncommon to find reports such as the one that follows in the OGPU reports on banditry. The case is particularly interesting, as the OGPU accused two brothers of banditry and hooliganism, while the brothers in turn described state representatives, associated with collectivization in the village, as 'bandits.' Here we see a 'switching of codes' as hooligans become bandits in the tension of collectivization, while the bandit label was in turn thrown at the state. In February 1930, 'at the moment of the organization of the collective farm in the village of Kniazhoe,' the brothers Zhukin, Nikolai, and Egor Mikhailovich arrived at the home of the organizer of the collective farmer Galkin. Galkin was away from his home, but the brothers grabbed his wife by the throat and began to choke her, saying, 'We are paying you back because your husband ... organizes the collective farm.' On 10 April, the Zhukin brothers approached a member of the local Komsomol, Sergei Dmitrevich Strukov, who was loading a cart, grabbed him, and tried to beat him. On the same day they approached a member of the governing board of the collective farm, Mitkin, and said, 'You are a bandit. You messed up [*izbudorozhil*] all of our village with your collective farm. All the same, you will not live long and neither will your collective farm.' Then they threw him to the ground and beat him. Only the intervention of the secretaries of the rural soviet, Nikolai Strukov and Ivan Iakunin, saved him from serious harm. On 20 April, the brothers Zhukin grabbed the collective farm activist Mitkin again and beat him unconscious. They stole twenty-eight rubles from him, which, the report makes a special effort to note, happened to be state property. On 21 April, the Zhukin brothers beat the collective farm member Gerasim Gerasimovich Kuzovshikov, saying, 'You were a poor peasant and an atheist, and now you want to grow rich. Fine, here is some work.' Then they threw him to the ground and beat him until they drew blood. The next day, in the neighbouring village of Grigorshchino, a fire broke out. The Zhukin brothers and fifty other peasants who had not yet joined the collective farm tried to disengage the horses from the fire truck. The horses were frightened by the cries and curses of the peasants on all sides. The OGPU report concluded that the two brothers had been terrorizing the collective farm members for months, noting that both brothers were middle peasants who steal wood, and both had been formerly charged with assault, theft, and other kinds of hooliganism: 'Why the brothers are not in police custody under charges of hooliganism in the village of Kniazhoe is beyond comprehension.'[75] It is interesting to note that both the bandits/hooligans and the men who supported the collective farm were linked to one another by kinship ties. The 'bandits' were brothers, and the local Komsomol member and the secretary of the rural soviet who were victimized were likely related to each other. Thus, both local crime and local government were built to some degree on kinship ties.

Conclusions

A host of intriguing revelations arise from a study of banditry in Riazan in the 1920s. The characters who peopled the Riazan countryside emerge from the sources – a cast of bandits, officials, ordinary citizens, and any combination thereof. A profile of who fell into the bandit lifestyle and why can be gleaned from the sources. One acquires a sense of what the average peasant valued, what he carried on his person, and what he thought about banditry and criminality. The 'switching of codes,' as bandit became outlaw and state became bandit, highlights the extent of the shock and crisis of collectivization in the countryside. The more detailed case studies of banditry provide the observer with a better sense of the role and the nature of the state in and through its interaction with what was finally most of Russia – the village. They provide a window on the village and to the nuances and intricacies of village politics. The importance and the strength of kinship ties, and their complex entanglement with local power and with the state itself at the local level, are revealed. The nature of the state at the local level is brought into sharp relief in its isolation and poverty, yet relative autonomy. Local power in the village, whether corrupt or not, pro-Soviet or not, operated on its own terms and conditions. If turning the face of the state to the countryside and the resulting flood of reports, letters, and revelations unveiled anything to the Bolshevik metropole in Moscow, it was the fact that as the state attempted to extend its authority into the village, those state structures were in turn rapidly incorporated into local politics as the state itself was drawn into the countryside rather than drawing the countryside into the state. Collectivization was a desperate attempt to address this crucial issue of power and control in addition to the host of economic and ideological elements involved in the decision to launch the first collectivization push in the fall of 1929.

The chapter that follows deals with a phenomenon as complex and revealing as banditry – and often overlapping with shared (mis)understandings of what was and was not banditry – the behaviours that fell under the rubric of 'hooliganism.' The criminal behaviours labelled banditry that were discussed above reveal much about life in the villages. Hooliganism exposes that much more about the fears and anxieties of the regime, conveyed as they were in the language and perceptions of criminality surrounding the notion of hooliganism.

Chapter Eight

Hooliganism: Toward the Cultured Life

For a cultured life, for a new everyday life, for sport instead of drunken hooliganism.

B. Zagor'e[1]

On 25 August 1924, the local priest, Father Kotov, walked into the Trukharev 'tea room' (*chainaia*), pointed to the poster on the wall, which commemorated the sixth year of the October Revolution, and yelled, 'Six years of hooligan power!' (*Shest' let vlasti khuliganov!*). He was sentenced to six months in jail, under Article 176 of the Criminal Code, for his act of 'hooliganism.'[2] As with the label of 'bandit,' the Bolshevik state had its own categories and fears thrown back in its face by members of a population who clashed with the new Soviet culture.

The origins of the term *hooligan* are uncertain. The word first appeared in police reports in England in the 1890s and in print for the first time on 26 July 1898 in London's *Daily News*. The word spread rapidly around the globe, first appearing in Russia circa 1900. In *Hooliganism: Crime, Culture, and Power in St Petersburg, 1900–1914*, Joan Neuberger analyses the meaning of the hooligan scare in the city at the turn of the century. She observes that in Russia, 'in contrast to London, New York, Paris, and Berlin, the power of hooliganism to provoke and explain has endured.'[3] Indeed, to the present day the charge and threat of hooliganism appears in Russia in moments of crisis and insecurity regarding crime and civility, although Geoffrey Pearson's work appears to contradict Neuberger's claims for Russian specificity. He traces the 'preoccupation with mounting lawlessness' associated with hooliganism scares in England from the 1840s to the late twentieth century. He finds that the crime scares, especially the hooligan scares, came in 'fits and starts' whenever there was a sense that the 'reins of government needed to be held more firmly.'[4] This chapter focuses on the concept, meanings, and implications of the crime of hooliganism for the Soviet countryside in the 1920s.[5] Here again, the idea of hooliganism and its rival interpretations, applications, and usage provide a window onto life in the villages as well as reinforcing the arguments regarding Bolsheviks fears of backwardness and sense of crime as a disease consuming the country from within.

The patterns surrounding the application of the concept of hooliganism in both pre-Revolutionary and Soviet times are not unique. Bill Schwarz identifies a very similar blueprint in his work on England at the end of the nineteenth century. In 1898 the London press set off a 'hooligan scare,' just as the press did in Neuberger's St Petersburg. A 'few scattered voices' identified the matter as exaggerated, including the police court commissioner, who saw the scare itself as manufactured by press hysteria.[6] In the British context, a debate emerged that was very similar to the one encountered in late-nineteenth-century Russia and later in the Soviet Union. Schwarz traces an interesting and sophisticated relationship between the concept of hooliganism and the idea of modernity in which *hooligan* became one of the 'keywords of modernity.' The hooligan's presence was seen as an indicator of lack of modern civility. The 'new invention' of the notion of hooliganism in the late nineteenth century, he argues, 'assumed the existence of an anti-social *disposition.* The consequent recourse to languages of animality or disease, powerfully adumbrated, implied that notions of wayward or incomplete human development lay at the bottom of the hooligan phenomenon. The force of the central category – the notion of the hooligan – suggests that at its most strident it could function as a mechanism for determining, in a modern vocabulary, characters and characteristics which were not properly part of human society.'[7] Thus, in the British context, hooligans become important signifiers of the uncivilized, of what needed to be remade and reforged in order to create a modern civilized citizen.

The concept of hooliganism played the same function in early Bolshevik Russia. Not only did Bolshevism have deep roots in modernist thought, the Bolsheviks were the creators of a revolution whose very success depended on the forging of a new man with a new consciousness.[8] As such creators, Bolsheviks were especially susceptible to the fear that the revolution, and the level of civilization that it was predicated on, were being undermined at every turn. Moreover, one of the Bolshevik's many dilemmas would be to explain crime in a socialist state when the standard socialist explanation for crime was to see it as rooted in economic conditions, in poverty, unemployment, and lack of access to upward mobility. As the standard explanation was no longer open to Bolsheviks, they often opted to see crime as rooted in a backward, anti-social(ist), peasant past instead. In Britain, Schwarz argues, the expansion of the state into what were formerly private spaces and the confusion of the late nineteenth century about what was high culture and what was low culture played into the need to define what was modern and civilized. In the Bolshevik case, revolutionary dreams thrust themselves into the private, and the very concepts of private and public became more and more blurred and overlapping.[9]

Toward the Cultured Life

Bolsheviks were also in a bit of a bind when it came to culture, raised as they were in the hegemonic 'aristocratic-bourgeois culture' of imperial Russia that would be superseded, according the Marxist thinking, by the new proletarian culture. The problem was how to define that culture and who should define it – the workers themselves or their revolutionary intellectual leaders? There were numerous elements of proletarian life or culture that were distasteful to Bolshevik intellectuals, such as anti-Semitism, drinking, brawling, and gaming.[10] Within just over a decade after the revolutionary victory of October, a carefully articulated Soviet culture would emerge that left no room for the 'uncultured' and 'backward' elements of the worlds of the toiling masses.[11] Thus for the Soviets too, the hooligan became a convenient shorthand signifier of the uncivilized. And the category of 'hooligan' spilled over easily into other concepts, fears, and threats. As Schwarz explains about the late-nineteenth-century British case, the hooligan had 'a whole regiment of kindred spirits' – prostitutes, male homosexuals, idlers – who were 'deemed unable to function as capable and efficient participants in the evolving modern world. Excluded from the norms of society, they were condemned to disciplinary controls of varying intensity. A sense of contagion was attached to them all, requiring a degree of insulation from the mainstream of the population so the latter would not cross the divide between the efficient and the deficient, augmenting the mass of the degenerate. For those condemned as hooligans there grew up a whole array of new regulatory institutions to keep them in check.'[12]

Notions of contagion and the need to isolate those who might be infectious from the rest of the population predominate in every sphere of Soviet life in the 1920s and 1930s. Responding to a survey on hooliganism conducted in the late 1920s, a thirteen-year-old girl wrote, 'So that we do not have hooligans, they must be attracted to clubs and time must be spent talking to them to make them listen to reason. But if some are found that cannot be changed, then they should not live, lest they infect others.'[13] In both Britain and the Soviet Union, suggestions on how to deal with hooligans ranged from corporal punishment to diverting hooligan energies into organized activities and sport. The young Soviet girl stretched the suggestions into the domain of capital punishment and associated the concept with contagion and disease.

From the examination of the development of the law against hooliganism, the campaign against hooliganism that was in full force by 1926, and the connections between hooliganism and the Soviet conception of *nekul'turnost*, or 'lack of culture,'[14] emerges yet another vivid snapshot of escalating concerns about crime, fear, and control through the 1920s. A familiar pattern of the period emerges. During the Civil War, hooliganism was interpreted as a serious threat to the Republic. By 1924, experts were taking a softer line on hooliganism, regarding it as a nuisance that clogged the prisons and wasted the courts' time. Within a year, however, the line began to harden, and, by 1926, the Soviet press was engaged in its own full-blown hooligan panic, which dovetailed nicely with other crime scares. These scares, in turn, merged with the move toward, and the rhetoric of, the First Five-Year Plan. The struggles with internal and external enemies and the implementation of rapid industrialization and wholesale collectivization required the purity and commitment of the entire population.

The Law

The first mention of hooliganism in Soviet law was in instructions of 4 May 1918 to the Revolutionary Tribunals of the Civil War on the 'struggle with pogroms, bribery, forgery, improper use of Soviet documents, hooliganism, and espionage.' M. Isaev, commenting in 1927, did not fail to point out that in such a threatening period for the regime, hooliganism was spoken of in the same breath as espionage. As one traces the development of the law on hooliganism in the 1920s, the law and conception of the crime go through changes that reflect the general tenor of the legal debates and of the development of Soviet state and society through the 1920s. When Article 176 on hooliganism was first framed in the 1922 Criminal Code, hooliganism was defined as 'pointless mischief and with a clear display of lack of respect toward individual citizens or toward society.' It carried a sentence of 'forced labour'[15] (*prinuditel'nye raboty*) or imprisonment of up to one year. As Isaev points out, at no time in 1922 did anyone speak of the necessity to battle hooliganism as a kind of *bytovoi* crime,[16] meaning as a result of the conditions of life in the Republic – conditions inherited, of course, from the past. This conception of hooliganism as a dangerous vestige of pre-Revolutionary culture took on significance for the countryside as the 1920s wore on.

The first mention of hooliganism in the weekly legal journal *Ezhenedel'nik sovetskoi iustitsii* occurred in December 1923. Here the district executive committees were called on to explain to peasants, through the communal gatherings, that destroying telephone and telegraph lines (a wonderful supply of wood) was punishable under Article 176 of the Criminal Code.[17] In the wake of a massive study of both the city and uezd courts of Moscow region and its recommendations, published in 1924, there was a short-lived tendency to weaken or decriminalize crimes that were clogging the courts and prisons. Hooliganism was one such crime. In their mammoth study of the workings of the justice system, Aron Solts and Shmuel Fainblit provided examples of typical hooliganism cases, which, they argued, wasted the time of the already overworked courts, the police, and the investigative organs. For example, a young man ordered a beer in a pub and walked away from the half-finished bottle to talk to a friend. A waitress removed the bottle and an argument ensued. The police were called and the young man was charged with hooliganism. The event occurred in September 1923 and the young man waited until June 1924 for the case to be called. By that time the case involved twenty pages of official forms and notes.[18] Fainblit was especially critical of rural hooliganism cases as representing particularly insignificant accusations. In keeping with this sentiment, the commission threw out 51 per cent of the rural hooliganism cases in the Moscow uezd courts. Fainblit argued that rural hooliganism fell into two categories: serious and non-serious. Serious hooliganism included the disruption of meetings of the Komsomol and other state- or party-sponsored events, digging up someone's garden, and throwing the village cats into a well. Here it appears that state and peasant both contributed to Fainblit's understanding of 'serious.' While the disruption of Komsomol meetings would likely be taken much more seriously by the state, an attack on a peasant's garden would be a real threat to a peasant family's standard of living. Non-serious hooliganism consisted of such trivialities as lifting the skirts of village girls or swearing, and Fainblit argued that in such cases, a small fine levied by administrative organs would be sufficient punishment.[19]

In the spirit of 1924, Article 176 was changed so that the concept of 'pointlessness' (*bestsel'nost'*) was removed, as well as the words 'toward individual citizens.' The article was divided into two parts. The first referred to 'simple hooliganism,' which was shifted to administrative jurisdiction and carried a penalty of up to one month of community service or a fine of fifty rubles. If the hooliganism was 'stubborn,' meaning recurrent or constant, if it was disruptive and continued despite warnings from the authorities, then the penalty was imprisonment for up to three months. Thus the trend in 1924 was to weaken rather than strengthen the law. By October 1925, however, the first suggestion was voiced, at a session of the Central Committee, to increase the penalty for 'stubborn hooliganism' to two to three years' imprisonment.[20]

Through 1926, concern over the rise in hooliganism was reaching a fever pitch, with most commentators writing alarmist articles about the steady rise of hooligan crimes. There were a few voices in the wilderness warning that the statistics were to be read with caution, as the campaign against hooliganism itself was contributing to the apparent rise.[21] In essence these voices were pointing out that the problem was semantic; if more and more activities were being labelled 'hooliganism,' then the crime would *appear* to be on the rise. The campaign put pressure on local organs to identify and prosecute hooliganism. Thus, all kinds of behaviour were labelled 'hooliganism' and charges of hooliganism were being levied at every turn because the crime was in the limelight. Already in January 1926, commentators were complaining that Article 176 was not sufficient as it stood to deal with the pervasive and ever-increasing occurrences of the crime of hooliganism. As one author in the legal journal *Proletarskii sud* claimed, 'Both the city and the countryside are groaning under the weight of hooligan crimes.'[22]

Article 176 was modified in August 1926. The new law allowed for the punishment of hooliganism under both administrative and criminal jurisdiction. For minor cases of hooliganism or mischief one could be sentenced up to three months in jail. Uncontrollable hooliganism that involved unruly or riotous conduct (*buistvo*) and excesses in behaviour (*beschinstvo*), and a refusal to halt such behaviour, could mean a sentence of up to two years in jail. Chief procurator of the RSFSR, N.V. Krylenko, who had himself participated in the Fainblit and Solts decriminalization project, reflected on the mistaken weakening of the law in 1925 in light of the new crime-wave fear: 'It was one of our juridical and political mistakes committed by our legal mechanism – a mistake that is now corrected by the law of August of this year, which again strengthened repressive measures.'[23]

A new directive allowed police to fine hooligans on the spot. Special offices were set up to process hooliganism cases faster and, as Krylenko explained, if you are arrested, your case will be in court by tomorrow and 'from there to jail.' Recidivists could be exiled.[24] In December 1926, the Council of People's Commissars of the RSFSR issued a resolution that allowed the police to ask for help from citizens in apprehending drunks and hooligans.[25] By the end of the year, one sixth of the male prison population had been sentenced under the charge of hooliganism.[26]

The discussion of the development of the laws against hooliganism reveals what kinds of crimes were considered hooliganism by law. In the countryside, hooliganism, which *genuinely* fell under Article 176, usually took the following forms: shouting and bawdy singing in the early morning hours, under the influence of a considerable amount of moonshine; destroying gardens; torturing animals; spitting on others; throwing rocks or mud; cursing; harassing women in word and deed; and especially worrying to the commentators, the disruption of cultural work in reading huts and Komsomol clubs.[27] However, both the press and the local people's courts had their own notions of what constituted hooliganism. 'Hooliganism' became the catchall for every kind of violent crime, in particular assault, rape, and banditry. A Commissariat of Justice circular of 9 November 1926 reminded courts that gang rapes and robbery by a group of hooligans should be tried under Articles 10 and 76 of the Criminal Code, which dealt with rape and banditry, respectively, and not under Article 176 for hooliganism.[28] One legal commentator in the journal *Proletarskii sud* captured the popular mood well. He noted that it was completely understandable that so many activities fell under the rubric of hooliganism because hooliganism was a 'mood' or a way of being rather than a readily understandable crime.[29]

The most infamous example of the misuse of the hooligan label was the 'Case of Chubarov Alley,' in which a group of young 'hooligans' brutally raped a young woman in Leningrad in September 1926. The press linked the case to the anti-hooliganism campaign, although the prosecutor argued that the case was more than rape; it was 'sexual banditry' and, as such, could be tried under Article 76, which carried the death penalty.[30] Five of the accused were sentenced to death. As Eric Naiman points out in his unravelling of the case, the rape in Chubarov Alley fit perfectly into the broader campaign against hooliganism that was then underway in the popular and legal press and went all the way up to the highest levels of the Bolshevik government. Naiman argues that the campaign had at least two objectives: to control crime and to increase the party's influence in the lives of young people.[31] Indeed, hooliganism was of special concern to the state and party, particularly because hooligans were usually young. In fact, hooligans were almost exclusively young males between the ages of eighteen and twenty-five.[32]

In his detailed analysis of the Chubarov Alley case, Naiman describes the pervasive language of infection and contagion linked to the hooliganism scare and the Chubarov Alley crime.[33] The NEP itself was on trial as a source of infection, and, as Naiman convincingly argues throughout *Sex in Public*, the NEP was a source of constant sexual and ideological anxiety, which were inextricably intertwined. The fact that hooligans were almost always male and the victims often female reflected gender anxiety as well. By 1928, Riazan had its own Chubarov Alley case. Under the pressure of the moral panic of the hooliganism scare, the history of crime for the last decade was reviewed; the central press struck gold in a 1924 case. According to a 1928 article in the central newspaper *Krest'ianskaia gazeta*, a horrendous series of events unfolded in the village of Shumosh' in Riazhsk in the late summer of 1924. The provincial misery began with the rape of 'Vera T.' by I.T. Chvizhin and I.F. Zemskov. In response to her cries, 'thirty adult hooligans and many young men' gathered, and instead of coming to Vera's aid, joined in the vicious sexual attack. 'The hooligans I.S. Luchkin, D.I. Miniaev, I.S. Vlasov, G. Vlasov, V.M. Prokofiev, and many others became participants in this vile brutality and miscellaneous deranged savagery against the unfortunate Vera T.'[34]

The fact that the name of the Chubarov Alley victim was Liubov (Love) and the name of the Riazan victim was Vera (Faith) supports Naiman's analysis that the purity of the time and the Revolution itself was on trial as the NEP began to unravel through 1926. Vera became psychiatrically ill as a result of the crime, and, although officials in the rural and district soviets knew of the brutality, no one had been punished. The author of the *Krest'ianskaia gazeta* article concluded,

> So there it is – the matter is not a Riazhsk one but a Riazan one.
>
> Again and again our request through *Krest'ianskaia gazeta* is to clean out completely these ulcers that remain in the villages of Riazan Province. Have no mercy on those who bring stench and anoint everyone with this fragrant ointment in order to deceive those around them. It is not a salve that is needed here but a red-hot iron rod, an unbending, sharp steel knife. To cut out and to cauterize – that's what is missing here.[35]

The fear of disease, contagion, corruption, and putrefaction went from the villages up to the uezds, through the province, and on to the nation itself. In the 1928 correspondence between the Riazan Provincial Court and the Party Control Commission responsible for a review and purge of the judicial organs, the party resolved that the Provincial Court would 'deal quickly' with the matter of the 'Shumoiskaia-Chubarovshchina.'[36]

The Countryside and Hooliganism in Word and Deed

One of the main concerns for contemporary observers of crime in the countryside in the 1920s was that, like bandits, hooligans were looked up to by some young members of the village. One local Riazan reporter noted, in the context of his concern over the need to 'tame' hooligans, 'In some localities, citizens not only do not struggle with hooliganism but transform the hooligan into some kind of hero.'[37] There was a growing sense that hooligans were exerting an 'ideological and moral influence' on members of the Komsomol and other local state and party organizations.[38] Local Komsomol clubs and 'houses of culture' became targets for criticism. One observer complained that adults refused to come to the local club and instead they simply asked what kind of house of *culture* it could possibly be. He described the local house of culture in the village of Vereshchuchinsk in Riazan Uezd: 'The young people conduct themselves here as in a sleazy bar [*v khoroshei kharchevne*] – they curse and swear, the floor is always wet with spit, the area is covered with cigarette butts, and the only things missing are sunflower seed shells. Not to mention the brawls and the various scandals, and in the club in the last little while a genuine prostitution ring has been cultivated.'[39]

The fear that the young representatives of power in the countryside were themselves becoming infected with the sick legacy of the past or were exhibiting the symptoms of this sick inheritance was especially alarming to the young Soviet state. And the involvement of representatives of the state and the party in hooliganism fuelled the Centre's fear that the young regime would be swallowed up by the darkness of the peasant masses. The campaign against hooliganism thus takes on an especially illustrative quality in the rural context.

As in the pre-Revolutionary period, local administration, from the district up to the province, held meetings on crime and notably hooliganism. Several causes of hooliganism were identified. Alcohol consumption was seen as the main problem, especially home-brewed alcohol, which was much stronger than what the state produced.[40] The participants in these meetings claimed that the energy of the population, especially of its youth, was not being properly channelled into healthy activities such as sport and culture, and instead young people turned to 'drink and hooliganism and sometimes to rape and murder.' Local representatives of power pointed to miscellaneous causes such as the weakness of administrative organs, in particular an underpaid and understaffed police force, combined with the very lax attitude of local courts toward the charge of hooliganism.[41]

Those who wrote about and those who governed Soviet Russia in the 1920s followed in the patterns of those who wrote and governed before them. In his study of crime in turn-of-the-century Russia, Stephen Frank discusses the perception of 'non-peasants and government officials' that there was a crime wave sweeping 'across the empire, leaving neither town nor rural hamlet untouched and threatening the very foundations of Russia's fragile civil society, if not civilization itself.'[42] This crime wave was also couched in the same general fear of hooliganism. The list of rural hooligan crimes for the pre-Revolutionary period is virtually identical to those listed above.[43] 'To explain the plague of hooliganism, Riazan District conferences pointed with near unanimity to the lack of culture [*nekul'turnost'*] among peasants.'[44] The Soviet commentators also unanimously pointed to 'lack of culture' as the cause of rural hooliganism. It is important to keep in mind, though, that what they meant was lack of *Soviet* culture.

In the pre-Revolutionary period, those who wrote about hooliganism in the village saw hooligan crimes as a result of a contaminating urban influence brought back to the village by migrant workers.[45] Thus before the October Revolution, the elite's fear of crime was linked to a fear of modernity and of the future.[46] The ruling and intellectual elite of the new Soviet regime blamed hooliganism on the past and, in particular, on a stubborn unwillingness of the peasantry to let go of this past and of their traditional ways of living. For the Soviet criminological observer then, it was the peasant background of workers that prompted them to disrupt meetings and to disturb the peace in their barracks with avid balalaika playing.[47] In his article that called on all organs of Soviet power to 'face the countryside,' Zinoviev warned of the influence of the peasantry whose 'moods travel by thousands of paths into the habitat [*sreda*] of the urban workers, manifesting itself in its reverberating influence in the factories and plants, creating for us at times very serious political difficulties.'[48] What these fears meant for the village was a war on village culture in the name of modernization and progress. The language of the discussion of hooliganism and *nekul'turnost'* makes this war explicit. Moreover, the language lays bare an internal colonization in which the new Soviet colonizers took it upon themselves to civilize the natives, in this case their own rural population. The campaign against hooliganism in the countryside, as it developed through the 1920s and especially after 1926, was easily adapted to this struggle; hooliganism came to be conceived of as a *bytovoi* crime, one rooted in culture and tradition.[49]

A closer examination of the language used in the hooliganism debate and the resulting portrait that the discussion painted of the countryside, as it developed through the 1920s, adds another dimension to our understanding of the Centre's sense of its rural near abroad. Beginning in 1924, commentators began to turn their attention to the crime of hooliganism and what it meant about and for a young Soviet society. S. Mokrinskii tried to delineate the differences between mischief (*ozorstvo*) and hooliganism. For him, *ozorstvo* was 'nothing more than a grimace of youth,' while hooliganism was a symptom of 'degeneration, a renunciation of culture and the weakening of personality,'[50] and the roots of hooliganism were in the failure of the new regime to eradicate the old life.[51] But this 'old life' was the life and culture of rural Russia. As Professor L.G. Orshanskii, a leading specialist on crime, explained, 'It is impossible to understand where this thick mass of hooligans comes from if you do not have in mind a generation whose predecessors emerged from our underdeveloped life in the same simple and archaic life of the peasant plough and bast shoes.'[52]

The countryside was seen as a dark, primeval place in which the only beacons of hope and culture were the local party and state organs. One writer noted that in the countryside young men disrupted the reading hut by disregarding lines for reading the paper and generally making a racket in this 'ray of culture in the wilderness' (*luch kul'tury v medvezh'em uglu*).[53] The same writer described hooliganism in general: 'Here we have unruly conduct under the influence of alcohol and young mischief making – all mixed up with scandals in public places such as gardens and theatres, beatings of passers-by and representatives of power, disruption of cultural work and noise in clubs, drunken walks that end in grievous bodily harm and even death. This endlessly varied display of the tainted side of our life and lack of culture [is] the sad legacy of former times.'[54] He went on to argue that salvation for the countryside lay in cultural-enlightenment work through the reading huts and clubs, where youth could be educated and organized 'in the matter of civilizing the countryside' (*v dele tsivilizatsii derevni*),[55] as 'holdovers from the past, in the form of hooliganism, are hindering the normal development' of Soviet society.[56]

In a 1928 People's Commissariat of Internal Affairs publication on crime in the countryside, the author embraced the changes in attitudes toward hooliganism that marked the post-1926 period. He saw hooliganism as the beginning of a long and dangerous slippery slope into murder and mayhem. Hooliganism in the countryside, he argued, grew out of the 'darkness and uncultured nature of our countryside.' He noted, 'Hooliganism, which we are used to understanding as simply mischief, conducted with a blatant disrespect for society, in the last little while has changed its character sharply to become a serious crime against society and state ... From harassment to obscene cursing, from covering white clothes with soot and tar, hooliganism little by little becomes deliberate damage and destruction of private, public, and state property, to the rape of women, to senseless beatings and even murder of one's fellow villagers.'[57] The author is mired in the confusion of the times and the changing shift in attitudes toward crime, and toward hooliganism in particular. He knows that in the early 1920s hooliganism was not seen as especially threatening, while by 1928 it is seen as a crime against society and state. Thus he believes that the crime itself must have changed rather than the state and its concerns.

Peasants too were caught in these shifting understandings of hooliganism. The 'girls' (*devushki*) of the village of Rykovo-Sabor'e in Riazan Uezd, wrote to the local paper in 1927,

> We are unable to leave our homes at night. If we do, the hooligan band led by Egor Sonchev, Vasilii Merteshev, Fedor Suslin, and Ivan Merteshev hooligan on us: They trip us, lift our skirts, and sting us with nettles.
>
> Save us!
>
> The Girls.[58]

The behaviour of the 'hooligans' would have been dismissed by the legal theorists of the early twenties as silly mischief not worth the court's time. What was new was the girls' sense and hope that this was a serious matter to be addressed by local power.

Krylenko himself was explicit about why it was important to control hooliganism. One must be able to 'walk calmly in the street without the risk of being spat upon; this is the question by which they will experience the strength of the political power of that class that rules and governs.'[59] To draw a parallel to the more general colonial case, a sub-prefect in North Africa expressed to Frantz Fanon, 'We must counter these natural creatures who obey the laws of their nature blindly, with a strict, relentless ruling class. We must tame nature, not convince it.' And Fanon adds,

'Discipline, training, mastering, and today pacifying are the words most frequently used by the colonialists in occupied territories.'[60]

To contemporary commentators, the most horrendous and graphic evidence of the lack of culture in the countryside was the custom of the village brawl (*draka*). And it was often under Article 176 for hooliganism, for lack of a better article under which to prosecute this behaviour, that peasants involved in village brawls were charged. Thus the age-old tradition became wrapped up in the general fear, and the general statistics of prosecutions, of hooliganism. In their introduction to *Khuliganstvo i ponozhovshchina* (Hooliganism and Knife-Fighting), an edited collection issued by the Moscow Provincial Court and the Moscow Institute for the Study of Crime and the Criminal,[61] the editors set an extremely alarming tone about the pervasive and violent crime wave that characterized Soviet society of the period. Given that the work was published at the height of the crime scare in 1927, this tone is not altogether surprising. And while the intention behind the authors' works was probably to spur reform and encourage development in the village, the result was part of a broader and ominous trend of dehumanizing the village, or confirming an already dehumanized view of the village. This dehumanization would make wholesale collectivization even more psychologically palatable in precisely the brutal form it adopted in the fall and winter of 1929–30.[62]

The editors' characterization of the countryside, and in particular the tradition of the village brawl, conveys an important side of the contemporary elite's perception of the village: 'The villages are places without any kind of cultural foundation where cruel, thoughtless carnage [*poboishche*] between neighbouring villages takes place. At weddings, christenings, saint's day celebrations, or even simple gatherings [*posidelki*], a sea of vodka flows and not infrequently they end with a knife in someone's stomach.'[63]

One of the contributors, V.I. Akkerman, studied the small village of 'N' in which, according to him, there was not a single 'cultural hearth,' not even a school, and the young people were interested in nothing but drinking and brawling.[64]

The tradition of the village brawl is revealing on a number of counts. On one hand, the elite perceptions of the village are laid bare. On the other, elements of village life and the significance to it of the brawl emerge from the sources generated by brawling. Sixty-eight per cent of brawling occurred in the summer and fall, when peasants were most likely to be out walking and gathering together and when the majority of festive occasions occurred. Brawling was popular at harvest time, as people were out and about and had money to spend on alcohol and festivities. Weddings were especially likely to dissolve into a brawl as a result of alcohol consumed and village customs surrounding wedding celebrations. It was the tradition that those in the village who were not invited to the wedding would come to the place of the festivities and demand alcohol from the revellers. If the alcohol was refused, the uninvited guests would begin to break dishes, chairs, tables, and windows, and a full-scale brawl would ensue.[65] In this way villagers who were nominally excluded from a celebration reminded those who were celebrating that their private festivities were in fact public events in which all members of the village could and should participate. The custom is reminiscent of the charivari of French local tradition. Young people would surround the home of the newlyweds and make noise with pots and pans, whistles and guns until they were paid off in money or food and drink to leave.[66] In the Soviet countryside, if a man from a neighbouring village courted a woman from another village, he had to 'pay off' the men there. In one village observed by M.Ia. Fenomenov, the payment was two bottles of vodka or moonshine from poorer peasants, one-half pail (*vedra*) from more wealthy peasants, and, from the wealthiest, the norm was half a pail of vodka or moonshine and one or two pails of beer. One could pay the market value in cash if one so desired. If the pay-off was not forthcoming, a brawl between the villages was likely to erupt, either at the time or at some later date.[67] The internal recognition and accommodation of varying degrees of wealth is worthy of note. This marriage fee or tax was not unique to Russian peasant society. For example, when outsiders married into villages in the Ariege region in nineteenth-century France, they had to pay a fee known as the *dret de rouminguero*, or the 'weed tax.'[68]

But most often brawls occurred between certain villages, because it was an established tradition that these particular villages fought on certain occasions. The brawls would typically begin with a group of young men of one village entering another village and playing the accordion and singing songs (*chastushki*) about fighting. The young men of one Riazan village that was invaded by the young men of the village of Gagarin, for example, would sing,

You boys of Gagarin	Vy gagarinskie rebiata
Come to us to stroll about.	Prikhodite k nam guliat'.
We have our little hatchets ready	U nas kolushki gotovy
And we'll collect little rocks too.	Eshche kamyshkov nabrat'.[69]

A student from the Leningrad Geographical Institute reported a similar pattern of the village brawl, based on his fieldwork in Leningrad Province in 1923. On the day of Makkabei[70] in the village of Krasilovo, there was a local celebration. A group of young men walked by, accompanied by the sounds of an accordion and several rows of girls. Many of the men in the group were carrying truncheons (*dubinka*) or steel pipes, prepared to fight the men of the village of Novitskoe. The young men 'howled' a *chastushka*:

From the sky a little star has fallen,	S neba zvezdochka upala,
And another one will fall.	i drugaia upadet.
Those from Krasilovskoe got it,	Krasilovskim popalo,
And those from Novitskoe'll get theirs.	i Novitskim popadet.

As the student walked through the village, he came across two rows of young men from the village of Novitskoe talking and laughing among themselves and playing the accordion. Once the two groups clashed, the whole village rushed to watch. Some entered into the melee while others simply watched and cheered on their side. According to the Leningrad student, 'Typically they fight until they are half-dead, and rarely is there a holiday without mutilation, and almost always they know that in the future in Pustoshka, on the feast of the Assumption [*na uspen'e*], there will be a fight between the Aliseevskie and the Pustoshenskie, and in Novinko on the Feast of the Protection [*na pokrov*], the Ivanteevskie will fight the Baluevskie, etc.'[71]

Village brawls also occurred sometimes over conflicts of long standing. In correspondence between the People's Commissariat of Agriculture and the Riazan provincial land department, the Commissariat called on the uezd land department of Kasimov to deal with a long-standing dispute between the villages of Miakovo and Volchkovo in Alekseevka District, Kasimov Uezd. The villages had been in conflict over the rights to a disputed meadow from before the Revolution, but a recent brawl between the two villages, in which two peasants were beaten to death and fifteen injured, had brought the matter to the attention of the Soviet authorities.[72]

Hooliganism and Knifefighting provides a vivid, detailed description of a typical village brawl in Central Russia. Near the church of Dmitrii Solunskii, between the villages of Ploskino and Biserevo, every year on the same day a fistfight (*stenka*) was held between the two villages in which young and old alike participated. In an interview, one man, referred to by the author as Citizen K., who had been arrested in connection with the brawl, explained that the *stenka* was an old custom that had a special place in Shrovetide celebrations (*na maslenitse*). Traditionally, peasants from two villages would gather. The brawl took place in a highly organized, ordered, accepted, and structured pattern. First, boys between the ages of ten and fifteen would face one another to fight. Next, young unwed men over fifteen would enter the fray. Only when the fight really heated up (or perhaps when the younger men had used up some of their energy) would the married men enter the arena. If a young man from one village had married a woman from the opposing village, he was still always obligated to fight for his own village and not for hers (*On dolzhen zashchishchat' interesy svoevo sela*). Citizen K. admitted that he was well aware of the savagery or wild nature (*dikost'*) of these brawls, which he himself had even written about in the local wall newspaper. But, he confessed, when he saw a brawl taking shape he could not simply stand by and 'roll a cigarette,' but rather felt compelled to take a most active part in the battle. He added that only after he received several bruises and got a good punch at someone else's nose or mouth would he feel himself 'calm' and 'powerful' (*oblechennyi*). Citizen K. told his interviewer that the tradition of the village brawl was one of the principal forms of amusement and diversion for young men in the village. He told them that when two large villages brawled, perhaps at Shrovetide, the inhabitants of all of the smaller villages of the area gathered just to watch. The best fighters had special status in the village, K. added, especially with the girls, who 'pay them a lot of attention.'[73]

The village brawl was a male affair in its active component, the actual physical fighting. It was largely young men who were prosecuted for the most violent cases of fighting. Only 13 per cent of such crimes were committed by men over thirty-one.[74] Men gained status, attention, and empowerment from the brawls. As with Amy Greenburg's brawling nineteenth-century Baltimore volunteer firemen, men in the Russian villages of the 1920s earned the respect of others 'through their physical strength and their ability to dominate others.'[75] But as the case of Citizen K. suggests, women had a role as spectators and as objects of rivalry and competition between villages. It is especially interesting to note that Citizen K. was a truly active member in the Bolshevik struggle for local cultural enlightenment. He organized a drama club through the village reading hut. He wrote regularly for and worked on the production of the local wall newspaper, and he helped with work in the local Komsomol cell.[76] The case of Citizen K. reveals much about village culture and the brawl. It illustrates the deep roots of the brawl in village tradition, as part of village festivities, holidays, and celebrations; its place in the traditions of rivalry, courtship, and marriage; and the significance and role of 'deep play' in the village. Clifford Geertz adapts Jeremy Bentham's concept of 'deep play' to the Balinese village. By deep play, Bentham referred to games that were entered into despite the fact that the outcome was pain and significant loss rather than gain, and, as Geertz points out, 'Despite the logical force of Bentham's analysis men do engage in such play, both passionately and often, and even in the face of law's revenge.'[77] Like cockfighting in Bali, the Russian brawl entailed tradition, honour, and status, and it too was played out despite possible legal repercussions.

For the sociologist and the anthropologist, games reveal much about the society in which they are played. Erving Goffman describes games as 'a field for dramatic action, a plane of being, an engine of meaning, a world in itself.' He writes that games are 'world-building activities' that display 'the structure of real-life situations.'[78] Victor Turner discusses the social function of games and of play and notes that fighting has long been an important part of play.[79] In his study of the attack on traditional culture in early-modern Europe, an attack that shared much with the Soviet war against traditional culture, Bakhtin explores the degree to which beatings and fighting were associated with festive occasions, spectacle, and carnival.[80] The Russian village brawl was a game, serving a number of social functions. Among them, it was a form of entertainment in a festive, carnival atmosphere.[81] The brawl was linked with courtship and marriage. Success in the brawl engendered status. And it provided an outlet for violence and vengeance within the boundaries of a game. If deaths occurred in the brawls, they were not an accepted part of the game.

Summarizing the meaning of the Balinese cockfight, Geertz writes much that is applicable to the Russian case: 'Every people, the proverb has it, loves its own form of violence. The cockfight is the Balinese reflection on theirs: on its look, its uses, its force, its fascination. Drawing on almost every level of Balinese experience, it brings together themes – animal savagery, male narcissism, opponent gambling, status rivalry, mass excitement, blood sacrifice – whose main connection is their involvement with rage and the fear of rage, and binding them into a set of rules which at once contains them and allows them play, builds a symbolic structure in which, over and over again, the reality of their inner affliction can be intelligibly felt.'[82]

Most alarming for the Bolshevik regime, its most active representatives, such as Citizen K. – upon whose shoulders the future of the link between town and country and the progress and enlightenment of the countryside would rest – were still so much a part of this traditional village culture. Moreover, these representatives helped to draw the state into local culture rather than the other way around.

Conclusions

As the case of Citizen K. suggests, village brawling highlighted the degree to which local state representatives were 'of the village.' A young village correspondent reported that in the village of Ostanovka, Podkidyshevo District, Riazan Uezd, there was a long-standing tradition of an annual brawl held every Whitsunday or the day of the Trinity (*na Troitse*). Young men from all the surrounding villages travelled kilometres to participate. In 1926 two hundred young men gathered. In order to incur the favour of the participants, the local cooperative brought out beer and comestibles.[83] There were also reports that chairmen of village soviets cheered on village brawls.[84] The charge of hooliganism criminalized activities such as the village brawl that were an important part of the 'sphere of sociability.'[85] Even more than banditry, hooliganism became a catch-all for labelling what was perceived as antisocial behaviour and, more importantly, as anti-Soviet behaviour – behaviour that was considered backward and pre-modern. Hooligan fears develop and blossom in times of perceived crisis, when regimes feel threatened and vulnerable. The second half of the 1920s was precisely such a time in Russia and the Soviet Union. The countryside seemed dark, impenetrable, infected, contagious, and threatening. The extent of the fear of hooliganism was reflected in the confused and varied application of the label to a wide range of perceived crime, from rowdy singing to gang rape. The word and the concept became increasingly charged emotionally and politically through the twenties. The conceptualization of the hooligan and hooliganism, and the hooligan fear itself, embodied and reflected the mounting tensions within Soviet state and society on the eve of the first collectivization drive. Moreover, the existence of individuals such as Citizen K., who in many ways stood for the state locally, illustrates the complicated and multi-layered nature of the state itself.

For the elite commentators on the Russian village, the brawl was the least abstract and most tangible sign of *nekul'turnost'* at best and village barbarism at worst. In the provincial meetings of judicial-administrative workers of the mid-1920s, time and again hooliganism and the village brawl were pointed to as the scourge of the countryside. One contributor to *Ezhenedel'nik sovetskoi iustitsii* said it best when he argued that the peasants had to be divested of their 'festive antics' (*prazdnogo bezdeliia*). The struggle with the village brawl was part of a larger attack on peasant culture. It is no accident that an acute observer of Russian life such as Bakhtin chose to write about Rabelais and his world and the clash between official and popular culture in early-modern France. And in turn, historians of the early-modern period looked to Bakhtin's work to understand this process.

The fear of crime and deviance was part of the Centre's conviction that it needed to better control its population, to discipline its citizens and servitors, and to order state and society in general. This drive to control and order became part of a civilizing mission, part of an internal colonization. The Bolshevik centre had to pacify, discipline, train, and professionalize local power structures, local knowledge, and the local culture and traditions through which peasants had forged a measure of autonomy. The campaign against hooliganism and its most prevalent statistical appearance in the countryside, the village brawl, were part of a general attack on peasant culture, tradition, and festive antics. *Samosud*, or vigilante justice, was yet another vivid activity observed by the Centre that drove home both its lack of control and its seemingly barbaric population and local power structures.

Chapter Nine

Rough Justice: The Village Disciplines Its Own

And they stole Veselka ... They stole his pride and glory.

Mozhaev, *Muzhiki i baby*[1]

The struggle with samosud, the struggle with vigilante justice is the struggle for the foundational principles and the beginning of revolutionary justice, for the authority of Soviet power.

G. Roginskii[2]

There is no point in waiting for help from *vlast'*. No matter how the peasant lives, righteous or not, *vlast'* robs him. Next time we catch a bandit we won't recognize any kind of police or courts, and we will settle with him ourselves.

Peasant, village of Zhamekin, Novgorod[3]

Despite its relative proximity, Moscow was indeed far away and, at times, the village did discipline its own. This chapter focuses on the internal workings of justice and what the investigation of them can reveal about the countryside. Jane Burbank has expressed concern that too many studies of the peasantry focus on an anomalous brutality that exoticizes a 'peasant other' and creates or reinforces the view that peasants are vicious and backward.[4] Burbank regards her own study of the kinds of cases that Russian peasants took to the district courts as an important corrective. She writes, 'Study of ordinary and, for most plaintiffs, voluntary engagement with the legal system reverses a long-term trend of finding resistant, exotic, or otherwise aberrant behaviors in the countryside. Scholars since the 1960s have moved away from condescending terms such as "primitive" or "barbaric"; nonetheless a residue of the customary, the lurid, and the separate clings tenaciously to work on peasants' legal activities.'[5]

Her warning is well taken, and my intention is not to focus on the lurid or to make claims or suggestions about peasant backwardness; and to be fair to those who have worked on horse theft and samosud in the past, their focus was more on understanding *why* peasants turned to samosud.[6] Moreover, peasant respect for the law on the kinds of issues taken to Burbank's volost courts is not necessarily incompatible with an acceptance of samosud that was applied to a very different set of crimes. I focus on these violent crimes here, *not* as a comment about the violent nature of the inhabitants of the countryside but in an attempt to understand *why* samosud remained an option in the 1920s. Equally important is the fact that Bolsheviks and intellectual commentators of the period were themselves immersed in the conviction that the countryside was primitive and brutal. Those perceptions, in turn, influenced central policy and general attitudes toward the countryside. Samosud cases are revealing on a number of levels. The details of the cases provide yet another window onto life into the village in the 1920s. The differences between the ways in which the crime was regarded in the local courts as opposed to in the higher courts, in particular regarding the role of state servitors in cases of samosud, tells us much about the regime's increasing fears and insecurities through the decade. I have chosen to focus on horse theft and arson as vehicles for exploring the notion of discipline within the village.

Of Horses and Men

In Riazan Province alone, there were one to three reported horse thefts per week through the 1920s.[7] The Riazhsk Uezd newspaper *Derevenskaia gazeta* identified horse theft as the most serious issue facing the countryside, followed by arson, corruption, drunkenness, and 'all of the evils that came with drinking, like brawling, maimings, rapes, and the disruption of meetings.' The article noted that peasants called for the death penalty to be used against horse thieves.[8] Naum Lagovier, a specialist on legal issues and the countryside in the 1920s, noted in 1928 that the state had strengthened the laws in the struggle against two of the 'scourges' of the peasant economy – wood theft and illegal brewing – and now it was time to deal with the third and 'most dangerous' scourge, the theft of large livestock – horses and cattle.

Between 1922 and 1927 in the RSFSR, excluding thefts in the Far East and the autonomous republics, the criminal investigation department recorded the theft of 323,256 head of large livestock. The number of horses stolen represented 10 per cent of the entire number of registered horses in the RSFSR, valued at nearly 9.5 million rubles. Moreover, these were just the reported crimes based on horses that were registered; it is likely that the numbers of horses and of thefts were much higher. One peasant wrote to the central-level newspaper *Bednota*, 'Due to horse theft, a peasant is afraid to own a good horse. To have a good horse is not to sleep at night.'[9] Memos to the local people's courts from the offices of the Riazan provincial Commissariat of Justice reminded them to take strong measures against horse thieves because the loss of a horse could mean ruin to a peasant household.[10] All manner of confusion and difficulties arose in the investigation of the thefts, for lack of resources and the volume of paperwork. One Arkhangelsk peasant complained that he travelled more than 230 kilometres to recover his horse, only to discover that the police had contacted him erroneously; the horse in question had been found two months before his was stolen.[11]

Writing to *Krest'ianskaia gazeta* in April 1924, the peasant A.V. Kokorev, from Chern' Uezd in Tula, described the atmosphere of suspicion surrounding outsiders and horse theft, the lengths he was willing to go to for the return of his horse, and the anguish caused when these issues dovetailed with police abuse of authority. Kokorev and some fellow villagers went to a neighbouring district to buy cows because the prices were better than in their own district. The men stopped overnight in a village along the way; unfortunately, a horse had gone missing in the area and, because they were strangers to the district, suspicion immediately fell on the visiting men. The chairman of the village soviet appeared and detained Kokorev and his friends until an agent from the criminal investigation department appeared. The agent spent two days looking over the documents the men had for their horses. He held the men under suspicion of carrying false documents because their papers did not contain the correct stamp. The men requested that the police call the authorities in Chern' and check the facts with them. Instead, the chief of police arrested the peasants, put them in jail, and promptly applied their horses to police work. The men sat in jail for five weeks. After his release, Kokorev travelled eight times with a rented horse and sleigh – which cost him forty puds of oats and thirty puds of grain – to ask for his horse's return. After two months, the police released the once-healthy horse, which, according to Kokorev's letter, was now close to death, and Kokorev had to pay an additional fee of twenty-eight rubles and seventeen kopecks to the police for the upkeep of his horse while she was in their care.[12]

Kokorev's story highlights a number of key features of life in the 1920s countryside. It shows the degree to which outsiders were easy prey in alien villages. It conveys the role documents played in rural life and the ways in which the possession of documents could be used against one as easily as not having the right documents. It reveals police abuse of authority, especially over such a key resource, and it brings the value of that resource home in a visceral way.

Horses were vital resources for both the state and the peasantry. For the peasant, horses represented status and a modicum of financial security. The words of one poor peasant talking about his position at the village assembly convey nicely the degree to which the horse represented power: 'We are not allowed to speak at the gathering [*skhod*]. Everyone smothers you with his voice. If you even open your mouth, they yell, 'You idler [*lodyr*].' If I had a horse, I would tear out the throat of each rich peasant.'[13]

For the state, horses were essential military resources, requisitioned in large numbers in both the First World War and the Civil War, as well as vital to the agricultural productivity of the nation. Keeping track of this four-legged resource proved to be yet another organizational challenge for the fledgling regime. Given that horses were such a crucial resource, they had to be counted, registered, and ticketed.[14] The counting was done through the military departments of the local administrative structure. The registration card, known as the *uchetnaia kartochka*, proved that a villager had registered his horse and recorded where it could be found in the event that the state needed to mobilize it. Naturally, the cards were a much-valued and much-coveted item in the countryside. Red cards were issued for healthy horses and white tickets for those excused from military service. Obviously, white tickets were more desirable than red, and peasants went out of their way to obtain them.[15] Registration cards came to be considered by peasants and local authorities as de facto proof of ownership and were known to villagers as the 'horse ticket' (*konskii bilet*) or 'horse passport' (*konskii pasport*). The 1920s saw a roaring business in counterfeit tickets and creative scams surrounding the documentation. One such scheme involved the preservation of official stamps; when district soviets were amalgamated, stamps (*pechaty*) of the obsolete soviets were preserved and then used to create false documents.[16] Entirely fake and forged tickets were created and sold. Tickets were sold to horse thieves by the owners of dying, lost, or slaughtered horses. Indi-

12. Peasant and horse, early twentieth century (photo archive of Evgeny Kashirin).

viduals reported their tickets lost in order to acquire a duplicate and sell the original.

One legal commentator argued that the *uchetnaia kartochka* actually facilitated horse theft. In theory, the goal of the *kartochka* was to prove that the owner of the horse had not hidden the horse from the military count (*uchet*). The author, Pavlovskii, pointed out that one must keep in mind how the count was done; it was conducted by the military departments (*voenotdely*) at a 'breakneck tempo.' For example, at the district level, three to seven hundred horses per day passed before the commission responsible for counting them, 'despite the limited means to process them.' Workers drafted from the district executive committees or other Soviet organs were not adequately trained or prepared for the job, with the result that there were all manner of mistakes and inaccuracies on the tickets. Moreover, many of the horses' owners lacked the skills to read over the descriptions of their horses for accuracy and simply signed the documents 'on faith' (*na veru*).

Pavlovskii provides examples of the kinds of problems that frequently arose because of the ticket system and the way it was administered. For example, a peasant who decided to take his horse to the market to sell often encountered there an agent of the police or criminal investigation department who would ask him if he was in fact the horse's owner. The peasant would present to the agent the ticket from the military department and suddenly the agent would declare that the horse had been stolen and arrest the peasant. The reason for the arrest would be that the horse had markings that were not indicated on the ticket. The villager was then required to prove that the horse actually belonged to him, with witnesses from his village and paperwork from the local administrative organs. According to Pavlovskii, the paperwork would drag on for a month or more, while 'the peasant "feeds the bedbugs" and "sits and bitterly complains of the injustice of the powers that be"' (*krest'ianin 'klopov kormit', sidit i gor'ko setuet na nespravedlivost' vlasti*). In actual fact, the peasant likely spent his time organizing the raising of enough money to bribe the police to let him go. Pavlovskii points out that it was much easier for a genuine horse thief to raise the bribe than a peasant who was trying to sell his horse.

Another common scenario involved confusion over the tickets. One peasant would buy a horse from another and would thus have a ticket with the old owner's name on it. Or he might claim that another villager or family member had asked him to bring the horse to market. The actual facts of the matter were extremely difficult to check. According to Pavlovskii's wry observation, the agent was usually left with two choices: Either arrest the man and hold him until the real owner of the horse could be verified or accept a bribe and forget the whole matter. Furthermore, the genuine horse thief often planted 'expert witnesses' around the market, who would verify that the horse was purchased from the peasant named in the document.[17]

Reports from Riazan through the 1920s confirm the complexities and conflicts surrounding the annual counting and registering of horses. In 1922, in the Zaraisk region, the chairman of the district executive committee was so worried about the registration going smoothly that he forced his workers to 'rehearse' the process for up to a week before the appointed days for peasants to bring in their horses. The chairman and the secretary of the committee were sleeping in their offices for nights before the registration days. When the day finally arrived, all roads leading to the registration point were clogged. The police and peasants harangued one another, exchanging curses. According to the report, the supervisor of the registration point 'ran around like a man possessed' (*begal kak ugorelyi*), complaining that the village soviets had not prepared the peasants with the correct information and that none of his workers had tables to write on. Once tables were found and set up, villagers were 'driven from table to table,' where they 'inundated the commission workers with a thousand questions of all different kinds, which the workers could not possibly answer, thanks to a lack of specialized knowledge.'[18]

Local representatives were not by definition anti-state in the 1920s. Some of them, like the members of the district executive committee who slept in their offices and rehearsed their duties, attest to a certain loyalty, or at the very least a concern about doing the job correctly. Yet despite all attempts to the contrary, the realities of local government had a life of their own. State representatives, party members in the village, and peasants were all part of the same local community and all fell prey to the traditional village communication system – rumour. In turn, the rumours themselves reflect the peasant suspicion of the state and state fears and insecurities.[19] In Skopin District the 1927 registration also caused mass confusion as the counting of horses dovetailed with the war scare. A party worker Davydkin charged into the local party office and handed in his key, saying that he had to leave the district, as he had been mobilized, and that other party members would soon be mobilized too. The result was panic and a spate of rumours. When the secretary of the local party cell called a meeting for the same evening, more rumours and panic followed. Rumours began to swirl in the villages and towns that there was a mobilization for war at hand. One woman who worked in a local factory asked to be excused to prepare dry underclothes for her husband.[20] A baggage handler at the Zaraisk train station said that the communists were afraid of the peasantry if there was a war, and that is why they were squeezing them and taking away their horses. And an 'active churchgoer' (*aktivnyi tserkovnik*) added that at the station there was 'a wagon that will take away all of the requisitioned horses and the young men.'[21]

At the Zemledelets reading hut, ten to twelve peasants gathered to listen to a middle peasant, A.P. Mikhailin, who said, 'Soon it will be the end of the Bolsheviks. England already has 15 ships at Solovki and the important birds have already flown away [*vazhnye ptitsy uzhe uleteli*]. At the factory Nedelia, in Moscow, at the time of the re-election of the party cell the workers stood in silence. The communists asked them again to name candidates and they just stood silently. No one raised a hand, no one voted for or against. They called in Rykov, who tried to convince the workers, but his attempts were met with silence, so he left.'[22]

Peasants from across the province repeated rumours of war with forces from Afghanistan, Poland, and England.[23] According to rumour, even a powerful Bolshevik such as Rykov could not convince workers to elect a new party cell. The workers themselves were said to use a peasant tactic that would become familiar to state representatives on the ground during the collectivization drive: they neither voted for nor against a motion.

In 1924, students from the Geographical Institute of Leningrad State University went on an extensive ethnographic excursion of the Leningrad region. They noted that villagers complained that theft was worse than they could remember and that toward evening every izba was locked tight, although the key was always easily uncovered under the step or behind a log. Losing a horse, in particular, was a terrifying prospect. The villagers relied on their own resources to find the missing animals. Often they would turn to the local wizard, sorcerer (*koldun*), or fortune-teller (*gadalka*) to help them. One such sorcerer swore to the students that on some days he had as many as 100 clients. He would ask the victim of the theft if the thief had left an item behind that could be used to reveal the culprit's reflection in a mirror: 'And on these grounds again springs up this peculiar kind of "self-help" ... There is a whole line-up of professionals, and some will travel sixty to seventy *versts* to find out who stole an item, who led a horse away, or to where missing cattle have disappeared. The fortune-teller uses cards to show the trail of the thief. In this way the thief is quickly found and energy is conserved. After this, an original procedure occurs: One approaches the thief [*usoveshchevat'*] to make him or her feel ashamed, so that he will return the stolen item. And the villagers (especially the fortune-teller) practically swore an oath to us that many stolen items were recovered this way.'[24] The student noted that 'many fortune-tellers are fed on missing livestock. For a day or two the peasant looks for the missing animal, and then shows up at the fortune-teller's with a dozen eggs.'[25]

Horse theft was the greatest threat and resulted in the most extreme measures against captured thieves. The student noted, 'Horse theft is also on the increase and it often occurred that a family would lose two to three horses and suddenly find itself in ruin. Villagers look for missing horses themselves, sometimes for several months, and sometimes for as long as a year. They go from village to village. It is difficult to find the horses because often they are dragged far from the village, distinguishing marks or brands are changed, and the horses are in such poor condition that their owners hardly recognize them. The courts often acquit in such cases or punish them so lightly that it does not even serve as a warning to the accused. Therefore, the matter often ends in samosud and battles to the death.'[26] Like the peasants of the pre-Revolutionary village, those of the Soviet 1920s turned to varied means of 'self-help' to deal with a threatening problem that was not, in the eyes of the peasantry, adequately dealt with through official judicial channels.

The theft of a horse was not an ordinary theft and was not regarded as such by peasants, who thought that the punishment for horse thieves should be severe, swift, and merciless.[27] Horse theft itself was a kind of violent crime against the individual because of the potential destruction the loss of a horse represented for the majority of peasant households, which regarded themselves fortunate if they owned just one horse.[28] Christine Worobec notes of the post-Emancipation peasantry that in an effort to protect their horses against theft, peasants would engage both in samosud and attempts to accommodate horse thieves. Peasants in Soviet Russia also engaged in both methods of defence.[29] A contributor to the journal of the Commissariat of Internal Affairs complained in the late 1920s that peasants tried to curry favour with known horse thieves to protect themselves or their villages against thefts. Villagers invited thieves to celebrations, supplied them with food, and employed them to look after their horses.[30] But it was those cases in which peasants engaged in vigilante action to punish horse thieves that most often came to the attention of the justice system.

Samosud

Samosud is the Russian term for vigilante justice, literally 'self-justice' from *samo* (self) and *sud* (justice). In the countryside, samosud generally involved an angry group of peasants who took it upon themselves to punish, usually by beating to death, suspected thieves, typically those who villagers believed were responsible for the theft of large livestock, especially horses.[31] Samosud has been studied in some detail for the post-Emancipation, pre-Revolutionary period.[32] Stephen Frank explores samosud in the context of a moral economy and the need to preserve equilibrium in a society in which the loss of a horse could be the difference between success or failure for a peasant household. Thus, horse thieves were symbolically cast out of peasant society for their crime and then punished in such a way that they would never return to their old habits. From a village perspective, samosud was a traditional way of punishing those who were threatening the delicate equilibrium of a community that still existed on the borders of subsistence.[33] By engaging in repetitive and subsistence-threatening thefts, the victims of samosud had symbolically placed themselves outside of the peasant community and were punished as a result.

On the night of 23 December 1923 in the village of Riassy[34] in Spassk, the villager Kuz'kov noticed that the fence on one side of his courtyard had been broken down. Concerned that his horse had been stolen, Kuz'kov checked his stable. Finding his horse standing there, Kuz'kov was still worried that an attempt had been made to steal her, and he began to search for footprints in the snow around the broken gate. He found footprints leading to the yard of his neighbour, Denisov. Kuz'kov quickly ran to the rural soviet to complain. On his way back home, he ran into a group of fellow villagers, among them Mikhail Lemeshov (a member of the Komsomol), Sergei Buniashin, and another Lemeshov, the party members. Kuz'kov asked the men if they would help him to find the person who broke his gate.

The men continued together and ran into another villager, Shatkov. They told Shatkov what had happened, and upon entering his own yard, Shatkov noticed that his horse was missing. News began to spread around the village that a horse had been stolen, and villagers quickly began to gather to search for the missing animal. The villagers suspected that the horse had been stolen by Denisov. Kuz'kov reported their suspicions to the chairman of the rural soviet, Ivan Buniashin. The chairman pulled Denisov aside and asked him if he had someone else's horse in his courtyard; Denisov replied that he did not. But when Buniashin went into the courtyard, followed by the gathered crowd, he found Shatkov's horse standing in Denisov's harness and saddle. The crowd grabbed Denisov and took him to Shatkov's home. There, it was revealed that two other villagers, Shishkov and Burov, had participated in the theft.

At this point, a member of the rural soviet left to alert the police constable, stationed in a neighbouring village. Before the police arrived, however, a sizable crowd had gathered, and when the news spread that Denisov, Shishkov, and Burov had stolen a horse, the crowd tried to drag the men into the street. The chairman of the rural soviet, Buniashin, managed to drive the crowd from the house, but the peasants regrouped outside, loudly demanding that the three men be 'put in the street.' Shishkov had already been accused of horse theft and the case was still pending before the Provincial Court. Moreover, he was suspected of murdering his own cousin. Denisov had already been tried in the people's court for theft. The crowd forced its way into Shatkov's house a second time, and this time succeeded in dragging Shishkov, Denisov, and Burov into the street, where all three were murdered.[35] The Provincial Court report stated that it was impossible to prosecute anyone in the case, as the murders took place in absolute darkness and the killers could not be identified.[36]

One by one, members of the village were interviewed in the investigation of the samosud, and each one provided a similar response. Shatkov himself claimed that when the crowd entered his home, they extinguished the light, so he could see nothing. Furthermore, he claimed, he remained inside while the murders occurred.[37] Others claimed that they went home the first time the crowd was dispersed and therefore knew and saw nothing.[38] Ivan Drynkov, a fifty-nine-year-old villager, reported that he heard the noise and followed it to Shatkov's house. There he saw Shatkov sitting on his stove with the crowd milling about. Suddenly, the crowd broke the lamp in his house and everything went dark. Drynkov claimed that he remained inside and did not go into the street with the crowd and therefore he too saw nothing.[39] The village closed around its own. The investigators could not even begin to identify potential suspects in the murders.

This Riazan case draws attention to a number of issues. The first place the peasant Kuz'kov went to report his suspicion was to the rural soviet, once again supporting the notion that it was an organization utilized by the peasants and seen as a reasonable place to turn for support and assistance in a local matter. The villagers Kuz'kov met on the road were members of the party and the Komsomol but also, and not surprisingly, members of the village community who were very much alarmed that a horse thief might be at work among them. While samosud was directed often against outsiders,[40] it was directed against insiders as well, who made themselves de facto outsiders by the nature of their crime. When insiders were the victims of samosud, they almost always had a long history of criminality within the village and in the eyes of the villagers. Two of the victims had already been charged with theft, including horse theft, and in this way had made themselves outsiders by violating the social contract of communal life in a serious way. One was suspected of even killing a relative. When investigators arrived in the villages to interview witnesses, the story told was often consistent on facts that in essence made it impossible to discover who was directly involved in dealing the death blows. The chairman of the rural soviet, in this particular case, appeared to be a voice of reason. He did his job, by all accounts, in his attempts to prevent the samosud and protect the suspected men until the police arrived.

The defence of samosud by peasants, and their assertion that samosud should be permitted and not punished, alarmed legal scholars.[41] In 1922, P. Erypalov noted that there was a strong conviction within the peasant population that the murder of a thief was not a crime.[42] Criminologist A. Shestakova found samosud particularly interesting because it often involved 'not one or two peasants but the whole village – the peasant community.' She claimed that the use of samosud was widespread among peasants and had a 'social-everyday' (*sotsial'no-bytovoi*) character, which made the crime especially entrenched and insidious because it was deeply rooted in peasant tradition and mentality.[43] She identified the typical reasons given by peasants in defence of a samosud. 'We killed him because we thought that such a thief and hooligan would not have to answer for his crimes.' Or, 'We killed him because he was a known thief and there was no other way to save ourselves.' Or, 'Yesterday he was sentenced, but after a month or two, he will be freed to steal from us again.'[44]

What made matters even more alarming in the eyes of the legal commentators at the Centre was that local courts were lenient on samosud in general, and particularly lenient on officials who were often involved. Samosud, like the village brawl, was another horrifying example to the elite of the base and bestial nature of peasant life. Moreover, the crime was especially problematic for Marxist legal scholars because it was a crime of the crowd. For the early revolutionaries, the crowd was a revolutionary actor capable of great heroism. This conception clashed with the violent justice of samosud, which was perceived and described as cruel and savage mob behaviour.[45] As the 1920s progressed, writers in the legal press became increasingly alarmed about two particular features of samosud cases. One was the light sentences that local courts meted out to villagers who participated in samosud, if the crime was punished at all, and the second was the frequent presence of representatives of Soviet power among the perpetrators of the crime.[46] One scholar noted that of the fifty cases of samosud he had studied from 1923, three involved village officials. In one case alone, a former people's court judge, the chairman of the village soviet, and a mounted police officer were participants in the samosud.[47]

Of the 1923 samosud cases reviewed by legal commentator Rodin, only two cases had been tried under Article 142, which referred to premeditated murder. The article carried a minimum sentence of eight years with strict isolation, because the case involved 'base incentives' or inflicted extreme suffering. Such cases were supposed to be heard at the provincial level. No case heard at the level of the people's courts was tried under Article 142. Instead, cases were heard under Article 143, which covered murder under conditions not specified in Article 142 and carried a minimum sentence of three years. Or cases were tried under Article 144, which covered murder under the influence of 'strong emotional excitement aroused by unlawful violence or gross insult on the part of the deceased,' which carried a sentence of up to three years. In fact, of those cases tried in the people's courts, a significant number of the accused were granted amnesties and the maximum sentence given to anyone was eighteen months.[48] The lenient sentencing of the courts toward samosud in the first half of the 1920s prompted the Commissariat of Justice through the Supreme Court to reassess and overturn a whole series of samosud cases in 1926. Most of the cases had been tried under Article 149, which dealt with cases in which a death was the unintended consequence of an assault and as such the death penalty did not apply. Those studying the crime were horrified to discover that in many cases members of the police, the criminal investigation unit, and members of the village soviets were participants in samosud.[49]

In his article on samosud, G. Roginskii argued that in the eyes of the population, those who commit samosud had taken on the 'halo' of a 'defender of the rights and interests of the citizen' and that this mood had utterly 'infected' the courts themselves. He presented an example from July 1925, in which two gypsies were apprehended in the village of

Kavezin as suspected horse thieves. A crowd of two to three hundred people apprehended the gypsies, beat them 'savagely,' then set them alight on a bonfire. Twenty-five people were charged under Article 142. Seven were acquitted and eighteen were charged under Article 144 instead of 142 and given sentences of two years' imprisonment. The lower court justified its decision by pointing out that horse theft was such a threat to the peasant – given that horses were the foundation of peasant survival – that he could not help but get 'overly excited' in the face of the crime.

Roginskii was especially concerned with this case, as a number of the accused peasants acted as people's investigators and a number of them had acted in the people's courts as assessors. Such peasants, he argued, should have been trained in these roles to uphold revolutionary law rather than vigilante justice. The Supreme Court overturned the ruling, prosecuting the men instead under Article 144 and saying that the lower court did not have the proper 'perspective' on the crime. The Supreme Court ruling noted that lenient sentencing in these cases gave the peasantry the wrong signal by seeming to support the idea that property was more valuable than life. Moreover, the court argued, Soviet power already adequately prosecuted and punished thieves, including horse thieves.[50]

The lower courts were even more lenient in cases of samosud by officials than in those involving ordinary citizens,[51] especially cases in which the victim was a suspected bandit or horse thief killed in custody. Roginskii points to the case in which a district chief of police ordered one of his constables to shoot the villager L'vov, who was suspected of murder and robbery. The police chief threatened to take the constable to court and charge him with neglecting his duties if he did not comply; the constable went to L'vov's home and shot him in front of his wife and children. The case went to the Provincial Court. The police chief and constable were charged under Article 106, Section 2, which covered excessive use of authority involving violence and carried a penalty of not less than three years in jail; in certain circumstances, the death penalty could be applied. The court, however, mitigated the sentence by applying Article 28 instead. Article 28 is worth reviewing in full: 'If, owing to the exceptional circumstances of a given case the Court becomes convinced of the necessity of imposing a penalty less severe than the minimum penalty provided in the particular Article of the Criminal Code which is applicable, or of the necessity of imposing another and less severe form of punishment, not designated in that Article, the Court may allow such exception to be made; provided, however, that the motives dictating such a course are exactly defined in the sentence pronounced.'[52] The court thus sentenced the men under these provisions and punished them with social sanction and banned them from working in the police or the investigatory organs for the next three years. The court explained its motives by stating that the men had not acted out of personal motives or a desire for profit or gain, but instead out of their desire to protect society and, 'despite their lack of understanding about the inviolability of the rights of the individual,' both men were 'honest people.' Roginskii attacked the lower courts for their sentimental motives and for their general tendency to see samosud in an 'attractive light' (*privlekatel'nyi svet*).[53]

This case is a particularly vivid example of the chasm between local interpretations of the seriousness of a crime and the interpretation of the same crime by legal thinkers at the Centre. The Criminal Code itself was harsh on those officials who exceeded or misused the powers granted them by their office. The lower courts found ways of undoing, mitigating, and reinterpreting this harshness to suit their view of the local situation. The Supreme Court overturned the ruling of the Provincial Court, emphasizing that samosud was a gruesome crime and even more appalling when it involved representatives of Soviet power. The commentary from the highest levels chastised the leniency of the lower courts. Moreover, the Supreme Court ruled that the men were sufficiently conscious to take responsibility for their actions: they were party members after all. The Supreme Court ruled against the men with reference to articles 5, 6, and 7 of the Criminal Code. Article 5 refers to 'socially dangerous elements' and the 'violation of the revolutionary system of law.' Article 6 refers to a 'socially dangerous act or omission that threatens the foundation of the Soviet political structure.' And Article 7 reads, 'A person is dangerous if he commits acts that are injurious to the community, or if his actions present a serious menace to the established laws of the community.'[54]

These cases capture the battle the state fought with itself as conceptions of justice and authority changed when one moved closer and closer to the village. Some representatives of Soviet power in the village saw eye to eye with the peasantry about the need to deal directly with bandits and horse thieves. And even the Provincial Court, not to mention the lower people's courts, were soft on these state representatives. The Centre became increasingly alarmed as the twenties wore on and as life at the lower levels was increasingly revealed and discussed in its alarming detail. The distance between the sense of revolutionary legality at the top and the sense of justice from below – and not even that far below when the provincial courts were involved – began to appear as a frightening abyss. Of course, the provincial courts were also dealing with ever-changing conceptions of justice and class. In the case outlined above, the court took the peasant background of the men involved into account in its lenient ruling. The Supreme Court, instead, based its ruling on the men's party status and positions as state representatives, which were considered key factors that should have raised them above the peasant population in their understanding of justice.

Samosud was a radical solution to the problem of large-scale or repetitive theft, utilized by villagers in an under-governed countryside in which it was deemed that the-powers-that-be did not sufficiently protect peasant interests. Significantly, those involved in samosud, in contrast to those involved in many of the other crimes discussed here, such as hooliganism and banditry, were often older, well-respected, and well-established members of the village community. The crime was perceived as a male-dominated one, and indeed, of the 400 people prosecuted for samosud in Rodin's 1923 study, only 8 were women. More importantly, many of those found guilty in Rodin's study were men over fifty years of age with large families, who were unlikely to be involved in other types of village crime. More than 40 per cent of those prosecuted for samosud had no prior record, showed no signs of mental illness, and had not been drinking.[55]

Angry villagers on the hunt for suspected horse thieves could easily be mistaken, and this was a concern expressed in the legal literature on samosud.[56] From the village of Polian, Shumash' District, Dmitrii Levushkin petitioned the people's court, seeking justice for the murder of his son. Levushkin claimed that his son, Andrei, was walking in a nearby village and was approached by a man who wanted to sell horses. Andrei Levushkin somehow ended up at the local rural soviet associated with the village. His father reported that he did not know what occurred at the soviet, but when Andrei emerged he was set upon by a group of local men and beaten. He died shortly after from his injuries in a Riazan hospital. Three men were found guilty under Article 164. This article addressed the 'failure to communicate to the competent institutions or persons the fact that a person is in a situation in which his life is threatened, and failure to render the latter such aid as it was possible to render, if such failure resulted in death or in grievous bodily harm.' Under Article 164, the crime was punishable with compulsory labour of up to six months.[57] The accused were thirty-six, forty-five, and sixty-five, all illiterate, non-party men, married, with homes, one or two horses, a cow, a pig, or a few sheep. The people's investigator argued that the evidence against the men was inconclusive and that, at any rate, they *believed* Andrei to have been a thief, which mitigated the beating and warranted sentencing under Article 164 rather than Article 144.[58]

The following detailed case captures the context of samosud, which was seldom the crime of passion that even the Criminal Code tried to suggest it was. Between 25 January and 28 January 1923, three members of the village of Uviaz, Zanino District, Kasimov Uezd, Arkhip Erikin, Petr Sten'shin, and Aleksandr Melekhev, were victims of samosud. On the night of 24 January, a general meeting of the inhabitants of the village of Uviaz was called to discuss the serious problem of theft in the village and to determine who was responsible for these thefts. The meeting became tense and violent.

A constable from the district police was called into the village to investigate the matter. He conducted a search of the homes of Mikhail Nikushin and Ivan Erikin. Stolen materials were found during the search and Nikushin was taken to the rural soviet for questioning. During his questioning, Nikushin pointed the finger at fellow villagers who had also participated in the thefts that had plagued the village, among them Arkhip and Ivan Erikin, Ivan Fateev, Konstantin Zinin, and Aleksandr Melekhev. He added that he knew a place where more stolen material was hidden. The police decided to allow Nikushin to show them the location, but on the way he escaped.

At the same time, the names of the men whom Nikushin had identified as his accomplices spread rapidly among the villagers, who had gathered at another general meeting. Those in attendance at the meeting collared the men and led them to the rural soviet to continue the meeting there. An enraged crowd broke into the room where the men were being questioned and beat Melekhev and Arkhip Erikin to death. Three days later, another general meeting was called at which Petr Sten'shin was accused of theft. Realizing that the risk of samosud was high, the chairman of the rural soviet attempted to take Sten'shin into protective custody, but the crowd was able to drag him outside. Only when the chairman of the rural soviet threatened everyone assembled with arrest did the crowd disperse, leaving Sten'shin unconscious in the courtyard. He died the next day of the injuries sustained during the beating.[59]

Once again, the people's investigator concluded that it was impossible to assign blame for the murders because they occurred in confusion under the cover of darkness. And once again, the village wall of silence closed around the matter. One member of the rural soviet testified that he saw nothing, and that when the suspects were taken from the building of the rural soviet he went home.[60] In his report to the chief of the Kasimov criminal investigation department, the chief of the uezd police expressed the villagers' frustrations and virtually defended their actions. He pointed to the prevalence of theft in the village of Uviaz and, at the same time, to the extreme torpidity of the justice system in investigating and prosecuting cases of theft. Moreover, all too often, he noted, thieves who were jailed were quickly 'amnestied,' whereby they returned to the village and immediately resumed their 'dirty deeds' (*griaznye dela*). The sympathetic inspector argued that theft attacked the roots of the peasant economy and was a threat to the 'Republic' in general. He noted that sometimes local power was involved in the samosud.[61]

A telegram from the chief of the district police, however, suggested that, in its way, the samosud was highly organized. He noted that the murdered men had been known thieves for the last three years, and the community had made a conscious decision to rid the village of them. Aleksandra Alekseevna Malekova, who had been named as an accomplice by Nikushin, petitioned the Kasimov prosecutor, also suggesting that the samosud was highly organized. She wrote that a village meeting was called on the night of 24 January, summoning villagers to 'discuss the thieves' (*idite na sobranie na schet vorov*). A presidium of six villagers was elected to deal with the matter, and Malekova named three of the men as key figures in the samosud. Malekova went on to state that she had been named at random by Nikushin in his attempts to save himself and that she was an innocent 'family woman.' She also accused the police of beating her during her interrogation and suggested that justice was slow in prosecuting those guilty in the matter because one of the guilty men was important in local politics and one was a member of the party.[62] The matter was resolved just over two years later, when eight villagers were charged under Article 144.[63] Interestingly, their profiles fit with the description of those involved in vigilante justice both in Russia and in other countries. They were not the young men of the bandit gangs. They tended to be over thirty and often over forty. They were married with children. In this case, the accused men had between two and five children each. They were fairly comfortable financially – by village standards – each with a house, a horse, and a cow, and no record of prior arrests.[64]

This particular file is especially interesting, as it includes a number of 'minutes' from the village gatherings and meetings of the rural soviet of Uviaz, as far back as 1920. In them, the murdered men, among others, are identified as thieves. In a meeting of 12 December 1920, serious concern was expressed about the return to the village of known thieves who had been granted amnesty. At this time, the rural soviet decided to organize a list of those parents who permitted their children to fall into hooliganism. The decision of the rural soviet was to sentence hooligans to forced community work and also to petition 'Soviet power' to take from Uviaz all the dangerous and threatening individuals who 'bring ruin to both the community and the state' (*nanosiat vred kak obshchestvu tak i gosudarstvu*) because the rural soviet did not have sufficient power to control or punish the individuals. The protocol was signed in the name of the village gathering of Uviaz.[65]

It is worth drawing attention to the intimate links between the rural soviet and the village gathering captured in this particular case. Peasants continued the meeting of the gathering at the building of the rural soviet. In this case, the chairman tried to prevent the samosud, but that is as far as his official role would take him. The members of the rural soviet, like their fellow villagers, 'saw nothing' on the night of the murders. The murder of the suspected thieves was the result of several years of frustration with the problem of theft in the village, which had been further compounded by the amnesties of the state. The OGPU reported that peasants regularly joked that it was 'better to go to prison than to the Red Army because the army doesn't grant leaves, but the prisons do.'[66]

In fact, OGPU reports compiled at the Centre and sent to high-ranking party members constantly drew attention to the connections among leniency with criminals in sentencing, amnesties, and samosud. In an uezd in Voronezh, for example, in only one month in 1925, 100 arrests were made. Ninety-five of those arrested were released and returned to their villages to 'further prey on and terrorize the peasantry.'[67] The same pattern was repeated across the country, and the report concluded that the organs of power failed to protect the peasantry, and therefore the 'struggle with crime necessarily moves toward samosud.'[68]

An exploration of horse theft and samosud reveals much about peasant and state in the 1920s. Once again, the extreme shortage of resources that plagued both comes into sharp relief. The Centre's drive to control resources and the floundering of local attempts to carry that drive through are evident in the confusion surrounding the counting and registering of horses. Once again, the ambiguous nature of local power is highlighted. Local peasant officials were themselves short of resources both as peasants and as officials of the state. Sometimes they used their positions of power to seize what they needed. The peasants' side in the struggle for resources is clear in their attempts to protect their horses from theft of any kind. The centrality of the horse in the peasant economy is palpable. Peasants were willing to go to any lengths, including murder, to guard this vital resource.

The samosud cases examined here show a village cohesion in the concerted testimony of villagers, designed to protect their own accused of being involved in a 'crime' many peasants saw as justifiable. The fact that local officials participated in samosud supports the notion that they were of the village in important – and for the state, frightening – ways. The Centre's increasing despondency about samosud, in general, and the involvement of state and party officials on the lower levels, in particular, is crucial here. The same pattern observed in changing and developing concerns about banditry and hooliganism can be observed in changing attitudes and concerns about samosud. Samosud becomes yet another graphic example of the 'uncivilized' mass that was felt to surround the Bolshevik Centre, an 'uncivilized' mass that sucked state organs and party members into itself, or even worse, included state and party representatives who shared their 'bestial' views and, at times, even facilitated them.

In the ideal socialist state, property would no longer have the significance that it held in an impoverished country with a large percentage of its population living on the edge of subsistence. The loss of a horse could push a peasant household over the edge into destitution. The Bolsheviks were extremely weak in the Soviet countryside, even in Riazan, a province not so far from Moscow. Nothing brought this weakness home to the Centre more forcefully than its inability to administer the localities and the peasants' blatant criticism, and ultimately rejection, of some of the administrative and judicial structures of the state as simply insufficient to protect them. The extreme measures sometimes adopted by peasants further confirmed the elite's view that the peasants were uncivilized, a view fostered and encouraged by the sensational central-level reports of the OGPU. Samosud cases were much more complicated than their representation as bestial violence. At certain moments peasant communities took it upon themselves to discipline other villagers. Arson was another form of ritualized violence in the village, with its own 'strict principles.' The crime of arson in the village has a certain duality to it. The thief's place as outsider was clear in the village and he or she would be punished if caught. Even if one lived in a village, by stealing a horse from a fellow villager one placed oneself outside of the community, and some arsonists were regarded in the same way.[69] Arson, however, was also a form of justice in and of itself.

Arson

Fires were a part of everyday life in the Russian village from time immemorial. And villages had the names to prove it: 'Pogorel'tsy,' 'Goreloe,' or 'Negoreloe.'[70] In his study of peasant economics, Shanin treats fire as a random factor of everyday life, which would throw a peasant household out of Chayanov's conception of the regular life cycle of the Russian peasant farm of the 1920s.[71] In his characteristic gloom in appraising the Russian peasant, his lot, and his life, Gorky wrote, 'Then a severe six-month winter sets in, the land is covered in a blinding white shroud, the snowstorms howl fiercely and man gasps from idleness and boredom in his close, dirty hut. Of all that he does there remains on earth only straw and the straw-thatched hut – and fires destroy that three times in the life of each generation.'[72]

In her cultural history of fire in Russia, focusing on the years between the Emancipation of the peasantry in 1861 and the eve of the 1905 revolutions, Cathy Frierson convincingly illustrates that fire was a central and revelatory element of pre-Revolutionary village culture. For her, peasants were 'paradoxical culprits in the fire question.' For educated contemporary observers, peasants and their relationship to fire were yet another measure of Russia's inadequacies in comparison to Western Europe. To their minds, peasants either engaged in 'insufficient action' – when accidental fires broke out or when they failed to work together to fight a fire – or they engaged in 'excessive action' in the case of arson aimed at other villagers. In both cases, peasants were seen as 'indicted agents of destruction who contributed to Russia's backwardness and robbed it of prospects for a fully modern future.'[73] In the late nineteenth century, the tsarist police and security services, ethnographers, elected local assemblies (*zemstva*), newspapers, and intellectuals generated statistics and studies on the 'fire question.'[74] A similar pattern can be traced in the 1920s. Police and security services kept detailed statistics on fire and investigated numerous cases of arson in the villages. Many of the structures and categories of investigation carried over from the pre-Revolutionary years. Many of the functions of the former zemstvos, such as insurance and fire protection, fell to the rural soviets. Thus the early years of Soviet rule in regard to fire again show remarkable similarities and continuities with the pre-Revolutionary era. The Bolsheviks grew up on the discourse of peasant backwardness illuminated by fire in the decades before the Revolution and the rural soviets inherited the pressures and frustrations that had confronted the zemstvos.

As Frierson correctly points out, arson has been most often studied and portrayed, both by Soviet and Western historians, as a source of protest and resistance either against the nobility or against Soviet power. The fact that most cases of arson were fires set by peasants against fellow villagers is not much discussed in the published analysis of arson and its uses. Frierson argues that when this kind of arson is factored back into our analysis, it illuminates a different kind of peasant agency outside of categories of class and resistance.[75] Her work provides essential context and background for the look at arson that follows. She draws a detailed portrait of the role that fire played in the Russian village for warmth, healing, sustenance, farming, faith, punishment, and revenge.

In the 1920s fire is yet another arena for understanding the internal workings of the village as well as Bolshevik fears of a malicious and autonomous peasant world. Arsonists chose to unleash the destructive force of fire against members of their own communities. Peasants turned arson on themselves in insurance scams, and they would turn arson against the state and its representatives in the conflagration of collectivization.[76] The 1920s represent both a period of normalcy (1921–6) and a period of intense crisis (1928–30). In the context of this chapter, arson is a means to reveal the internal workings of the village in a period of relative calm and it shows how fire was turned against the state when the pressure from the Centre intensified at the end of the decade.

I begin here with cases tried in local courts. These detailed cases reveal more about the inner workings of the Riazan village than they do about the crime of arson specifically. The particulars provided by the cases are supplemented with material from a Supreme Court study of arson. The Supreme Court material lacks the colour of the lower-level arson cases but provides much more detail on the timing, motives, and impact of arson. As with other violent crimes explored in this work, the crime of arson transforms over time, becoming increasingly politicized and changing from a weapon of village justice to a powerful weapon against collectivization.

Arson on the Ground

On 19 March 1925, the people's investigator (*narsled*) Razsmotrev, of the first precinct (*uchastok*) in Sasovo, began investigating a series of fires that had raged in the village of Gavrilov through the summer of 1924. The citizens of Gavrilov had written over one hundred letters to the district police with the names of those they believed were responsible for the fires. The letter writers complained that twenty-five fires had already been set and that the 'bandits' responsible had promised twenty-five more in a note they had attached to a telegraph pole. The note added that, with the new fires, the 'whole village would be destroyed to its foundations.' On the basis of testimony collected from a large number of villagers, the investigator concluded that more than fifteen citizens of the village of Gavrilov participated in setting a series of fires, targeted at specific fellow villagers.

As the investigator explored the circumstances surrounding individual fires, however, individual motives, arguments, and jealousies emerged as the causes of the devastation, revealing a world of village conflicts and enmities. On 5 September 1924, for example, there was a fire at the home of the villager Maslov. Suspicion fell on Ivan Berestianskii, Pavel Studenetskii, and Sergei Studenetskii because one night the men had prevented Maslov from crossing a village field. Berestianskii threatened Maslov, telling him that they were there to 'clean up the road.' The village was rife with rumours of the group's guilt.[77] Another fire broke out on 24 October 1924, on the Zaitsev property. One villager, Nazvanov, claimed that he had seen Stepanida Siniakova a few minutes before the fire hide from him 'in a suspicious way' behind a pile of bricks. Moreover, Nazvanov added, he had seem Siniakova arguing with Zaitseva repeatedly in the days before the fire.[78] Interestingly, however, in the letters to the district police, Nazvanov was often named as one of the 'bandits' who terrorized the village.[79]

When a fire broke out at the Vavilkin farmstead on 26 October 1924, the villager Anikeev was the prime suspect. Fellow villagers testified that two days before the fire, Vavilkin's fifteen-year-old son had argued with Anikeev. They claimed that on the day of the fire, another of Vavilkin's sons saw Anikeev emerging from behind the burning threshing barn. On 31 October 1924, fires were set at the homes of two villagers, Tatarnikov and Merlin. Ivan Timakov, Ivan Berestinskii, and Sergei Studenetskii were accused of setting them. The motive behind these fires, it was argued, was revenge for a beating that Timakov had received at the hands of the Tatarnikov and Merlin.

This Provincial Court case is revealing on a number of levels. First, it highlights the official link between arson and banditry, although whether or not this link was real is another matter. The OGPU reports always placed the cases of arson within the general context of reports on banditry, even though arson was prosecuted under a separate article of the Criminal Code. Moreover, if the arsonists were in fact a loose bandit gang, the case highlights the degree to which bandit gangs were also 'of the village.' The 'bandits' were village members with typical village grievances, seeking revenge for these grievances in a traditional and very destructive way. Once again, the important role of kinship ties and ties of friendship in village interactions on the sides of both the victims and the perpetrators is illuminated. The conflict that triggered the arson, and the arson itself, involved extended family or friendship links. Arson was a common and frequently applied method of local, unofficial justice.

On the night of 7 November 1923, a fire broke out on the property of Efim Vasil'evich Maksimov in the village of Ermolovo and spread to that of his neighbour and brother, Petr Vasil'evich Maksimov. On 25 October 1924, almost a year later, the Skopin people's investigator arrived in Ermolovo to investigate the case. Efim Maksimov – who had been charged in 1905 for 'strike activity' but acquitted – claimed that a month before the fire a fellow villager, Danil Egorovich Buianov, told him that he knew there were some people who planned to do Maksimov harm. Buianov claimed that he was trying to talk them out of it, but that two other villagers were angry at Maksimov and his son.

It seems, however, that two days before the fire Buianov went to the home of Protazov and told him that Maksimov would burn. Another villager, Suzov, testified that when he was at the home of Maria Buianova, he heard Buianov claim that if it were not for him, Maksimov would have burned a long time ago. Moreover, Sizov's[80] nine-year-old daughter told her father that she had overheard Buianov say, on the day of the fire, 'Today Maksimov will burn.' Buianov, however, claimed that he never told Maksimov that someone intended him harm, but rather Maksimov had told him that someone intended to burn *him* down. Buianov added that he had heard a rumour that perhaps a villager by the name of Ulianov knew something. The investigator's notes continue in this confusing fashion, with Vasilii Maksimov stating that Buianov said in his presence that he knew people who were planning to burn him down. Moreover, the arsonists vowed to ensure that no water would be available to Maksimov on the night of the fire. The Skopin investigator concluded that there was insufficient evidence to press the charge of arson against anyone he interviewed and sent the case on to the Provincial Court. It is worth noting that villagers often gave investigators false and usually humorous names.

The depositions collected by the Provincial Court add more characters to the mix. Suspicion fell on Danil Egorovich Buianov, who testified that at 10 p.m. on the night of the fire, he first went to the home of

Petr Mironovich. From there he went to visit Andrei Kuprianov, and, after passing the time there, he went on to the home of his own brother, Petr Buianov, with whom he visited until 1 a.m. He then proceeded to Maksimov's house and bought some fish from him. Buianov stated that while he was with Maksimov, his threshing barn began to burn. Ivan Sizov testified that, after the fire, he ran into Buianov, who claimed that he did not set the fire, but that he knew who did. According to Sizov, Buianov did not say who that person was. Sizov, however, had already been charged in the courts for giving false information in a preliminary judicial investigation (Article 178 of the Criminal Code). He had also been charged in the past for wood theft. Once again, Sizov's daughter, now ten, testified that she was at Maria Buianova's on the day of the fire and had heard her son tell his mother that today Maksimov would burn. Maria's nine-year-old son confirmed that Sizov's daughter was indeed at their home on that day. Maria Burianova denied that her son had said anything of the sort to her about the burning of Maksimov. She too had been formerly charged under Article 178 for providing false testimony, as had another questioned villager, Korpovich. Finally, Vasilii Maksimov – party member and secretary of the village soviet – testified that he had questioned Buianov at a village meeting about the fire and that Buianov had seemed frightened. Thus, he concluded with certainty, Buianov was guilty, at least of not warning Maksimov.

In the case notes two villagers emerge from the tangled web and were accused of setting the fire at Maksimov's. The rural soviet secretary sent an official form bearing witness to the fact that two villagers, Efim Protosov (unless he is the Protazov mentioned earlier)[81] and Egor Ulianov, were always carrying explosives around with them and that they had set the fire. The rural soviet secretary was Vasilii Maksimov, the father of the victims of the arson. The two men identified by Vasilii Maksimov were ultimately charged under Article 197 for the deliberate destruction of property by fire. Ultimately, Buianov was charged under Article 164 for his failure to warn Maksimov that he was in danger.[82]

The case of Maksimov's fire is a confusing and convoluted one, but it provides us with a wealth of detail about the village and the nature of familial networks, friendships, and power. First, the initial investigation occurred nearly one year after the fire – not an unusual occurrence for a police force ever short of resources and personnel. Second, two of the main witnesses were children, one of whom was contradicted by his mother. Several of the remaining witnesses had been charged in the past with providing false testimony and thus were known to be loose with the truth. The purpose of including such a case is not to solve the mystery of the Maksimov's fire, but instead to bring the reader into the village itself. What emerges from the case are not the guilty, but rather the voices of villagers in a more or less 'normal' situation, as opposed to one of crisis. The fire was long past; Maksimov may have already rebuilt. What is revealed once again is the power of kinship, as family members protect and support each other repeatedly through their testimony. The Maksimov clan was well placed in the village, with ties to party and state. Vasilii was secretary to the village soviet and a party member. Efim, himself, may have been involved in revolutionary activity in 1905. Efim was fairly well off by village standards, with only two children, his own izba, a horse, a cow, a calf, a bull, a pig, and five sheep. The success and status of the Maksimov clan may have made them the objects of jealousy, but it also helped them in the investigation, as Vasilii was able to use his position and authority as secretary of the village soviet to defend his sons.

Beyond the workings of power and kinship in the village, the reader also catches a glimpse of simple, day-to-day village life, in particular of the high degree of socializing that characterized village interaction. Danil Buianov, for example, went to four different homes between 10 p.m. and 1 a.m., socializing and acquiring fish, likely for further socializing.[83] Sizov's daughter spent the day in the home of the Buianovs with their son of her age. The reference to whether or not Maksimov would find water, and presumably help, for fighting the fire alludes to the communal fire-fighting operations that could, but did not always, quickly come into play when a fire did erupt. The rapidity with which villagers came to the aid of a fellow villager likely said a lot about his or her place, or how highly he or she was regarded, in the village. Finally, what is revealing is the way in which the village was both open and closed to the investigator. Peasants were willing to chat with the investigator on all manner of convoluted details that provided him with little assistance in his actual investigation. It took the courts over a year and over seventy pages of double-sided testimony, statements, questioning, cross-examining, and official documents of every kind imaginable to finally lay charges in the case.

Fire from Above

Moving to more general studies of arson, one finds additional details about the crime and the countryside in the 1920s. The State Insurance Agency recorded the number of reported fires for the years 1922 to 1928.[84] It should be kept in mind that these were recorded cases and that there would have been many more fires that were simply dealt with by the villagers themselves and never recorded. Moreover, the large jump from 1923 to 1924 in the number of recorded fires would likely have had much more to do with improved reporting and recording than with an actual increase in the number of fires.

Frierson has an excellent discussion of the challenges of interpreting statistics of fire and arson in the pre-Revolutionary period. She notes that the incidence of fire caused by peasant 'carelessness' – a category of the official statistics that carried over into the Soviet period – appeared to increase after 1870. This increase, she argues, was a result of increased reporting and not a real rise in the incidence of accidental fire or arson, although burning one's property in order to collect compulsory state insurance might have driven the figures up too. It was clearly in the peasant interest to report a fire to investigators as accidental or the result of carelessness, as punishment took the form of a small fine; arson was a criminal offence that could mean exile to Siberia. The effect of these investigative results, Frierson argues, was to further convince a reading public and the bureaucracy of peasant backwardness, incompetence, and passivity while simultaneously obscuring peasant agency.[85]

As was the case in the pre-Revolutionary period, when educated and state observers in Soviet cities turned to face the countryside they saw fires that emblazoned both the symbolic and the real destructive potential of the peasant majority. Between 1922 and 1924, the number of recorded fires more than doubled, and from 1922 to 1928 the number almost quadrupled. The State Insurance Agency reported 30,255 fires in 1922–3, 68,464 in 1923–4, 93,475 in 1924–5, 96,632 in 1925–6, 116,228 in 1926–7, and 120,000 projected for 1927–8.[86] The accuracy of those numbers can be debated, but the impact that they had on the state officials who observed and processed them cannot; as in the pre-Revolutionary period, Russia appeared to be burning.

As much as 70 to 80 per cent of these fires fell under the rubric of 'deliberate arson' (*umyshlennyi podzhog*), and certain villages in Moscow and Riazan provinces were especially singled out for 'burning' between eighteen and twenty times in the course of a summer.[87] Interestingly enough, arson statistics were much lower in the pre-Revolutionary period, when more than 85 per cent of fires were listed as accidental or 'other.'[88] In the Soviet statistics then, the peasants appear more violent and more deliberate; perhaps such a portrayal could help to justify the violence soon to be deployed against them. In June 1926, there were 310 fires in Riazan Province. As a result of the fires, 1,346 homes were destroyed as well as 3,930 additional buildings, such as barns, bathhouses, and storage sheds. The fires cost the State Insurance Agency almost 140,000 rubles. Twenty-three of the fires were reportedly caused by children playing with fire, 6 by lightning, 58 because of carelessness, 52 because of uncleaned chimneys and stoves, 108 as a result of arson, and the causes of the remaining 63 were unknown.[89]

A study of arson cases sent to the Supreme Court from the provincial courts of Riazan, Voronezh, Nizhegorod, Tambov, Kursk, Siberia, and the North Caucasus provides a good overview of the motivations and context of arson in the mid-1920s, extracted from the local complexities that permeate the raw cases explored above. Ninety-four per cent of the 1926 cases took place in the countryside, confirming that arson was still very much a rural phenomenon at this time. Arson typically took place in the fall, around harvest time. Peasants were distracted and busy with the harvest, and, more importantly, the arsonist's victim had the most to lose if the household's barn was full of grain.[90] Statistics on age and gender suggest that men were more likely than women to set a neighbour's property ablaze. But when the statistics on conviction are broken down and correlated by age and gender together, they reveal an interesting result. A much higher percentage of male convictions were of men under twenty-five, but most female arsonists were over forty. This difference suggests that arson for women was a crime of desperation, especially for older women, women on their own, widows, or spinsters. Marginalized women were especially disempowered within the village. Fire was an appealing and often anonymous weapon. Arson allowed women to get revenge in one of the few violent and destructive means still within their power. Trading blows with those who marginalized or threatened them physically was not a realistic option, but a well-placed match could effectively get the message across.[91] For men, arson was more an angry, impulsive reaction to a threat to their honour, as we saw in some of the Riazan cases above.

Figures based on social group are always even more problematic than the average statistic. First, there was no satisfactory way found to measure wealth in the village in the 1920s.[92] Second, middle and poor peasants were the majority of arsonists because they made up the bulk of the peasantry. A breakdown of victims according to social grouping would perhaps be more revealing but was unfortunately not included in the study. Obviously, the most severe sentencing was reserved for cases in which there was loss of life. Still, arson was prosecuted quite seriously in general, with the bulk of the perpetrators receiving sentences of one to five years' imprisonment. In 1927, arson was prosecuted under Article

175. Part 2 of that article was applied if the fire was a danger to the public but did not result in loss of life. Part 3 was applied if there was a loss of human life or a loss of public property. Of those charged under Article 175, Part 2, 97.1 per cent were found guilty.

One of the most interesting features of the cases of arson is the degree to which fire targeted a particular victim. Traditionally, commentators were appalled at the crime of arson because fire could so easily spread from household to household, and there were incidences of massively destructive fires, especially those set accidentally by children, or at least those attributed to children. Yet a look at the impact of the arson cases on the property of the neighbours of those targeted is revealing. The statistics suggest that the peasant arsonist usually knew what he or she was doing and minimized the risk to those around the victim. More than 85 per cent of fires that caused loss of property and not life destroyed only the property of the targeted household. Judging by the small number of arson cases that did involve loss of human life – in the eleven cases prosecuted under Article 175, Part 3, in which six lives were lost – arsonists did not intend to murder their victims. When deaths did occur, it seems they were usually accidental. The victims were often children who had been left alone in the house, or the deaths were a result of a fire that had blazed out of control. The peasant arsonist was thorough, as witnessed by the fact that in the vast majority of cases *all* of the victim's property was destroyed. The fact that in so many cases all of the victim's property was lost, yet the fire did not spread to neighbouring households, was an even greater testament to the arsonist's skill and the quick response of other villagers.[93]

In her study of the turn-of-the-century countryside in Upper Bavaria, Regina Schulte explores what cases of arson reveal about the world of the peasant village. She points out that arson was a crime that chiefly threatened inhabitants of the countryside, rather than urban dwellers, because of the impact and effectiveness of such a punishment in the rural setting. 'Anyone setting fire to a farm was striking at the very heart of peasant life – not just property but the farmer's very identity.'[94] Schulte's conception rings especially true for the Russian village where the household (*dvor*) was in many ways literally synonymous with a peasant's identity. The power of the household represented prestige, status, wealth, and position in the village. Each household and its representative was a constituent part of the village community (*obshchina*), of the peasant world (*mir*). Arson was a spectacular reminder of both the frailty of the link between the peasant and his place in the community and the need for the protection and assistance of that community.

Arson, used as a form of popular justice, samosud, was a means by which peasants settled scores with other peasants without turning to the courts or even to unofficial mechanisms of conflict management within the village. Arson was a quick and dirty way to make one's point in an argument and to wreak revenge. Arson was also used against peasants who failed to play their part in village prudence, village solidarity, or village charity. These findings parallel those of Frierson, who argues that arson in the village was controlled and directed, showing 'peasant mastery over fire.' Moreover, arson reveals and confirms peasant agency 'beyond protest or resistance.'[95] The motives for setting fire to someone else's property are remarkably consistent over time and place. Schulte identifies vengeance as the prime motive for arson in the villages of Upper Bavaria, as do Frierson and Frank in their studies of the pre-Revolutionary Russian countryside.[96] Conflicts addressed by arson ranged from quarrels over land or the ruining of gardens and crops by the grazing of another's animals to disputes over fodder or honey.[97] In an especially Soviet example, a member of the raion soviet was burned down because he refused two brothers a needed document.[98]

It is worth commenting on the cases of fire set for insurance money. In the years before the Revolution, peasants set fire to their own property to collect zemstvo insurance. Compulsory fire insurance had been introduced as part of the Great Reforms. Frierson argues that the decision to burn oneself out for insurance money is more evidence of peasant agency and shows peasants to be 'calculating risk takers' who could take requirements imposed by the state and turn them to their own advantage.[99] Peasants in Riazan of the 1920s were not strangers to the same ruse in order to collect Soviet state insurance.[100] In May 1925, in the village of Ermolovo, the home and courtyard of Afanasii Kul'kov caught fire. Thanks to the quick reaction of his neighbours, the fire was extinguished and the walls remained standing. The next morning everyone in the village was surprised to find that the walls were now dust. It seems Kul'kov had destroyed the walls because they were of poor quality and he knew that one received a lower premium if the adjuster from State Insurance came and found walls at all. Also, on a May night in 1925, Pelagia Ivanovna Koshkina's 'dilapidated wooden house' caught fire. Despite requests from the family that the house be allowed to burn to the ground, fellow villagers put out the fire. That night, while the rest of the village slept, the family succeeded in reigniting the fire and the entire structure burned to the ground. The rural soviet and the district police did nothing to report or investigate. They had other matters they found far more pressing than insurance fraud that provided other peasants a few extra rubles from the state.[101]

The nature of arson and its victims would take an interesting turn in Riazan of the late 1920s, as the targets of arson became increasingly politicized over time. As the tax squeeze, in the years leading up to the first collectivization drive, began to press down on the peasants of Riazan, the targets of arson became more and more political. In the fall of 1928, in the village of Chernaia Sloboda in Sasovo, four fires erupted simultaneously. The local state farm was set on fire, as was the building of the people's court, part of the office of a people's investigator, and, for good measure, the apartment of the local chief firefighter. The last is again testament to the precarious position of a state servitor, who could be both a help and a hindrance, friend or foe, depending on the circumstances and on his conduct. The corridor and part of the people's court building were destroyed. The OGPU report noted that 'among the population there was a panic.' All of the local soviet buildings were put under guard and 'stubborn rumours' circulated that a 'terrorist group had arrived to destroy the Soviet establishment.'[102] By 1930, villagers, in their frustration, continually resorted to an age-old popular punishment to express their displeasure with those among them who had broken with tradition and community to support the collectivization effort. The villages of Riazan were on fire. In the last week of March and the first two weeks of April alone, the home of the chair of the rural soviet, a poor peasant woman, was burned by fellow villagers, who saw her as instrumental in their loss of voting rights.

On 29 March, in the village of Luzha, Rybnoe District, the home of a poor peasant woman burned while she was at a collectivization meeting. A fellow villager, Petrushkin, was arrested under suspicion of arson. On 4 April, a note appeared in the village mailbox that the whole village would burn if Petrushkin was not released. On 9 April, in the village of Sobchak, Spassk, three threshing barns with 3,000 puds (almost fifty metric tons) of collected grain were destroyed by fire. In the village of Gavrilovka, on 10 April, the home of a woman activist was burned to the ground. In Staryi Kistrus, also on 10 April, six homes burned, one belonging to the chairman of an agricultural cooperative who was a party member. In the village of Shrovka, Sapozhok, the home of the secretary of the local Komsomol cell was set ablaze.[103] It is worth noting the relatively high number of women who were targets of politically motivated arson. Women may have been regarded much more harshly for going over to the side of party and state. But women on their own – as these women seemed to be – were also more likely to support state policy because of their marginal position in the village and were more likely to be punished by the village for the same reason.

Suspicious fires continued to break out all through the month of April 1930. Again, on 10 April, in the village of Antonov three fires flared together. Five homes and six holding pens for large livestock, which held the cattle of the de-kulakized, were destroyed. On 14 April, the threshing barn of a collective farm activist burned. In the village of Berevozka, on 15 April, seven threshing barns burned. In the village of Dolgino, the threshing barn of a village soviet chairman went up in smoke. Nine households and six threshing barns burned in Mikhailovo District on 18 April. Among those targeted was a member of the party who had participated in collectivization.[104] The OGPU noted that the whole month of April was marked by the frequent destruction of collective farm buildings by fire. Moreover, peasants branded as kulaks were setting their own buildings on fire rather than turn them over to the collective farm, and, in general, there was an alarming increase in the number of peasants who were setting their property on fire in an attempt to collect insurance. The OGPU put pressure on the local people's courts to deal faster with arson cases and to set up show trials on the topic.[105]

Arson continued to plague the countryside through the summer, but not at the same high rate as in April. Still, in the village of Studenka, on the night of 24 May, the collective farm administrative building, the village soviet, and the cooperative buildings burned to the ground.[106] In June and July, similarly suspicious and destructive fires were reported in the Tuma, Sapozhok, Pitelino, Riazan, Shatsk, Chuchkovo, Sasovso, and Rybnoe districts.[107] On 19 August 1930, a massive fire spread across twelve districts, destroying 980 homes along with storage buildings and threshing barns and almost twenty metric tons of grain; the OGPU suspected arson.[108]

Conclusion

A look at the incidences and motives of arson provides a more detailed understanding of the interpersonal tensions and conflicts within the village community. Generally, the village united against a horse thief. Arson was a more complicated crime. While horse thieves placed themselves *outside* the village community through their deeds, arsonists were simultaneously insiders and outsiders. In some cases, arsonists were regarded as dangerous enough to merit samosud against them, but in many cases arson was a common way of settling intra-village conflicts, as its motives and frequency illustrate. Arson, far more than horse theft, was a kind of justice that villagers used against each other with substantial frequency. Whereas the cases of samosud against horse thieves show a united village, which included local officials – much to the horror of the Centre – arson reveals a more complex and fragmented side of village life, of the conflicts, rivalries, and tensions that marked everyday existence. Arson was both a crime in peasant eyes *and* a way of administering justice against members of the community who violated village norms. Arson also became an effective weapon against the state when the state and party took on an increasingly threatening form as the 1920s drew to a close. This increasingly threatening form revealed itself in the policies and implementation of wholesale collectivization as the pressures of the push for the collective farms sparked a conflagration in the villages of Pitelino in February 1930.

Map 2 Pitelino

Chapter Ten

Pitelino

Let's go home. It smells like murder here.

Wife of the rural soviet chairman in Zabelino, 16 March 1930[1]

On the night of 27 January 1930, a member of a collectivization brigade raped a peasant woman in the village of Malye Mochily in the Pitelino district of Riazan. Her husband returned home to find the man hiding in their cellar. According to the OGPU report on the incident, a 'massive scandal resulted that compromised the whole brigade.'[2] The brigade, however, was in fact already compromised by its tendency to indulge in 'tactless activities.' Brigade members, for example, demonstrated a penchant for firing off their guns in the middle of the night; the local peasants used these nocturnal gunshots as an excuse to stop attending meetings on collectivization. The incident in Malye Mochily set the scene for a rebellion against collectivization that would encompass more than twenty villages in the region, rage openly for six days, simmer for months, and involve thousands of peasants.

The Centre launched a massive campaign to collectivize the peasantry in the winter of 1929–30. Industrial workers and urban activists were sent en masse to the countryside to aid local party and soviet officials in the business of collectivization.[3] In Moscow region, the zealous Regional Party First Secretary K.Ia. Bauman directed collectivization, pushing Riazan especially hard to be a model and challenge to other districts in the race for the rapid collectivization of his region.[4] Perhaps even more than elsewhere in the Russian Republic, the implementation of wholesale collectivization in the Moscow region led to massive 'excesses' (*peregiby*), to use a Soviet euphemism. It also led to a peasant rebellion of major significance in Riazan's Pitelino District. Throughout these pages, I have argued that the rural soviet was largely 'of the village.' During the collectivization drive, emergency elections were held to reconstitute the rural soviets with trustworthy supporters of the policy. These elections were not always successful. In Pitelino, however, the rural soviet had been reconstituted to support the policy of collectivization and, as such, no longer protected the villages of the region. For the people of Pitelino, there was no shock absorber between villagers and the aggressive policies of the Centre.

The Uprising: From Ground Zero

Pitelino is located about 160 kilometres due east of the city of Riazan, which in turn is located 200 kilometres southeast of Moscow. In 1929, Riazan Province (*guberniia*) had a population of almost two million people. In 1930, the province became an *okrug* within the newly formed Moscow Oblast. Riazan county was subdivided into smaller administrative units or raions. Pitelino was one of the smaller of Riazan's twenty-seven districts. It was about 934 square kilometres, with one rural soviet located, on average, every 32 square kilometres. The district was characterized by a fairly high population density: 22,976 men and 26,593 women lived in Pitelino District, virtually all classified as rural inhabitants as opposed to migrant workers or town dwellers.[5] From January 1930, the relationship between collectivizers and the local peasantry in Pitelino was tense as events moved relentlessly toward a violent confrontation. On 22 February, peasants from across the district began to gather on the few narrow streets of the village of Veriaevo. Early in the day, rumours circulated that the collectivization brigade working with the rural soviet was 'gathering cattle to slaughter and ship to Moscow.'[6] Over the course of the day, more and more peasants filled the village streets. One version of events later claimed that brigade members had seized cattle to be redistributed to poor peasants. The gathered cattle escaped, and, when the brigade members went chasing after the beasts, a crowd gathered to watch the spectacle.[7]

A second version of events claimed that the problems in Veriaevo occurred as a result of the 'tactless conduct' of the plenipotentiaries involved in collectivization work. Furthermore, the unrest did not involve cattle but rather the collection of seed grain. Whatever the case may be, there is no doubt that the brigade and rural soviet members were indeed 'tactless.' They went from door to door in the villages of the district and emptied the barns, most belonging to 'middle' peasants, of *all* remaining grain.[8] Thirty of these middle peasants were then fined for not contributing to the grain reserve collection. Brigade members and rural soviet officials combed the homes of villagers in their relentless search for hidden grain, even breaking open the locked trunks in which peasant families kept their most treasured possessions. The collectivizers seized not only seed grain reserved for the next planting but also baked bread, which they often took by force. When women resisted, the brigade members dragged them around by their braids.[9] According to an OGPU report, the local rural soviet told peasants that they had twenty-four hours to turn over their grain. Those who failed to do so were subject to fines and searches. Locks were broken on storehouses, which were then 'picked clean' (*vygrebalo vse do chista*). The report went on to note that livestock was collectivized without adequate preparation and with no thought given to shelter or fodder. Moreover, during de-kulakization, a significant number of middle peasants and the families of Red Army soldiers (sectors of the rural population who should officially have been safe from seizure) were stripped of virtually everything and left standing quite literally in their underclothes.[10]

By 22 February, the villagers of Veriaevo had been pushed beyond the limits of their endurance and they chased the collectivizers out of the village. The collectivizers ran toward the neighbouring village of Gridino. But the peasants of Veriaevo rang the church bells to alert their neighbours, leading to the gathering of a massive crowd in Gridino as well. Part of the Veriaevo crowd chased after the fleeing collectivizers, while the remaining villagers destroyed the barn in which the confiscated seed grain had been stored. The crowd then broke the windows at the local rural soviet and smashed whatever they could find in the building. They seized property that had been stripped from peasants labelled as kulaks and dispossessed, returning it to its owners. The crowd then proceeded to beat the rural soviet chairman and the wife of a party member for good measure. The disturbance lasted until five or six in the evening. Meanwhile, in the village of Gridino, the church bells summoned a crowd twice the size of the one gathered in Veriaevo. The crowd beat one brigade member severely and chased the remaining members on to the village of Pavlovka. Both villages settled down toward evening. But throughout the night, small groups of local peasants patrolled Veriaevo. In fact, for days the peasants of Veriaevo staffed checkpoints and barricades and refused to allow officials into the village until they had agreed to address the issues of the violations, excesses, and scandalous behaviour (*bezobrazie*) of the brigade and rural soviet members. Whenever officials approached the village, the church bells in Veriaevo rang out and the peasants of Gridino came running.[11] Peasants in the surrounding villages expressed their solidarity with Veriaevo and Gridino. Already on the Saturday evening of 22 February, for example, in the village of Andreevka, located about eight kilometres from Gridino, a crowd marched through the village holding a black flag.[12]

With rebellion threatening the entire district, an armed detachment to deal with the unrest was formed in the neighbouring district of Sasovo, made up of members of the railway security forces and the Sasovo militia. The force was dispatched to Pitelino under the leadership of the secretary of the district party committee, Vasil'chenko, and the chairman of the district soviet executive committee, Subbotin. On Sunday[13] morning, the detachment arrived in Veriaevo, which was calm. Within moments of the detachment's arrival, however, a crowd of women gathered. When three of the officers decided to look for the local cooperative store to find food, the women blocked their path. The officers responded by firing five shots into the air. With that, the church bells rang out, and a part of the crowd rushed toward the shots. The remaining peasants demanded that the detachment lay down its weapons or leave the village immediately. The secretary of the party committee and the chairman of the district soviet executive committee took fright and quickly retreated to Gridino. There, the bells had already summoned a crowd, which attempted to detain the retreating officials, stopping their horses and throwing sticks at them. The detachment then withdrew to the district centre of Pitelino. In response to the bells of the villages of Veriaevo and Gridino, a crowd of *several thousand* peasants coalesced in Veriaevo from at least ten surrounding villages, including Maleevka, Andreevka, Ferm, Mikhailovka, Dmitrievka, Pavlovka, Seniukhino [*sic*],[14] and Lubonos. According to an OGPU report, the Veriaevo priest had played an active role in the unrest, shouting, 'Stand up for the Orthodox faith!' from the church steps.[15] Unfortunately, the documents do not detail how this enormous crowd was dispersed, although more troops were dispatched and stationed in Pitelino, and the OGPU dispatched 150 specially trained officers to the area.[16]

On 23 February, at 11 p.m., villagers called a general meeting in Gridino, which was attended by more than three hundred people, mainly women. At the meeting, the women demanded that the chairman of the district soviet executive committee, Subbotin, and his assistants, Ol'khin and Kosyrev, be put on trial in the next forty-eight hours.[17] The women threatened to hang these officials on meat hooks if they fell into their hands. They also demanded the return of their recently socialized grain reserves, noting that the grain was simply rotting in its current storage conditions. At the end of the meeting, the villagers resolved to elect a new rural soviet immediately and to launch an investigation into the excesses of the collectivization drive.[18] It is worth drawing attention to the fact that the *villagers themselves recognized the pivotal role of the rural soviet and sought re-elections in order to promote and protect their interests.* Such actions further illustrate and support the arguments made throughout that the rural soviet was recognized, valued, and embraced as a key institution for the peasants of Riazan up to and even during the first collectivization drive.

For the next few days, the villagers set about undoing collectivization. On the night of 23 February, in the village of Ferm, a group of women warned the former head of the district soviet executive committee that they intended to take back their grain reserves. At midnight, a crowd of 100 strong, including peasants from the neighbouring villages of Rusanovka and Sukhusha, arrived to seize the grain reserves. At the same time, in the village of Stanishchi, a crowd of women destroyed the communal holding pen for collectivized cattle and beat the local agronomist, while in the village of Obukhovo, peasants rallied to prevent the dispossession and de-kulakization of one of their neighbours.[19] On 24 February, in the village of Pet, a crowd of over four hundred peasants repossessed 100 dairy cows, redistributing them to their former owners along with 130 out of 180 confiscated horses.[20] The crowd went to the rural soviet and asked that the grain reserves be removed from the church, which was being used to store the collectivized grain.[21] In the same village, at 11:00 a.m. on 26 February, there was a meeting of poor peasants. Seventy women gathered from the villages of Veriaevo, Stanishchi, Kamenka, and Gogolka and stormed the meeting, demanding that the church be reopened and grain reserves redistributed. The women were persuaded to disperse, but they vowed they would 'return in the morning to take the grain reserves by force and settle up with the members of the collectivization brigade.'[22]

Previously, on the morning of 25 February, the Gridino peasants had looted the home of the collective farm chairman, Kosyrev, whom they had already demanded be put on trial for his part in the excesses.[23] On the same day, a group of women in the village of Nesterovo took back the cows taken from kulak families and returned them. To emphasize their point, they broke a window at the home of a rural soviet member.[24] The women of Znamenka also reclaimed confiscated cattle, while the village schoolchildren tore up posters and portraits of Soviet leaders.[25] According to an OGPU report, that night a group of 'kulaks' from Gridino, Vysokoe, Veriaevo, Pavlovka, Rusanlovka, and Nesterovo met secretly to plan an uprising. At this illegal meeting, villagers called for the destruction of the rural soviet, the redistribution of the seed grain, and the reinstatement of voting rights for all peasants. Again, elections to the soviet were valued and taken seriously. According to the report, the group also called for a slaughter of local and visiting Soviet and party workers.[26]

At noon on 26 February, in the village of Potap'evo, a group of women gathered near the cooperative store. Armed with fence posts, they headed to the rural soviet, where they demanded the return of their grain reserves. Brigade workers convinced the crowd to disperse. On 27 February, the unrest turned deadly. OGPU officers arrived in Potap'evo to investigate and root out the 'anti-Soviet elements' allegedly behind the unrest. When it was discovered that the OGPU had arrived, the church bell was sounded and peasants thronged to the rural soviet, where the OGPU force was preparing its investigation.

Once again, we see the rural soviet in the desperate vice between power from above and the needs of its constituency below. The battle for space is graphically illustrated here. The rural soviet buildings were one of the few physical spaces where the OGPU could gather to conduct organizational and administrative work. It was also the place where peasants had met and exchanged news, had smoked a little with *vlast'* and quarrelled a little with *vlast'*, where peasants had gathered to deal with the paperwork necessary to talk to higher powers. The rural soviet as place was contested in the struggle for space, resources, and souls that was collectivization.

The crowd dispersed when the agents fired into the air, but quickly reconvened. At this point, the OGPU agents fired into the crowd, wounding one man and killing a woman.[27] The bells rang out once more and the crowd armed with clubs then swelled with peasants from the surrounding villages. A platoon arrived and ordered the crowd to disband, but to no avail. The platoon was ordered to divide the crowd in half, triggering chaos and a skirmish; shots were fired and the peasants scattered. In the confusion one villager was killed and another wounded. On the same day, OGPU agents were forced out of the villages of Vysokoe and Znamenka.[28]

For days, peasants milled about the village streets in the February cold. In Veriaevo, the crowd called out, 'We welcome Soviet power without collective farms, grain collections, and local communists.'[29] It was not until March that the regime began to gain the upper hand on events, instituting a repressive clampdown on the district. In all, 333 people were arrested in connection with the Pitelino uprising. Of this number, 247 were recorded as middle peasants and 9 as poor peasants, suggesting some solidarity across 'class lines' in the village.[30] The aftershocks of the uprising continued through March, as the OGPU asked for reinforcements in the area. On 21 March, in Pitelino village, the poor peasants demanded immediate monetary payment for work done on the collective farm, a free share of the harvest, the opening of churches, and the return of their local priest, who had been arrested by the OGPU. The report claimed that 'in the evenings the whole population gathers to talk about the past and about collective farm life.'[31] In every district, rumours swirled about that on Holy Thursday (*velikii chetverg, na strastnoi nedele*) there would again be an uprising like the February rebellion. March was also marked by repeated attempts by Pitelino peasants to prevent the deportation of kulaks from their district.[32]

At the same time, the unrest in Pitelino contributed to a massive exodus from the collective farms, one that was more pronounced there than in any other district.[33] In a report of 20 February, Pitelino District was said to be 100 per cent collectivized.[34] Yet by April, the percentage of collectivized farms in Pitelino had fallen to 6.[35] The OGPU complained incessantly about the negative impact of the Pitelino uprising on the surrounding districts, where it had created a 'tense' mood among the peasants and empowered the perceived enemies of collectivization, supporting their hope that 'soon Soviet power will fall.'[36] Through April and May, struggles raged over the designation of collective farm land. There were bitter clashes between those few peasants who remained on the collective farms and those who had signed out, and family members who had left tried to encourage their kin to support them. In Veriaevo on 20 May, the collective farm member A.P. Klimov was approached by a relative, I.V. Klimov, who said to him, 'You took the best land from us, land on which we had already planted millet. You left us without kasha. We will not forget this. It would be better for you to leave the collective farm. Others will follow you.'[37]

In June 1930, OGPU reports told of a 'grain crisis' in the district.[38] A report of 22 June stated that 'a whole host of villages' in Pitelino District, among them Veriaevo and Pet, 'are experiencing a massive shortage of grain. Peasants are going to the rural soviet and begging for bread, even if just to feed their children.' On 3 June, the peasants of Stanishchi had expected the peasants of Veriaevo to raid the starch factory in Pet. The report went on to predict that peasants would soon begin to take back their grain from the collection points.[39]

Local officials were scapegoated for the course of events in Pitelino District. At a May 1930 trial of those accused of using excessive or illegal force in the course of collectivization, the chairman of the district soviet executive committee, Subbotin, received a sentence of five years in a corrective labour camp; his assistant, Ol'kin, the people's court judge (*narsud*), Rodin, and the head the district OGPU, Iurkov, received three years each; the district party committee secretary, Vasil'chenko, received a sentence of six months' hard labour; and the chairman of the Veriaevo rural soviet, Aleshin, and several other local Veriaevo officials were fired.[40]

The Official Versions

Based on the OGPU reports and telegrams sent from the troubled districts in the heady days of the February rebellion, a portrait emerges of a fairly spontaneous peasant rebellion that spread like a fire from village to village. The reports suggest that the rebellion was caused by the 'tactless behaviour' of those responsible for collectivizing agriculture in the district and that the rebellion was supported and engaged in by almost all of the region's peasants. Support crossed class lines and was rooted in the desire of the local peasantry to address the 'excesses' of the collectivizers and to protect their own political and economic interests. As Tania Kozlova, an eyewitness, told me in 2005, 'They had no need for the collective farm; they wanted to push that power aside, they wanted their own.'

A slightly different story, one that appeared nowhere in the OGPU reports, surfaced at a late February meeting of Riazan district party secretaries. The secretary of the Pitelino District Party Committee blamed the agitation in Veriaevo on a former deputy to the tsarist state duma who had a 'two-story house' and who, in fact, the secretary claimed, was such a large landholder that he was practically the equivalent of a noble landowner (*pomeshchik*). This former deputy supposedly conducted agitation among the peasants after being de-kulakized. According to the district party secretary, the trouble began when loyal poor peasants showed local officials that there was grain buried in the forest. When it was brought to the grain collection point, the wealthy peasant who had hidden the grain demanded that it be returned. When it was not returned, the peasants began to spread rumours that there would be house searches for grain. Spurred on by the rumours, peasants seized the expropriated horses of the de-kulakized and returned them to their former owners.[41] By retelling the story in this way, the district party secretary downplayed the events in Pitelino, blaming them all on acceptable, traditional enemies – the '*pomeshchik*' and the 'kulak' – when, in fact, the uprising had involved almost all of the inhabitants of the unruly villages. What is interesting here is the way in which history was being rewritten practically as it happened. In fact, by the time the report on the Pitelino uprising reached the Centre, kulaks were blamed entirely for the unrest.[42]

Another account of the riot was written in 1957 by A.N. Ianin, a former party worker, who witnessed the events in the district. His account was part of an official history of the origins of regional party organizations and collective farms in the Pitelino district, and the riot was presented as an example of dangerous kulak opposition to the collective farms. While Ianin wrote of a rebellion that he claimed occurred in early March, his recollection was likely a kind of stylized montage of the February events. His account is an interesting and problematic view of these events. Although it was written twenty-seven years after the uprising, it is significant precisely because it captures the essence of the official Stalinist depiction of peasants and peasant rebellion.

Ianin claimed that the trouble began when the secretary of the Pitelino District Party Committee was replaced by one Fediaev, 'who was considered a talentless worker even in the district.' According to Ianin's recollection, the new chairman of the district soviet executive committee, Subbotin, was a 'mediocre' member of the local police who had been transferred to Pitelino from Shatsk – in other words, both incompetent and an outsider. And the district worker Ol'kin, 'a man little acquainted with agriculture,' was named the chief of the district land department (RAIZO).[43] It is worth noting that district power structures had been recently reconstituted. This 'troika' 'began to throw its weight around [*khoziainichat'*] in Pitelino District. Without any preparatory work among the population, [the troika] began to lead wholesale collectivization there, where they did not permit a common meeting ground, embittered the population, and provoked an open uprising against Soviet power.'[44]

Ianin maintained that the dissatisfaction that the troika produced in the population was further exploited by a group of 'conspirators' consisting of the 'kulak' Os'kin, 'who was a former member of the Tsarist State Duma';[45] the 'kulaks' Papkin and Miagkov; the local priest from Veriaevo; a White Guard officer and former 'emissary of Antonov,' who was hiding to avoid prosecution; and 'some kind of "woman-kulak" (*zhenshchina-kulachka*) with a criminal past.' This list of the guilty implicated in the events in Pitelino offered a virtual catalogue of recognizable and acceptable enemies of the Soviet state. Ianin left no stone unturned as he unmasked those behind the extraordinary events: political-economic enemies (the kulaks), political-historic enemies (White Guards and emissaries of Antonov, all rolled into a unique hybrid), former tsarist officials (members of the tsarist duma), religious enemies (the local priest), wayward women, recidivist criminals, and even gypsies.[46] Ianin made a point of mentioning that one of the villages was a 'gypsy village.' Further, demonstrating a literary flair with just a hint of the supernatural, Ianin added a host of more traditional characters to the mix: 'In these villages there appeared mysterious wanderers [*stranniki*], informants [*informatory*], soothsayers [*predskazateli*] spouting the most unimaginable nonsense [*nesusvetnaia chepukha*], spreading wild rumours, gossip [*spletni*] that women and children would be socialized.'[47] According to Ianin, February was marked by 'rabid' agitation among the population against the collective farm and against collectivization in general.

Ianin dated the Pitelino riot as taking place at the beginning of March. According to his variant, a crowd of two or three thousand peasants gathered from eleven villages. The crowd was made up 'mostly of women,' armed with clubs, axes, pitchforks, and firearms and carrying icons and banners. Drawn by the ringing of the church bells of Veriaevo, the women walked to Gridino singing 'God, Save the Tsar' (*Bozhe, tsaria khrani*). In Gridino, the size of the crowd grew 'at lightning speed' as it prepared to march on Pitelino to demand the 'freeing of the arrested priests.' Ianin adds that 'in fact' the crowd intended to capture and take over the district centre and commit a 'pogrom,' exterminate (*istrebit'*) communists, and slaughter (*perebit'*) 'all of the soviet workers it despised.'[48] According to Ianin, the procession and the riotous demonstrators were led by a 'woman-kulak.' 'From one pocket of the skirt of this *Pitelinskaia Alena-bogatyr* stuck out a pistol, from the other pocket, another pistol; in her waistband, bullets, like the most authentic bandit-robber.'[49] This gender-bending, semi-mythical woman does not appear in any of the OGPU reports. She is, however, a fascinating character: a relic of the past, the untamed woman of the Soviet 1920s who was tamed in both fiction and reality by Ianin's time.[50] There is certainly a mocking tone in Ianin's prose as he recalls the masculine role of this 'Alena-bogatyr' of Pitelino, the *bogatyr* being the *male* hero of early Russian folklore.

In Ianin's account, a local police constable and an agronomist from the district went to meet the crowd. They were met with cries of 'Beat them!' Further, he noted, 'And after this, the dense striking of stakes was heard, the crash of craniums, and the police constable [*militsioner*] and agronomist were no more. They were killed by the mutineers, who continued on their way to sweep away all that they hated in their path.'[51] Ianin writes that the mutineers intended to surround Pitelino and take it by storm, but they were confronted by a detachment of 300 Red Army soldiers from Sasovo led by the chairman of the okrug soviet executive committee, Shtrodakh, and the secretary of the okrug party committee, Gilinskii. According to Ianin, Shtrodakh 'rudely' asked the crowd, with his revolver in hand,

> 'Why are you rioting [*buntuete*]? You don't like the collective farms?' To which members of the crowd responded, 'And you come here with your gun to terrify us and drag us into the collective? ... We won't go! ... Down with the collective farm! Down with the kommuna!'
>
> The Alena-bogatyr began to taunt Shtrodakh: 'Here is your collective farm! Have a look!' the woman-kulak-mutineer declared impudently and without shame, lording it over everyone, [and] suddenly raising her skirt, showing Shtrodakh her naked body amidst an explosion of laughter and mocking whoops from the crowd of like-minded villagers. Shtrodakh could not control himself in the face of her impudence and shamelessness, and he shot his revolver at the mutineer who was insulting him and killed her.[52]

This action inflamed the crowd. Only repeated volleys from the detachment finally forced the gathered villagers to scatter; they regrouped to attack the collective farm, taking back grain and cattle and destroying account books. 'Three collective farm chairmen and several collective farm members, communists, and Komsomol members were killed.'[53] If Shtrodakh did indeed shoot and kill a peasant woman engaged in a traditionally effective, peaceful, harmless, and age-old tactic of protest, the 'moral' violation of the peasant community was even further reinforced by his actions.

Ianin's account, written almost thirty years after the Pitelino events, continued the reconstruction of the rebellion already initiated at the February meeting of the district party secretaries. With graphic gusto, he detailed the acceptable explanations for a (in his eyes) gratuitously violent peasant revolt. He depicted a backward, ignorant peasant mass easily led astray by agitators and the archetypal enemies of Soviet power: backward and untamed peasant women, over-zealous and corrupt local officials, kulaks, and tsarist remnants. But is there more behind and beyond the official version of events? Do the events at Pitelino contribute something to our understanding of the Soviet countryside at the time of the Great Break?

Understanding Pitelino

From 1928 to the fall of 1929, a crisis had developed in Riazan, rooted in forced grain requisitioning and grain shortages as well as increasingly heated and united peasant opposition to state grain, tax, and rationing policies. In May 1929, the head of the county OGPU, Remizov, conducted an 'emergency tour' of Riazan. He reported that there was a reawakening of kulak and religious counterrevolution in the countryside. He noted that peasant protest, ostensibly over the closing of churches and usually involving significant numbers of women and rural soviet members, inevitably developed into heated criticism of state policy. At these gatherings, peasants complained repeatedly about the shortage of bread, high taxes, and the export of grain. Protest often resulted in demands for the 'communists' to leave the village.[54]

The OGPU reports claim that poor peasants feared that state policy would lead to starvation and, as a consequence, had little faith in the regime.[55] The tax policy that was supposed to boost and engender class war in the countryside in the previous two years had not been successful.[56] It would have been more palatable to the Centre if the OGPU had discovered that opposition in the countryside was coming only from wealthy peasants and especially from the regime's ideological scapegoat, the kulak. Yet the reports quite candidly reflect the degree to which the countryside was still a place of complex and local loyalties and conflicts. One report noted that even though the poor in the village were 'barbarically exploited' by the kulak, they continued to support and respect wealthy peasants.[57] The Riazan peasantry was not prepared economically or ideologically for the shift to collectivized agriculture. Although there were clearly tensions and social divisions in the village, these differences were submerged in the face of a greater threat from the outside.[58]

In Riazan, peasants resisted collectivization in myriad ways that were similar to those of peasants elsewhere.[59] Families initiated fictional partitions of land and property.[60] They slaughtered their livestock. In early January, in Pitelino District, for example, there was a mass slaughter of small livestock such as sheep and younger animals. The local peasants were reported to say, 'We'll go to the collective farm but without our livestock. It's all the same. We die of hunger.'[61] Fearing that they would be labelled kulaks, people also fled their homes and villages. There were 150 such cases recorded by the OGPU by the end of February 1930.[62] A number of Riazan peasants even engaged in a hunger strike to protest collectivization.[63] Women refused to let the members of the collectivization brigades talk about the collectivization process.[64] Peasants spoke of the arrival of the collective farm as the coming of the Antichrist, where all would be branded with the mark of the devil.[65] There were acts of terrorism, arson, and beatings of brigade and collective farm members.[66] Between 1 February and 14 March, there were twenty-six registered cases of 'terrorist acts' in Riazan.[67] Threats and calls to action lamenting the fate of the peasant were glued to fences and walls. These anonymous writings called for a return to the 'old life' and threatened those 'who drink the blood of the peasant.'[68] The OGPU knew of at least thirty-six such postings in February and early March. There was also mass unrest, usually consisting of crowds of a hundred to a thousand peasants that gathered to harass the collectivization brigades and to undo collectivization. There were thirty-four recorded occurrences of such unrest in Riazan in February and the first half of March. Typically, during 'mass unrest,' women reclaimed collectivized cattle and redistributed them to their original owners. And when, at the end of February, the collective farms were declared 'established,' women refused to let the collectivized horses plough the fields. But by the end of February, peasant households were already signing out of the collective farms. They were further emboldened by Stalin's 'Dizzy with Success' article of 2 March 1930.[69]

The theme of peasant resistance has become prominent in discussions of collectivization.[70] The extent of this resistance and the variety of its forms are impressive. The most overtly threatening form of resistance was, of course, the violent uprising that involved hundreds, and in some cases thousands, of peasants. Yet not all peasants rebelled, raising the question not of why peasants engaged in mass rebellion but of why, in fact, so many *did not.*[71] There were more than 6,350 villages in the province of Riazan, yet there were only thirty-four cases of 'mass unrest' involving approximately 175 (or 3 per cent) of Riazan villages, and none were of the scale of the uprising in the Pitelino district. How can a rebellion like Pitelino be explained?

Although official transcripts laid the blame on incompetent officials, backward women, kulaks, and other class enemies, the earliest reports of the Pitelino unrest, the daily *svodki* from the OGPU, quite accurately described a situation in which *all* villagers, regardless of social and economic conditions, united in their struggles against the collectivization brigade and the rural soviet. In this regard, the unrest in Pitelino mirrored peasant unrest elsewhere in the Soviet Union. This similarity was the case with other features of the rebellion as well. Rumours, for example, were immensely important in the events in Pitelino District. The rumour that allegedly sparked the rebellion was that the plenipotentiaries were 'gathering cattle to slaughter and ship to Moscow,' suggesting that peasants were aware to some degree of their colonial relationship to Moscow and actively resented it.[72] The rumours about cattle encouraged peasants to come together in protest. Cattle, like horses, were a crucial resource is this northern district of Riazan Province. Further, the rumours described by Ianin capture and encapsulate the fears of both peasants and the Centre. Villagers feared that women and children would become communal property, and the Centre feared a 'slaughter' of its representatives. Or perhaps both sides claimed that these were their fears in order to justify extreme actions. Rumours about accepted and traditional enemies and their role in the unrest began to shape the historical record by the end of February 1930.

Peasant women were at the forefront of protest in Pitelino, just as they were across the rest of the Soviet Union during collectivization. Peasant men and women took advantage of the traditional view of women as less threatening and less politically responsible than men. Men were much more likely to be arrested for protest than women and tended to stay on the sidelines unless the women were threatened. Only then could peasant men step in on the grounds that they were defending their womenfolk.[73] The graphic symbolism of peasant protest must have frightened the authorities, as peasants used and inverted the regime's own tactics and language.[74] Pitelino peasants paraded under black or white flags and defied the regime by setting up barricades and demanding that all who entered show their documents – a procedure that was becoming an everyday part of Soviet life. Demanding the return of the 'old ways,' of tradition, the church, and the priest, Pitelino peasants explicitly rejected the new Soviet order. The children's reaction to the posters of the great leaders further suggests that peasants knew that responsibility ran all the way to the top in the destruction of their communities. Traditional features of Soviet power became the subjects and the objects of peasant protest. The red flag parades of communist festival were replaced by the black flag of anarchy and the white flag of counter-revolution. The requisite

Soviet posters were torn from the walls and shredded by children, who, like women, could not be held entirely responsible for their actions.

What the events in Pitelino capture vividly is the high degree of solidarity *among* the villages of the district. Over and over the villagers worked together, uniting over and above any rivalries that may have existed prior to the rebellion. Messengers skied between villages with news of events.[75] Village church bells constantly warned neighbouring villages of danger or of collectivization events, bringing their inhabitants rushing to confront the collectivizers. Peasants from more than twenty villages called meetings among themselves, made plans, and issued demands. Peasants were political and they knew how to organize.

There was a host of common experiences for the peasantry across the Soviet Union during the first collectivization drive. Yet violent uprisings were relatively uncommon. What exactly sparked violent unrest? The most obvious explanation is the most commonly accepted one: the excesses of the collectivizers. And there was certainly much variation in the behaviour of collectivization brigades. Even within Riazan itself OGPU reports lamented that the brigade in Mikhailov District 'cries with the population' and socializes with them.[76] The brigades in Pitelino, however, violated the moral economy of the villages in the district both morally and economically. In Pitelino, peasants were pushed beyond the line of subsistence as their last grain was removed from their barns and trunks and even baked bread was seized from their homes. But, just as importantly, the peasantry was morally violated. A brigade member raped a local woman in Malye Mochily,[77] and the detachment sent by the state killed at least two Pitelino peasants. It is the active and violent cooperation and participation of rural soviet members in the excesses in Pitelino that is most important in explaining why there was violent rebellion here. The organization that was typically *of* the village, the rural soviet, turned *on* the village.

Rural soviet officials accompanied the collectivizers as they went door-to-door taking the peasants' last seeds of grain. Peasants were incensed that it was the rural soviet that demanded that all grain be turned over within twenty-four hours. When property was destroyed and windows broken, it was the rural soviet or homes of rural soviet members that were targeted. Rural soviet officials were physically attacked. What angered peasants most was that their own local government had betrayed them when it should have protected them. The first official action recommended by the protesting peasants was the dissolution of the existing rural soviet and its reconstitution with peasants who would better serve local interests. The most repetitive feature of the OGPU reports on collectivization and peasant resistance nationwide is the constant complaint that the village soviets acted as a 'brake' on collectivization. This 'foot dragging' of the rural soviet may very well offer a clue to why more villages did not erupt in rebellion across the Soviet Union during the first wave of collectivization in 1929 and 1930.

The role of the rural soviet in the 1920s and during the first collectivization drive is pivotal and worthy of further consideration as we attempt to refine our conceptualization of village and state. Despite the regime's attempts to change the composition of the rural soviets through the 1920s, in 1929 the majority remained 'of the village' – that is, rural soviet members were villagers themselves, had personal relationships with the peasants of the surrounding villages, and often made decisions rooted in custom and tradition rather than in central ordinance or instruction. In fact, much of the lower state apparatus was 'suspect' as being more of the village and the region than of the state. Consider the head jailer of the Kasimov district, denounced in an OGPU report, who brought vodka for his prisoners, delivered notes among them on the progress of their cases, and took several home to spend nights at his house.[78] This kind of non-standardized informality of the old order was what the regime faced locally and what it believed it had to overthrow in the name of modernization, standardization, and progress. This traditional order was not always a benevolent or gentle one, but it was an order that existed and even developed and strengthened in the countryside in the 1920s.

Many village soviets were staffed by wealthy peasants with strong patronage networks. These individuals used their positions to protect family and circles of friends and allies as best they could.[79] Before the first collectivization drive, rural soviet chairmen helped fellow peasants avoid grain requisitioning. In some cases, they issued permission to village members to acquire grain 'necessary for their own personal use.'[80] In October 1929, a report on the grain-requisitioning campaign stated, 'Almost all village soviets up to this time have made no independent attempts to implement measures decreed by the Central Committee in Moscow and the Council of People's Commissars against the kulak section of the village; they [rural soviets] do not use the rights granted to them.'[81] OGPU reports are replete with laments about the *khvostism*, or 'backwardness' (*khvost* literally means 'tail'), of the local governmental structure and of the rural soviets in particular.[82] By December 1929, OGPU reports were complaining that the *aktiv* – those who were in theory active supporters of Soviet power, such as rural soviet chairmen, local police officers, and local party members – were speaking out against collectivization. Increasingly, members of the rural soviet refused to turn over their grain.[83] Moreover, according to the OGPU, members of the rural soviets were sympathetic to the plight of the 'class enemy': 'Many of the lower party and soviet organs deal poorly with the crimes of the kulak class. Inventories of property, which should be done because of the wilful hoarding of grain, in the majority of cases are never realized, and the property is not sold. Kulaks are given breaks and extensions.'[84] In the same report the OGPU complained that rural soviet members supported their relatives, who were kulaks, accepted bribes in return for assistance, lowered grain-requisitioning norms levied on local kulaks, and spread grain-procurement obligations out among middle and poor peasants.[85] Members of the rural soviet in the village of Vysokoe, Shatsk District, were explicit about their relationship to the countryside: 'These are our people and if we apply the control figures [for grain quotas] in their entirety, then the peasants will tear us to pieces.'[86] Of course the OGPU presented these examples as evidence of anti-Soviet behaviour when, in fact, most simply reveal the common workings and power structure of the pre-collectivization village. The examples presented suggest that the rural soviets were very much of the village and, as a result, were in fact a serious brake on collectivization.

As late as February 1930, the OGPU complained that the majority of rural soviets continued to deter peasants from joining the collectives and that both local party members and rural soviet members were slaughtering their own livestock.[87] For example, six members of the Berezovo rural soviet refused to enter the collective farm. Two of them, Voronko and Bazanov, spoke out against collectivization at every meeting, calling it '*barshchina*' (a direct reference to labour obligations under serfdom) and 'violence' (*nasilie*).[88] Makarov, a member of the rural soviet of the village of Velikii Studenets located in Sasovo District, joined the collective farm, but at each meeting he spoke out against it, calling it a 'whorehouse' (*publichnyi dom*). He urged his fellow villagers not to enter the collective farm, telling them that the collective farm meant 'hunger and ruin.' The OGPU agent's conclusion was that as 'a result of his activities, more than half of the households in the village did not enter the collective farm.'[89]

Rural soviet chairmen represented a voice of reason, complaining over and over that targets for collectivization and requisitioning were too high and impossible to enforce. They continued to assign quotas in customary ways, by 'eater,' that is, by the number of members of a given household, instead of by class.[90] A report of 1 March, from the Riazan county prosecutor, lamented that a whole host of rural soviets 'violate the class line' in this way.[91] In fact, rural soviet chairmen were in the most difficult situation imaginable, caught in a vice between the weight of the mass of the peasantry, on one hand, and the weight of the regime, on the other. Their position was precarious and dangerous, as they were often the sole representatives of Soviet power locally and were at best torn between regime and village.

On 16 March 1930, at 11:00 p.m., a meeting of the village activists was called to discuss collectivization in the village of Zabelino, Sarai District. Practically the whole village appeared outside the meeting. Cries of 'We have no kulaks here – sign us all out of the collective farm, or else we will not let you out of the rural soviet alive' rang out from the crowd. The wife of the rural soviet chairman, perhaps taking the side of the crowd or perhaps simply fearing for her husband's life, said to him, 'Let's go home. It smells like murder here.' But the chairman refused to leave the scene and instead struck her. Villagers in the crowd began to shout, 'Down with the collective farm! The brigade members write about us to the OGPU!' The crowd demanded the right to leave the collective farm. Finally, the chairman of the rural soviet gave the list of those who had signed up for the collective farm to the gathered peasants. They signed out of the collective and woke all of the sleeping members of the village so they could sign out too. Among the 126 households signed up for the collective, 110 signed out.[92] Here, the chairman of the rural soviet attempted to act as a state representative and enforce state policy only so far before taking it upon himself to act in a way he believed would redress the situation. His wife's graphic admonition captures the ugly and tense dangers of the village during the first drive.

Like rural party members, the rural soviet staff believed at this early stage that they had a voice in the general power structure of the state and that they could reason, negotiate, and act in prudent ways with impunity. The rural soviets were pivotal during the first collectivization drive partly because of the role the regime now expected them to play. As the most basic grassroots element of the state structure, they were expected to be the hubs of collectivizing activity, and in some cases they did facilitate OGPU and brigade work. More often, however, members of the rural soviet were a very vocal and crucial source of opposition in the village. Disloyalty within state organs made the regime very nervous, and disloyalty within state organs at the village level empowered the peasantry.

On 21 February, in the village of Nekliudovo, Kasimov District, a candidate member of the party, Mileshkin, together with a member of the rural soviet, Ivantsov, asked a villager to write a positive recommendation (*otzyv*) for an accused kulak arrested for hostile agitation against the collective farm. Both Mileshkin and Ivantsov signed the letter and it was circulated around the village. The OGPU reported that seeing 'the signature of the party member and a member of the rural soviet, the majority of the peasants signed the recommendation.'[93] In the village of Zabelino, the chairman of the rural soviet signed into the collective farm himself, but advised other peasants not to sign up. He told them, 'Don't sign up for the collective farm. If we don't have eighty households who want to enter the collective farm, then we will be saved from it.' The OGPU claimed that as a result of the rural soviet chairman's actions, collective farms in the area grew very slowly.[94] Villagers used the state's expectations against the state itself. If party and rural soviet members were supposed to be examples, then peasants would follow their examples when it suited them. When the brigade members in one village began to insist upon full entry into the collective farm, local villagers said to them, 'There you have Sedel'nikov, a party man. He is not entering the collective farm, and there is no way we are entering either.'[95] The regime underestimated the degree to which the rural soviets were 'of the village.' There was massive turnover in rural soviet membership as peasants endeavoured to quit their posts or were purged and as the regime scrambled to fill the rural soviets with loyalists. The rural soviet was a kind of bridge between peasant and state through the 1920s, a bridge that had to be dismantled as part of the collectivization drive.[96]

In Pitelino District, however, the rural soviet was not 'of the village' and had been reconstituted in a recent unscheduled election of the kind that was taking place all over the Soviet Union in late 1929 and early 1930. Members of the rural soviet assisted the collectivization brigade and participated in the excesses. Rural soviet members smashed locks and confiscated not only grain but flour and even baked bread. They participated in de-kulakization, which took place at night without the participation of the 'masses,'[97] meaning without even a show of democracy. In Pitelino, rural soviet members did not soften the blow of collectivization by dragging their feet or assigning grain quotas according to custom. Studies of peasant unrest have identified the factors that push peasants to rebel. James Scott has argued that peasants resist when they are pushed beyond the line of subsistence, when the 'moral economy' of the village is violated.[98] Yet many villages were pushed beyond the line of subsistence in the Soviet Union during the first collectivization drive, and relatively few of them rebelled. While pushing peasants beyond the line of subsistence is crucial to explaining the rebellion in Pitelino, the complicity of the local rural soviet as it backed central policy in the villages of Pitelino was a central factor underlying the rebellion. In the region, village officials violated the moral economy and pushed peasants beyond the line of subsistence. If these factors explain why the rebellion occurred, then the irony is that the regime was saved from more rebellions like the one in Pitelino by the one feature of the village that the OGPU complained most bitterly about – the way in which rural soviets acted as a brake on the collectivization process by refusing to cooperate, by allowing peasants to avoid the collectives, by helping wealthy peasants to disguise their wealth, by dividing grain-requisitioning demands by 'eater' as opposed to class, by providing false documents, and by accepting any kind of excuse to alleviate harsh policy from the Centre. These tactics stopped peasants from taking to the street and engaging in open confrontation with armed forces. Such rural soviet members were weeded out over time as the regime gained a stranglehold on the countryside, but at this crucial juncture they may very well have saved the Soviet regime by softening the onslaught of collectivization. The foot-dragging village soviets held their villages together and ironically may have sacrificed them to the state and to the collective farm in the long term.

It was a tribute to the effectiveness of the rural soviet that so many villages did not erupt into rebellion. Many rural soviet members did continue to try to moderate the policies from above, while the Centre tried through rapid and constant elections to make them reliable conduits of centralized power. The behaviour of the rural soviets drove home to the regime the degree to which they had to solidify and restructure the rural administration if they were to capture the peasantry. The first collectivization drive was the climax of the first stage of a process already engaged by the policies of high taxation and grain requisitioning, by the fears of bandits and hooligans, and by the fear of officials who participated in samosud. As one village priest astutely articulated to his flock, 'They have dragged you into a bag. All they have to do is tie the knot.'[99]

Reading Pitelino through Time

One of Riazan's greatest native sons is the village-prose writer Boris Andreevich Mozhaev. His two-volume novel, *Muzhiki i baby*, was written as a 'historical chronicle' of the events of 1929–30 in Pitelino.[100] Mozhaev was born in Pitelino on 1 June 1923 and witnessed the events of collectivization through the frightened eyes of a child. His father, Andrei, was arrested in connection with his opposition to collectivization and appears in *Muzhiki i baby* as Andrei Borodin, a member of the rural soviet who takes a moderate position on collectivization.[101] Mozhaev grew up in Pitelino, attended school in Potap'evo, and worked as district school teacher until his military service in the Far East. In 1943 he was sent to a higher military engineering school in Leningrad and was later evacuated to Iaroslavl. In the 1960s he returned to Riazan. His first Riazan story was *Zhivoi* (Alive), better known as *Iz zhizni Feodora Kuz'kina* (From the Life of Fedor Kuz'kin), one of the most controversial works of village prose, published in 1966. Mozhaev's fiction wrestled with the suffering of collectivization; Fedor Kuz'kin, like Andrei Borodin, is an intelligent, honest, hard-working peasant, who is arrested for his incomprehension and questioning of the decisions surrounding collectivization.

Throughout his career as a village-prose writer, Mozhaev faced criticism and censure. He began writing *Muzhiki i baby* in 1976, and by this time Mozhaev was free of the mythical enemies that parade through Ianin's narrative. But he was not free of some of the conventions that characterize socialist realism. There are no women mutineers or *bogatyrs*, only rioting peasant women and one distressed young communist, Mariia, who battles for decency and order and loses her love in the violence. And while there are some pure love interests, such as Mariia and Uspenskii, that purity itself results in violent death. There is no overt 'naturalism' in Mozhaev, although he does restore an off-colour sense of humour to the peasantry. He boldly embraces local peasant dialect, thereby rejecting the classic Soviet language that was supposed to be part of socialist-realist literature.[102] Mozhaev, for example, writes a beautiful dialogue that represents both the bawdy side of peasant dialogue and the local flavour of Riazan speech. The exchange is between the forest patroller, Sen'ka Knut, a solitary old man (*bobyl*), and two young women to whom he gives a ride on his *tarantass*:

– Knut, have you ever been in love?
– What?
– How come you never married?
– I got old, girls.
– Knut, is it true that men who are afraid of women dry up?
– What?
– The watering can ...

– Girls, I still have enough for the sowing.
– Water?
– Ah, you wild things![103]

Another indicative moment of such 'local colour' occurs at a meeting of the local Tikhanovo *aktiv*. Senechka Zenin, the secretary of the local party cell, gives a long speech, in a series of long speeches, about events in China and the importance of purchasing the third industrial bond. One peasant woman, Tarakanikha, falls asleep and snores loudly, causing much hilarity among the gathered villagers. When the group is chastised, one asks,

– So it turns out that Tarakanikha has a class face, so it is forbidden to laugh at her?
– And what kind of ass does she have?[104]

The collective farm organizers are not amused.

Still, many of Mozhaev's characters would indeed be at home in a socialist-realist novel. Ozimov, for example, is a police chief who is in misery at the role he is forced to play during collectivization. He is killed by the crowd and buried in his uniform in a coffin lined with red satin. He is a communist martyr who is sacrificed because of the excesses of a few. In some ways Mozhaev is not free of parts of the official line either. The excesses in Pitelino are the fault of a few over-zealous local activists like the secretary of the local party cell. Zenin criticizes the local collective farm for not turning over its surplus to the state, but instead wasting money on 'women's apparel'; the collective farm had bought cloth to make uniforms for the collective farmers – red dresses for women, black pants for men.[105] Mariia, the kind-hearted communist girl, tells Zenin, when he is pushing forced grain requisitioning, that he is worse than the village thief Van'ka Zhadov because at least Van'ka had the decency to rob people at night, not in the daytime, and to stab people openly with a knife.[106] So Mozhaev works within many of the strictures of socialist realism; there are good communists who would have made socialism work, perhaps, if not for fools like Zenin. There is one good, caring, loving communist woman; other women are background.

Yet some of the subtleties that can be gleaned from the archival record, and are missing from Ianin's account, are found in the depth and richness of *Muzhiki i baby* and more beyond. Mozhaev lived in these villages and when one visits them, one immediately grasps the fidelity of his descriptions. Mozhaev writes that the pre-Revolutionary merchant,

13. Pitelino central square, 2004 (photo by the author).

Kamanin, who had a large house, practically gave it to the RIK (raion executive committee). Kamanin had wanted to build a new house across from his old one, but the RIK said no because the square had to be kept for demonstrations. The Pitelino village square where Kamanin had his house is the administrative centre of the district to this day.[107]

The reader finds colourful and varied markets; the role of the village churches; rural soviet meetings that resist the decisions of the November plenum and drink to Soviet power; the overlapping of the rural soviet and the gathering; distress over the loss of voting rights; local police officers; short-staffed criminal investigation units; samosud; samogon; horse theft and retribution; the horse thief who is aided by the forest warden; threats of arson; taxation; arguments over the buying of state bonds; the central role of women in resistance to collectivization; and the unenviable position of being a decent rural soviet chair. Evdokim Akimov, chairman of the Gordeevo soviet, for example, refuses to search from household to household for 'excess' grain. When asked to account for his failure to act, he says, 'I am the chairman of the rural soviet ... If you do not believe in me, then replace me with the village librarian or someone else who will grope around in stoves and beds.'[108] When the violence of February is in full swing, Andrei Borodin looks to the chair of the Tikhanovo soviet, Pavel Krechev, as *vlast'* in the village. Borodin argues that the soviet is real power locally and not members of the Communist Party; but the chairman, cowed by the collectivization brigade, just looks at the floor.[109]

Mozhaev's descriptions of the Pitelino uprising echo the *chastushki* still remembered in the region and the telegrams and documents of the archives. In Mozhaev's narrative, the peasants of Gordeevo run to Veret'e and tell their neighbours that they are being dragged into the collective farm by force. The younger men hide in the forest. Old men and women run to the holding pen (*kormushka*) that had been built for the collectivized livestock and smash it to pieces, throwing the broken boards into the street. The peasants take back their grain, some recognizing their own bags. The collectivization brigade leader arms himself and calls in the police. The chief of police sees men on the edge of the forest with axes and pitchforks and hears the sound of the church bell. Villagers call for new elections of local power through the gathering and in another moment ask to elect a rural soviet based on the rules of 1925, with no voters denied their voting rights.

The actual days of the uprising in Mozhaev's narrative become more literary and more symbolic than the archival documents and the memories of the women that begin the epilogue. The chief of police, Ozimov, a relatively sympathetic character in the novel, is shot by a frightened villager. Women capture the leading local collectivizer, Zenin, and flog him, such that he lies on his stomach in the nearby hospital, cursing. The crowd invades the hospital looking for him. The crowds use the church bells to call the villagers to gather and thus the bell-ringer, Ivan Kukurai – a kind of holy fool, half-blind and deaf, and constantly surrounded by small, taunting children – is naturally a target for the troops' attempts to control the situation. Dmitrii Uspenskii is shot protecting Ivan. Ozimov and Uspenskii are buried on the same day. Still, Mozhaev points the finger at the OGPU. Zenin writes the okrug administrative department (*adminotdel*) a telegram complaining of terror acts in the district, including the theft of apples from the former noble estate, the shooting out of a window during a Komsomol play, and the beating of collective farm agitators. When the local police investigate, however, the apples, it turns out, were taken by young people organizing a *posidel'ka* and were returned; the window was broken by a stone, not a gun, and by 'drunken hooligans,' not kulak enemies; and the beating was only one punch in the nose, pretty mild as far as village brawling went. Implicitly, the arrival of the OGPU is the reason for bloodshed in Mozhaev's version. The telegram is what brings the OPGU agents to the villages, and their presence leads in turn to the escalation of violence and the loss of life.

Throughout the novel, Uspenskii represents Mozhaev's point of view. He shares not a few characteristics with his creator. Uspenskii loves history and philosophy, and he is the village school teacher. It is through this character that Mozhaev's own position, confused and in tension, is revealed. Uspenskii had fought on the Bolshevik side in the Civil War. He was the son of a priest who responds, when his class origins are held against him, by pointing out that Chernyshevsky and Dobroliubov were also sons of priests.[110] The chairman of the raion party committee, Vozvyshaev, tells Krechev to confiscate Uspenskii's house and use it as a base from which to organize the collective farm. Krechev, however, hesitates. He sees Uspenskii as a good man who signed up for the state bond, which everyone else had run away from like a 'demon from incense.' On the one hand, then, Uspenskii represents hope for socialism of a certain kind. On the other hand, he is martyred trying to save a holy fool and after coming to the conclusion, 'I am neither Red nor White, Mama. I am too Russian.'[111]

Mozhaev, like many village-prose writers, was an Orthodox believer and he has strong traces of Russian nationalism running through his work. The tension for Mozhaev in *Muzhiki i baby* is between faith in a better Leninist line and the rejection of Bolshevism as something altogether foreign. The explicit line in the novel is that the party's left wing was responsible for the policy at the top that led to the excesses of the first collectivization drive. Together with over-zealous local officials, who bring in the OGPU, they create the violence at the bottom. In discussing *Muzhiki i baby* in 1988, Victor Danilov argued that Mozhaev's novel represented a dangerous fantasy: 'Very characteristic – and dangerous – is the fantasy of B. Mozhaev's novel *Muzhiki i baby,* where the responsibility for the violence that peasants were subjected to in the course of collectivization in the winter of 1929–30 is transferred from the real perpetrators (Stalin and his closest associates, in first place, Molotov and Kaganovich) to Trotsky, Zinoviev, Kamenev, Iakovlev, and Kaminskii, of whom the first three by 1927 already had no relationship to the political decisions made, and Trotsky had been deported from the Soviet Union in February 1929. All of these fantasies were not born in *perestroika. Perestroika* and *glasnost'* only made them visible.'[112]

Some of the danger here may be anti-Semitism; Trotsky, Zinoviev,

Kamenev, Iakovlev, were all Jewish.[113] Could Mozhaev have blamed Stalin in 1976 or even 1980 for the path collectivization took? Was he bound by fear, by the residue of socialist realism, by convention, by the limits of his historical training and his archival access (Mozhaev did work in the Riazan archive), by his own prejudices? His official analysis of collectivization followed the accepted line. If anyone at the top was mistaken it was the Left Opposition, and mistakes were made by over-zealous communist officials at the lower levels. Still, Mozhaev was brave in implicating the OGPU to the extent that he does in *Muzhiki i baby*.

In his epilogue, Mozhaev concludes his 'historical chronicle' with what would become the official line of early glasnost. Collectivization involved excesses, which were a violation of the Leninist line. Lenin had advocated gradual transformation without coercion. If Lenin's line had been followed, then violence could have been avoided and agriculture peacefully collectivized. And the novel concludes by pointing out that, despite the excesses, the collective farms were constructed more slowly, and successfully, in the years that followed the violence of the first drive. Yet if one pushes Mozhaev's critique of the Left, one may come to a Russian-nationalist critique that rejects Bolshevism as fundamentally anti-Russian.

Uspenskii laments,

> Everything connected with the people, its way of life, its faith and religion, all of this is alien to our left-wingers. Not only do they not accept the faith of the people, but they are also hostile to the most sublime manifestations of the people's national spirit. To them Tolstoi is a religious fool, Dostoevskii an obscurantist, even Pushkin expresses the culture of the nobility. And this is without even mentioning their hatred of all Russian philosophers, from Khomiakov to Bulgakov. For them the Russian historical experience is merely foul soil which has to be cleared away, and that's where their historical intolerance, lack of moderation, and desire to create a social miracle comes from. So where do little kids and old men and women come in? We'll just create history as fast as possible according to our own plan. At the moment people believe in it, and if anyone doesn't we'll make them … Just a little bit more and we'll be in paradise. We only need to force everyone into a collective farm. Give us a miracle. A little bit more and we'll be there. That's where the rot is. That's the whole point.[114]

When Boris Mozhaev wrote *Muzhiki i baby* between 1976 and 1980, there was still much that could not be said about collectivization and about the unrest in Pitelino as well. Mozhaev's novel and the nuances that it introduced to the understandings of the villages of the 1920s and the collectivization drive of 1929–30 were prophetic of the historiographical developments that were to come. Initially, during glasnost Lenin was still sacred, as he was for Mozhaev. It was only when Lenin, and Leninism, became part of the 'original sin'[115] of 1917 that openness and restructuring took on a life of its own, which could not be controlled from above.[116] For some this discussion of Mozhaev may seem like literary criticism rather than historical analysis. But, there is no need for such strong disciplinary boundaries to be vehemently declared and defended. Furthermore, Mozhaev's work reveals much about Pitelino, its impact on one who witnessed it, and how these experiences of collectivization helped to create and shape a village prose writer in the 1960s as well as his return in the early years of glasnost. One can gain insights into significant transition moments in the history of the Soviet Union with their changing conceptions and presentations of the countryside and its history.

Conclusion

What does the Pitelino rebellion tell us about collectivization and the countryside in the 1920s? The documents generated by the events in Pitelino during the days of the unrest provide the researcher with a rare, intimate gaze into the villages of the district. These materials bring us closer to the realities of collectivization on the ground than historians have ever been before, outside of the collections of published primary documents that provide the raw and bloody data.[117] The documents reveal what elements of collectivizer behaviour prompted peasant unrest – a violation of the moral economy, both morally and economically. They show that a rural soviet that cooperated with aggressive collectivization activists increased the possibility of violence, suggesting that rural soviets that resisted may actually have prevented or limited extreme violence and unrest. Villagers took the rural soviets seriously and tried to re-elect a soviet that would defend them.

The events also illustrate the key role played by women in resistance to collectivization. When the village was under attack, women were prevalent in the panicked reports of the OGPU. Until this point, women were difficult to find in many of the archival records that I consulted. They were in court less often than men for violent crimes, and the crimes for which they did appear, such as wood theft or illegal brewing, were dealt with usually in mass sentencing and thus women's individual voices were not heard. Yet it is the women who are left today to preserve and pass on the memories of the experience of collectivization. Despite the fact that the women were at the forefront of the rebellion in Pitelino, no one remembers the story as a tale of women's protest, except perhaps Ianin, and even then his heroine was a most peculiar mix of mythical, she-male *bogatyr* and shameless flasher. In Mozhaev, the women can talk dirty and they can flog Zenin, but they cannot wax philosophical on the past and future of Russia. The eyewitnesses (the OGPU and Ianin) report that a woman was shot and killed, but in Mozhaev's version the victims are men. Women preserve the memory of the rebellion, but always as a tale of '*muzhiki i baby*,' of men and women.

The official reactions to Pitelino reveal much about the recording and creation of history itself. Within days of the uprising, Riazan party officials began to reconstruct the events; they cast the unrest as prompted by the evil influence of the traditional enemies of the Revolution. This reconstruction focused the blame on a limited number of individuals, rather than entire villages, and made the unrest in some ways less frightening and, more importantly, made the dream of building collectivization salvageable. Enemies were given names and faces and they could be removed or purged and then a new civilization could still be built. Ianin's account of 1957 illustrates the development and solidification of a particular reading of Soviet history. Ianin's official version is bloody and sensational, peopled with acceptable enemies and flavoured with a strong dose of male fantasies.

Boris Mozhaev's grappling with the uprising of his childhood provides us with a remarkable window on an individual who was injured by collectivization, yet grew up a Soviet man. Mozhaev was caught between his attraction to orthodoxy and the Russian past, both likely nurtured in his intense friendship with Solzhenitsyn, who lived across from Mozhaev during Solzhenitsyn's exile in Riazan, and his loyalty to the Leninist ideal. He also grew up on socialist realism and he could not escape its influence entirely. Much of the conflict, tension, and promise of the early years of perestroika are foreshadowed in *Muzhiki i baby*. Mozhaev's painstaking portrait of the Riazan countryside confirms and augments what was found in the archival record. His eyewitness testimony and experience reinforce the portrait of the province painted in the pages of this book.

The explicit position of the officials, of Ianin, of Mozhaev, and even of some present-day eyewitnesses was that the unrest reflected pointless, elemental peasant revolt. But both *Muzhiki i baby* and the archival record cannot help but capture local politics, organization, sophistication, and complexity. I would go further and argue that the record captures a strong commitment by villagers to organized politics and due process. And that tradition continues to this day.

Pitelino Redux: A Postscript

In the summer of 2004 I met Natasha Zhuravleva. She is the village schoolteacher in Malyi Studenets, a small village in Sasovo, a district that borders Pitelino. I told her that I was in the region to find out more about an uprising that took place there in 1930. I met Natasha through her cousin Viacheslav Egorkin, who lived in the city of Riazan but had been born and raised in Malyi Studenets along with Natasha on the former collective farm, 'Bolshevik.' Neither had ever heard of the Pitelino uprising even though Natasha was fiercely devoted to the history of her region. I asked them if they would go with me to look for survivors, so that together we could hear their story, and they agreed. We travelled in the summers of 2004 and 2005 to search for those who remembered.[118] Natasha's family represent a kinship network of sorts that continues the tradition of village intellectuals and of local rural inhabitants committed to the functioning of their village, largely on their own and against significant odds. Natasha was educated in the city of Riazan and she could have moved away from the countryside. Instead, she came back there to teach because, as she so eloquently put it, 'If we, still here in the wilderness, forget what is honour, patriotism, so that children go to the city and say, proudly, "Yes, I am from Malyi Studenets." – "And where is that?" – "In Sasovo District." And start to talk so people are interested. And not simply stand with eyes downcast, saying, "We are from the countryside." So this does not happen, I tell them that they have to read a lot, know a lot. So some city boy or girl, you can silence them because you know better. And then you will not be ashamed that you were born in the countryside.' Natasha's mother, Raisa, is the chairperson of the rural soviet. And they do not appear to benefit in any significant way from their positions of 'power.' They serve their constituency at great personal cost and sacrifice. Despite the fact that Pitelino is no more than 500 kilometres from Moscow, it is a wilderness of sorts; until the late 1970s the best way to reach the area was by small plane as there were no paved roads. In the summers of 2004 and 2005, we journeyed to Pitelino to conduct interviews with those who remembered the uprising of 1930. All of the people we interviewed were women, for there were no men living who remembered the events.

Alessandro Portelli maintains that 'historical work using oral sources is unfinished because of the nature of the sources; historical work excluding oral sources (where available) is incomplete by definition.'[119] Talking to the people of Pitelino helped to bring the events full circle from the telegrams of the 1930s to the memories of the present day. Given the ways in which history and narrative have been forged and controlled over the course of Soviet history, oral history has a great deal to offer the historian. In general, oral history has provided vital information on those groups in society that have not left an extensive written record, and especially for those whose 'written history is either missing or distorted.'[120] Moreover, oral history reveals the often hidden 'psychological costs' of events, which are evident if we listen closely to the words of Mozhaev and to the women living in the villages of Pitelino District today. For the women to whom we spoke, there is lingering fear, confusion, revision of history, and even defiance. Niura Marfina's mind jumps back and forth between two traumatic events: what she saw in Stalingrad where she was sent to rebuild after the Great Patriotic War, and the events of collectivization. There is much that Marfina cannot say, and when she cannot say something about Pitelino, she jumps to a memory of a fellow villager whom she met in Stalingrad after the war who *did* want to talk about the rebellion. And as Portelli reminds us, sometimes 'the most precious information may lie in what the informants *hide*, and in the fact they *do* hide it, rather than in what they *tell*.'[121] The repeated insistence from most of the women that we spoke to about Pitelino was that their families did *not* go to the rebellion, *never* resisted collectivization, and *always* and at all times obeyed the authorities. These repetitions should prompt the reader to listen to what is being hidden as much as to what is being said.

There is an extensive literature on memory, collective memory, commemoration, and the creation of history.[122] But we are not yet to the point where the inhabitants of Pitelino are creating a memorial to the victims of collectivization, nor was a statue devoted to the successes of collectivization ever built, unless you consider the now-rusting and desolate farms themselves. The one sculpture I remember from the collective farms near Pitelino is known colloquially as 'Give me (some food), mama' (*Podai mama*), dubbed thus by the hungry children of the farm. One of those children, now grown, who was born in the 1970s, still remembers walking to school barefoot, and he added, 'At least we were *all* barefoot.' What I found in interviewing those who remembered the Pitelino uprising were fragmented, troubled memories – memories, in most cases, that made certain to emphasize that family and even the entire village always constituted obedient and willing members of the collective farms.

There is also an extensive literature on the connections among history, trauma, and memory.[123] In the Soviet and post-Soviet case, we have an especially rich context for analysis because the repressing and the re-understanding of the memory of events was explicitly encouraged. Ianin, for example, re-remembers the events of collectivization in a mythologized and acceptable way for his time, position, and place. Perhaps his need to write about the events was motivated by the trauma of witnessing them; we cannot know. We could make a stronger case for Mozhaev's need to write about the events of collectivization that he witnessed as a seven-year-old boy, and he writes about them in the contours of the spaces within which he found to work during the thaw, the difficult Brezhnev years, and finally the opportunities for openness in the 1980s. Finally, the memories of the women who 'remember' the uprising make the process of constructing memory even more explicit and more complicated because they suggest a self-consciousness about the accepted version of events versus a different telling. The oldest of the women says, 'I am ninety years old, so I can tell you.' She can give the traumatic version of events because she has nothing to lose. But the two younger women, even though they are in their eighties, are not so free. They can speak of aspects of the violence of collectivization in embedded and fragmented and symbolic ways. Collectivization is a tale of hunchbacks, witches, yet 'our' people took from us. One could have believed in kulaks then, and now 'know' that they never existed. One could remember that they shot some 'rich millers,' Well, 'not rich, they had a mill.' One could remember a man in Stalingrad who wanted to talk about events that happened more than fifteen years earlier in the villages of Riazan.

These women of Pitelino were left largely on their own to remember the past. Yes, they suggest that we check in with the local administrator. Yes, they certainly speak much more freely of the event now than they would have in 1950, but the construction of memory that so preoccupies historians of the West inspired by Pierre Nora is not the same in Pitelino. In fact, Natasha Zhuravleva tells Tatiana Kozlova that we came a long way to talk to her. She asks if we came from the district centre. Our friend says, no from further away than that. From the capital of the province, she asks? No further. Moscow? When Natasha tells her that we came from across the ocean, from Canada, she just stares in confusion. This memory is not the stuff of national commemoration. That is not to say that historians cannot write fruitful studies of commemoration and remembering Soviet history both of the official creation of collective memory as well as popular means of preserving 'unofficial remembrances,'[124] just not in Pitelino and not now.

A more appropriate framework to look at the memories of the Pitelino uprising is articulated by Nathan Wachtel, who points out that a recollection is not assumed to be an 'accurate reflection of the past' but rather 'part of present reality.'[125] At each level of the construction of the uprising one can see this principle at work as the realities of the moment shape the narrative of the event. Accepting that these narratives are constructions of a given moment does not mean that they cannot be used to reveal a great deal for the historian. As Natalie Davis and Randolph Stern explain, 'People do worry about the fit between what actually happened and received narratives about the past. The process of adjusting the fit is an ongoing one, subject to continual debate and exchanges in which memory and history may play shifting, alternately more or less contentious roles in setting the record straight. Sometimes this task is best performed by the unreflective, erratic operations of memory, sometimes by rules of recording and interpretation that, since the Renaissance and the Enlightenment, belong to historical discourse.'[126]

Our journey began in the village of Pet, where the ruins of the starch factory are still visible from the grounds behind the shell of a once-majestic church. When we asked a local inhabitant where the rural soviet was located, the response was a very suspicious, 'Who are you and why are you looking for it?' No further information was forthcoming. It was in the village of Pet in July 2004 that we met Anna Petrovna. She had recently moved to Pet from Gridino. She spoke of her relative, who had found the stones to build a house with a partition and a storage barn and its own cellar. 'He made a home with a partition inside, a storage barn. Under the storage barn he made a cellar, all by his own strength, and then they de-kulakized him. Dragged him off to Siberia. They threw his children out of the house.' She emphasized that despite the fact that the family was labelled 'kulak,' it had nothing. 'We had no beds, feather pillows, and blankets, not like we do today; instead, they slept in the clothes that they lived in, made out of rough homespun cloth. They lived very poorly then. And everything was stolen.' Anna Petrovna trips over the word *stolen* and changes it to *destroyed.* She chastises herself for believing in kulaks: 'Who were kulaks then? I can't believe it now; then I was stupid. What for? Throw people out of their homes, send them off to Siberia, there, de-kulakized.'[127] And she begins to articulate an impor-

14. Church in Pet, 2004 (photo by the author).

tant and reoccurring thread. 'To create this life, they dragged us to the collective farm by force.'

Anna Petrovna came out against the concept of kulak, the process of de-kulakization, the cruelty in the face of local poverty, the injustice, and exile to Siberia. She had revised her thinking, admitting that at one time she did believe that the people who were exiled were kulaks. But when we asked her about the Pitelino rebellion, she assured us that no relative of hers participated. We asked her if she remembered the rebellion. She said, 'Only through the stories. A woman came to us, and my mother said, "Oi, what's happening in the village? And with pitchforks, and sticks, and axes."' But 'our peasants, my grandfather, did not go, nor Papa. They were not at the uprising. They were afraid.' She is adamant about the futility of the rebellion, 'What can you do with sticks? Idiots.' She shakes her head and tells us that many people ended up 'there,' meaning in Siberia or exile, because of 'that rebellion.' She returns again, worried, to the theme of her family's participation: 'I remember, my parents, they did not go. They were not at the uprising. No one was there, none of my relatives. They all lived right next to me; my grandfather had four brothers. They all lived together, and no one went to the uprising, never, no one. They were obedient people. They were so obedient, they went nowhere. Never against the authorities. If they were told to be somewhere, they were there. If you are told to do something, you do it.' Then Anna Petrovna's manner of speaking changed. She began to almost sing in a rhythmic way, like a chant that helps one remember, as she listed what her family had contributed to the collective farm.[128] 'Even though all of the strips of land had been sown, and the peas, and sheep and winter crops, and spring crops, everything – all of it, all was handed over, and the horses, and our things, everything. They gave it to the collective farm. And then they went to work there, Grandpa, Mama, and Papa.'

Anna Petrovna is still guarded about who participated in the rebellion, and she still feels the need to underscore the fact that her relatives were good, obedient, and submissive. We continued talking to her about when the roofs of the village were no longer built from thatch but metal, when electricity came to the village, when mechanized farm equipment was more common. 'Some years after the war,' was the answer. She spoke of the war years when women did all of the farmwork by hand with scythes and continued to do so long after the war. We asked her if there had been hungry years after the war. She said, 'No, we had potatoes, and some people had radishes.' Then she suddenly returned to the collectivization of the district. 'In the thirties there was hunger, after they came through with the Red broom.' The 'Red broom' (*krasnaia metla*) was a way of referring to Bolshevik means of 'cleaning up' trouble, or in this case sweeping up 'everything' in the village. 'They went from household to household,' she told us. 'I remember. They ferreted everything out. Flour. They turned the woodpile over in our courtyard. I remember, everything we hid, they found, although we were hungry. I was five years old and I said to one of those men, "Uncle, please leave some for us or we will die without bread. Uncle, don't take everything from us, leave us some. We are dying." Still they took everything ,and whatever they found they put in a bag.' There is an eerie echo in the archival record of Anna Petrovna's words. The OGPU reported that in a Sapozhok village in February 1930 'the de-kulakization brigade confiscated all property, including dresses and boots. Ill-clad and shoeless children ran after the carts that were carrying away the goods, crying, "Uncle, give me back the boots. I am cold."'[129]

We asked Anna Petrovna if the collectivizers were local. She said, yes, that some of them were 'ours.' The only one she recalls, though, was 'an old, old woman, a hunchback.' For Anna Petrovna, who was only five years old at the time of the uprising, it is as if the enemy has adopted the frightening form of a local witch. In reality, a woman on her own with a hunchback could have been very likely marginalized and perhaps victimized in the village, and it would be logical if she had decided to throw her lot in with Soviet power. We asked Anna Petrovna if there had been good times in her life. She immediately replied that there were good times and bad times, but that life itself, 'Life was wonderful. You just have to know how to live it.' Anna Petrovna is not beaten. She finished talking to us with an impassioned argument with one of our team about the impossibility of reviving the farms without capital and technology.

In the summer of 2005, we returned to travel to the villages of Gridino and Veriaevo. The oldest woman in Gridino had lost her memory, and her daughter sent us to find Niura Marfina. She embeds her recollections of the events in another traumatic memory, Stalingrad 1943. We asked about the uprising and she said abruptly, 'They came to the school and killed a police officer. And then the rich ones … Well, rich; they had a mill. They shot those millers too.'[130] Suddenly, her mind shifts. 'And you know what happened? In 1943, in the war, in Stalingrad, they herded us there to a construction site. I was only nineteen. And we came there to work and build.' The memories are entangled because a young man from a neighbouring village happened to find himself in her work brigade. His name was Petukhov, from Veriaevo, and he wanted to talk. She admitted to him that his village was only a kilometre from hers. He asks her if she remembers. 'A little,' she answers, 'I was eight or nine. Our parents did not let us out of the house,' because the villagers had gathered with pitchforks and stakes. We asked Marfina if her parents or relatives participated in the uprising. Her denial extended to all of her fellow villagers as well. 'Our parents did not go anywhere. Only those from Veriaevo, ours, no, no, no. Ours, from Gridino, they did not go anywhere.'

Her mind jumps back to Stalingrad and to Petukhov, who had wanted to recall the uprising with her in 1943. She insisted that her village had not participated. 'We, I say, are not like that, I say. And my parents are not any kind of strikers, no way.' He wants to talk in particular about a family who had been exiled. Still, Marfina's memory skips around the topic. 'They were exiled,' she says. 'Maybe he was at that age. What more can I tell you? I can't.' We ask Marfina why there had been an uprising at all. And she repeated, anxiously, that it was not our people but 'those Veriaevo people.' When we asked why the villagers of Veriaevo had risen up, Marfina gave up on remembering. 'And that I don't know, my dear one. My granddaughter, dear one, I don't know. No, remember, I am eighty years old.'

From Gridino we went on to Veriaevo. We stopped to ask a group of women for directions and asked about the uprising. They advised us to see the chief administrator of the district, who would have something to say on the matter. The only one left who remembers, they tell us, is Tatiana Kozlova. In the village of Veriaevo, Tatiana Kozlova agrees to tell us her recollections of the uprising because 'I am ninety years old and I can tell you.' Her son helps her onto the front step to sit and talk to us and tells us that she is the 'oldest one' and it is 'time to die.' Kozlova's movements are slow, but her memory is sharp and she instantly carries us back to the days of the uprising. On the first day, collectivization began violently and abruptly. 'When the collective farms were formed, they found the kulaks and de-kulakized them. And horses, cows, they took them. They fenced them in. Whoever had a bigger home, they took everything for the collective farmers. They took everything.'

On the following morning, the men and women walked around the village, angry and armed with sticks. The collectivization brigade was still on site and words were exchanged. 'One peasant hit one with a stick. He

15. Church in Gridino, 2004 (photo by author).

16. Inside the church in Gridino, 2004 (photo by author).

kind of killed him. He never came back. They put him in prison.' She remembers the martyr wrapped in a sheepskin coat and taken away to a hero's burial. It is as if the days replay themselves vividly in her mind, and she returns to the day following the death. She slips into the present tense as armed men raced to the village to put down the unrest. 'Here, the next morning, it was a holiday, Sunday, I went to midday service. The police came from Pitelino. On horses, sleighs, everything was frozen. It was so cold. The sleighs are approaching, drawn by horses, the police, they are coming, coming.' She recalls that everyone was gathered in the most central location of the village – the church and the square beside it – the very grounds to which the church bells summoned villagers in times of crisis, to fight fires, to defend the village. 'They began to urge us: don't do this … But it was too late, everyone turned up with sticks, the women and the men … And ours killed a police officer … There happened to be this beam there, and they killed him. And then they were all fighting, mass confusion. They left, and then they gathered again. And the police left. We gathered to go to Gridino, to have an uprising there … and there was confusion again.' Kozlova confirms the archival testimony that villagers of Gridino were also very active alongside the people of Veriaevo. 'They came from Gridino here … Now, when we had that uprising, they came from Gridino. Our people gathered and went to Gridino. We were afraid. They came … to beat us.'

Kozlova remembers how order was restored. Armed men returned and selected the supposed ringleaders. 'And the next day, the police came back and began to pick people out; they took a lot of people away. Arrested them. Some were able to return and some vanished.' Kozlova is well aware that the uprising had set the tone for collectivization and the establishment of Soviet power in the region, and she remembers that there had once been an alternative in the villages. She comes back to a thought that echoed those of Anna Petrovna. 'The collective farm was created anyway after all this … They had no need for the collective farm, they wanted to push that power aside, they wanted their own.' She recalled how the old women had destroyed the holding pens created to temporarily house the collectivized livestock, just as Mozhaev had described it. In fact, it could have been one of the wooden boards thrown into the street from the pens themselves that was used to kill the police officer in Kozlova's version of events. When we told Tatiana Kozlova that the people in Gridino denied participating in the uprising, she laughed and said that her village even had a song (*chastushka*) about the event that proved they had participated because it ended with the line, 'We helped the people from Gridino, and broke our bare feet.'

When we parted, we thanked Kozlova, wished her good health and more time to tell her story. Her answer, 'No, I've had enough.'

Conclusion

Writing as many of Riazan's villagers back into history as possible has been a fundamental goal of this study. Thus Ivan Abramovich Guskov, the Sasovo peasant whose detailed letter on taxation and his village opens part 2, is as important, if not more important, a historical actor in these pages as Vladimir Il'ich Lenin or Grigorii Zinoviev. The physical spaces of the village, the buildings of local government, courts, gathering places, meadows, and forests are the constant backdrop. Relations among peasants, kinship networks, community expectations and demands, and the peasant experience of the state at various levels were an important component of daily life in the Riazan village.

These chapters have identified and explored specific issues that provided the context for peasant contact with the Bolshevik regime in the 1920s. *Face to the Village* has focused on a particular region and explored the assumptions and conclusions of the field in a regional context. The concentration on a single province meant that general questions could be formulated and engaged in a more specific and detailed way. The immense variety and complexity of life and politics within the villages of Riazan bring into sharper relief the complexity of the Soviet Union as a whole.

Part one of *Face to the Village* makes the regional focus even sharper by concentrating on specific local institutions (broadly defined) – the police, courts, and rural soviets. These institutions not only came into contact with peasants as parts of the state, they overlapped with the peasantry in a significant way. Most of the people who staffed these institutions, at the lowest levels, shared cultural background and convictions with the wider peasant community. The 'peasantness' of these representatives proved especially horrifying to the Centre, which had counted on these cadres to be the proponents of its civilizing mission. Those peasants who were politically active – members of their rural soviet, people's court judges, members of the cooperatives, police – especially if they approached their position honestly, were in the unenviable position of representing the village, on one hand, and being the civilizing missionaries of the Centre's dreams as well as the frontline of resource extraction, on the other. Thus the police, the courts, and the rural soviets became battlefields in the struggle for space, control, and identity between a significant part of the population and the regime in the 1920s. State, party, and society melded together, in part, because for the Bolshevik Centre there should be little difference among them. Ordering and systematizing the party/state meant ordering and systematizing society. For precisely this reason local officials, who in theory represented the state and often in practice were of the village, presented such an intractable challenge and prompted such anxiety at, and ultimately reaction from, the Centre.

Special attention has been paid here to the ambiguities of the position of those caught in the middle, between the regime and the peasantry, of those who actually staffed the state at the lowest levels. When the Bolsheviks turned to face the countryside in 1924 and 1925, they were shaken by what they found. In fact this initial attempt, undertaken in good faith to better understand the countryside, fuelled state insecurities and fears. Ironically, the Centre became ever suspicious of those who were supposed to be its representatives of both Soviet authority and the civilizing mission. The fact that local forest wardens, members of the rural soviets, police constables, and people's court judges had closer ties to the community and to peasant culture, rather than to the state and state culture, was an alarming discovery. Peasant culture was considered too backward, too stubborn, too impure, too traditional, far too irreverent for the modern state, and highly inappropriate for the modern citizen. Peasants and especially peasant state representatives had to be trained, professionalized, disciplined, and punished. So that they would behave appropriately, peasants had to be civilized and socialized. The degree to which the Centre was 'successful' in this mission is also an essential question for further study. Do elements of traditional peasant culture survive collectivization, and if so, in what forms? What was the outcome of the state's civilizing mission in the post-collectivization years? The oral histories gathered in Pitelino hint at the complicated impact of the collectivization, and recent de-collectivization, of the countryside.

Face to the Village challenges the traditional view of the countryside in the 1920s. Typically the rural soviets have been regarded as passive and ineffectual. I argue that they were important institutions for politically minded peasants in the villages of the 1920s. In some cases, villagers even maintained their own rural soviets, independently, with no assistance from the state. In connection with the reappraisal of the role of the rural soviet, the book also challenges the view that peasants in the 1920s were apolitical. There was a core of peasants who were profoundly interested in local politics, for good or ill, meaning as honest representatives or for personal gain. And here I include within the category of 'honest' those chairmen who distributed tax breaks to the village and forged documents for villagers labelled 'kulak' and targeted for persecution.

Another theme running through the book is the issue of resources. Part two focuses on conflict over resources – taxation and wood. The peasants themselves were resources, in the bodies they could contribute to the army, in the labour they could contribute to agricultural and industrial production, and in the crops they could produce. They were also competitors for resources. They competed with the state through the wood they stole, the horses they valued, and the samogon they distilled. The clash over horses captures much about the concerns and needs of the state and of the population. Peasants were concerned with holding onto this precious resource at all costs. The state was concerned with counting it in the event of military engagement. On the one hand, peasants saw the capture and murder of horse thieves as justifiable in light of the fact that formal policing and legal structures could not protect them. On the other hand, legal experts and the reports of the OGPU became increasingly concerned about samosud, or vigilante justice, as yet another graphic sign of village barbarism. Most shocking for these observers was the fact that local officials participated in samosud. Local courts, which were supposed to be the champions of the civilizing mission, were lenient on peasants involved in samosud and even more lenient on officials who participated. Like hooliganism, samosud was labelled in the second half of the 1920s, a '*bytovoi*' crime, a crime rooted in peasant tradition, peasant everyday life, peasant mentality, and peasant culture. As such a war against this culture could be justified.

The book supports a more nuanced periodization of the period of the New Economic Policy. The years 1921–4 were spent trying to address the damage caused by the policies of the civil war. Between 1924 and 1925, there was a window of potential negotiation between peasant and state; but the information gathered, in part because of a commitment to 'face the countryside,' and the growing tension over resources provide additional insight into how and why the NEP would unravel. The year

1926 marks the beginning of the end of the NEP and the end of negotiation. The periodization itself is not what is new; rather, it is the way in which the changes are illustrated in these pages that is novel. Inspired by methodologies borrowed from history, anthropology, and ethnography, and using the records that the Bolshevik regime and its population left of themselves, *Face to the Village* identified the central issues of the day and used them as windows onto the early Soviet countryside.

In order to better understand Russia in the 1920s, it helps to reach beyond the confines of the field of Soviet history and draw on a range of theoretical and comparative literatures. To better understand Bolshevik state-building, one has to place the process in the context of combined under-development and recognize the ways in which such an undertaking was informed by modernism, utopian dreams, and violence. The policies and activities of the Bolshevik Centre in the 1920s involve a combination of tactics and goals. These strategies and aims range from state-building techniques and demands in the early modern sense, to high-modernist commitments to progress and industrial development in the post-enlightenment sense. Such a situation leads the researcher to comparisons with the histories of developing nations of the twentieth century in general. Consistently, the Centre's need and drive to simplify a diverse, complex province with its diverse and complex villages – much less a diverse and complex empire – came face to face with local complications. The Centre ultimately chose to steamroll over local knowledge with all of the brute force of simplicity. Thus we see the Bolshevik Centre wrestling with the challenge of extracting resources from its peasantry in terms articulated by Charles Tilly and methods identified by Mikhail Bakhtin in their studies of early-modern Europe. At the same time, Bolsheviks were dreaming of a modern dairy and mechanized farming in the language and vision of Eisenstein's *General Line*. Despite the many differences among leading Bolsheviks, rank-and-file supporters, and Bolshevik intellectuals of the 1920s, they were united in their commitment to the conviction that Russia could move forward to socialism, progress, and development, and avoid the evils of capitalism.

This book demonstrates the brittleness of Soviet power in the 1920s – the Centre's sense of vulnerability and insecurity – on one hand, and the 'peasantness' of local power, on the other. From the onset, the Bolsheviks were trapped between a theoretical commitment to mass participation and their profound distrust of those masses, especially the 'vacillating' peasant population. The way in which the regime solicited, procured, collated, and processed information – especially material gathered and distributed by the security organs – seriously shaped and nurtured this self-perception and in turn influenced policy decisions.

The Soviet regime was obsessed with itself. It talked about itself constantly. It studied itself, monitored itself, praised and criticized itself incessantly in meeting after meeting, gathering after gathering, study after study, and in countless journals and newspapers.[1] The researcher can sift through this material, determine what is Bolshevik speak, understand and process it, and read the evidence that the Bolshevik regime and its citizens produced about themselves in another way. Reading in another way brings us closer to an understanding of what the inhabitants of the Soviet Union saw around them and how they absorbed, processed, and articulated their world.

Language has been an essential element in this study. The regime's struggle with the peasantry and with its perceived backwardness played itself out in a literal purification of local power structures and the purification of language itself. The new Republic needed a respectable Soviet language, cleansed of local dialects and colloquial expression.[2] Literate commentators on the 1920s – ethnographers, party observers, journalists – often saw the world around them through a Bolshevik lens. The linguistic influence of this perspective has to be decoded and sifted in order to extract the phenomena being observed from the confines of state categories and state constructs. Exploring self-consciously the use of language is essential in dealing with slippery concepts such as hooliganism and banditry. The very words became entangled with, and became part of, the rising fears and insecurities that fuelled vague and frequent applications of the charge of criminal behaviour, especially under the rubric of hooliganism, and the increasingly harsh punishment of offenders through the 1920s. Understanding the use of language both consciously and unconsciously by peasants and at each level of administrative structures is vital to better understanding events of the 1920s and beyond.

In their letters to *Krest'ianskaia gazeta,* peasants used the language of the regime to argue their cases. Ivan Abramovich Guskov illustrates the degree to which he was painfully aware of the variables that would complicate the Centre's appraisal of his situation. Thus, his village had no kulaks, no migrant workers, no sources of income outside of agriculture, and the local peasants raised cattle for much-needed fertilizer and nothing more. Villagers wrote and spoke in ways that challenged the state within the boundaries of the regime's own semantics. Sometimes they used the regime's promises, its official transcript, to challenge it. At other times, they pointed out in naked terms the consequences and implications of central policies and central categories. In 1925, a village correspondent, K.N. Koldashov, from the village of Ermalovo (*sic*)[3] in Skopin, pointed out that state policy was contradictory; peasants were encouraged to use modern technology to improve their farms and then the same peasants were punished for becoming kulaks. The correspondent asked *Krest'ianskaia gazeta* to clarify exactly what a kulak was, requesting that the answer be published in the paper so that peasants would all understand, because as far as he could perceive it, the concept amounted to something like a formula: 'If you work, you will be a kulak, and if you don't work and ruin your farm then you will be considered a bedniak.'[4]

The anatomy of a peasant rebellion against collectivization that concludes this study ties the book together in a number of ways. The study of the Pitelino rebellion involved an even more focused spatial approach, this time on a single district and the response of villagers there to collectivization. The spaces of conflict, the buildings of the rural soviet, the newly declared collective farms, and the villages themselves are essential to grasping the Pitelino rebellion. The final chapter continues the pattern, established in the earlier chapters, of writing as many individuals into the narrative and bringing the reader as close to the riotous grounds of the district as possible. Peasant hopes for any serious negotiation on acceptable terms were shattered by the sudden and violent nature of collectivization. Many local officials in 1929 were still 'of the village,' and they did their best to protect their constituency and to soften the blow of collectivization as far as they could. Thus, the theme of the role, nature, and place of local officialdom is laid bare in the final chapter. The oral testimonies of the present-day survivors of the uprising illustrate how the events have been remembered in different ways. We are privileged to hear the voices of the villagers themselves talk about their past and their present. Interestingly, most of the interviewees are still cautious about admitting participation in the unrest of 1930, even when they can readily admit that they do not believe in 'kulaks' or that the present-day regime has abandoned them. Only Tatiana Kozlova, liberated by her ninety years, can tell the whole story without fear.

The Centre had a dream of a modern, civilized Russia, and was in the process of building and staffing a state that was to be harnessed to the fulfilment of the dream. The country was profoundly short of accessible resources outside of its recalcitrant, opinionated peasantry, with which the regime constantly clashed anyway over the remaining limited resources, such as horses, grain, and wood, and over definitions of acceptable behaviour. Politically minded peasants were rightfully wary of the Bolshevik regime in the 1920s, but they were also willing to watch, wait, and negotiate with it, if possible. But watching, waiting, and negotiating takes time. Smoking a little with *vlast'* and quarrelling a little with *vlast'* can be long and drawn out. Those who walked the halls of power in Moscow and those who supported state and party hierarchies decided they did not have this kind of time.

Appendix

TABLE 1 Riazan crops as percentage of sown area, 1929

Crop	%
Rye	44.7
Oats	19.4
Potatoes	13.8
Millet	9.3
Buckwheat	3.2
Legumes	2.2
Hemp	1.7
Flax	1.0
Vegetables	1.0
Tobacco	0.2
Wheat	0.1
Sugar beets	0.1
Misc. grasses and roots	3.3

Source: *Statisticheskii 1927–28–29*, 244–7

TABLE 2 Riazan diet, February 1924 – average use per peasant in lbs per day

		Lbs per person per day
Bread products		
	Bread baked with rye	1.817
	Other flour products	0.188
Vegetables		
	Potatoes	2.604
	Cabbage, preserved and fresh	0.342
	Salted cucumbers	0.024
	Onions and garlic	0.005
	Other root vegetables	0.030
Other products		
	Butter	0.022
	Sugar	0.007
	Apples	0.002
	Dried mushrooms	0.001
Meat and fish		
	Pork and mutton	0.046
	Other kinds of meat	0.035
	Herring	0.001
	Salted fish	0.001
	Fresh fish	
Other animal products		0.002
	Tallow (*salo*)	0.003
	Milk	0.482
	Farmer's cheese (*tvorog*)	0.006
	Sour cream	0.002
Other		
	Salt	0.049
	Tea and coffee	0.002

Source: Adapted from *Statisticheskii ezhegodnik Riazanskoi gubernii za 1923–1924 gg.*, 92–3.

TABLE 3 A communal budget, 1926–7

	Rubles
Wages for commune representatives	5,377
Miscellaneous expenses of the commune representatives	2,644
Support of the village postal service	23,725
Wages for the members of the rural soviet	10,388
Miscellaneous expenses of the rural soviet	9,179
School needs	2,282
Political enlightenment	740
Support for the census commission	106
Repair of bridges and road construction	3,616
Fire protection	4,744
Maintenance of taxpayers lists	248
Land matters	40,051

Source: Rezunov, *Sel'skie sovety i zemel'nye obshchestva*, 16

TABLE 4 Tax collection in Riazan for 12 October 1928 (rubles)

Uezd	Total assessed per raion	Tax (*nalog*) 28–9	% collected	Arrears collected	Other amounts collected	Fines collected	Totals collected by uezd
Zaraisk	489,568	195,323	40.0	894	348	98	196,663
Kasimov	244,721	98,693	35.0	859	–	–	99,552
Riazhsk	748,056	258,109	34.5	2,904	–	–	261,013
Riazan	935,497	279,755	29.9	1,655	680	–	282,090
Sasovo	1,053,704	312,596	29.6	1,350	743	–	314,689
Skopin	731,850	278,396	38.0	600	924	–	279,920
Spassk	576,042	168,429	29.2	2,030	629	–	171,082
Total	4,809,438	1,591,301	33.1	10,291	3,313	98	1,605,009

Source: GARO, f. R-4, op. 1, d. 106, l. 8. Note the mixing of uezd and raion, reflecting the period of administrative-territorial transition.

TABLE 5 Household income to percentage of tax paid, 1928–9 (%)

Households according to income	No. of households	Tax paid in 1927–8 (%)	Tax paid in 1928–9 (%)
Up to 250 rubles	55.8	22.5	13.6
251–400 rubles	28.3	31.3	26.4
401–700 rubles	13.4	31.5	37.2
More than 700 rubles	2.5	14.7	22.8

Source: Mar'iankhin, *Ocherki istorii nalogov s naseleniia v SSSR*, 129.

TABLE 6 Russian dependence on wood in comparative context, 1916

	Household heating (%)	Industry (%)	Transport (%)
European Russia	48.0	28.0	24.0
Germany	10.5	73.0	16.5
England	7.0	79.0	14.0
United States	7.0	73.0	20.0

TABLE 7 Causes of arson

Causes		Number of cases
Personal arguments		51
Arguments over land and property		20
Hooliganism		19
To cover up another crime		19
	Murder	6
	Theft or robbery	10
	Financial wrongdoings in the cooperative	3
To receive insurance		12
Jealousy		21
	Refusal to marry (woman to a man)	5
	Refusal to marry (man to woman)	6
	Women burning the property of other women they believe to be involved in a sexual relationship with their husbands	10
Burning of a mill to end competition		4
Burning of the village soviet		6
For a refusal to give samogon or money for drinking		4
For appearing as a witness in court		4
For a refusal to give bread or a place to sleep		5
Surrounding samogon production		2
Miscellaneous (one case for refusing entry to a spectacle without a ticket)		8

Source: 'Doklad o sudebnoi praktike po prestuppleniam, predusmotrennym st. 175 UK, po dannym UKK Verkhovnogo Suda za 10 mesiantsev 1927,' *Sudebnaia Praktika* no. 1 (15 Jan. 1928): 9–10.

Glossary

adminotdel (administrativnyi otdel): Security department
aktiv: Peasant activist
baba (pl. *baby*): Derogatory term for a (peasant) woman
batrak: Landless, agricultural labourer
bedniak: Poor peasant
chastushka (pl. *chastushki*): Improvised popular songs
Cheka (*Chrezvychainaia komissiia po bor'be s kontrrevoliutsiei i sabotazhem*). Extraordinary Commission to Combat Counterrevolution and Sabotage 1917–22, the first incarnation of the Soviet secret police under Feliks Dzerzhinskii
chekist (pl. *chekisty*): Agent of the Cheka
de-kulakization: Expropriation of the kulaks
desiatina: One hectare
dvor: Peasant household
edoka: Literally 'eater,' a mouth to feed in the peasant household
finagent: Financial agent, tax inspector
Gosstrakh: State Insurance Agency
GPU (*Gosudarstvennoe politicheskoe upravlenie*): State Political Administration, 1922–3
green serpent (*zelenoe zmeia*): Colloquial term for samogon
guberniia: Province
Gubplan: Provincial Planning Commission
gubsud: Provincial Court
ispolkom (*ispolnitel'nyi politicheskii komitet*): Executive committee of a soviet
izba: Peasant hut
izbirkom (*izbiratel'naia komissiia*): Electoral commission

khutor: Farm separated from the traditional village landholding system
kolkhoz: Collective farm
Komsomol (*Kommunisticheskii soiuz molodezhi*): Union of Communist Youth
Komsomolets: Male member of the Union of Communist Youth
Komsomolka: Female member of the Union of Communist Youth
kulak: Derogatory term for a wealthy peasant
lapti: Bast shoes
militsioner: Police constable
militsiia: Civil police force
muzhik: Derogatory term for a male peasant
Narkomfin: People's Commissariat of Finance
Narkomvoenmor: People's Commissariat of Military and Naval Affairs
Narkomzem: People's Commissariat of Agriculture
narsled: People's investigator
narzasedatel': People's assessor
narsud: People's court
NKVD (*Narodnyi komissariat vnutrennykh del*): People's Commissariat of Internal Affairs
oblast': Administrative-territorial part of an okrug; Riazan became an oblast within Moscow Okrug in 1930
OGPU (*Ob"edinennoe gosudarstvennoe politicheskoe upravlenie*): United State Political Administration; state security organ, 1923–34
okrug: Large administrative-territorial unit created in 1930
Old Believers: Members of the sect who worshipped according to pre-schism religious belief
otkhodnik: Peasant working for wages outside of the village
otkhodnichestvo: Outmigration for work, usually temporary or seasonal
pud: 16.38 kg
Rabkrin / NK RKI (*Narodnyi komissariat raboche-krest'ianskoi inspektsii*): People's Commissariat of Worker-Peasant Inspection
raion: Geographical division smaller than an uezd and larger than a *volost'*, which were introduced in June 1930 when Riazan became an okrug
RAIZO (*Raionnyi zemel'nyi otdel*): District land department
RAO (*Raionnyi administrativnyi otdel*): Police department
rural soviet / sel'sovet (*sel'skii sovet*): Rural council, the lowest level of the state structure
samogon: Moonshine, home-distilled alcohol
samooblozhenie: Self-taxation

scissors crisis (1923): The prices paid for grain were low and the prices demanded for manufactured goods were high.
selispol (*sel'skii ispolnitel'*): Village deputy
sel'kor (*sel'skii korespondent*): Village correspondent
seredniak: Middle peasant
skhod: Village assembly
SNK (*Sovet narodnykh komissarov / Sovnarkom*): Council of People's Commissars – coordinating body of the commissariats
sobranie: Meeting
soviet (*sovet*): Elected council with administrative functions
starosta: Peasant elder
svoi: Ours
uezd: Geographic area in size between volost and guberniia
uezdispolkom: Executive committee for the uezd level
usad'ba: Land around a peasant household
valenki: Felt boots
verst: Measure of distance approximately 1 km
VIK (*Volostnyi ispolnitel'nyi komitet*): District executive committee / volost-level soviet
vlast': Power
volmilitsiia: District police
volost': Smallest geographic district above the village level – translated as 'district'
VTsIK (*Vsesouiznyi tsentral'nyi ispolnitel'nyi komitet*): All-Union Central Executive Committee – highest level of the state administration
war scare (1927): A fear that the Soviet Union would face imminent war
zaem: State bond
zemel'noe obshchestvo: Commune
zhenotdel: Women's department (of the party)

Notes

Introduction

1 This call to 'face the countryside' first appeared on 30 July 1924 in articles published simultaneously in *Pravda* and *Leningradskaia pravda*. See Carr, *Socialism in One Country 1924–26*, 1:195. Zinoviev's exact words were, 'The time has come to compel the entire range of our organizations to turn their face to the countryside' (*Pora, pora zastavit riad nashikh organizatsiei bol'she poverniutsia litsom k derevne*). See G. Zinoviev, 'Neurozhai i nashi zadachi,' *Pravda*, 30 July 1924. Grigory Zinoviev (1883–1936) was an 'old Bolshevik.' He had chosen the Bolshevik side when the Russian Social Democratic Workers Party (RSDRP) split at its second congress in 1903 into Bolsheviks and Mensheviks. He was close to Lenin and worked tirelessly for the cause, but he disagreed with Lenin over the timing of the October Revolution, issuing a handwritten declaration against it, along with Lev Kamenev. He was executed in August 1936 for his supposed role in the murder of Sergei Kirov. He was rehabilitated in 1988.

2 It is doubtful that Lenin had changed his mind about the peasantry from his 1919 view. 'The town cannot be equal to the country. The country cannot be equal to the town under the historical conditions of this epoch. The town inevitably *leads* the country. The country inevitably *follows the town*' (italics in original). Lenin, 'The Constituent Assembly Elections and the Dictatorship of the Proletariat,' in *Collected Works*, 30:257. Lenin goes on to argue that the peasantry, being petty-bourgeois vacillators (30:268–9), needed to be won over 'if possible' and at the very least 'neutralized' (30:263).

3 Zinoviev, 'Neurozhai,' *Pravda*, 30 July 1924.

4 L. Artimenkov, 'O revoliutsionnoi zakonnosti v derevne,' *Ezhenedel'nik sovetskoi iustitsii* (hereafter *ESIu*) 10 (1925): 241. Artimenkov's major complaint

was that rural soviets and district executive committees constantly formulated and passed illegal resolutions (242).

5 B. Shavrov, 'Volostnaia militsiia,' *Administrativnyi vestnik* 4 (Apr. 1925): 36.

6 Stalin himself disliked the film. He criticized the fact that the lead actress was 'too peasant' and that the field work was still being done by hand. Rossiiskii gosudarstvennyi arkhiv sotsial'no-politicheskoi istorii (RGASPI), f. 558, op. 11, d. 828, l. 39.

7 Raleigh, *Provincial Landscapes.* Raleigh argues that regional histories allow for 'decentering standard narratives of the Soviet historical experience' (4). And he too emphasizes that talk about the local does not mean leaving out the Centre. He emphasizes the ways in which 'local studies actually help create and recreate the center, because the relationship between center and periphery is symbiotic and dialectical' (6). All too often, those who engage in regional studies are repeatedly asked to justify their choice by proving that their focus is broadly representative or 'typical' in some way. Raleigh addresses this issue head on. He writes that the contributors to *Provincial Landscapes* make a conscious attempt to 'avoid the misguided efforts to justify our labors by stressing the "typicality" of the localities we have chosen to investigate' (ibid.).

8 Riazanskaia okruzhnaia organizatsionnaia komissiia, *Materialy k organizatsii Riazanskogo okruga,* 12.

9 See, for example, Heinzen, *Inventing a Soviet Countryside*; Lewin, *Russian Peasants and Soviet Power*; and Rees, *State Control in Soviet Russia.*

10 The arguments I make about scarcity and dearth are not those of statisticians interested in absolute and comparative data about dearth. Instead, I am interested in how a shortage of resources determined and shaped behaviors in the countryside.

11 See, for example, Cohen, *Bukharin and the Bolshevik Revolution,* Pipes, *Russian Revolution*; Rabinowitch, *Bolsheviks Come to Power*; Rabinowitch, *Prelude to Revolution*; Rigby, *Lenin's Government*; Schapiro, *Communist Party of the Soviet Union*; Schapiro, *Political Elites in the USSR*; Tucker, *Stalin as a Revolutionary*; Tucker, *Stalin in Power,* to name but a few.

12 See for example, Fainsod, *Smolensk under Soviet Rule,* 141; Haimson, 'Problem of Social Identities,' 13–19; Lewin, *Russian Peasants and Soviet Power,* 36; and Fitzpatrick, *Stalin's Peasants,* 28, where she writes, 'Most peasants had lost interest in politics.' Work by Josh Sanborn and Scott Seregny challenge the view that peasants were isolationist: Sanborn, 'Mobilization of 1914'; Seregny, 'Zemstvos, Peasants, and Citizenship.'

13 Gaudin, *Ruling Peasants,* 5. Peasants 'came into contact with state agents, laws, and institutions to a degree they had never before experienced. As the

government established new offices, new courts, and new laws for the countryside, villagers made immediate and massive use of them. They flooded local authorities with complaints, appeals, and petitions against their neighbors, their communes, and their elders.'

14 In his work on the Viatka countryside, *Russia's Peasants,* Retish also finds that peasants worked with Soviet institutions to further their own specific agendas. As he puts it, 'In order to help resolve problems with their communes, neighbors, and families, and to better their situation, peasants invited the Bolshevik state into their homes' (162). He concludes that peasants changed the early Bolshevik state as much as it changed them and that villagers did not want be on their own in some mythical autonomous village, but rather they engaged with the new state, accommodated, negotiated, and altered it (esp. 267–8).

15 Burbank, *Russian Peasants Go to Court*; Gaudin, *Ruling Peasants*; and Retish, *Russia's Peasants.*

16 There is an extensive literature on space and place. For an overview, see Cresswell, *Place.* See also Lefebvre, *The Production of Space*; and Rodman, 'Empowering Place.'

17 See 'Note on Administrative Changes in Riazan' at the end of chap. 1.

18 Penner, for example, opted in her study of the Don to use the word *farmer* rather than peasant to avoid the derogatory connotation of the word. 'Pride, Power and Pitchforks,' xiii.

19 See Shanin, *Awkward Class*; Shanin, *Defining Peasants*; and Shanin, *Peasants and Peasant Societies.*

20 Shanin, *Peasants and Peasant Societies,* 3–8; and *Defining Peasants,* esp. chap. 4.

21 For more on the debate between citzen and subject, see Glebov, 'Interview with Peter Sahlins,' 43–4. The interview's subtitle, 'Subjecthood That Happens to Be Called Citizenship,' is particularly evocative here (39). See also Yanni Kotsonis, '"No Place to Go"'; and Kotsonis, '"Face-to-Face."'

22 Frierson, *All Russia Is Burning,* 10–11.

23 See Mozhaev, *Muzhiki i baby,* 67–71, for a literary portrayal of such an occurrence. Retish also challenges the overly simplified division of state and peasant into aggressor and victim in *Russia's Peasants,* 10–11.

24 I try to avoid attempts at judging or categorizing the village, either as an idyllic 'world we have lost' (Laslett, *World We Have Lost*), or as a 'Hobbesian world of unconstrained envy, rebuke, and retribution in which peasants acted against their fellows, often for the most inglorious reasons' (Frierson, *All Russia Is Burning,* 8). Both Frierson and Gaudin emphasize the highly conflictual nature of the Russian village. While I do not agree necessarily with a Hobbesian label, I do think their works are important,

nuanced correctives to the more homogenized and peaceful portrait of village life.

25 Hoffmann, *Peasant Metropolis.*

26 For an account of their fate, see Viola, *Unknown Gulag.*

27 See the articles and commentaries in *Kritika: Explorations in Russian and Eurasian History* 1, no. 1 (Winter 2000). As Michael David-Fox notes in his commentary, 'Any black-and-white dichotomy between resistance and complicity, and historical formulas predicated upon it, effectively vanishes,' 161.

28 Kotsonis, '"No Place to Go,"' 561–2.

29 A long-standing and heated debate on 'backwardness' is once again raging. See the debate between Gorshkov and Martin, 'Debating "'Backwardness,"' based on a lengthy online debate involving numerous historians of Russia and the Soviet Union. As Gorshkov notes, the 'Bolsheviks characterized themselves as modernizers' (4) and *chose* to portray the countryside and the Russian past as backward. It is the implications of this choice/belief on the part of the Bolsheviks that I am concerned with and not any conviction or desire to call the Soviet countryside backward or portray it objectively as such. In fact, my goal is quite the opposite, to show that the Russian village was complex and functioned on its own terms through the 1920s with an awareness of central power and a desire to work with it until state policies turned against the peasantry so decisively. My study complements the work of Kotsonis, *Making Peasants Backward.* Kotsonis argues that in the diverse work of the pre-Revolutionary cooperative movement, very different groups were united by a firm belief in peasant 'backwardness.' He writes, 'These attitudes were structured by a circular reasoning that began and ended with "backwardness," for backwardness brought forth the cooperator, backwardness explained why peasants seemed unable to assimilate what they were told, and backwardness necessitated the permanent supervision and management of extraneous authorities' (135). For more on the connection between the Bolsheviks and modernity, see David L. Hoffmann, 'European Modernity and Soviet Socialism,' in Hoffmann and Kotsonis, *Russian Modernity,* 245–60. For more on the Bolshevik obsession to eliminate backwardness, see David-Fox, 'What Is Cultural Revolution?'; and Keller, 'Islam in Soviet Central Asia, 1917–1930.'

30 For more on utopianism in the Soviet context, see Stites, *Revolutionary Dreams.*

31 Scott, 'Afterforeword,' 400. Critics of Scott emphasize that the state *itself* is illegible and accuse Scott of oversimplifying and reifying the concept. See the collection put together by Das and Poole, eds., *Anthropology in the Margins of the State*; and Sivaramakrishnan, 'Introduction,' 325.

32 Holquist, 'State Violence.'
33 Ibid., 30.
34 Weiner, 'Nature, Nurture, and Memory in Socialist Utopia,' 1114.
35 See the Riutin platform, document 3, in Getty and Naumov, *Road to Terror*, 57.
36 Viola, *Peasant Rebels under Stalin*, 3.
37 See, Mallon, 'Promise and Dilemma,' 1512.
38 Scott, *Seeing like a State*, 1.
39 Tilly, 'Reflections,' 71.
40 See Kotsonis, '"Face-to-Face"'; and Kotsonis, '"No Place to Go."'
41 See the discussions of the amalgamation of districts (*ukreplenie*) in 1924 and the 'rationalization' of districts into raions (*raionorovanie*) at the end of the 1920s, covered in chapter 1. See also Vandergeest, 'Real Villages.' Max Weber's definition of the modern state also emphasizes the notion of territory. A state needs to be able to define the territory over which it has jurisdiction. See Weber, *Theory of Social and Economic Organization*, 156. On Stalinism as a civilization, see Kotkin, *Magnetic Mountain.*
42 Weber, *Theory of Social and Economic Organization*, 156. Thinkers who wrestle with defining *state* often link Weber's ideas on a monopoly over the use of force to the notion of military force. See, for example, Mann, 'Autonomous Power of the State,' 112; or Rogan, *Frontiers of the State in the Late Ottoman Empire*, 2–5. My thanks to Amanda Sala for drawing my attention to the latter. See also Buck-Morss, *Dreamworld and Catastrophe*, 4–5. And Holquist's opening quotations and subsequent contextualization in 'State Violence as Technique,' 19–20.
43 See Frank, *Crime, Cultural Conflict and Justice*; and Frank, 'Confronting the Domestic Other.' See also Viola, *Peasant Rebels under Stalin*, esp. chap. 1. Frank and Viola draw the parallels between the Tsarist and Soviet regimes, respectively, and colonialism. This approach leads the researcher into a rich comparative literature and down a path, already forged by Shanin, toward seeing Russia as sharing the problems of other developing nations. See Shanin, *Russia as a Developing Society*.
44 Scott, *Seeing like a State*, 82. Michael David-Fox also supports this line of argument in the Soviet context in 'What Is Cultural Revolution?' 183. Douglas Northrop writes that to consider the notion of internal colonization is 'a potential productive approach but risks blurring the distinctions between modernizing states and colonial empires.' See *Veiled Empire*, 23n28. I would argue that the blurred distinction is precisely what is productive.
45 See document 19, in Viola et al., *War against the Peasantry*, 99.
46 George Yaney and Stephen Frank explore the nature of the 'civilizing

mission' in the Tsarist context. See Frank, 'Confronting the Domestic Other,' 74–107, for an excellent look at the high-modernist dreams of pre-Revolutionary thinkers and attempts to 'colonize the countryside,' esp. 76; and *Crime, Cultural Conflict and Justice.* For Yaney's contributions, see *Systematization of Russian Government*; and esp. *Urge to Mobilize.* For a detailed study of how the civilizing mission developed through the 1930s and the forms it took, see Hoffmann, *Stalinist Values*; and Gorham, 'Mastering the Perverse,' 139. Naiman explores similar themes in 'Crime, Utopia, and Repressive Complements.' 'In their self-protective operations, utopian texts [and states] frequently seek to attack those categories of human interaction that bind them to reality and thwart the individual's (or society's) attempts at isolation from temporal, spatial, or bodily contamination: categories as broad as language, history, disease, sexuality and crime' (512). For a study of the state use of coercion in resource extraction and internal colonization, see Gouldner, 'Stalinism.' What is missing from Gouldner – and emphasized in this work – is the idea of the civilizing mission.

47 Dziga Vertov writes of the electric man in 'We: Variant of a Manifesto,' in *Kino-Eye*, 8. And Trotsky builds palaces on ocean floors in *Literature and Revolution*, 254. 'Man, who will learn how to move rivers and mountains, how to build peoples' palaces on the peaks of Mont Blanc and at the bottom of the Atlantic.'

48 'Samooblozhenie sel'skogo naseleniia,' *Krest'ianskii iurist* 2 (31 Jan. 1928): 3.

49 Slezkine, 'Imperialism as the Highest Stage of Socialism,' 230.

50 In his study of western Siberia, 'Modernity and Backwardness,' Shearer argues that 'the Soviet government acted toward Siberia in ways analogous to the Western European colonial experience' (198). Viola develops the idea that collectivization was a civil war – a kind of colonization, a war on peasant culture and peasant traditions. In *Peasant Rebels under Stalin*, she traces Bolshevik attitudes toward peasants, which in turn enabled officials at the Centre and cadres in the field to dehumanize their 'enemy' and wage war against them; see esp. 29–44. See also her introductions to the documents in *The War against the Peasantry*.

51 Scott, *Seeing like a State*, 77.

52 Fenomenov, *Sovremennaia derevnia*, 2:38.

53 Buck-Morss, *Dreamworld and Catastrophe*, 60 and 67. My thinking about time was originally inspired by an informal paper given by Eric Naiman at the joint graduate student conference of Stanford and Berkeley in 1993.

54 Ibid., 58.

55 For a graphic visual presentation of the concept, see the film *Old and New* (*Staroe i novoe*). Eisenstein intercuts the tractor breaking down the fences

of individual peasants with intertitles that say 'Forward,' 'Forward.' For the continued plague of muddy roads, read the 'diary' of Ignat Danilovich Frolov, in Lahusen, Garros, and Korenevskaya, *Intimacy and Terror*, 11–65.

56 Platonov, *Chevengur*, 45.

57 Gosudarstvennyi Arkhiv Riazanskoi Oblasti (GARO), f. R-2541, op. 1, d. 789, ll. 5–7 ob.

58 Bol'shakov, *Sovetskaia derevnia 1917–1924*, 88.

59 Fenomenov, *Sovremennaia derevnia*, 2:95.

60 Bol'shakov, *Derevnia posle oktiabria*, 5.

61 In 2006, the editors of *Ab Imperio* devoted the fourth volume of the journal to concepts of subjecthood, citizenship, state, and nation. They frame the discussion as that of 'the most de-personified form of societal organization, the state, and its perception in individual experience' (17). In the discussions, the '"state" emerges as a sum of total projections by members of the polity, as a result of interactions between different societal groups, and as a hostage of the "human factor" of those who speak on its behalf' (18). Boundaries between 'state' and 'society' make it 'impossible to unambiguously discriminate between societal and civic loyalties' (19).

62 That is not to say that they are not important or worthy of study. Sumpf's interesting article 'Confronting the Countryside,' on reading huts finds that the process largely 'took shape mainly "on paper" (e.g. in various administrative reports) and possibly in the fantasies of some local "visionaries"' (477). He concludes that 'rural political education was genuinely able to take hold of the village only when some local initiative, occasionally individual but more often stemming from the whole village collective, invested this work with locally relevant peasant meaning, centred on satisfying everyday needs and especially on enabling some sort of compromise with the new Soviet authorities' (498). His conclusion complements my own findings.

63 Pearson, *Hooligan*, 233.

64 For the origins of this formulation, see Geertz, *Interpretation of Cultures*; Geertz, *Local Knowledge*; Rittersporn, *Stalinist Simplifications*; Scott, *Moral Economy*; and Scott, *Seeing like a State*.

65 See Brown's discussion of the 'trope of backwardness' and the *kresy* in *Biography of No Place*, 5–9. To repeat, I do not accept the label of 'backwardness'; rather, like Brown, I find the 'trope' to be a means used at the time to dismiss or simplify difference, complication, and diversity.

66 Platonov, *Chevengur*, 140.

67 Seminar in agrarian studies, 1997.

68 In particular, Davis, *Return of Martin Guerre*; Ginsburg, *The Cheese and the Worms*; and Ladurie, *Montaillou*.

69 Of course there are innumerable aspects of village life that could not be looked at here, such as details of land-holding, marriage, the family, etc. Many of them have been dealt with elsewhere. For a start, see Atkinson, *End of the Russian Land Commune;* Engel, *Between the Fields and the City*; and Worobec, *Peasant Russia.*
70 Geertz, *Interpretation of Cultures*, 9–10.
71 Rogers, 'Historical Anthropology Meets Soviet History,' 649.
72 Engelstein, 'Combined Underdevelopment,' 343n21. Engelstein defines Trotsky's articulation of combined development as a 'term to describe how "backward" countries might skip over stages traversed by advanced nations in order to arrive at the socialist goal without enduring the requisite intervening development. It implies the coexistence of elements associated with separate time periods in the Western sequence.'
73 Ibid., 343.
74 For a similar discussion of sources, see Brown, *Biography of No Place*, 13–17.
75 Tilly, 'Reflections on the History of European State-Making,' 8.
76 Glebov, 'Interview with Peter Sahlins,' 43–4.
77 A word about references to the materials of the Riazan archives that occur throughout this book is in order. I had phenomenal access to materials in Riazan for which I am eternally grateful. When I was working in the archives, the party and state archives were officially united into a single State Archive of Riazan Oblast (GARO), although each former archive retained its own reading room, building, and staff. The two are to be physically united in one building by 2010. Thus it is not possible for the reader to distinguish party documents from state documents merely from the reference, as all appear as GARO references. Moreover, I had such complete access to the state documents that I was able to see the raw materials from which party documents and reports were created. This fact became very clear when working in the former party archive. Essentially, I have utilized the raw materials more than the party reports, lectures, and summaries based upon them.
78 For a detailed look at letters as a source, see Lenoe, 'Letter-Writing and the State.' Lenoe argues that the letters best serve as 'direct windows on the everyday functioning of Soviet society, the instruments of power, and the ways in which agents of the Soviet state acted to shape the public identity of their subjects' (140).
79 See the introduction by Kriukova, *Krest'ianskie istorii*, 4–8, for a detailed description of the *Krest'ianskaia gazeta* archive and it strengths.
80 See the discussion in Park and Brandenberger, 'Imagined Community?' 554–9. See also Holquist, 'Information Is the Alpha and Omega of Our Work.'

81 Park and Brandenberger, 'Imagined Community?' 554.
82 Ibid., 555–6.
83 Sarah Davies, *Popular Opinion in Stalin's Russia.* See also Viola's discussion of *svodki* and 'Popular Resistance in the Stalinist 1930s,' 55–8. Viola and Davies focus more on the svodki of the 1930s, which, I would argue, have a much deeper and consistent ideological imprint than those of the 1920s, especially the svodki written up to 1926.
84 See Bol'shakov, *Kraevedcheskoe izuchenie derevni,* 79–82. There was an intense rivalry between the two and by 1930, Bol'shakov was viciously attacking Fenomenov in his work. One wonders if it is an accident that the kulak family in Fenomenov's village was given the surname Bol'shakov. See, for example, Fenomenov, *Sovremennaia derevnia,* 1:117.
85 Bol'shakov, *Sovetskaia derevnia (1917–1924),* 12.
86 GARO, f. R-5, op. 1, d. 305, l. 12.

1. The Setting

1 See Fitzpatrick, 'Civil War,' 57–76. Holquist explores ideas about surveillance and the modern state. See 'Information Is the Alpha and Omega of Our Work.'
2 Davies, *The Development of the Soviet Budgetary System,* 85–6.
3 A.V. Lunacharskii, 'Deviataia godovshchina Oktiabr'skoi revoliutsii,' *Sovetskoe stroitel'stvo,* nos 3–4 (Oct.–Nov. 1926): 14.
4 For an excellent discussion of ideas of purity and the rhetoric of the debates, see Naiman, *Sex in Public,* esp. 266–7. See also Gorham, 'Mastering the Perverse,' esp. 139.
5 See document 10 in Viola et al., *War against the Peasantry,* 55–6. For an excellent and detailed discussion of the entire process, see Viola's introduction to the volume.
6 A growing body of literature provides a complex understanding of the politics of collectivization as they took shape in Moscow through the 1920s. See, for example, the five-volume series by Danilov, Manning, and Viola, *Tragediia Sovetskoi derevni,* and the English edition prepared by Viola et al.
7 Riazanskaia gubernskaia planovaia komissiia, *Materialy k planu narodnogo khoziaistva Riazanskoi gubernii,* 4:6. I specify the year in the text because borders and internal boundaries were constantly shifting through time. See the note on administrative changes at the end of this chapter.
8 *Iz istorii kollektivizatsii sel'skogo khoziaistva Riazanskoi oblasti,* 5.
9 Popov et al., *Dva veka Riazanskoi istorii,* 135.
10 Russian measures are left for accuracy: 1 desiatina = roughly 1 hectare; 1

pud = roughly 16 kg. The impact and implications of this forest clearance is seen in chap. 4.

11 Stepanova, 'Sel'skoe khoziaistvo i derevnia v XIX veke,' 518–19.

12 For the most detailed, exhaustive, and thoughtful collection of statistical material that actually allows for comparison province by province, see Wheatcroft, 'Grain Production and Utilisation in Russia and the USSR before Collectivization.' For the comparison on horses, see 3:239.

13 Ibid.

14 Popov et al., *Dva veka Riazanskoi istorii,* 145.

15 *Uchenye zapiski,* 18:40.

16 Popov et al., *Dva veka Riazanskoi istorii,* 66.

17 Ibid., 70.

18 *Uchenye zapiski,* 18:40.

19 Peasants would venture from their native villages to supplement their income with temporary work in factories or other enterprises. For more on the concept of *otkhodnichestvo,* see Johnson, *Peasant and Proletarian.*

20 Popov et al., *Dva veka Riazanskoi istorii,* 70–7.

21 Tul'tseva, 'Obshchina i agrarnaia obriadnost' Riazanskikh krest'ian na rubezhe XIX–XX vv,' 46.

22 Popov et al., *Dva veka Riazanskoi istorii,* 164.

23 Ibid., 164–72.

24 Ibid., 170. See the collection edited by Margulis, Lebedeva, and Tumarkina, *Krest'ianskoe dvizhenie.*

25 Margulis, Lebedeva, and Tumarkina, *Krest'ianskoe dvizhenie,* 6.

26 Ibid., 10–12.

27 Ibid., 11.

28 Ibid., 11–18.

29 See Popov et al., *Dva veka Riazanskoi istorii,* 185; and Fulin, 'Fevral'skie dni 1917 g. v Riazani,' 3:5.

30 Tul'tseva, 'Obshchina i agrarnaia obriadnost',' 47.

31 Gaudin, '"No Place to Lay My Head."'

32 Tul'tseva, 'Obshchina i agrarnaia obriadnost',' 46. For more on communes and the Stolypin reforms, see Esther Kingston-Mann, 'Peasant Communes and Economic Innovation: A Preliminary Inquiry,' in Kingston-Mann and Mixter, *Peasant Economy,* 23–51.

33 Fulin, 'Fevral'skie dni,' 4; and Suslov, 'Bor'ba za khleb v Riazanskoi gubernii,' 79–80.

34 Fulin, 'Raspredelenie chastnovladel'cheskikh zemel',' 69.

35 Stepanova, 'Sel'skoe khoziaistvo i derevnia v XIX veke,' 481; Fulin, 'Fevral'skie dni,' 4; Fulin, 'Raspredelenie chastnovladel'cheskikh zemel',' 52.

36 Suslov, 'Bor'ba za khleb v Riazanskoi gubernii,' 81.
37 Radkey, *Elections to the Russian Constituent Assembly*, 42.
38 L.G. Promasov, *Vserossiiskoe uchreditel'noe sobranie*, 365.
39 See Perov and Kuznetsov, *Istoriia*, 1:42–7.
40 Note Lenin's retort to the Socialist Revolutionaries (SRs) on this score: 'A fine party, indeed, which had to be defeated and driven from the government in order that everything in its program that was revolutionary and of benefit to the working people could be carried out!' In Lenin, *Collected Works*, 30:265. For more on the SRs, see Figes, *People's Tragedy*; and Melancon, *The Socialist Revolutionaries and the Russian Anti-war Movement, 1914–1917*.
41 *Iz istorii kollektivizatsii sel'skogo khoziaistva Riazanskoi oblasti*, 5.
42 Fulin, 'Raspredelenie chastnovladel'cheskikh zemel',' 59:22.
43 Ibid., 59–60.
44 Suslov, 'Bor'ba za khleb v Riazanskoi gubernii,' 81–92.
45 Ibid., 60.
46 See ibid., 83–90, for a detailed description of the struggles.
47 Ibid., 68.
48 Ibid., 80–100.
49 Ibid.
50 Perov and Kuznetsov, *Istoriia*, 134.
51 Suslov, 'Bor'ba za khleb v Riazanskoi gubernii,' 84. The 1926 census provides different numbers, putting the number of rural inhabitants at 1,620,000 and urban at 149,500, or 8.4 per cent of the province's population. See Riazanskaia okruzhnaia organizatsionnaia komissiia, *Materialy k organizatsii Riazanskogo okruga*, 11–12.
52 Perov and Kuznetsov, *Istoriia*, 135–6. For more on the Tambovshchina, see Danilov and Shanin, eds., *Krest'ianskoe vosstanie v Tambovskoi gubernii v. 1919–1921 gg*; and Landis, *Bandits and Partisans*. Antonov was killed in a shoot-out with the Cheka on 22 June 1922.
53 See the interesting letter from a Skopin peasant in Kriukova, *Krest'ianskie istorii*, 122.
54 Sokolov, 'Vosstanovlenie i dal'neishee razvitie sel'skogo khoziaistvo,' in *Nekotorye voprosy kraevedeniia i otchestvennoi istorii. Uchenye zapiski*, 3:50.
55 Khoroshilov, 'Sozdanie material'no-tekhnicheskikh i politicheskikh predposylok massovoi kollektivizatsii,' 51.
56 See G.Z., 'Prokuratura v derevne Riazanskoi gub.,' *Vlast' sovetov* 17 (1926): 21.
57 Sokolov, 'Vosstanovlenie i dal'neishee razvitie sel'skogo khoziaistvo,' 3:47–55.
58 *Statisticheskii 1926–1927*, 262–71.

59 Table 1 in the appendix lists crops and their cultivation as a percentage of sown land on the eve of collectivization, providing a good glimpse of crop diversity, or lack thereof, in Riazan. Table 2 provides a statistician's attempt to quantify the Riazan peasant diet. Once again, accuracy is difficult to vouch for, but the singularity of the diet makes an impression.

60 *Statisticheskii 1927–28–29*, 244–7.

61 Riazanskaia gubernskaia planovaia komissiia, *Materialy k planu narodnogo khoziaistva Riazanskoi gubernii vyp. V sotsial'no-ekonomicheskaia struktura krest'ianskogo khoziaistva Riazanskoi gubernii*, 10.

62 Ibid., 7, 63–4, 130–4.

63 See ibid., 11–64. On bee-keeping, see 37. On density, see Riazanskaia okruzhnaia organizatsionnaia komissiia, *Materialy k organizatsii Riazanskogo okruga*, 12.

64 This position was held by A.V. Chaianov, although the Riazan statisticians who worked on the books above were not full-blown members of his school. For the debate on measuring wealth, see A.V. Chaianov, *Krestianskoe khoziaistvo* (Moscow: Ekonomika, 1989); Cox, 'Awkward Class'; Harrison, 'Chaianov,' 127–61; Shanin, *Awkward Class*, 45–62.

65 Sokolov, 'Vosstanovlenie i dal'neishee razvitie sel'skogo khoziaistvo,' 3:54–5.

66 Khoroshilov, 'Sozdanie material'no-tekhnicheskikh i politicheskikh predposylok massovoi kollektivizatsii,' 50.

67 *Iz istorii kollektivizatsii sel'skogo khoziaistva Riazanskoi oblasti*, 6.

68 Khoroshilov, 'Sozdanie material'no-tekhnicheskikh i politicheskikh predposylok massovoi kollektivizatsii,' 73.

69 Ibid., 58–61.

70 Ibid., 81.

71 GARO, f. 4, op. 3, d. 13, ll. 714–15.

72 For comparative percentage data, see, 'Svedeniia Narkomzema RSFSR o khode kollektivizatsii v RSFSR na 1 marta 1930,' in Danilov, Manning, and Viola, *Tragediia sovetskoi derevni*, 2:289. The only regions higher than the Central Moscow region were the Central Black Earth, the North Caucasus, Bashkir ASSR, Tatar ASSR, and the Crimea.

73 GARO, f. 2, op. 1, d. 66, l. 124.

74 Lynne Viola, 'Kollektivatsiia i Riazanskii okrug,' in *Riazanskaia derevnia v 1929–1930 gg*, ed. Viola et al., xl.

75 Davies, *Socialist Offensive*, 215.

76 Stepanova, 'Sel'skoe khoziaistvo i derevnia v XIX veke,' 518–20; *Iz istorii kollektivizatsii sel'skogo khoziaistva Riazanskoi oblasti*, 283–4; *Riazanskaia entsiklopediia*, 1:25–36. See also Riazanskaia okruzhnaia organizatsionnaia komissiia, *Materialy k organizatsii Riazanskogo okruga*, 4–8.

77 *Riazanskaia entsiklopedii*, 37–8.
78 Zhevniak, *Atlas Riazanskoi oblasti*, 6.

2. The Police

1 Quoted in P. Zaitsev, 'Derevne nuzhen kul'turnyi militsioner,' *Administrativnyi vestnik* 4 (Apr. 1925): 6.
2 Quoted in G. Iakovlev, 'O tak nazyvaemoi voenizatsii,' *Administrativnyi vestnik* 1 (Jan. 1928): 58.
3 Frank, *Crime, Cultural Conflict, and Justice*, 30; Weissman, 'Regular Police,' 46. I have chosen to translate the Russian *militsiia* with the English *police* for a number of reasons. The English word *militia* conjures up an image of a trained paramilitary organization or a volunteer force. Russian *militsionery*, or constables, were ordinary individuals, paid but not well, poorly educated, ill-trained, and not especially disciplined in both the years before the Revolution and after. A special thank you to Peter Solomon for exchanges on this issue.
4 Weissman, 'Regular Police,' 52–4. This chapter focuses on the regular police almost entirely and much less on the secret or security police. For more on the security police, see Lin, 'Fighting in Vain.'
5 Frank, *Crime, Cultural Conflict, and Justice*, 32.
6 Weissman, 'Regular Police,' 48–9.
7 Quoted in Weissman, 'Regular Police,' 56. For more on police working for other ministries, see Frank, *Crime, Cultural Conflict, and Justice*, 32; Perov and Kuznetsov, *Istoriia Riazanskoi militsii*, 1:17; and Weissman, 'Policing the NEP Countryside,' 175.
8 Weissman, 'Regular Police,' 50.
9 Frank, *Crime, Cultural Conflict, and Justice*, 33. More study needs to be conducted of these pre-Revolutionary peasant police representatives to fit them into the debates on whether or not they were indicative of a closed and abandoned village or whether their positions drew them into the state. Gaudin makes brief reference to the tenners (*desiatskie*) as another financial burden on the commune. See *Ruling Peasants*, 16 and 139. Burbank does not make a clear distinction between regular police and elected village assistants in *Russian Peasants Go to Court*. Frank and Weissman tend to see the peasant police representatives in the context of the autonomous village.
10 Weissman, 'Regular Police,' 52–9; and Weissman, 'Policing the NEP Countryside,' 176. The police tended to resort to what Weissman labels the 'law of the fist' (*kulachnoe pravo*).
11 Frank, *Crime, Cultural Conflict, and Justice*, 34–5.

12 See Hagenloh, *Stalin's Police,* 20–30, on this issue.
13 For more on the concept of dual power and the police in Petrograd in 1917, see Tsuyoshi Hasegawa, 'The Formation of the Militia in the February Revolution: An Aspect of the Origins of Dual Power,' *Slavic Review* 32, no. 2 (1973): 302–22, esp. 302–6. See also Hagenloh, 'Police under Stalin.'
14 GARO, f. 2145, op. 1, d. 1-a; f. R-4883, d. 185, l. 121, in Perov and Kuznetsov, *Istoriia Riazanskoi militsii,* 5–26.
15 In GARO, f. R-1, d. 87, l. 108, in Perov and Kuznetsov, *Istoriia Riazanskoi militsii,* 29.
16 For more on the Red Guard, see Wade, *Red Guards and Workers' Militias in the Russian Revolution.*
17 GARO, f. 2114, in Perov and Kuznetsov, *Istoriia Riazanskoi militsii,* 35 (*Upivaites' vlast'iu*).
18 GARO, f. 2144, op. 1, d. 54, in Perov and Kuznetsov, *Istoriia Riazanskoi militsii,* 57.
19 A.S. Antonov, who led a 'green revolution' against Bolshevik forces during the Civil War, was a uezd police chief after the February Revolution and through October 1917. He and the chairman of the uezd committee on desertion worked together to create forged documents to help young men avoid conscription into the Red Army. Antonov's forces made incursions into parts of Riazan. GARO, f. R-2114, op. 1, d. 202, ll. 5–6, in Perov and Kuznetsov, *Istoriia Riazanskoi militsii,* 135; and Figes, *Peasant Russia, Civil War,* 335–6.
20 For a detailed description of this period in Riazan and the tides and fortunes of the police, see Perov and Kuznetsov, *Istoriia Riazanskoi militsii,* 4–133. On the highest rate of deserters, see 108–9. On losing officers, see 108–22 and passim.
21 GARO, f. R-2114, op. 1, d. 37, ll. 394, 432; d. 54, in Perov and Kuznetsov, *Istoriia Riazanskoi militsii,* 57–74. The letter from the police chief is on 62–4.
22 GARO, f. R-2114, op. 1, d. 28, l. 113, in Perov and Kuznetsov, *Istoriia Riazanskoi militsii,* 74–6.
23 GARO, f. R-2114, op. 1, d. 10, ll. 98–99, in Perov and Kuznetsov, *Istoriia Riazanskoi militsii,* 79.
24 According to Perov and Kuznetsov, *Istoriia Riazanskoi militsii,* 108–9. For more on desertion, see Sanborn, *Drafting the Russian Nation.*
25 Perov and Kuznetsov, *Istoriia,* 59–71.
26 GARO, f. R-2114, op. 1, d. 54 and d. 9, in Perov and Kuznetsov, *Istoriia Riazanskoi militsii,* 108–16.
27 For more on these divisions, see Hagenloh, *Stalin's Police,* 123–7.
28 See GARO, f. R-55, op. 1, d. 212, l. 16, for a report from Pronsk. See Perov

and Kuznetsov, *Istoriia Riazanskoi militsii,* 12, for a report from the police in Riazhsk.

29 GARO, f. R-2114, op 1, d. 2020, in Perov and Kuznetsov, *Istoriia Riazanskoi militsii,* 127–33. Melnikov's report is on 98.

30 Ibid., 128–37.

31 GARO, f. R-4, op. 3 (1922), d. 1, l. 14.

32 Hagenloh, *Stalin's Police,* 36–40.

33 GARO, f. R-55, op. 1, d. 212, l. 18.

34 GARO, f. R-63, op. 1, d. 3, l. 85 ob.

35 Perov and Kuznetsov, *Istoriia Riazanskoi militsii,* 142–3.

36 For material on the origins and structure of the Soviet police, see I. Kiselev, '10 let Raboche-krest'ianskoi militsii,' *Administrativnyi vestnik* 10–11 (Oct.–Nov. 1927): 29–32; Shelley, *Policing Soviet Society,* 22–23; and Weissman, 'Policing the NEP Countryside,' 176–83. On the criminal investigation department, see I.N. Iakimov, 'Zadachi i deiatel'nost' Ugolovnogo Rozyska v gorode i derevne,' *Administrativnyi vestnik* 4 (Apr. 1927): 39. See also Perov and Kuznetsov, *Istoriia Riazanskoi militsii.,* 142–5. For information on the rivalry between the NKVD and the GPU/OGPU, see Lin, 'Fighting in Vain'; and Hagenloh, *Stalin's Police,* 47–65.

37 Perov and Kuznetsov, *Istoriia Riazanskoi militsii,* 148.

38 'Obiazannosti militsii,' *Administrativnyi vestnik* 4 (Apr. 1925): 76–7. I. Kiselev complained constantly of the same problem. See I. Kiselev, 'Material'noe polozhenie militseiskikh organov,' *Administrativnyi vestnik* 4 (Apr. 1927): 19–23; Zabkov, 'K voprosu o sblizhenii s naseleniem,' *Administrativnyi vestnik* 3 (Mar. 1925): 58.

39 I. Liubomov, 'Bol'noi vopros,' *Administrativnyi vestnik* 3 (Mar. 1928): 23.

40 Shpilko, 'O raspredelenii militsii v sel'skikh mestnostiakh,' *Administrativnyi vestnik* 12 (Dec. 1925): 50–3.

41 GARO, f. R-55, op. 1, d. 77, l. 172.

42 GARO, f. R-55, op. 1, d. 212, ll. 1 ob.–16.

43 A.E. Zvenchik, 'Professional'nye zabolevaniia sredi rabotnikov militsii,' *Administrativnyi vestnik* 7 (July 1925): 31. See GARO f. R-55, op. 1, d. 212, l. 14 ob., for a report from Pronsk on officers falling ill in 1923.

44 On the village deputies, see Weissman, 'Policing the NEP Countryside,' 182; I. Zaitsev, 'O sel'skikh ispolniteliakh,' *Administrativnyi vestnik* 2 (Feb. 1926): 17–20; V.M. Boretsov, 'Na pomoshch' derevne,' *Administrativnyi vestnik* 12 (Dec. 1925): 79–80; and Kononov and Korotaev, 'Kollektivizatsiia sel'skogo khoziaistva i administrativnye organy,' *Administrativnyi vestnik* 4 (Apr. 1930): 17–20.

45 GARO, f. R-4, op. 43, d. 407, l. 5.

46 'Tsirkular NKIu No. 48,' *ESIu* 9 (7 Mar. 1925): 231–2.
47 Zaitsev, 'Derevne nuzhen kul'turnyi militsioner,' 3–6.
48 Ia. Kutafin, 'O strukture admotdelov,' *Administrativnyi vestnik* 1 (Jan. 1928): 23.
49 GARO, f. R-55, op. 1, d. 212, l. 14 ob.
50 GARO, f. R-63, op. 1, d. 3, l. 177.
51 Ibid., ll. 175–9.
52 Ibid., ll. 65–71 ob.
53 GARO, f. R-63, op. 1, d. 49, ll. 97–101 ob. See also ll. 3–23 for similar reports.
54 B. Shavrov, 'Volostnaia militsiia,' *Administrativnyi vestnik* 4 (Apr. 1925): 39.
55 Ibid., 36.
56 Weissman, 'Policing the NEP Countryside,' 181; and V. Khalfin, 'Tekuchest' lichnogo sostava ugolovno-administrativnykh organov RSFSR,' *Administrativnyi vestnik* 6 (June 1925): 21.
57 RGASPI, f. 17, op. 85s, d. 123, l. 13. It is interesting to compare how much the district police were paid in comparison to other district workers. The district chief of police might have earned anywhere from fifty to eighty-five rubles per month, while the village constable earned anywhere from thirteen to twenty-one. The people's court judge earned about seventy rubles per month and the forest warden about forty-five rubles per month. See Kiselev, 'Material'noe polozhenie militseiskikh organov,' 20. In some areas in Riazan the turnover was 130 per cent. GARO, f. R-63, op. 1, d. 3, l. 169. In 1925 salaries for a district officer ranged from thirty-three to thirty-five rubles per month in Leningrad and Moscow, and from to nine to twelve rubles per month in the provinces. See B. Shavrov, 'Volostnaia militsiia,' *Administrativnyi* vestnik 4 (Apr. 1925): 39.
58 On prices, see Riazanskoe gubernskoe statisticheskoe biuro, *Statisticheskii ezhegodnik Riazanskoi gubernii za 1923–1924 gg.*, 106–8.
59 Kiselev, 'Material'noe polozhenie militseiskikh organov,' 21.
60 GARO, f. R-55, op. 1, d. 212, l. 16 ob.
61 Khalfin, 'Tekuchest,' 21. For a contemporary look at the impact of having few resources in the comparable circumstances of a developing nation, see the Jamaican film *Third World Cop*, in which the identity of a potential witness is protected by putting a cardboard box over his head.
62 GARO, f. R-4, op. 111, d. 979, l. 1 ob.
63 GARO, f. R-63, op. 1, d. 49, l. 119.
64 Stepanov, 'O podgotovke lichnogo sostava v derevne,' *Administrativnyi vestnik* 6 (June 1928): 49.
65 Perov and Kuznetsov, *Istoriia Riazanskoi militsii*, 166.

66 A. Semenov, 'Material'noe polozhenie rabotnikov militsii,' *Administrativnyi vestnik* 9 (Sept. 1928): 23–7. On the shortage of horses for the criminal investigations departments, see N. Batrakov, 'Mozhno-li rabotat' v takikh usloviiakh?' *Administrativnyi vestnik* 3 (Mar. 1925): 60–1.

67 GARO, f. R-4, op. 43, d. 407, l. 5. For more on the shortage of horses, see Kiselev, '10 let Raboche-krest'ianskoi militsii,' 35; and S. Krylov, 'Rabota militsii v obraztsovykh distriktiakh,' *Administrativnyi vestnik* 9–10 (Sept.–Oct. 1925): 79–80.

68 Kiselev, 'Material'noe polozhenie militseiskikh organov,' 21–2.

69 N.A. Nikolaevskii, 'S"ezd rabotnikovuezdnykh ugrozyskov v g. Ranenburge,' *Administrativnyi vestnik* 1 (Jan. 1928): 6–63.

70 'Krest'ianskii spravochnik,' *Kollektiv,* 16 October 1924.

71 Rossiiskii gosudarstvennyi akhiv ekonomiki (RGAE), f. 396, op. 3, d. 67, l. 20.

72 GARO, f. R-63, op. 1, d. 100, ll. 1–34.

73 GARO, f. R-63, op. 1, d. 3, l. 169 ob.

74 GARO, f. R-4, op. 3 (1924), d. 4, l. 174.

75 GARO, f. R-4, op. 3 (1922), d. 1, ll. 20 ob.–21 ob.

76 GARO, f. R-55, op. 1, d. 177, l. 124.

77 Weissman, 'Policing the NEP Countryside,' 187.

78 GARO, f. R-4, op. 3, d. 10, l. 98.

79 GARO, f. R-4, op. 3. d. 6, l. 68.

80 Ibid., l. 104.

81 Bol'shakov, *Sovetskaia derevnia 1917–1924,* 90. On defining *chastushki,* see Tirado, 'The Village Voice,' 1.

82 Similar to the English term *home brew, samogon* comes from the Russian *self* (*sam*) and the verb to brew (*goniat'*).

83 For an excellent overview of the nationwide campaign and its legislation, the press hysteria surrounding illegal brewing, and the campaign's motivation from and significance at the Centre, see Weissman, 'Prohibition and Alcohol Control.' Phillips explores the urban context in *Bolsheviks and the Bottle.* Vertov included a scene of children in the struggle against alcohol in early *Kino-Eye* films as well as a prolonged sequence on the effects of alcohol on village women.

84 See, GARO, f. R-4, op. 3 (1922), d. 1, l. 201, for the recipe and prices. A 1924 article in the local Skopin newspaper calculated that 105 million puds of grain were wasted each year in samogon production and that the Soviet Union could be 1.5 times richer without it. 'Skol'ko stoit samogon,' *Kollektiv,* 2 Nov. 1924.

85 Perov and Kuznetsov, *Istoriia Riazanskoi militsii,* 147.

86 Solts and Fainblit, *Revoliutsionnaia zakonnost'*, 43–8; and Solomon, 'Criminalization and Decriminalization,' 15–17.
87 Solts and Fainblit, *Revoliutsionnaia zakonnost'*, 49–50.
88 GARO, f. R-4, op. 3, d. 1, l. 374.
89 V. Mokeev, 'Prestupnost' v derevne,' *ESIu* 16 (25 Apr. 1925): 419.
90 GARO, f. R-4, op. 3, d. 8, l. 235.
91 In his study of private correspondence in the 1920s, V.S. Izmozik identified alcohol and drunkenness as the most oft-repeated theme. Izmozik, 'Voices from the Twenties,' 288.
92 GARO, f. R-4, op. 3 (1925), d. 6, l. 6.
93 Ibid., l. 40.
94 Mokeev, 'Prestupnost' v derevne,' 418.
95 'Po bor'ba s samogonom net mer,' *Sovetskaia derevnia,* 12 (12 April 1924): 4.
96 'Samogon p'em,' *Sovetskaia derevnia* 26 (9 Aug. 1924): 3.
97 GARO, f. R-4, op. 3, d. 6, l. 248.
98 Ibid., l. 268.
99 GARO, f. R-4, op. 3 (1925), d. 6, l. 41.
100 GARO, f. R-4, op. 3 (1922), d. 10, l. 98.
101 The Russian term is *vedro*. One *vedro* usually contains about twelve litres.
102 Litvak, 'Samogonovarenie i potrebelenie alkogolia v Rossiiskoi derevne 1920-kh godov,' 74–7; Perov and Kuznetsov, *Istoriia Riazanskoi militsii,* 146–7; GARO, f. R-55, op. 1, d. 177, ll. 403–4 ob.
103 See GARO, f. R-4, op. 3 (1923), d. 10, l. 15 ob., on the 'age-old tradition,' l. 12 on citizen participation, and l. 26 on the participation of local power in samogon dealings.
104 P. Zaitsev, 'Derevne nuzhen kul'turnyi militsioner,' 3; '... *kazhdyi militsioner, osushchestvliaiushchii ukazannye zadachi, dolzhen byt' ne tol'ko khoroshim sovetskim chinovnikom, no takzhe khoroshim obshchestvennym deiatelem i politikom.*'
105 Odinokov, 'Temnye piatna na sel'skoi militsii po gazetam s mest,' *Administrativnyi vestnik* 8 (Aug. 1925): 75–6.
106 GARO, f. R-4, op. 3 (1925), d. 6, l. 104.
107 Ibid., ll. 67–8.
108 Ibid., l. 6.
109 For more on the idea of an official transcript, see Scott, *Domination and the Arts of Resistance.*
110 Weissman, 'Prohibition and Alcohol Control,' 357.
111 Voronov, *O Samogone,* 11.
112 GARO, f. R-4,op. 1, d. 1965, ll. 40–124.
113 GARO, f. R-2461, op. 5, d. 185, l. 76 ob.
114 GARO, f. R-4, op. 3, d. 6, l. 5, ll. 68, 102.

115 RGASPI, f. 17, op. 85s, d. 123, l. 13.
116 Ibid., l. 14.
117 Voronov, *O samogone*, 5.
118 Ibid., 18–19.
119 Ibid., 24.
120 Ibid., 25–6.
121 I.F. Kiselev, 'Vopros voenizatsii militsii,' *Administrativnyi vestnik* 12 (Dec. 1927): 28–30
122 Ia. Kutafin, 'Itogi rabot 2-go Riazanskogo gub. s"ezda admrabotnikov,' *Administrativnyi vestnik* 8 (Aug 1928): 41–4; and I. Kiselev, 'Rol' militsii v bor'be s prestupnost'iu,' *Administrativnyi vestnik* 4 (Apr. 1929): 62–3.
123 GARO, f. R-63, op. 1, d. 49, ll. 4, 23, 126 ob.
124 Pirogov, 'Sel'skie ispolniteli,' *Administrativnyi vestnik* 1 (Aug. 1928): 16.
125 Perov and Kuznetsov, *Istoriia Riazanskoi militsii*, 182–6.
126 GARO, f. R-298, op. 1, d. 4231. Of those 1,085, 87 were dismissed for 'weakness in work'; 33 for lacking authority or unethical behavior; 96 for connections with criminal elements; 42 for inappropriate class origins; 450 for drunkenness; 140 for corruption; 213 as 'alien elements'; and 24 for miscellaneous reasons.
127 For details, see Lin, 'Fighting in Vain.'
128 Perov and Kuznetsov, *Istoriia Riazanskoi militsii*, 186.
129 Ts. I., 'Osnovnye printsipy novoi programmy po sluzhbe militsii,' *Administrativnyi vestnik* 3 (Mar. 1929): 27–30. The journal had been accused of being too apolitical. See Lin, 'Fighting in Vain,' 148.
130 Perov and Kuznetsov, *Istoriia Riazanskoi militsii*, 187–90.

3. The Courts

1 L.A., 'Sud v derevne,' *Krest'ianskii iurist* 5 (15 Mar. 1928): 15.
2 Burbank, *Russian Peasants Go to Court*; Frank, 'Popular Justice'; Frank, *Crime, Cultural Conflict and Justice*; Frierson, *All Russia Is Burning!*; Frierson, 'Crime and Punishment'; Frierson, '"I Must Always Answer to the Law"'; Frierson, 'Red Roosters'; Popkins, 'Code versus Custom?'; Popkins, 'Peasant Experiences'; Popkins, 'Popular Development of Procedure'; Worobec, 'Horse Thieves'; Worobec, *Peasant Russia.*
3 Popkins, 'Code versus Custom?' 408.
4 Yaney, *Systematization of Russian Government*, 363.
5 Frank, *Crime, Cultural Conflict and Justice*, 212–15.
6 A claim supported in the works of Bushnell, *Mutiny amid Repression*; and Verner, *Crisis of Russian Autocracy.*

7 Burbank, *Russian Peasants Go to Court*, xiv.
8 Ibid.
9 Ibid., 10.
10 Frierson, '"I Must Always Answer to the Law,"' 327–8.
11 Frank, *Crime, Cultural Conflict and Justice in Rural Russia.*
12 Frierson, *All Russia Is Burning!*; and Gaudin, *Ruling Peasants.*
13 Gaudin, *Ruling Peasants*, 7.
14 Ibid., 210.
15 Popkins, 'Code versus Custom?' 424. Retish finds the same pattern for 1917–21 in his work on Viatka in *Russia's Peasants.*
16 See Osipovich, 'Narodnyi sud'ia v derevne,' 8–9, for an explicit statement of this civilizing mission.
17 Gaudin, *Ruling Peasants*, 211.
18 Bol'shakov, *Sovetskaia derevnia*, 103; Bol'shakov, *Derevnia 1917–1927*, 308. Bol'shakov gives the example of the citizens of the village of Iakshino who petitioned to have the Lidinkin family exiled from the village because the Lidinkin children stole money from another villager's cupboard. The district executive committee accepted the petition.
19 See Solomon, *Soviet Criminal Justice under Stalin*, 17–27, for a study of the development of the courts in the early Soviet period. See also Hazard, *Settling Disputes in Soviet Society*, 2–148, for an extremely detailed look at legislation on the courts from 1918 to 1921.
20 Bol'shakov, *Derevnia 1917–1927*, 309.
21 See Hazard, *Settling Disputes in Soviet Society*, 150–1.
22 For further examples, see Frank, *Crime, Cultural Conflict and Justice in Rural Russia*, 48; and Solomon, 'Criminalization and Decriminalization,' 11–12.
23 GARO, f. R-4, op. 1, d. 485, l. 220 ob.
24 Tan-Bogoraz, *Staryi i novyi byt*, 104.
25 Hazard, *Settling Disputes in Soviet Society*, 190–3; and Carr, *Socialism in One Country 1924–26*, 1:82–3.
26 GARO, f. R-4, op. 1, d. 485, ll. 101–2.
27 Ibid., l. 220.
28 Ibid., l. 220 ob.
29 Ibid., l. 221.
30 Ibid., l. 309. Bol'shakov discusses the problems associated with this delivery system due to the confusion at the district executive committees over delivery of items which resulted in many witnesses falling through the cracks. Bol'shakov, *Derevnia 1917–1927*, 313. On the comparable situation in Tver, see 310–13.
31 GARO, f. R-4, op. 1, d. 485, l. 221. ll. 312–312 ob. The situation could still

be worse: the court of the fifth division of Kasimov Uezd had no furniture, save for a bed and a trunk; see ll. 56–6 ob.

32 Ibid., l. 221.

33 Ibid., ll. 325–6.

34 Ibid. On typewriters, see l. 51 ob.; on legal literature, see ll. 221, 234 ob., 309, 312; on firewood, ll. 221, 313; on the absence of portraits, see l. 51 ob.; and RGAE, f. 396, op. 4, d. 111, l. 69.

35 GARO, f. R-4, op. 1, d. 485, l. 221.

36 Ibid., ll. 221–221 ob.

37 Ibid., ll. 103–103 ob. The statistical profile given here fits with Solomon's observations on the education and party profile of people's court judges. See Solomon, *Soviet Criminal Justice*, 34–5.

38 V. Osipovich, 'Propaganda sovetskogo prava na fabrike i v derevne,' *ESIu*, 13 (4 Apr. 1925): 321–2. In 1928, the investigators were attached to the office of the procuracy. See Solomon, *Soviet Criminal Justice*, 42–3, on the dual subordination of investigators to both the judge and the procurator until 1928, when they were transferred to the procuracy's jurisdiction entirely.

39 Malikov, 'Golos sledovatelia,' *ESIu* 25 (21 June 1924): 584–5.

40 GARO, f. R-298, op. 1, d. 3821, l. 23.

41 Ibid., l. 24. For similar examples, see GARO, f. R-4, op. 1, d. 485, l. 50. A. Genov points out that one cannot judge the assessors too harshly, since the bulk of them live so far away from court and 'in work periods like fall or spring they consider it superfluous [*izlishnii*] to study justice [*zanimat'sia sudami*].' See also 'Krest'ianstvo v narodnom sude' and 'O narodnykh zasedateliakh,' *ESIu* (3 Apr. 1924): 2.

42 GARO, f. R-298, op. 1, d. 4025, l. 15 ob.

43 GARO, f. R-298, op. 1, d. 3821, ll. 3–20, and d. 4025, ll. 3–35.

44 GARO, f. R-298, op. 1, d. 4025, l. 35.

45 'Pervoe Moskovskoe gubernskoe soveshchanie zashchitnikov sovmestno s predstaviteliami ob okazanii iuridicheskoe pomoshchi naseleniiu,' *ESIu* 50–51 (27 Dec. 1925): 1551–1553.

46 GARO, f. R-5, op. 1, d. 60, ll. 12–17.

47 Ibid., ll. 1 and 10.

48 V. Beliaev, judge of the third district of Moscow Uezd, *ESIu* 27 (9 July 1924): 633–4.

49 M. Begichev, 'Zagromozhdenie sudov,' *Kollektiv*, 16 Oct. 1924.

50 It is not unusual for a court system in a time and place where central authority is weak to make rulings more in keeping with the local context than with central demand. See, for example, Brewer and Styles, where 'the practice of local courts sometimes deviated considerably from the letter of

the law as enacted or interpreted in Westminster; and most legal officials were rank amateurs who were as much concerned with the preservation of local harmony as they were with the (often divisive) business of litigation,' as quoted in Yang, *Crime and Criminality in British India*, 13. This fact once again emphasizes that Soviet Russia and Russia in general should not be studied as a peculiar and unique historic example.

51 See Solts and Fainblit, *Revoliutsionnaia zakonnost'*, for a summary of the commissions' findings.

52 See Solomon, 'Criminalization and Decriminalization,' 16–24, for an exploration of this process.

53 RGASPI, f. 17, op. 85s, d. 180, l. 14.

54 Ibid.

55 Ibid., l. 15.

56 Ibid., l. 16.

57 Ibid., l. 17.

58 Ibid., l. 19.

59 GARO, f. R-298, op. 1, d. 3821, ll. 15–17. Karnov wrote an impassioned forty-page report.

60 Ibid., l. 31.

61 Ibid., l. 32.

62 Ibid., ll. 32–5.

63 Ibid., ll. 35–40.

64 GARO, f. R-2462, op. 7, d. 43, l. 72.

65 GARO, f-R-2462, op. 7, d. 39, ll. 107, 108.

66 Ibid. ll. 231–41 ob. See also Fainsod, *Smolensk under Soviet Rule*, 178–80, for 1928 reports on people's court judges in Smolensk, where connections to the local community were a constant problem. Fainsod comments, 'The procuracy obviously faced a real problem in breaking the ties of the lower judicial organs to the countryside' (180).

67 M. Shaliupa, 'Sel'skie narodnye sudy,' *Sovetskoe stroitel'stvo* 8 (Aug. 1929): 23–30.

68 On the village social courts and their development, see Solomon, 'Criminalization and Decriminalization,' 27–31.

69 Ibid., 82–98.

4. The Rural Soviet

1 Gaudin, *Ruling Peasants*, 47. Gaudin deals in detail through the book with the role played by land captains in the pre-Revolutionary countryside.

2 Cited in E. Elistratov, 'Staraia i novaia volost',' *Vlast' sovetov* 6 (Sept. 1924):

103–4. Elistratov describes the *skhod* as exploitative and controlled by the elder who in turn was the lackey of the local land captain.

3 Figes, *Peasant Russia*, 71–4. Figes also finds the peasantry engaged in rural politics. Mikhail Kalinin, chairman of the Central Executive Committee of the USSR (TsIK), was often referred to as 'starosta.'

4 There is much material available for details on the Centre's position on the rural soviets and their theoretical functioning. For a start, see *Sobranie zakonov i rasporiazhenii RSFSR / SSSR*; and A. Beloborodov, 'O sel'skikh sovetakh,' *Vlast' sovetov* 2 (May 1924): 46–53.

5 GARF f. 393, op. 50. d. 38, l. 1; and Elistratov, 'Staraia i novaia volost',' 102–17.

6 N. Lagovier, 'Rol' sel'sovetov v bor'be s prestupnost'iu,' *Sovetskoe stroitel'stvo* 10 (Oct. 1929): 19–20.

7 Although the *zemel'noe obshchestvo* and the *skhod* overlapped in fact, I have tried to use *commune* where *zemel'noe obshchestvo* was used in the material, and *gathering* when *skhod* was used.

8 G. Amfiteatrov, 'Zemel'noe obshchestvo i sel'sovet,' *Revoliutsiia prava* 2 (1928): 99–100; Rezunov, *Sel'skie sovety i zemel'nye obshchestva*, 24; Taniuchi, *Village Gathering in Russia*, 4. For surveys of material on the matter, see Kabanov, 'Dokumentatsiia sel'skogo skhoda'; Koznova, 'Krest'ianskaia pozemel'naia obshchina,' 292–308.

9 Lewin, *Russian Peasants and Soviet Power*, for example, depicts the rural soviet as becoming a party organ staffed by *bedniaks* (poor peasants) and *batraks* (landless peasants) and ignored by the majority of the peasantry as a mere 'executive body' carrying out work assigned to them from above (81–2). But in the next breath, he writes, 'The bedniak who was the party's favorite candidate for this post (sel'sovet chairman), frequently could not afford to fill it and it often fell to the more comfortably off peasant.' If the more 'comfortably off' peasants wanted the position, does this not suggest peasant interest in and use of the institution? Keep, *Russian Revolution*, embraces a similar contradiction. On the one hand he sees rural soviets dominated by returning Red Army centralizers (450–1, 463) and then is surprised to find a rebellion led by a local soviet (451–5). He argues that the Bolsheviks controlled the rural soviets generally, but the system was a 'weak reed to lean upon' (459).

10 Carr, *Socialism in One Country*, 2: 304–5. See also Figes, *Peasant Russia, Civil War.*

11 Carr sees the renewed emphasis on the state at the local level as motivated in part by the events in the village of Dymovka, surrounding the highly publicized murder of a rural correspondent (*sel'kor*) and trial of his accused

murderers. See Carr, *Socialism in One Country*, 2:318. On Dymovka, see the coverage in *Pravda, Izvestiia, Bednota,* and *Krest'ianskaia gazeta* in the fall of 1924.

12 Carr, *Socialism in One Country*, 2:322.

13 N. Levertov, 'Sel'skii sovet Moskovskoi gubernii,' *Vlast' sovetov* (Sept. 1924): 138.

14 'Sel'skie sovety rabotaiut plokho,' *Derevenskaia gazeta*, 14 Aug. 1927, 3.

15 See Maria Belskaia, 'Arina's Children,' in *In the Shadow of Revolution*, ed. Fitzpatrick and Slezkine, 226–7, about the occupation of village houses by the local soviet, which became even more ominous during the collectivization drive.

16 Golubykh, *Ocherki glukhoi derevni*, 9–12.

17 Ivanov, 'TsIK Soiuza SSR i ego rabota po stroitel'stve sovetov,' *Sovetskoe stroitel'stvo* 4 (Apr. 1927): 56.

18 GARO, f. R-4, op. 3, d. 6, l. 63. In 1923, a rumour circulated in the village of Temeshovo, Sasovo Uezd, that there would be two elections, one for the non-party government and one for the communists. See GARO, f. R-4, op. 3. d. 8, l. 62.

19 GARO, f. R-4, op. 3, d. 6, ll. 74–6.

20 Ibid., l. 15.

21 RGAE, f. 393, op. 3, d. 526, l. 79.

22 Ibid., l. 75.

23 GARO, f. R-4, op. 3, d. 6, ll. 115–115 ob. At the Centre, observers were increasingly alarmed at this political interest (*aktivnost'*) among middle and wealthy peasants. See 'Vybory v sovety,' *Sovetskoe stroitel'stvo* 5 (Dec. 1926): 8.

24 'Vybory v sovety,' *Derevenskaia gazeta*, 17 Jan. 1926, 2.

25 GARO, f. R-4, op. 3, d. 8, l. 212.

26 F.T. Ivanov, 'Vazhneishie itogi vyborov 1927 goda (Kuda razvivaiutsia sovety),' *Sovetskoe stroitel'stvo* 8–9 (Aug.–Sept. 1927): 22.

27 See Alexopoulos, *Stalin's Outcasts*, for a detailed look at those deprived of their rights.

28 RGAE, f. 396, op. 3, d. 526, l. 42.

29 A. Ivanov, 'TsIK Soiuza SSSR i ego rabota po stroitel'stve sovetov,' *Sovetskoe stroitel'stvo* 4 (1927): 57.

30 See Alexopoulos, 'Ritual Lament'; and Alexopoulos, *Stalin's Outcasts.*

31 M.I. Kalinin, 'O vyborakh v sovety,' *Sovetskoe stroitel'stvo* 4 (1927): 5–26. For an excellent study of the local process of de-kulakization, see Viola, 'Second Coming,' 65–98.

32 Lagovier, 'Rol' sel'sovetov,' 22–5.

33 Amfiteatrov, 'Zemel'noe obshchestvo i sel'sovet,' *Revoliutsiia i prava* 2

(1928): 103. See also 'Pis'ma iz derevni za den',' *Bednota*, 27 Mar. 1925, 4. The latter article cites letters complaining that fathers and husbands would not let women attend village meetings. One correspondent from Smolensk reported that husbands threatened to burn their wives and the entire household if they insisted on attending meetings.

34 Figes, *Peasant Russia, Civil War*, 211.

35 Murugov and Kolesnikov, *Apparat nizovykh sovetskikh organov*, xv.

36 RGAE, f. 396, op. 3, d. 526, l. 2, and Murugov and Kolesnikov, *Apparat nizovykh sovetskikh organov*, xv.

37 Agitprop TsK RKP(b), *Agitatsiia i propaganda v derevne*, 32.

38 RGAE, f. 396, op. 2, d. 153, ll. 16–17; and Lagovier, 'Rol' sel'sovetov,' 16–28.

39 See Carr, *Socialism in One Country*, 2:318–44. Taniuchi also deals in detail with the development of the elections to the soviets in *Village Gathering in Russia*, 72–80.

40 GARO, f. R-4, op. 3 (1925), d. 8, l. 24.

41 GARO, f. R-4, op. 5 (1926), d. 7, l. 28.

42 Ibid., l. 40.

43 Ibid., l. 42.

44 For a study that discusses holdovers from the old regime within the Commissariat of Agriculture, for example, see Heinzen, *Inventing a Soviet Countryside*, esp. chap. 1.

45 GARO, f. R-5, op. 1, d. 84, l. 41.

46 GARF, f. 393, op. 50, d. 30, l. 1. In the central level *svodki*, there were numerous reports of kulaks and 'members of anti-Soviet parties' who 'try to concentrate power in their own hands ... come to meetings "mobilized" with members of their family.' See RGASPI, f. 17, op. 85s, d. 180, l. 73.

47 'P'ianoe selo,' *Kollektiv*, 12 Oct. 1924.

48 'Veselyi chlen sel'soveta,' *Kollektiv*, 10 Dec. 1924. Once again, Bakhtin provides a possible reading of such behaviour when he writes, 'The men of the Middle Ages participated in two lives: the official and the carnival life. Two aspects of the world, the serious and the laughing aspect, coexisted in their consciousness.' Bakhtin, *Rabelais and His World*, 96.

49 GARO, f. R-4, op. 3, d. 6, ll. 175–175 ob.

50 GARO, f. R-4, op. 3, d. 6, l. 283 ob.

51 There is a significant literature that engages with the meaning of drinking and culture in pre-Revolutionary and early Soviet society. Frank, Phillips, and Snow find drinking to be an essential component of peasant and worker culture, and all find elite attitudes against drinking as representing a cultural divide. Frank, 'Confronting the Domestic Other,' 14–107; Phillips,

Bolsheviks and the Bottle; Snow, 'Alcoholism in the Russian Military.' McKee argues that there were also attempts from below to take a stand against drinking in pre-Revolutionary society and thus a 'clash of cultures' was not inevitable. He does conclude, however, that a clash of cultures did occur because the lower classes and elites were unable to or 'not even allowed to try to build a common culture.' See McKee, 'Sobering Up the Soul of the People,' 233.

52 Rezunov, *Sel'skie sovety i zemel'nye obshchestva*, 27.

53 RGAE, f. 396, op. 2, d. 82, l. 261 ob., in Kriukova, *Krest'ianskie istorii*, 105.

54 Village correspondents or *sel'kory*, as they were known, were the village reporters for Soviet newspapers. There was a significant network of such correspondents already in the 1920s. Chapter 7 tells the tragic story of one such unfortunate Riazan correspondent. For more on village correspondents, see Coe, 'Struggles for Authority in the NEP Village,' 1151–71.

55 RGAE, f. 393, op. 3, d. 526, l. 88.

56 'Kulatskie radeteli,' *Kollektiv*, 10 Dec. 1924.

57 '"Kulakam nado dat' otpor" – Kak v derevne zachasuiu provodiatsia obshchie sobraniia,' *Kollektiv*, 16 Oct. 1924.

58 RGAE, f. 396, op. 3, d. 526, ll. 93–93 ob.

59 A. Chernyshov, 'Sel'sovet Troekurovskoi volosti bezdeistvuiut,' *Dervenskaia gazeta*, 2 July 1927, 6.

60 S. Sharov, 'O sel'skom biudzhete,' *Sovetskoe stroitel'stvo* 2–3 (Feb.–Mar. 1927): 113–15. RGASPI, f. 17, op. 85s, d. 318, also discusses illegal obligations assessed according to class.

61 Taniuchi, *Village Gathering in Russia*, 61–2. For a detailed look at self-taxation, see 53–67.

62 'Samogon p'em,' *Sovetskaia derevnia* 26 (9 Aug. 1924): 3.

63 Rezunov, *Sel'skie sovety i zemel'nye obshchestva*, 30. It seems that the practice of making local collections did not disappear in the post-collectivization village. In the 1947 film *Sel'skaia uchitel'nitsa*, a village school teacher goes to the local bar to take up a collection to send a promising young student to sit an exam.

64 Alexander G. Beloborodov had been a Bolshevik delegate to the Constituent Assembly. He was elected chairman of the Urals executive committee in 1918 and would play a key role in the fate of the Romanov family. On his early years in Soviet power, see Pipes, *Russian Revolution*, 748–86 and passim. During the Civil War he 'was a major player in decossackization. Definitely no softie' (Peter Holquist, personal correspondence). From 1923 to 1927, he was RSFSR people's commissar for internal affairs. Expelled from the party in 1927 and 1936 as a Trotskyite, he was executed in 1938. See also Getty and Naumov, *Road to Terror*, 596.

65 RGASPI, f. 17, op. 85s, d. 123, ll. 17–18.

66 See V. Mokeev, 'Zakon o sel'skikh obshchestvennykh sobraniiakh (skodakh),' *ESIu* 20 (1927): 596–7, for a discussion of the decree and its contents. 'Sel'sovet – rukovoditel' skhoda,' *Derevenskaia gazeta*, 21 Apr. 1927, 6.

67 Kozhikov, 'Sel'skie sovety i zemel'nye obshchestva,' *Na agrarnom fronte* 5 (1928),: 67; Rezunov, *Sel'skie sovety i zemel'nye obshchestva*, 24.

68 G.N. 'Kak provoditsia v zhizn' zakon o rasreshenii prav mestnykh sovetov,' *Krest'ianskii iurist* 12 (30 June 1928): 15.

69 N. Lagovier, 'Sel'sovety i skhody,' *Krest'ianskii iurist* 5 (15 Mar. 1928): 11. Lagovier maintained that the peasants who ran the soviets simply did not know the law. But such laws were not necessarily worth knowing, in light of local complications.

70 Rezunov, *Sel'skie sovety i zemel'nye obshchestva*, 31.

71 GARO, f. R-5, op. 1, d. 84, l. 30.

72 I. Akimov, 'O sel'skom biudzhete i vzaimootnosheniiakh sel'sovetov s zemel'nymi obshchestvami,' *Sovetskoe stroitel'stvo* 4 (Apr. 1928): 33–50.

73 M. Boldyrev, 'Revoliutsionnaia zakonnost' v oblasti upravleniia i administrirovaniia,' *Administrativnyi vestnik* 5 (May 1925): 11.

74 Male, *Russian Peasant Organization*, 147–8.

75 Riazanskii gubernskii statisticheskii otdel, *Statisticheskii ezhegodnik Riazanskoi gubernii za 1926–1927*, 416.

76 A policy designed to create a manageable number of regional divisions (*raiony*) between the uezd and district (*volost'*) level with one rural soviet in each raion thus reducing the number of soviets. In the letter from Riazan that begins chapter 5, Ivan Abramovich Guskov refers to such a situation.

77 Sharov, 'K voprosu o sel'skom obshchestvennom khoziaistve,' *Vlast' sovetov* 6 (Sept. 1924): 126.

78 A look at a communal budget from 1926 to 1927, table 3 in the appendix, supports such a claim.

79 The final chapter deals in detail with the role of the rural soviets during collectivization in Riazan.

80 For the contours of the debate, see K. Apshenek, 'Perestroika sovetskogo apparata v sviazi so sploshnoi kollektivizatsiei,' *Sovetskoe stroitel'stvo*1 (Jan. 1930): 64–8; V. Budagov, 'Nado perestroit' sistemu rukovodstva nizovym sovetskim apparatom,' *Sovetskoe stroitel'stvo* 1 (Jan. 1930): 79–86; and I. Dolin, 'Sel'skie sovety v raionakh sploshnoi kollektivizatsii,' *Sovetskoe stroitel'stvo* 12 (Dec. 1929): 75–86.

81 'Novye zadachi sovetov v sviazi s kollektivizatsiei,' *Sovetskoe stroitel'stvo* 2 (Feb. 1930): 1–7.

82 See Viola, 'Campaign of the 25,000ers,' 164–5. (This material did not

appear in the published book based on this dissertation. My thanks to Lynne Viola for sharing the dissertation with me.) See also Davies, *Socialist Offensive*, 226.

83 See N. Kulagin, 'Selo pod kulatskoi piatoi,' *Sud idet* 5 (1930): 11–13; and V. Zerkov, 'Kulastskii sel'sovet,' *Sud idet* 7 (1930): 8–9.

84 I. Akimov, 'Novyi zakon o sel'skikh sovetakh,' *Sovetskoe stroitel'stvo* 4 (Apr. 1930): 5–18.

85 RGASPI, f. 17, op. 85s, d. 180, ll. 1–6, and d. 318, l. 25. The central-level *svodki* were replete with complaints about the unlawful assessment and collection of fines by the rural soviets.

86 GARO, f. R-61, op. 1, d. 555, ll. 1–33.

87 Ibid. ll. 42–42 ob. on Markin; on the Soldatov brothers, l. 44; on Geras'kin and the group of middle peasants, l. 54. For more such reports, see ll. 55–7; and GARO, f. R-63, op. 1, d. 139, l. 1 ob.

88 Izdanie offitsial'noe, *Razdel 1: Rukovodiashchie ukazaniia po pereustroistvu i pod"emu sel'skogo khoziaistva Riazanskogo okruga; Razdel 2: O rasshirenii prav sel'sovetov na territorii Riazaskogo okruga*, 10–11.

89 GARO, f. R-5, op. 1, d. 35, l. 20.

90 In November 1929, Soviet troops moved into Manchuria to defend Russian interests in the Chinese Eastern Railway. The area covered by the line had been occupied by Chinese forces in July 1929.

91 GARO, f. 2, op. 1, d. 85, ll. 49–50.

92 See Duara, *Culture, Power and the State*, 165, for an interview with a village official along these lines.

93 M. Boldyrev, 'Kak dolzhny rabotat' admorgany v derevne,' *Administrativnyi vestnik*, 7 (July 1925): 10–11.

94 S.T., 'Sel'sovety, kotorye protiv bednoty,' *Vlast' sovetov* 25 (Nov. 1925): 18–19.

95 TsIK decreed in 1926 and repeated again in 1930 that people could regain their voting rights if they were able to illustrate that they were loyal to Soviet power and had performed socially useful labour for the last five years. Alexopoulos, 'The Ritual Lament,' 119. See also Alexopoulos, *Stalin's Outcasts*, esp. 31–41.

96 My findings fit very well with those of Young, *Power and the Sacred*, who shows how religious activists used rural institutions like the soviet to raise resources for their cause and even became members themselves to use the soviets to promote religion in the villages of the 1920s. She too illustrates how villagers used the state's 'institutional forms' against it. Young makes the same connection made throughout this book regarding 'impatience' with rural realities that help us understand the decision to collectivize the

countryside and attempt to violently shatter a kind of rural civil society. See esp. 277–9.

97 Frierson, *All Russia Is Burning!*; and Gaudin, *Ruling Peasants.*

5. Taxation

1 GARO, f. R-4, op. 3, d. 8 (1927), l. 2. *Chastushka* sung in the village of Krivopole, Ranenburg Uezd. There is most likely a religious parody here: Trotsky is asking good, and implicitly Christian, people for alms. My thanks to Evgeny Dobrenko for intepretation help with the *chastushka.*

2 Bol'shakov, *Derevnia posle Oktiabria,* 93. Peasant in the village of Ivanovka, Nikol'skaia District, Kursk.

3 The maintenance of soviets, which had technically been eliminated by the amalgamation of districts, was a common phenomenon in Riazan. The issue is discussed in the previous chapter's section on rural soviets. See also S. Sharov, 'K voprosu o sel'skom obshchestvennom khoziaistve i sel'skom sovetskom apparate,' *Vlast' sovetov* 6 (Sept. 1924): 126.

4 RGAE, f. 396, op. 3, d. 521, ll. 141–142 ob.

5 For attitudes to insurance costs, see GARO, f. R-4, op. 3, d. 6 (1925), ll. 19–21.

6 Newcity, *Taxation in the Soviet Union,* 2–3.

7 GARO, f. R-4, op. 3, d. 5, l. 7.

8 Mar'iankhin, *Ocherki istorii nalogov s naseleniia v SSSR,* 53.

9 GARO, f. R-4, op. 3, d. 5, l. 8.

10 GARO, f. R-4, op. 3 (1926), l. 22. The collection breakdown per uezd: Dankov, 74.7%; Elat'ma, 76.3%; Kasimov, 93.5%; Mikhailov, 80.2%; Pronsk, 85.3%; Ranenburg, 82%; Riazan, 88.9%; Riazhsk, 73.6%; Sapozhok, 67.8%; Shatsk, 91.7%; Skopin, 80.9%; Spassk, 76.3%; Spas-Klepiki, 97.2%; Zaraisk, 90.0%.

11 GARO, f. R-4, op. 3, d. 10 (1926), l. 91.

12 GARO, f. R-4, op. 3, d. 6 (1925), l. 248 ob. And this practice was part of Tsarist taxation policy. See Kotsonis, '"Face-to-Face,"' 224.

13 Bol'shakov, *Derevnia posle Oktiabria,* 93.

14 GARO, f. R-4, op. 3, d. 6 (1925), ll. 1, 10.

15 Uritskii, *Chto dolzhen znat' krest'ianin o nalogakh,* 29.

16 GARO, f. R-2461, op. 5, d. 239, ll. 6–28.

17 GARO, f. R-4, op. 3, d. 8 (1927), ll. 273–274 ob.

18 Carr, *Socialism in One Country 1924–26,* 1:250. See also, Davies, *The Development of the Soviet Budgetary System,* 114–17.

19 Uritskii, *Chto dolzhen znat' krest'ianin o nalogakh,* 23–4.

20 Liakhova, *Finansovo-nalogovaia rabota volosti,* 1–56; and Uritskii, *Chto dolzhen znat' krest'ianin o nalogakh,* 18–24.
21 GARO, f. R-4, op. 3 (1925), d. 6, l. 10.
22 'Kulatskie radeteli,' *Kollektiv,* 10 Dec. 1924.
23 GARO, f. R-4, op. 3 (1925), d. 6, ll. 66–7.
24 'Dela derevenskie,' *Derevenskaia gazeta,* 7 Jan. 1926, 4.
25 GARO, f. R-4, op. 3 (1925), d. 6, ll. 19–20.
26 V. Mokeev, 'Blizhe k derevne,' *ESIu* 39–40 (9–16 Oct. 1924): 922.
27 RGASPI, f. 17, op. 32. d. 99, l. 9.
28 Liakhova, *Finansovo-nalogovaia rabota volosti,* 154–63.
29 GARO, f. R-4, op. 1, d. 485, ll. 43–4. An expanded list, issued to the police in 1927, detailed what could and could not be seized. Police were reminded not to confiscate tools and books necessary for a given profession. They were asked not to confiscate axes, hammers, planes, and chisels from carpenters; needles, glue, leather, and boot trees from bootmakers; instruments and books from doctors, dentists, and vets; or musical instruments from musicians. Every citizen of the republic had the right to the following: at least one set of winter and summer wear, one jacket, one hat, three changes of underwear, one pair of felt boots, and one pair of leather boots. Each family member was entitled to keep one spoon, knife, fork, teacup or glass, stool, bed, pillow, and two towels. The household was entitled to keep a samovar or kettle for boiling water, a primus or kerosene stove, a lamp, one dining table, two tablecloths, two tea towels, two kitchen towels, two buckets, one trunk or something to keep outerwear in, and the most necessary cookware (pots, a cast-iron pot, oven fork, poker, and a kneading trough), wood for cooking and warmth for a period of one month, and enough food to feed each member of the family for one month: one pud and five funts of flour (or one pud, twelve funts of grain), one pud of potatoes, five funts of buckwheat groats, three funts of salt, one funt of oil (or four funts of sunflowers), and ten funts of vegetables of any kind. Each household in 1927 could still keep, according to law, one cow and one horse plus a specified amount of feed, a plough, a harrow, a cart, a sledge, and small implements such as scythes, sickles, axes, rakes, pitchforks, and shovels, as well as unharvested grain and seed grain. GARO, f. R-63, op. 1, d. 49, ll. 85–86 ob.
30 Bol'shakov, *Derevnia posle Oktiabria,* 182–3.
31 GARO, f. R-4, op. 1, d. 990, ll. 113–41.
32 GARO, f. R-4, op. 3, d. 6 (1925), ll. 282 ob.–283.
33 GARO, f. R-4, op. 3, d. 6 (1925), ll. 52–3. It is worth noting that Borets Dis-

trict was so problematic. In the chapter on banditry, one catches a glimpse of local government in Borets, and it is possible that a high-ranking 'bandit' convinced his OGPU colleagues that the district was in terrible shape and could not pay its taxes.

34 Carr, *Socialism in One Country*, 249–69, 296–328; and Danilov, 'Sovetskaia nalogovaia politika v dokolkhoznoi derevne,' 184.

35 Newcity, *Taxation in the Soviet Union*, 7–21; Mar'iankhin, *Ocherki istorii nalogov s naseleniia v SSSR*, 46–61; and Uritskii, *Chto dolzhen znat' krest'ianin o nalogakh*, 3–13.

36 Mar'iankhin, *Ocherki istorii nalogov s naseleniia v SSSR*, 105.

37 Danilov, 'Sovetskaia nalogovaia politika v dokolkhoznoi derevne,' 185.

38 Penner, 'Pride, Power and Pitchforks,' 390–1, traces a similar pattern.

39 Mar'iankhin, *Ocherki istorii nalogov s naseleniia v SSSR*, 127–8.

40 GARO, f. R-4, op. 3 (1926), d. 10 (1926), ll. 373–4.

41 GARO, f. R-4, op. 3 (1927), d. 8 (1927), ll. 3–4.

42 See in particular the July and October 1927 editions of Riazan and Sapozhok's *Derevenskaia gazeta*. For more on newspapers and their impact on central-level politics, see Lenoe, 'Letter-Writing and the State.' Lenoe recounts that newspaper reports on peasant attitudes to the agricultural tax, among other topics, went to high party leaders such as Stalin, Molotov, Bukharin, and Kaganovich, and 'from the content of the intelligence reports themselves, the party's leaders felt that foreign subversion, peasant resistance, intra-party conflict, and the erosion of their base of support among factory workers actually threatened their rule' (154).

43 'Usilim sbor naloga!' *Derevenskaia gazeta*, 12 Oct. 1927, 6.

44 Grain requisitioning has received the most attention in the available literature and will not be explored in detail here. For more, see Davies, *Socialist Offensive*; Lewin, *Russian Peasants and Soviet Power*; Moshe Lewin, '"Taking Grain": Soviet Policies of Agricutural Procurements before the War,' in Lewin, *Making of the Soviet System*, 142–77; and Viola et al., *War against the Peasantry*, 20–2, 57.

45 GARO, f. R-5, op. 1, d. 106, ll. 10–14.

46 RGASPI, f. 17, op. 3, d. 667, ll. 10–12, in V. Danilov, Manning, and Viola, *Tragediia sovetskoi derevni*, 1:136. See also Danilov's discussion of the directive on p. 31 of his introduction.

47 RGASPI, f. 17, op. 2, d. 375 (pt 2), ll. 50 ob.–66 ob., as excerpted in Viola et al., *War against the Peasantry*, 99. At the same plenum, Bukharin objected:

> Tribute is a category that has nothing in common with socialist construction. But unfortunately, the pithy catchword of 'tribute' proved to

be not merely 'literary.' Connected with it is the subsequent change in the taxation of the peasantry, the growing difficulties with the supply of bread, the reduction in the sown area, and the dissatisfaction of the peasantry (now we will have to reduce taxes). Nobody has discussed the question of 'tribute.' Nobody has the right to demand that a member of the party makes common cause with this 'tribute.' Meanwhile, the situation has become such that no one can say a word against the 'tribute' because Comrade Stalin has pronounced this word. The fiery Comrade Petrovsky (*Leningradskaia pravda*) has written against the 'tribute' but quickly found himself in the position of deputy editor of the Saratov Krai planning committee press organ (a journal with a circulation of one thousand). Meanwhile, this formula overturned all the previous party decisions, and this is why it produced such an immense impression. Naturally, I could not agree with this formula and viewed it as an omen of further 'extraordinary' policies. At the July plenum, Comrade Kaganovich was aiming for the repetition of extraordinary measures, 'just in case.' Although it was necessary to emphasize peace with the middle peasant, people laughed at this. (114)

48 See Ivnitskii, *Repressivnaia politika sovetskoi vlasti v derevne (1928–1933)*, 29–30.

49 Ibid., 30.

50 V.P. Danilov does an excellent job of illustrating this process across the country as a whole in his introduction to *Tragediia sovetskoi derevni*, 1:13–67.

51 See, for example, GARO, f. R-5, op. 1, d. 47, ll. 20, 24.

52 GARO, f. R-4, op.1, d. 1965, ll. 225–30.

53 GARO, f. R-4, op. 1, d. 106, l. 9.

54 Table 4 in the appendix provides a graphic look at tax collection in Riazan for October 1928. Keeping in mind that tax collection was over-fulfilled in 1928–9, the table suggests how much pressure was placed on the countryside to pay up in early 1929. Table 5 captures the continuing shift of taxes to households perceived as being wealthy. By 1930, an estimated 2.8 per cent of households branded as 'kulak' were paying 26 per cent of the country's taxes. Note the squeeze on the wealthier middle peasants in 1928–9.

55 Danilov, 'Sovetskaia nalogovaia politika v dokolkhoznoi derevne,' 187–8.

56 Liakhova, ed., *Finansovo-nalogovaia rabota volosti*, 148–50. For more on peasant convictions that insurance was a clever state ploy to raise revenue, see Penner, 'Pride, Power and Pitchforks,' 396–8.

57 'Samooblozhenie sel'skogo naseleniia,' *Krest'ianskii iurist* 2 (31 Jan. 1928): 3.

58 'Kampaniia po samooblozhenii: ee nedochety,' *Krest'ianskii iurist* 12 (30 June 1928): 7. See also Ivnitskii, *Repressivnaia politika*, 27–8.

59 Penner, 'Pride, Power and Pitchforks,' 409. Penner notes the same phenomenon: 'Neither should rebellion by farmers against the new, externally defined terms of their self-taxation policy be cited in support of the myth of farmers' irresponsibility. As often as not during the NEP years, the driving force behind the bridges that were mended, the schools that were repaired, maintained and supplied with fuel for the winter session, came from the farmers themselves.'

60 GARO, f. R-4, op. 3, d. 9, ll. 90–1.

61 See, for example, Kalinin's pitch on the second industrial bond in M.I. Kalinin, 'Vtoroi zaem industrializatsii,' *Krest'ianskii iurist* 16 (31 Aug. 1928): 1, in which he explains to peasants that Soviet power needs their help to raise 500 million rubles with 25 ruble bonds, in five easy payments of 5 rubles each, to build more factories and promote agriculture.

62 RGASPI, f. 17, op. 85, d. 318, ll. 22–4. Rates of success for collections varied across Riazan. In December 1928, the figures ranged from 33.9 per cent of targets collected in Borets (already known as a problematic location; see the chapter on banditry) to 81.7 per cent collected in Sapozhok. Most localities came in between 50 and 70 per cent. GARO, f. R-5, op. 1, d. 47, l. 50.

63 GARO, f. R-4, op. 3 (1929), d. 11, l. 19.

64 Ibid., ll. 19–27.

65 Ibid., l. 15.

66 GARO, f. R-4, op. 3, d. 11, ll. 14–15.

67 Ibid., ll. 93–4. It seems that the sale of state bonds remained an unpopular task in the early 1930s as well. The impoverished, marginalized, and shunned Pavel Morozov was recruited to sell bonds in 1932. See Druzhnikov, *Informer 001*, 36–7.

68 GARO, f. R-4, op. 3 (1929), d. 11, l. 142.

69 Ibid., l. 180.

70 Ibid.

71 Penner, 'Pride, Power and Pitchforks,' 399.

72 This theme will be further developed in the final chapter, which focuses on the dynamics of a village rebellion.

73 GARO, f. R-4, op. 1, d. 1965, l. 37.

74 GARO, f. R-4, op. 3 (1929), d. 11, l. 36.

75 Ibid., l. 181.

76 Ibid., l. 142.

77 Ibid., l. 119.

78 He may even have transmogrified into the legendary 'Os'kin' of Ianin's narrative! See the final chapter.

79 Borders, *Village Life under the Soviets*, 126.

80 Danilov, 'Sovetskaia nalogovaia politika v dokolkhoznoi derevne,' 164.
81 Ivnitskii, introduction to 'Tianut s muzhika poslednie zhily,' in *Nalogovaia politika v derevne (1928–1937)*, ed. Ivnitskii, Sorokina, and Tiurina, 3–17.
82 Ibid., 15.
83 Kotsonis, '"Face-to-Face,"' 233.
84 Ibid., 228.
85 Ibid., 229.
86 Ibid., 239–40.
87 Ibid., 240.
88 Ibid., 241–2. See also Kotsonis, '"No Place to Go,"' 536–60.
89 '"Face-to-Face,"' 242–3, and '"No Place to Go,"' 558.
90 '"Face-to-Face,"' 243–4, and "No Place to Go,"' 559–60. Peter Holquist traces similar patterns in grain requisitioning policy through the Tsarist regime to the civil war. The Tsarist regime opted to override rather than utilize market structures in acquiring grain. The Provisional Government did the same, as did the Soviet regime. *Making War, Forging Revolution*, 35–44.
91 Kotsonis, '"No Place to Go,"' 565.
92 Ibid., 567.
93 Ibid., 568–9.
94 Ibid., 571–4.
95 Ibid., 573–4.

6. The Forest

1 Translations of the technical language of forestry have presented a challenge. Moskalev called himself a *smotritel,'* which would translate as 'keeper or custodian.' In the official literature, what I have chosen to translate as 'forest guard' appears in Russian as *lesnoi strazh, lesnaia strazha, lesnoi storozh.* The guard was divided between foresters (*lesniki*) and patrollers or wardens (*ob"ezdchiki*), known together as the forest guard. I have chosen to refer to an individual as a 'forest guard,' regardless of whether he was a *lesnik* or an *ob"ezdchik,* because their functions overlapped in the 1920s. They worked together and had the same powers in the apprehension of wood thieves, the main focus of this chapter. *Lesnichestvo* refers both to the forest district in the 1920s and to the forest administration offices in charge of a forest district. Bonhomme, *Forests, Peasants, and Revolutionaries,* 168n84, also discusses the distinctions and similarities between *lesnik* and *ob"ezdchik.* For an amazing tale of the intricacies of forest conflicts, see Balzac, *The Peasants.*
2 All measures in this case were converted from *vershok.* One *vershok* is equal to 4.4 centimetres.

3 GARO, f. R-343, op. 1, d. 3183, ll. 5–5 ob.

4 Ibid., l. 9.

5 See, for example, Retish's work on Viatka, *Russia's Peasants*, esp. chap. 4.

6 See Olenetskii Gubpolitprosveta, *Lesozagotovitel'naia kampaniia 1921–22 operativnogo goda v Olenetskoi gubernii*, 3, for a good comparison of Russian dependence on wood in 1916 to other countries (reproduced in table 6 in the appendix).

7 See *Les krest'ianam*, 1.

8 See for example, Guha, *The Unquiet Woods*; Harrison, *Forests*; Mooser, 'Property and Wood Theft'; Pathak, *Contested Domains*; Sahlins, *Forest Rites*; and Whited, *Forests and Peasant Politics.*

9 Linebaugh, 'Karl Marx, the Theft of Wood, and Working-Class Composition.'

10 Marx, *Collected Works of Marx and Engels*, 1:225. Marx begins his series of articles on the matter in a way relevant to the present study:

> At the very beginning of the debate, one of the urban deputies objected to the title of the law, which extends the category of 'theft' to include simple offences against forest regulations. A deputy of the knightly estate replied, 'It is precisely because the pilfering of wood is not regarded as theft that it occurs so often.' By analogy, the legislator would have to draw the following conclusion: It is because a box on the ear is not regarded as murder that it has become so frequent. It should be decreed therefore that a box on the ear is murder. From the point of view recommended above, which mistakes the conversion of a citizen into a thief for a mere negligence in formulation and rejects all opposition to it as grammatical purism, it is obvious that even the pilfering of fallen wood or the gathering of dry wood is included under the heading of theft and punished as severely as the stealing of live, growing timber.

11 Jane Costlow's work provides a rich and fascinating look into the 'forest question' in the nineteeth century in both scientific literature as well as works of fiction and visual art. See 'Imaginations of Destruction' and 'Who Holds the Axe?'

12 See, for example, Barr and Braden, *Disappearing Russian Forest*; Bonhomme, *Forests*; Harris, 'Growth of the Gulag'; Pallot, 'Forced Labour for Forestry'; and Weiner, *Models of Nature.*

13 Stephen Frank and Cathy Frierson have explored the matter briefly for the pre-Revolutionary period. See Frank, *Crime, Cultural Conflict and Justice*, 24, 63–5, 104–13; and Frierson, 'Crime and Punishment in the Russian Village,' 58–9.

14 Keep, *Russian Revolution*, 204.
15 See, for example, Stepanova, 'Riazanskoe krest'ianstvo v gody vtoroi revoliutsionnoi situatsii,' 16–18.
16 S.N., 'Les i okhota,' in *Les. Sbornik statei*, 9.
17 GARO, f. R-4, op. 3 (1923), d. 4, l. 19.
18 For historical background on forest protection before the Emancipation, see Bonhomme, *Forests*, 14–20; Narodnyi Komissariat Raboche-Krest'ianskoi Inspektsii RSFSR, *Lesa mestnogo znacheniia*, 7; and Treplyakov et al., *History of Russian Forestry*, 6–7.
19 French, 'Russians and the Forest,' 1:24.
20 Bonhomme, *Forests*, 18–27; Frank, *Crime, Cultural Conflict, and Justice*, 109–14; French, 'Russians and the Forest,' 24–38; Narodnyi Komissariat Raboche-Krest'ianskoi Inspektsii RSFSR, *Lesa mestnogo znacheniia*, 7–8; and Treplyakov et al., *History of Russian Forestry*, 6–9. See also Yaney, *Urge to Mobilize.*
21 Frank, *Crime, Cultural Conflict, and Justice*, 105–11. See also Frierson, 'Crime and Punishment in the Russian Village,' 58–9.
22 Bonhomme, *Forests*, traces these debates in detail.
23 These findings mirror those emphasized by Holquist in *Making War, Forging Revolution.*
24 See, for example, Men'shikov, 'Obshchestvo druzei lesa,' in *Les. Sbornik statei*, 15–16, who wrote, 'The only path to the conservation of the forests is to overcome the peasant instinct to destroy it ... to explain to him day after day that the forest is not the enemy but the friend of the agriculturalist.'
25 GARO, f. R-298, op. 1, d. 3696, ll. 3–5.
26 Bonhomme, *Forests*, 14–166. Bonhomme tends to be very sympathetic to the voices of the early conservationists.
27 *Lesnoi kodeks RSFSR s izmeneniiami na 1 fevralia 1918: Izdanie ofitsial'noe* (Moscow: Novaia derevnia, 1928), especially articles 1, 4, 8, 10, 23, 24, 33–5, 69–73. For more on access and distribution, see V. Fedorov, 'Lesa mestnogo znacheniia,' *Krest'ianskii iurist* 3 (15 Feb. 1928): 10–12; *Les Krest'ianam* (which reminded the peasants on the first page, '*Samovol'no rubit, pod sud ugodish*" [Cut wood yourself, wind up in prison]); RSFSR Narodnyi Komissariat Zemledeliia, *Lesnoe Khoziaistvo RSFSR i perspektivy ego razvitiia*, 65–151.
28 Narodnyi Komissariat Raboche-Krest'ianskoi Inspektsii RSFSR, *Lesa mestnogo znacheniia*, 34.
29 A. Tomilin, 'Lesnye dela: Do sikh por mnogo zhalob na lesnikov,' *Bednota*, 6 Feb. 1925, 3. Although this office was located in Tver, a similar scenario played out across central Russia. Other contributors to *Bednota* made similar complaints, saying that the forest district offices were becoming kiosks for

the issuing of wood-cutting tickets. See N. Voznyi, 'Kak uluchit' otpusk lesa? O kollektivnom otpuske,' *Bednota*, 13 Dec. 1924, 1.

30 'Golosa o lese: V chem prochina samovol'nykh porubok,' *Bednota*, 30 Jan. 1927, 3.

31 Narodnyi Komissariat Raboche-Krest'ianskoi Inspektsii RSFSR, *Lesa mestnogo znacheniia*, 46–7.

32 GARO, f.R-298, op. 1, d. 4130, ll. 32–3 ob. In 1924, in Sapozhok the cooperatives organized wood supply, but the inhabitants of the area complained that they added a tax of 10 per cent to the charges, so citizens tried to bypass the cooperative and went directly to the offices of the forest administration instead. See also statistics (1925–6) on thefts from the area's (Riazhsk) forests from GARO, f. R-342, op. 1, d. 6672, ll. 5–5 ob., and in table 7 in the appendix.

33 GARO, f.R-298, op. 1, d. 4130, l. 39 ob.

34 Narodnyi Komissariat Raboche-Krest'ianskoi Inspektsii RSFSR, *Lesa mestnogo znacheniia*, 32–3.

35 Ibid., 53–4. See also S.P. Kavelin, 'Lesnye dela. Mozhno li vyrastit' derevo i prodat' ego?' *Bednota*, 17 July 1924, 3, and the entire issue of *Bednota*, 10 Jan. 1925.

36 See, for example, Kudriavtsev, 'Lesu nuzhen khozian,' *Bednota*, 29 Apr. 1927, 3; and Fedorov, 'Lesa mestnogo znacheniia,' 10–12, for a detailed look at the duties and responsibilities of the rural and district soviets toward the forest.

37 GARO, f. R-343, op. 1, d. 6672, l. 5 ob.

38 In his ethnographic study, Fenomenov mentions the 'plunder of the forests' and the stockpiling of wood. See *Sovremennaia derevnia*, 1:69.

39 Bol'shakov, *Derevnia posle Oktiabria*, 194. Rural soviets received reminders in Riazan in the 1920s to verify their consituents' claims to poverty before issuing them the documents necessary to receive free or discounted wood. See, for example, GARO, f. R-343, op. 1, d. 3183, l. 31.

40 Tan-Bogoraz, *Staryi i novyi byt*, 104.

41 See GARO, f. R-63, op. 1, d. 49, ll. 57–60 ob.; and 'O poriadke presledovaniia narushenii v lesakh gosudarstvennogo lesnogo fonda,' *ESIu* 51 (27 Dec. 1926): 1429–31.

42 *Ugolovnyi kodeks RSFSR* (Moscow, 1924), 20.

43 Ovchinkin, 'O lesorubkakh,' *Proletarskii sud*, July–Aug. 1924, 23.

44 GARO, f. 2461, op. 6, d. 121. See also d. 120, in which the court made the same ruling on another group of thieves who had been sentenced by the people's court en masse. In fact, the reason that so few cases are used in this chapter to provide insight into who stole wood is that most sentencing consisted of group sentences with a list of names and the fine noted beside

the accused. Few exchanged words were recorded.

45 For more on the decriminalization, see Solomon, 'Criminalization and Decriminalization.'

46 See Goliakov, *Sbornik dokumentov po istorii ugolovnogo zakonodatel'stva SSSR i RSFSR, 1917–1952 gg.*, 177.

47 E.K., 'St 99 Ugolovnogo Kodeksa,' *ESIu* 20 (24 May 1925): 554–6.

48 N. Lagovier, ' Administrativnye vzyskaniia v bor'be s samovol'nymi porubkami,' *Vlast' sovetov* 30 (1927): 7–8.

49 GARO, f. R-343, op. 1, d. 4852, l. 62.

50 Narkomiust Kurskii, Tsirkuliar No. 51, 'O poriakde raspredeleniia konfiskovannoi ili otobrannoi u lesonarushitelei drevesiny i vsyskannykh s nikh denezhnykh summ,' *ESIu* 14 (11 Apr. 1926): 445.

51 'O lesorubakh, militsii i vzyskannykh den'gakh,' *Bednota*, 5 July 1928.

52 GARO, f. R-298, op. 1, d. 4853, l. 83.

53 Ibid., l. 36.

54 Lagovier, 'Administrativnye vzyskaniia,' 7–8.

55 GARO, f. R-343, op. 1, d. 7427, l. 10.

56 GARO, f. R-343, op. 1, d. 6672, l. 31.

57 See GARO, f. R-342, op. 1, d. 7417, ll. 59–61 ob.; and Fedorov, 'Lesa mestnogo znacheniia,' 10–12; and 'Novoe polozhenie o lesakh mestnogo znacheniia (postanovlenie Sovnarkoma RSFSR ot 30 dekabria 1927 g.),' *Krest'ianskii iurist* 4 (29 Feb. 1928): 9–12.

58 A. Iodkovskii, 'Bor'ba s lesnymi narusheniiami,' *Krest'ianskii iurist* 2 (31 Jan. 1928): 8–9.

59 'O lesorubakh, militsii i vzyskannykh den'gakh,' 3.

60 See N. Lagovier, 'Nedosoly i perebarshchivaniia v bor'be s lesokhishcheniiami,' *Bednota*, 9 Sept. 1927, 1.

61 See Bonhomme, *Forests*, 182–93. Instructions on dealing with forest violations came from NKZ, NKIu, NKFin, NKTrud, the police, and the forest departments. See GARO, f. R-63, op. 1, d. 49, l. 30. Within Narkomzem alone, instructions were issued by the forest inspectors, the forest area administration, and the land administration offices on all levels. See RSFSR Narodnyi Komissariat Zemledeliia Upravlenie Lesami, *Meropriiatiia po lesnomu khoziaistvu RSFSR*, 144. This publication calls for systematization, rationalization, supervision, discipline, and control; see 144–53.

62 Narodnyi Komissariat Raboche-Krest'ianskoi Inspektsii RSFSR, *Lesa mestnogo znacheniia*, 58–9.

63 RSFSR Narodnyi Komissariat Zemel'nogo Upravleniia Lesami, *Lesnoe khoziaistvo RSFSR i perspektivy ego razvitiia* (Moscow, 1927), 2:123; and GARO, f. R-1440, op. 1, d. 116, ll. 28–9.

64 GARO, f. R-343, op. 1, d. 3183, l. 31.
65 Ibid., l. 33.
66 GARO, f. R-343, op. 1, d. 4852, l. 124, and f. R-343, op. 1, d. 6672, l. 25.
67 GARO, f. R-343, op. 1, d. 6672, l. 27.
68 Ibid., l. 51.
69 GARO, f. R-61, op. 1, d. 441, l. 257.
70 Forest guards were seen as a major cause of forest fires. The guards themselves blamed the fires on garbage fires that ran out of control or some other kind of negligence. As Cathy Frierson points out, however, such excuses are typical of peasants who well knew that negligence was much more positively regarded than arson. See *All Russia Is Burning*, 55–7.
71 GARO, f. R-343, op. 1, d. 4852, l. 125.
72 GARO, f. R-343, op. 1, d. 3700, ll. 49–109; GARO, f. R-4, op. 3 (1923), d. 4, ll. 6–7; GARO, f. R-343, op. 1, d. 3183, l. 80.
73 GARO, f. R-343, op. 1, d. 3183, l. 33.
74 GARO, f. R-298, op. 1, d. 4130, l. 20 ob.
75 Tomilin, 'Lesnye dela,' p. 3.
76 GARO, f. R-343, op. 1, d. 3183, l. 4.
77 GARO, f. R-342, op. 1, d. 6672, l. 4.
78 GARO, f. R-61, op. 1, d. 441, l. 260 ob.
79 GARO, f-343, op. 1, d. 6672, l. 79. See also A. Kondratiev, 'Lesokhishcheniia i bor'ba s nimi,' *ESIu* 49 (28 Oct. 1927): 1312–13, who supported confiscation of axes and saws.
80 GARO, f. R-63, op. 1, d. 49, l. 64, and f. R-298, op. 1, d. 4854, ll. 12–16 ob., for a ten-page document itemizing the obligations of the rural and district soviets.
81 RSFSR Narodnyi Komissariat Zemledeliia Upravlenie Lesami, *Lesnoe khoziaistvo*, 123–5.
82 GARO, f. R-343, op. 1, d. 3183, ll. 1–2 ob.
83 GARO, f. R-343, op. 1, d. 4852, l. 92.
84 See Bonhomme, *Forest, Peasants, and Revolutionaries*, 165–6; Costlow, 'Who Holds the Axe?,' 20–1; and Frank, *Crime, Cultural Conflict, and Justice*, 111–13. See also GARO, f. R-55, op. 1, d. 177, l. 71.
85 GARO, f. R-298, op. 1, d. 3690, l. 12. For more examples of such letters, see the excerpts in the newspaper of the Riazhsk and Sapazhok party committees, 'Unichtozhenie lesov,' *Sovetskaia derevnia* (18 Jan. 1924): 3.
86 GARO, f. R-342, op. 1, d. 3183, l. 20.
87 Ibid.
88 Ibid., l. 23.
89 GARO, f. R-298, op. 1, d. 3690, ll. 15–18.

90 Evidence such as this letter supports arguments made by Jane Burbank on pre-Revolutionary peasant 'legal culture' as well as arguments made by Aaron Retish and Corinne Gaudin about peasant willingness to engage with state power. See Burbank, *Russian Peasants Go to Court*; Gaudin, *Ruling Peasants*; and Retish, *Russia's Peasants.*

91 GARO, f. R-343, op. 1, d. 3182, ll. 83–4.

92 GARO, f. R-343, op. 1, d. 3183, l. 70.

93 GARO, f. R-343, op. 1, d. 3180, ll. 1–14; and 'Sud nad banditom,' *Rabochii klich,* 1 and 2 July 1925.

94 GARO, f. R-343, op. 1, d. 3180, ll. 23–40.

95 'Lesnye dela: Ne delaite iz lesnykh rabotnikov vorov!' *Bednota,* 8 Aug. 1924. Note the date, shortly following the Kudom massacre, and thus still sympathetic to the conditions of the guard.

96 On turnover, see RSFSR Narodnyi Komissariat Zemledeliia Upravlenie Lesami, *Lesnoe khoziaistvo RSFSR v 1927/28 godu* (Moscow, 1928), 10.

97 GARO, f. R-343, op. 1, d. 4852, ll. 19–20, 30.

98 Ibid., ll. 96, 98.

99 Ibid., l. 30.

100 Ibid., l. 106.

101 Ibid., ll. 2–2 ob.

102 Ibid., l. 48.

103 'Les, krest'iane i lesnye rabotniki,' *Bednota,* 27 Aug. 1925; and 'Les trebuet khoziaiskoi ruki,' *Krest'ianskaia gazeta,* 25 Sept. 1925, 3. For more complaints on the corrupt nature of the forest guard, see GARO, f. R-4, op. 3 (1925), d. 6, l. 40; GARO, f. R-61, op. 1, d. 441, l. 241; 'Lesa v opasnosti,' *Derevenskaia gazeta,* 1 Aug. 1926, 1; 'Ubrat' strozha Ivana Boikova,' *Derevenskaia gazeta,* 1 Aug. 1926, 5; Kondratiev, 'Lesokhishcheniia i bor'ba s nimi,' 1312–13; N. Lagovier, 'Nedosoly i perebarshchivaniia v bor'be s lesokhishcheniiami,' 1; GARO, f. R-298, op. 1, d. 4591, l. 107; GARO, f. R-343, op. 1, d. 4852, l. 125.

104 GARO, f. R-343, op. 1, d. 3183, ll. 71, 84.

105 Mozhaev, *Muzhiki i baby,* 104–5.

106 Tomilin, 'Lesnye dela,' 3. For more on the mutual protection between foresters and patrollers, see GARO, f. R-61, op. 1, d. 441, l. 242.

107 GARO, f. R-343, op. 1, d. 3700, ll. 11–12.

108 Ibid., ll. 67, 81.

109 Narodnyi Komissariat Raboche-Krest'ianskoi Inspektsii RSFSR, *Lesa mestnogo znacheniia,* 54–5.

110 In his conclusion to *Forests,* 232–3, Bonhomme does raise the question, 'Should forest-related tensions be added to the usual list of factors cited by

historians who seek to explain the state's decision in favor of collectivization.'

111 See Goliakov, *Sbornik dokumentov*, 177.

112 GARO, f. R-343, op. 1, d. 6672, l. 61.

113 GARO, f. R-343, op. 1, d. 7427, l. 10.

114 GARO, f. R-298, op. 1, d. 4853, l. 78.

115 GARO, f. R-343, op. 1, d. 4852, l. 135.

116 GARO, f. R-298, op. 1, d. 4591, ll. 2–158.

117 GARO, f. R-298, op. 1, d. 4853, l. 36.

118 GARO, f. R-1440, op. 1, d. 441, ll. 258–9, and op. 1, d. 116, ll. 28–9.

119 GARO, f. R-298, op. 1, d. 4853, ll. 24–33; f. R-61, op. 1, d. 441, l. 242; and RSFSR Narodnyi Komissariat Zemledeliia Upravlenie Lesami, *Meropriiatiia*, 154–7.

120 RSFSR Narodnyi Komissariat Zemledeliia Upravlenie Lesami, *Lesnoe khoziastvo RSFSR v 1927/28 godu*, 112–14.

121 GARO, f. R-298, op. 1, d. 4853, l. 140.

122 GARO, f. R-5, op. 1, d. 161, ll. 19–24. See also f. R-298, op. 1, d. 4854, ll. 1–4.

123 GARO, f. 298, op. 1, d. 4853, l. 35.

124 See, for example, A.T., 'Zhaluiutsia na neporiadki s otpuskom lesa,' *Bednota*, 5 Feb. 1928, 2.

125 GARO, f. 298, op. 1, d. 4853, ll. 41–8.

126 Ibid., l. 42.

127 GARO, f. R-298, op. 1, d. 4592, ll. 3–16. I have translated the word *svoi* here as 'insiders.' A better but more awkward translation would be 'our own' or 'our people.' Parentheses in the original.

128 GARO, f. R-5, op. 1, d. 156, l. 20.

129 GARO, f. R-5, op. 1, d. 4, ll. 2–23. Much of the material on scarcity running through this chapter echoes Alexopoulos's findings in *Stalin's Outcasts*, especially regarding the savings of resources by denying them to the disenfranchised. See, for example, 29.

130 From Len, ed., *Predstavleniia vostochnykh slavian*, 182, quoted in Worobec, 'Witches, Sorcerers, and Demons,' 17, quoted with permission. In the Rabkrin, Narkomzem, and court materials no one made reference to forest spirits or demons. Such references were perhaps part of a different kind of dialogue, involving alternate identities and a different context.

131 Gille, 'From Nature as Proxy to Nature as Actor,' 9.

132 Costlow, 'Who Holds the Axe?' 19.

133 See, for example, GARO, f. R-2461, op. 6, d. 2806, ll. 1–4, and d. 121, ll. 4–15; f. R-2541, op. 1, d. 380, l. 9, and d. 160, ll. 1–1 ob.

134 Ovchinkin, 'O lesorubkakh,' 23.
135 GARO, f. R-343, op. 1, d. 6672, l. 5. In Riazhsk, for example, in 1923–4, 17,629 people were charged in 2,953 cases of forest violation, showing the degree to which wood theft was a 'group crime' by necessity, of course, given the labour involved.
136 Lahusen, Garros, and Korenevskaya, *Intimacy and Terror,* 144.

7. Bandit Tales

1 'Smert' sel'kor Shchelokov,' *Derevenskaia gazeta,* 17 Nov. 1927, 1.
2 Some may claim that this story is a fabrication created in light of pressures to launch a press campaign on banditry. Local documents confirm the existence of the gang and the events as recorded in the press. Moreover, the case is so revealing on multiple levels precisely *because* the press chose to highlight this case within such a campaign.
3 'Smert' sel'kor Shchelokov,' *Derevenskaia gazeta,* 17 Nov. 1927, 1.
4 'Delo Riazhskikh banditov: Otchego soshel s uma sel'kor Shchelokov,' *Derevenskaia gazeta,* 2 Sept. 1927, 2. See also 'Slovo-sudu! Delo Riazanskikh banditov,' *Bednota,* 3 Sept. 1927; and 'Delo Riazanskikh banditov,' *Krest'ianskaia gazeta,* 6 Sept. 1927, 2.
5 'Delo Riazanskikh banditov,' *Krest'ianskaia gazeta,* 27 Sept. 1927, 4.
6 'Delo Riazhskikh banditov,' *Derevenskaia gazeta,* 16 Sept. 1927, 2.
7 'Delo Riazhskikh banditov,' *Bednota,* 13 Sept. 1927, 3.
8 Ibid.
9 'Delo Riazhskikh banditov: Otchego soshel s uma sel'kor Shchelokov,' 2.
10 'Delo Riazhskikh banditov,' *Derevenskaia gazeta,* 10 Sept. 1927, 2–3.
11 'Sel'kor Shchelokov vyzdorovel,' *Derevenskaia gazeta,* 6 July 1927, 4.
12 GARO, f. R-4, op. 3 (1927), d. 8, l. 28.
13 'Delo Riazhskikh banditov,' *Derevenskaia gazeta,* 10 Sept. 1927, 2. See also 'Delo Riazanskikh banditov,' *Krest'ianskaia gazeta,* 27 Sept. 1927, 3, for a description of the opening of the trial; and 'Delo Riazanskikh banditov,' *Krest'ianskaia gazeta,* 27 Sept. 1927, 4, for the number of witnesses.
14 'Delo Riazanskikh banditov,' *Krest'ianskaia gazeta,* 27 Sept. 1927, 4.
15 'Delo Riazhskikh banditov,' *Bednota,* 6 Sept. 1927, 4
16 On the murder of Petin, see 'Delo Riazhskikh banditov,' *Derevenskaia gazeta,* 21 Sept. 1927, 2; and GARO, f. R-4, op. 3 (1927), d. 8, ll. 32, 78.
17 'Delo Riazhskikh banditov,' *Derevenskaia gazeta,* 21 Sept. 1927, 2.
18 'Delo Riazhskikh banditov,' *Bednota,* 13 Sept. 1927, 3.
19 'Delo Riazhskikh banditov,' *Derevenskaia gazeta,* 21 Sept. 1927, 2; and 'Delo Riazanskikh banditov,' *Krest'ianskaia gazeta,* 27 Sept. 1927, 4.

20 'Delo Riazhskikh banditov,' *Bednota*, 17 Sept. 1927, 4.

21 GARO, f. R-4, op. 3 (1928), d. 8, l. 50; see ll. 34–55 for the full OGPU report on the continuation of bandit activities by a band called '*Butyrskii trest.*'

22 See Solomon, *Soviet Criminal Justice under Stalin*, 65–6, for a discussion of the 1927 amnesty.

23 An article in the NKVD journal *Administrativnyi vestnik* complained about the involvement in corrupt activities and links with bandit gangs by local officialdom across the Soviet Union. The article describes the bandit group '*bim-bombisy*,' better known by its shorter name '*bim-bom.*' The gang was founded in 1923 by a former employee of the GPU, Abramchik Lekher, who, upon his dismissal from the GPU, organized a bandit gang with his father in his home village. In the ranks of the band were many employees of 'various soviet and cooperative' establishments, including the village and raion soviets. The band, it seems, stole horses from villagers and cooperatives, and nothing was done because of the collusion or inclusion of local officials with the band. The gang members socialized at the home of the local gendarme, where they drank and 'partied' (*bezobraznichali*) with the gendarme's two daughters. When the gang was finally apprehended, the arrested included a worker from the reading hut, a member of the Komsomol, an employee of the raion land department, the head of the raion police, the chair of the rural soviet, a GPU agent, a people's court judge, the head of the local party committee, and 'many other representatives of local power.' The article emphasized that there would be no clemency for members of the state involved in banditry and that they would in fact be shot. See N.O. 'Razoblachennye bandity,' *Administrativnyi vestnik* 6 (June 1925): 63–7; see also, 'Shaika "Bim-Bom,"' *Bednota*, 26 July 1925; and 'Sud,' *Bednota*, 30, 31 July, 2, 4, 6, 13, 14, 18, 29, 30 Aug. 1925.

24 For a discussion of kinship ties and witnesses in court cases, see Schulte, *The Village in Court*, 13–14. On family influence in local politics see GARO, f. R-5, op. 2, d. 5, l. 168. In his study of banditry in northeast Brazil, Singelmann also finds strong family ties and connections between banditry and the local police, who were often recruited from among the same sections of the local population; see 'Political Structure and Social Banditry,' 75–6.

25 GARO, f. R-4, op. 3, d. 13, l. 586. See also Landis, *Bandits and Partisans*, 145–6, 276–8, for information on the role of women in the *Antonovshchina* in Tambov.

26 For a discussion of banditry in the pre-Revolutionary period, see Frank, *Crime, Cultural Conflict and Justice*, 124–32.

27 Landis, *Bandits and Partisans*, 118.

28 Ibid., 78–9.

29 GARO, f. R-4, op. 3, d. 10, l. 26.
30 For more details, see A. Uchevatov, 'Moskovskii banditizm,' *Proletarskii sud*, Mar. 1925, 38–44. Uchevatov pays special attention to Moscow itself with a detailed breakdown of robberies by days of the week, times of day, weapons, etc.
31 Hobsbawm, *Primitive Rebels*, 15; and Hobsbawm, *Bandits*, 17. See Blok, 'The Peasant and the Brigand,' 494–503; Ranajit Guha, *Elementary Aspects of Peasant Insurgency in Colonial India*, 5–6; O'Malley, 'Social Bandits,' 489–501; and Sant Cassia, 'Banditry, Myth and Terror,' 773–95, just to name a few.
32 Hobsbawm, *Primitive Rebels*, 5.
33 See Anthony, 'Peasants, Heroes and Brigands,' 123–48, for similar findings among Chinese bandit cases.
34 Blok, *The Mafia of a Sicilian Village 1860–1960*. In his 1972 article, Blok argues that Hobsbawm's 'social banditry' is not a useful category of analysis. I disagree; I think it is *one* useful category. In addition, there are many more, including Blok's, to help us understand various *types* of banditry, and these types may well overlap. See Blok, 'The Peasant and the Brigand,' 497–8.
35 As Blok noted, 'All outlaws and bandits required protection in order to operate and to survive at all.' *The Mafia of a Sicilian Village*, 99.
36 A brief look at what was taken from peasant homes or peasant travellers in the period also provides a glimpse into village life and village living standards.
37 GARO, f. R-4, op. 3 (1928), d. 13, l. 583.
38 This document is worthy of study in itself for its remarkably personal tone in the reporting of these events and its seemingly intimate connection with local politics and interrelations among villagers, all presented in a remarkably unsophisticated way.
39 GARO, f. R-4, op. 3 (1928), d. 13, l. 584.
40 GARO, f. R-4, op. 3, d. 10, ll. 135–6. Shearer also notes similar concerns in the 1930s in 'Crime and Social Disorder in Stalin's Russia,' 128.
41 See 'Doklad UKK Verkhsuda RSFSR o praktike UKK vo votorom polugode 1926 g.' Utverzhden v zasedanii Prezidiuma Verkhovnogo Suda RSFSR 10 maiia 1927g., *Sudebnaia Praktika* RSFSR (31 May 1927): 4–7, for more details on average sentencing, frequency of the death penalty, and the length of time it took such cases to be investigated and brought to trial.
42 Uchevatov, 'Moskovskii banditizm,' 39.
43 GARO, f. R-4, op. 3, d. 10, l. 215.
44 GARO, f. R-4, op. 3 (1925), d. 8, l. 207. For more on robberies along the

province's roads, see GARO, f. R-4, op. 3 (1925), d. 6, l. 177; and GARO, f. R-4, op. 3, d. 8. ll. 77–8.

45 GARO, f. R-4, op. 3, d. 10, l. 215.

46 GARO, f. 4, op. 3, d. 11, l. 185.

47 GARO, f. 4, op. 3 (1925), d. 6, l. 177. See also Sahlins, *Forest Rites*, for extensive material the precarious position of forest guards in rural France from the sixteenth to the nineteenth centuries.

48 'Shaika vorov,' *Sovetskaia derevnia*, 6 (23 Feb. 1924): 3.

49 GARO, f. R-4, op. 3 (1925), d. 6, l. 18.

50 GARO, f. R-4, op. 3, d. 13, l. 448.

51 GARO, f. R-4, op. 3, d. 13, ll. 485–6. See also GARO, f. R-5, op. 2, d. 5, l. 1390.

52 'Doklad UKK Verkhsuda RSFSR,' 6.

53 GARO, f. 4, op. 3, d. 10, l. 215.

54 Ibid. For example, the peasant Kopytin was robbed of his horse by two armed men in Konoplino District, Riazhsk Uezd, on the night of 24 September 1924. GARO, f. R-4, op. 3 (1925), d. 6, l. 18. On the night of 30 December 1925 a band of seven to nine well-armed men robbed Danil' Grishin of the village of Chernyshevka, Ranenburg Uezd, of two horses and property worth 10,000 rubles. The leader of the gang was one Nobichkov, an escapee from the Riazan state penitentiary (*Riazgubtiur'ma*). On 9 June 1925, a man and his wife were robbed of their horses in Sasovo. On the same day near the village of Lukhovits, Zaraisk Uezd, three people, including a child, were found murdered in a struggle over horses. GARO, f. R-4, op. 3 (1925), d. 8, l. 184 ob. Because of the special nature of horse theft and its impact on the countryside, this issue is treated separately.

55 See, for example, GARO, f. R-4, op. 3 (1925), d. 6, l. 59.

56 Ibid.

57 GARO, f. R-5, op. 2, d. 4, ll. 444–5.

58 GARO, f. R-5, op. 2, d. 5, l. 1391.

59 GARO, f. R-5, op. 2, d. 5, l. 1389. See GARO, f. R-5, op. 2, d. 5, l. 1562.

60 GARO, f. R-4, op. 3, d. 10, l. 26.

61 See the local Skopin newspaper *Kollektiv*, 'Krest'ianstvo v narodnom sude,' *Kollektiv*, 8 Apr. 1925, in which peasants demand better protection from banditry and argue that the struggle with banditry and horse theft should take first place in the *narsud* and *gubsud*. See also the local Sapozhok paper, 'Nepravil'nyi prigovor tak-li nuzhno nakazat' grabitelei,' *Derevenskaia gazeta*, 22 June 1927, 3.

62 GARO, f. R-4, op. 3, d. 13, l. 586.

63 See, for example, RGAE, f. 396, op. 5, d. 117, ll. 2–6.

64 RGAE, f. 396, op. 5, d. 117, l. 2.
65 See GARO, f. R-5, op. 2, d. 5, ll. 76–9.
66 It is worth noting that Figes gets Hobsbawm wrong when he writes, 'Nor is it to argue that all "banditry" should he seen as a form of social protest by the oppressed, as Hobsbawm is inclined to argue: some bandits were, by any criteria, criminals, and were never seen – nor saw themselves – as avengers of the poor.' Figes, *Peasant Russia, Civil War*, 341. In fact in his June 1980 postscript to *Bandits*, Hobsbawm disagrees strongly with the notion that all forms of banditry are forms of social protest. See Hobsbawm, *Bandits*, 143.
67 Joseph, 'On the Trail of Latin American Bandits,' 20–1.
68 See Fitzpatrick, *Stalin's Peasants*, 234–5, and Viola, *Peasant Rebels under Stalin*, 176–9, for brief discussions of banditry under collectivization. See also Shearer, 'Crime and Social Disorder in Stalin's Russia,' 127–8.
69 GARO, f. R-5, op. 2, d. 5, l. 1546.
70 Ibid., ll. 1373–4.
71 Ibid., l. 1377. This report mentions the desperate need for the creation of special groups made up of trustworthy party members and members of the RAO (*raionnyi administrativnyi otdel*) to combat banditry in the region.
72 GARO, f. R-5, op. 2, d. 5, l. 25.
73 Ibid., l. 592.
74 Ibid., l. 846.
75 Ibid., ll. 790–1.

8. Hooliganism

1 B. Zagor'e, 'O khuliganstve,' *Proletarskii sud*, Jan. 1926, 3.
2 'Khuligan,' *Kollektiv*, 2 Nov. 1924.
3 Neuberger, *Hooliganism*, 3. Neuberger's focus is on urban hooliganism, and her work looks closely at what hooliganism reveals about urban life in the years immediately before the Revolution. My focus here is on rural hooliganism in the years immediately after the October Revolution. For more on hooliganism, see Humphries, *Hooligans or Rebels?*; Nye, *Crime, Madness, and Politics in Modern France*; and Tanner, 'The Offense of Hooliganism and the Moral Dimension of China's Pursuit of Modernity, 1979–1996,' 1–40.
4 Pearson, *Hooligan*, 230.
5 LaPierre traces the nature and meaning of hooliganism in the Khrushchev years. See 'Making Hooliganism'; 'Private Matters or Public Crimes'; and 'Redefining Deviance.' Most of the exisiting work on hooligans and hooliganism focus on the concepts in the urban context.

6 Schwarz, 'Night Battles,' 101. Neuberger also traces the crucial role of the press in its contribution to the 'moral panic' surrounding hooliganism. *Hooliganism*, 15–22, 25–70.

7 Schwarz, 'Night Battles,' 106. Italics in original.

8 See Mally, *Culture of the Future*, and Stites, *Revolutionary Dreams*.

9 For more on an ongoing and fascinating debate in the Soviet context on private and public, see the contributions to Siegelbaum, ed., *Borders of Socialism*, esp. Brian LaPierre's article in the volume, 'Private Matters or Public Crimes: The Emergence of Domestic Hooliganism in the Soviet Union, 1939–1960,' 191–207. LaPierre argues that by the late 1950s and early 1960s 'the apartment began to replace the street and the courtyard as the center for hooligan activity' and extended the demand for civility into the public/private space of the home.

10 Sheila Fitzpatrick has wrestled a great deal with this issue. See her collected articles in *The Cultural Front*, esp. chap. 2, 'The Bolsheviks' Dilemma: The Class Issue in Party Politics and Culture,' 16–36. In *Peasant Metropolis*, Hoffmann finds that drinking and other aspects of rural culture continued to be combatted under the rubric of hooliganism, 135, 173.

11 Hoffmann deftly traces the shift from the iconoclastic ideals of the 'cultural radicals' of the early revolutionary years to a culture that emerged in the 1930s and embraced much more traditional ideas and values about family, morality, and authority. He locates this shift firmly in the modern. He frames Stalinism as 'a particular response to more general challenges facing modern state leaders and a particularly violent implementation of modern state practices.' *Stalinist Values*, 13–14.

12 Schwarz, 'Night Battles,' 117.

13 P. Liublinskii, 'Khuliganstvo i ego sotsial'no-bytovye korni,' in *Khuliganstvo i khuligany*, ed. Tolmachev, 57.

14 Throughout this chapter, I will use the Russian *nekul'turnost'*, as it is a central trope in the Soviet lexicon.

15 In this case, forced labour would likely be a kind of community service in the area.

16 M. Isaev, 'Khuliganstvo,' in *Khuliganstvo i khuligany*, 12–13.

17 'Bor'ba s khuliganstvom na putiakh soobshcheniia,' *ESIu* 49 (20 Dec. 1923): 1144.

18 Solts and Fainblit, *Revoliutsionnaia zakonnost' i nasha karatel'naia politika*, 76.

19 Ibid., 87–8.

20 Isaev, 'Khuliganstvo,' 13. Apparently the administrative fines were lower in rural areas and rather than a fine of 100 rubles or forced labour of up to one month, as in urban areas, the fine in rural areas was ten rubles or

forced labor up to two weeks. See B. Zagor'e, 'O khuliganstve,' *Protelarskii sud* 11–12 (June–July 1926): 4.

21 Among those arguing about the pervasive rise in hooliganism: A. Stel'makhovich, 'K voprosy bor'by s khuliganstvom,' *Protelarskii sud* 17–18 (Sept.–Oct. 1926): 1–2; Shestakova, 'Prestupleniia protiv lichnosti v derevne,' 1:215. E. Shirvindt warned that the press was playing a major role in the hooligan scare, in 'Nekotorye itogi bor'by s khuliganstvom,' in *Khuliganstov i khuligany*, 69. See also Naiman, *Sex in Public*, 250–88; and Solomon, *Soviet Criminal Justice under Stalin*, 58. Gorsuch discusses the campaign against hooliganism and press hysteria, *Youth in Revolutionary Russia*, 167–8. She also pinpoints 1926 as a turning point in attitudes toward hooliganism; her focus is largely on urban youth.

22 Zagor'e, 'O Khuliganstve,' *Proletarskii sud*, Jan. 1926, 2.

23 N.V. Krylenko, 'Chto takoe khuliganstvo?' in *Khuliganstvo i prestuplenie: Sbornik statei*, ed. Kiylenko, 15–16.

24 Ibid., 30–1.

25 Perov and Kuznetsov, *Istoriia Riazanskoi militsii*, 1:172.

26 Gorsuch, *Youth in Revolutionary Russia*, 167.

27 Stel'makhovich, 'K voprosy bor'by s khuliganstvom,' 1–2; B. Zagor'e, 'Bor'ba s khuliganstvom i novyi zakon o khuliganstve,' *Protelarskii sud* 11–12 (June–July 1926): 3–5; Zagor'e, 'O khuliganstve,' *Proletarskii sud*, Jan. 1926, 2–3.

28 Isaev, 'Khuliganstvo,' 14, on the same tendency to combine minor offences such as mischief and serious offenses like rape under the label of hooliganism. See also Neuberger, *Hooliganism*, 116, for similar observations.

29 'It is entirely clear. Hooliganism in its essence is a way of being' (*I eto vpolne poniatno. Khuliganstvo po sushchestvu svoemu – eto nastroenie*'). Zagor'e, 'Bor'ba s khuliganstvom i novyi zakon o khuliganstve,' 3.

30 Naiman, *Sex in Public*, pp. 253–54.

31 Ibid., 258–9. See also Gorsuch, *Youth in Revolutionary Russia.*

32 Most of the existing studies were of urban hooligans. For more on who they were, see Krylenko, 'Disput o khuliganstve,' 22; and 'Bor'ba s khuliganstvom i novyi zakon o khuliganstve,' in *Khuliganstvo i prestuplenie: Sbornik statei*, ed. Krylenko, 4; Zagor'e, 'O khuliganstve,' 2; See also T. Segalov, 'Prestupnoe khuliganstvo i khuliganskie prestupleniia,' in *Khuliganstvo i khuligany*, 64–6. Segalov also discusses the small number of women charged with hooliganism and claims they were almost all prostitutes and that many of them were suffering from cocaine addiction, dovetailing nicely with Bill Schwarz's observations quoted above.

33 Naiman, *Sex in Public*, 262.

34 I. Gorevoi, 'Tam, gde bylo delo Riazhskikh banditov: Bandity Ermolovy i Shumoshskaia-Chubarovshchina,' *Krest'ianskaia gazeta*, 21 Jan. 1928, 5.

35 Ibid.
36 See GARO, f. R-2462, op. 7, d. 43, l. 23.
37 'Khuligany budut usmireny,' *Derevenskaia gazeta,* 2 Sept. 1926, 1.
38 Zagor'e, 'O khuliganstve,' 2. See also Stel'makhovich, 'K voprosy bor'by s khuliganstvom,' 1, who claimed that 'hooligan bands' were attracting youth into their ranks.
39 'Nevozmozhnoe khuliganstvo tvoritsia v Vereshchuchinskom klube,' *Derevenskaia gazeta,* 7 Jan. 1926, 4.
40 Alcohol did in fact play a role in hooliganism cases. For example, in eleven provinces of central Russia during the first quarter of 1926, among the 39,846 people who were arrested for hooliganism, 30,600 were drunk. During the second quarter of 1926, 90,597 were arrested and 62,305 of them were drunk. See Krylenko, 'Disput o khuliganstve,' 19. On the link between hooliganism and alcohol in the countryside before the Revolution, see Neuberger, *Hooliganism,* 124–5.
41 A. Chernyshev, 'Voprosy bor'by s khuliganstvom na soveshchaniiakh po bor'be s prestupnost'iu,' *Rabochii sud* 21 (1926): 1275.
42 Frank, *Crime, Cultural Conflict, and Justice,* 279.
43 Ibid. 281, 289. See also Neuberger, *Hooliganism,* 114, for the governor of Ufa's remarkably similar list of hooligan behaviours.
44 Frank, *Crime, Cultural Conflict, and Justice,* 282.
45 Weissman echoes this claim: 'In the case of hooliganism, however, exposure to city life among peasants who retained ties to the village was undoubtedly a major causal factor.' Weissman, 'Rural Crime in Tsarist Russia,' 237.
46 Burds, 'The Social Control of Peasant Labor in Russia,' 58–62; Frank, *Crime, Cultural Conflict, and Justice,* 282–3. See also Engel, 'Russian Peasant Views,' 449; and Weissman, 'Rural Crime in Tsarist Russia,' 228–40. For a discussion of hooliganism and village versus urban interpretations, see Neuberger, *Hooliganism,* 126–7.
47 See Segalov, 'Prestupnoe khuliganstvo i khuliganskie prestupleniia,' in *Khuliganstvo i khuligany,* 71–2.
48 G. Zinov'ev, 'Neurozhai i nashi zadachi,' *Pravda,* 30 July 1924.
49 M. Kiriushkin (g. Zaraisk, Riazan gub.), 'O bor'be s khuliganstvom v derevne,' *Vlast' sovetov* 21 (1926): 17–18.
50 S. Mokrinskii, 'Ozorstvo i khuliganstvo,' *ESIu* 37 (1924): 878.
51 Ibid., 879. Shestakova makes exactly the same argument in 'Prestupleniia protiv lichnosti v derevne,' 216.
52 L.G. Orshanskii, 'Khuligan (Psikhologicheskii ocherk),' in *Khuliganstvo i prestuplenie,* 62.
53 Zagor'e, 'O khuliganstve,' 2.
54 Ibid., 2–3.

55 Ibid., 2.
56 Zagor'e, 'Bor'ba s khuliganstvom i novyi zakon o khuliganstve,' 3.
57 Kabanov, *Bor'ba s ugolovnoi prestupnost'iu v derevne,* 8.
58 'Khuliganstvo shaika: Izbav'te nas ot nei,' *Derevenskaia gazeta,* 27 July 1927, 5.
59 Krylenko, 'Disput o khuliganstve,' 17.
60 Fanon, *Wretched of the Earth,* 303.
61 For more on the institute, see Kowalsky, '"Who's Responsible for Female Crime?"' 366–86.
62 On the dehumanization of the Russian peasantry on the eve of collectivization, see Viola, *Peasant Rebels under Stalin,* esp. 29–36.
63 Moskovskii gubernskii sud i Moskovskii kabinet po izucheniiu lichnosti prestupnika i prestupnosti, *Khuliganstvo i ponozhovshchina* (Moscow: Mosrabototdel, 1927), 5. Frank also found that, in order to illustrate the 'degeneration' of a 'dissolute peasant youth,' pre-Revolutionary reformers published 'graphic details of the brutal, mass fistfights and turf battles between gangs from rival villages, the frequent stabbings and maimings, and the rash of other crimes that accompanied the revelries of teens and young adults during village fetes.' Frank, 'Confronting the Domestic Other,' 84–5.
64 V.I. Akkerman, 'Ubiistvo v drake,' in *Khulganstvo i ponozhovshchina,* 138.
65 B.S. Man'kovskii, 'Derevenskaia ponozhovshchina,' in *Khuliganstvo i ponozhovshchina,* 118.
66 See Sahlins, *Forest Rites,* 37; and Natalie Davis, 'Charivari, Honor and Community,' 42–57. For an account of charivari in nineteenth-century Russia, see Frank, 'Popular Justice, Community and Culture.'
67 Fenomenov, *Sovremennaia derevnia,* 2:12–13.
68 See Sahlins, *Forest Rites,* 36.
69 Fenomenov, *Sovremennaia derevnia,* 2:12.
70 The Orthodox Church marks the day of the seven Maccabean martyrs in mid-August. The day is associated with the peasant-calendar day 'Spas-Makovei.' In the village, poppy seeds (*mak*) are taken to the church to be blessed and then baked into pies or bliny. The sanctified poppy seeds are also used for magic and healing, thus embodying a wonderful mix of Christian and traditional culture. For more, see Tul'tseva, *Riazanskii mesiatseslov,* 232.
71 Tan-Bogoraz, *Staryi i novyi byt,* 111–12.
72 RGAE, f. 478, op. 3, d. 3213, l. 288.
73 Man'kovskii, 'Derevenskaia ponozhovshchina,' 118–20.
74 Ibid., 115.
75 Greenburg, 'Fights/Fires,' 162.
76 Man'kovskii, 'Derevenskaia ponozhovshchina,' 119–21.

77 Clifford Geertz, 'Deep Play: Notes on the Balinese Cockfight,' in Geertz, *Interpretation of Cultures*, 433. On Bentham, see 432–3.
78 Goffman, *Encounters*, 26, 27, 34.
79 Turner, *From Ritual to Theatre*, 28, 32. Turner points out that the Anglo-Saxon etymology of 'play' originates in fight or battle, 33.
80 Bakhtin, *Rabelais and His World*, 196–203.
81 See Robert C. Davis, *War of the Fists* on bridge battles in Venice up to the seventeenth century, which shared an atmosphere similar to that of the Russian village brawl.
82 Geertz, *Interpretation of Cultures*, 449–50.
83 L. Ranovskii, 'Za 7 verst skhodilis' na draky,' *Derevenskaia gazeta*, 8 July 1926, 3.
84 'Siuda metla nuzhna. Predsedatel' sel'soveta rukovodit kulachnimi boiami,' *Derevenskaia gazeta*, 24 Mar. 1926, 3.
85 As Robert Muchembled explains, those in power detached violence from the 'sphere of sociability' and synchronized it with the 'notion of criminality.' 'Anthropology of Violence,' 68.

9. Rough Justice

1 On the theft of Andrei Borodin's beloved mare, which opens Mozhaev's *Muzhiki i baby*, 11.
2 G. Roginskii, 'Samosudy,' *ESIu* 40 (1926): 1153.
3 RGASPI, f. 17, op. 5, d. 180, l. 29.
4 Burbank, *Russian Peasants Go to Court*, 4. One may also wonder why it is so crucial to Burbank to find and highlight the liberal subject. For more on this issue, see Anna Krylova's provocative article, 'The Tenacious Liberal Subject in Soviet Studies.'
5 Burbank, *Russian Peasants Go to Court*, 15.
6 Frank, 'Popular Justice, Community and Culture'; Frierson, 'Crime and Punishment'; and Worobec, 'Horse Thieves and Peasant Justice.'
7 GARO, f. R-4, op. 3, d. 8, ll. 206, 434.
8 'Za revoliutsionnuiu zakonnost' v derevne,' *Derevenskaia gazeta*, 1 Oct. 1926, 2. Appeals appear again and again in peasant letters for harsher penalties against thieves and bandits. See, for example, RGAE, f. 396, op. 5, d. 117, l. 2, and d. 92, ll. 67–9 (Letters to *Krest'ianskaia gazeta*). See also Sokolov, *Golos naroda*, 179, in which the editor discusses the repeated appeals in peasant letters for the death penalty. He writes, 'There is no other way to explain other than that this "execution psychology" (*rasstrel'naia psikhologiia*), in large part, was inherited from the epoch of civil war and war communism, permanently present in the popular consciousness.'

9 Lagovier, *O Samosudakh*, 4.
10 GARO, f. R-4, op. 1, d. 485, l. 29.
11 N. Lagovier, 'Nizovoi sovetskii apparat v bor'be s konokradstvom,' *Vlast' sovetov* 30 (1928): 19.
12 RGAE, f. 396, op. 3, d. 67, l. 20.
13 V. Mokeev, 'Blizhe k derevne,' *ESIu* 39–40 (9–16 Oct. 1924): 922.
14 For more on the modern state's obsession with counting, see Holquist, '"Information Is the Alpha and Omega"'; and Holquist, 'New Terrains and New Chronologies.'
15 'Pereuchet loshadei v Riazhskom uezde,' *Sovetskaia derevnia* 2 (7 Jan. 1924): 4; and GARO, f. R-4, op. 3, d. 11, l. 162.
16 GARO, f. R-4, op. 3 (1922), d. 1, l. 97, and f. R-63, op. 1, d. 49, l. 81.
17 Pavlovskii, 'Uchetnaia kartochka i konokradstvo,' *ESIu* 39–40 (1923): 14–15. See also 'Bor'ba s konokradstom,' *Administrativnyi vestnik* 1 (Jan. 1926): 81–2, where the author claims that the majority of the peasants in their 'obscurity' look at their cards and say: about this thing with the little holes in it, I can understand nothing. And I am afraid to waste 50–100 rubles on a horse and just cannot bring myself to do it' (*po etoi shtuke s dyrochkami poniat' nichego ne mogu i tratit' 50–100 rub. na loshad' boius' i ne reshaius*), 82. See also N.N. Semenov, 'Konskii bilet (pasport) i registratsiia perekhoda loshadi, kak mera preduprezhdeniia konokradstva,' *Administrativnyi vestnik* 7–8 (July–Aug. 1927): 58–62, for further discussion of the system's defects and more suggestions on how to improve and use the system against horse theft.
18 GARO, f. R-4, op. 3, d. 11, l. 165.
19 For discussions of the role of rumour in peasant life and politics, see Lefebvre, *Great Fear of 1789*; and Yang, 'A Conversation of Rumors.' In the context of the Soviet countryside, see Fitzpatrick, *Stalin's Peasants*, esp. 286–96; and Viola, *Peasant Rebels under Stalin*, esp. 53–60.
20 GARO, f. R-4, op. 3, d. 11, l. 164.
21 Ibid., l. 166.
22 Ibid., l. 167.
23 Ibid., ll. 167–9.
24 Tan-Bogoraz, *Staryi i novyi byt*, 102–3.
25 Ibid., 103.
26 Ibid., 102–3.
27 On the value of horses in peasant society and attitudes toward punishing horse thieves, see Frank, 'Popular Justice,' 257, 259; and Worobec, 'Horse Thieves and Peasant Justice,' 284.
28 For a graphic and colourful conceptualization of the horse in peasant life,

see the wonderful and banned 1934 film *Happiness*, discovered and released on video in 1991.

29 Worobec, 'Horse Thieves and Peasant Justice,' 286.

30 N.N. Semenov, 'Samodeiatel'nost' naseleniia kak faktor bor'by s konokradstvom,' *Administrativnyi vestnik* 3 (Mar. 1928): 48.

31 Shestakova, 'Prestupleniia protiv lichnosti v derevne,' 1: 220; Gernet, 'Statistika gorodskoi i sel'skoi prestupnosti,' 34. Gernet recounts a case from 1917 in Kazan in which three travellers from the city of Sviiazhsk passing through the nearby countryside made the mistake of asking a villager about horses in the village. The villager decided they were connected to horse thieves and consulted his fellow villagers. All three travellers were burned alive. See G. Kudriavtsev, 'Zverskaia rasprava,' *Krestianskii iurist* 19 (15 Oct. 1928): 5, for a report of a Tver peasant woman, believed to have stolen a cow, who was severely beaten. Lying injured on the ground, she begged the victim of the theft for mercy; he kicked her in the face with his boot, saying, 'Ack, vermin, you steal a cow, you're going to remember' (*Vuu, gadina, korov vorovat, 'budesh' pomnit*).

32 See, for example, Frank, 'Popular Justice, Community and Culture'; Frierson, 'Crime and Punishment'; and Worobec, 'Horse Thieves and Peasant Justice.' Frank, Frierson, and Worobec have more references to cases of shaming, as well as cases of punishment and injury, in which the victim was not killed. Frank and Frierson have explored the practices of shaming and punishing insiders with the familiar mechanism of charivari and rough justice. They have based their studies on surveys of peasant custom, undertaken toward the end of the nineteenth century (see Frank, 'Popular Justice,' n7; Frierson, 'Crime and Punishment,' n3; and Worobec 'Horse Thieves,' n1). I had less access to the kinds of cases that did not make it to the courts or that did not come to the attention of the authorities, and were of a more mundane and day-to-day nature, such as the punishing of insiders with shaming. The cases that came to the attention of the provincial courts and the legal scholars of the twenties were much more likely to be those that resulted in the death of the subject of the samosud, and it will be those cases that are focused on here. Moreover, survivors of less severe forms of samosud were unlikely to report the attack to the authorities. They did not want to draw the attention of the formal system to the crimes they had committed and probably feared retribution from the community if they went to the authorities. As Frank points out, challenging the decision to punish challenged the authority of the community itself (see Frank, 'Popular Justice,' 244; and Frierson, 'Crime and Punishment,' 67–8).

33 Frank, 'Popular Justice,' 263. Muchembled makes this point in 'Anthropology of Violence,' 59.

34 Dal' gives the meaning of *riasa* for the Riazan region as 'a swampy, wet place.' See Vladimir Dal', *Tolkovyi slovar' zhivogo velikorusskogo iazyka*, 4th ed. (1914; St Petersburg: Diamant, 1996), 3:1781. My thanks to Denis Kozlov for discovering the village name and meaning.
35 GARO, R-2462, op. 5, d. 504, ll. 37–8.
36 Ibid., l. 38.
37 Ibid., l. 29.
38 Ibid., l. 33 ob, l. 38.
39 Ibid., l. 36 ob.
40 Frank, 'Popular Justice, Community and Culture,' 239–65.
41 Lagovier, *O Samosudakh*, 5. Lagovier reacts to what he perceived as an alarming trend in peasant letters that 'Soviet power should allow samosud' (*sovetskaia vlast' dolzhna razreshat' samosudy*).
42 P. Erypalov, 'Volna samosudov,' *ESIu*, 24–5 (30 June–7 July 1922): 18.
43 Shestakova, 'Prestupleniia protiv lichnosti v derevne,' 219–20.
44 Ibid., 220.
45 On the problem of the crowd and samosud, see Rodin, 'Ubiitsy samosudom,' *Pravo i zhizn'* 7–8 (1925): 96.
46 P. Erypalov, 'Volna samosudov,' *ESIu* 24–5 (30 June–7 July 1922): 18. Erypalov complained that more than half of samosud cases went unpunished and that chairmen of village soviets participated in samosud. See also 'Ubil odin,' *Sud idet* 18 (Sept. 1928): 1006–7.
47 Rodin, 'Ubiitsy samosudom,' 97.
48 Ibid. See *Ugolovnyi Kodeks RSFSR* (Moscow, 1923), 28–9. Translations based on *The Criminal Code of the Russian Socialist Federative Republic*, 36–7.
49 Roginskii, 'Samosudy,' 1153.
50 Ibid., 1154.
51 Central-level OGPU reports also remark on the tendency of representatives of local power to participate in cases of samosud. See, for example, RGASPI, f. 17, op. 85, d. 180, l. 22.
52 *Ugolovnyi Kodeks RSFSR*, 22, 7; translations from *Criminal Code of the Russian Socialist Federative Republic*, 27 and 8.
53 Roginskii, 'Samosudy,' 1155.
54 *Ugolovnyi Kodeks RSFSR*, 6, translations from *Criminal Code of the Russian Socialist Federative Republic*, 4. Roginskii, 'Samosudy,' 1155. Roginskii also describes another example of a *gubsud* ruling on a chairman of a rural soviet, Iu., and the secretary of the rural soviet, D. It seems that D., under instructions from Iu., shot an arrested man at the marketplace and, in order to cover up the crime, they claimed he had been shot while trying to escape. Their actions fell under articles 142 and 116 of the Criminal Code, but

they were charged under Article 28. One was sentenced to six months and the other to one year. The motive for the court's ruling was that there were many thieves at the marketplace and peasants were demanding that they be dealt with. The Supreme Court overturned the case and charged them under Article 106, Part 2, with three-year prison terms each.

55 Rodin, 'Ubiitsy samosudom,' 97, 96.

56 See Lagovier, *O Samosudakh.*

57 *Ugolovnyi kodeks RSFSR,* 31. Translations quoted from *Criminal Code of the Russian Socialist Federative Republic,* 40.

58 GARO, f. R-2461, op. 5, d. 122, ll. 11–33.

59 GARO, f. R-2461, op. 5, d. 121, ll. 2–2 ob.

60 Ibid., l. 15 ob.

61 Ibid., l. 76. One may wonder why criminals would return to their villages. Peasant criminals were released from jail just outside the cities. They had no resources and nowhere to go. At least in the village they had kinship networks and established criminal networks to return to.

62 Ibid., l. 75.

63 Ibid., ll. 67–71. Article 144, as discussed above, was the most lenient article under which to prosecute samosud.

64 Ibid., ll. 68–71.

65 Ibid., ll. 61–63 ob. This level of organization and official sanction of samosud was not uncommon. The OGPU reported a number of such cases. On 18 April 1925, in the village of Novoselok in Tula, the entire *obshchestvo* agreed to samosud against a fellow villager, Lobanov, who had been suspected of stealing and threatened arson against the village. One evening there was a fire. Members of the village found Lobanov in the forest and led him back to the village where the following *postanovlenie* was issued: 'The whole community sentences Lobanov to death for theft and arson.' There were 50 signatures. In a similar case in Nizhegorod, there were 150 signatures. RGASPI, f. 17, op. 85, d. 180, ll. 35, 36.

66 RGASPI, f. 17, op. 85, d. 180, l. 29.

67 Ibid., l. 31.

68 Ibid., l. 32.

69 In Viatka, for example, in 1925, in the village of Asinera, a fire broke out. The local peasants suspected a fellow villager, Nikifor Lebedev, his wife, Uliana, and their twelve-year-old son, Egor, because they were not at the fire. By order of the chair of the rural soviet the suspects were summoned to the blaze. Nikifor refused to come out of the house, but Uliana was brought to the fire and thrown in. She managed to run out of the blaze. Then the chairman of the rural soviet hit her with a beam and again threw her into

the fire. A day later Egor was summoned, supposedly for questioning by the police, but he was led to the edge of the forest and beaten; he died from his injuries. RGASPI, f. 17, op. 85, d. 180, l. 142. (Note the role played by the chairman of the rural soviet.) The case was included in central-level OGPU reports precisely because of his involvement.

70 I.N. Iakimov, 'Podzhog,' *Administrativnyi vestnik* 7 (July 1928): 31. The meaning of the names is difficult to convey: roughly, 'those that have burned,' 'the one that burned,' and 'the one that didn't burn.'

71 Shanin, *Awkward Class,* 113.

72 Gorky, 'On the Russian Peasantry,' 13.

73 Frierson, *All Russia Is Burning,* 6–7.

74 Ibid., 10–11.

75 Ibid., 8.

76 See Frierson's careful discussion of the historiography on arson in broader European, Russian, and Soviet contexts. Ibid., 103–7.

77 GARO, f. R-2461, op. 6, d. 639, l. 117.

78 Ibid.

79 Ibid., ll. 25, 105.

80 Up to this point the investigator's notes refer to a 'Suzov,' then the notes switch to 'Sizov.' I have retained the investigator's usage in the text.

81 The investigators' notes are a written nightmare. Spellings of village names and people vary to such a degree that the researcher is never sure if a new person or place has been added to the mix or simply a new variation in the spelling of a person or place already mentioned.

82 GARO, f. R-2461, op. 6, d. 639, l. 117, and ll. 1–70.

83 The witnesses interviewed for a 1923 case of horse theft in Riazan Uezd paint a similar picture. They provide a glimpse of who is out and about in the village streets. At least ten young men, who ranged in age from fifteen to twenty, were questioned. Their statements were consistently vague, although the suspect was seen with a horse in the streets between 11 p.m. and 1 a.m. The suspect, who himself was only twenty, claimed he had been socializing with friends in various homes until 5 a.m. Once again the researcher catches a glimpse of an active nocturnal social life that was often restricted to men, which revolved around visiting one another's homes and often drinking until the wee hours. GARO, f. R-2461, op. 3, d. 177.

84 Figures are taken from 'Derevnia v ogne,' *Vlast' sovetov* 14 (1929): 18. For more on Gosstrakh, see Iakimov, 'Podzhog,' 32.

85 Frierson, *All Russia Is Burning,* 55–6.

86 'Derevnia v ogne,' 18

87 Ibid.

88 Frierson, *All Russia Is Burning*, 55.
89 '310 pozharov za iiun,' *Derevenskaia gazeta*, 15 July 1926, 4.
90 'Doklad o sudebnoi praktike po prestupleniam, predusmotrennym st. 175 UK, po dannym UKK Verkhovnogo Suda za 10 mesiatsev 1927,' *Sudebnaia Praktika* 1 (15 Jan. 1928): 8–9.
91 For the difficult and marginal position of women in the village, see Bohac, 'Widows and the Russian Serf Community'; Farnsworth, 'Litigious Daughter-in-Law.' Frierson works the category of gender through her analysis in *All Russia Is Burning*. For a discussion of women as arsonists and disempowerment in the pre-Revolutionary village, see Frierson, 'Red Roosters,' 112.
92 For a discussion of the debate, see Cox, 'Awkward Class or Awkward Classes?'; Harrison, 'Chaianov'; and Shanin, *Awkward Class*, 45–62.
93 'Doklad o sudebnoi praktike po prestupleniam, predusmotrennym st. 175 UK,' 8–12.
94 Schulte, *Village in Court*, 26–7.
95 Frierson, *All Russia Is Burning*, 107.
96 Frank, *Crime, Cultural Conflict and Justice*, 134; Frierson, *All Russian Is Burning*. John Archer's findings are different. While the findings in the Russian village of the 1920s concur with those of Frank and Schulte, they do not concur with Archer's claim that in nineteenth-century East Anglia 'arson was, generally speaking, an act of social protest perpetrated against an individual expressing a wider sense of social grievance.' Archer, *By a Flash and Scare*, 8. Archer, however, is dealing with farm labourers and social protest again those who hired them. In the Russian village, arson was a personal crime, a way of settling a score, viscerally, quickly, and outside of the official court system.
97 Table 7, in the appendix, captures the variety and complexity of motives for arson in the Soviet countryside, ranging from disputes over land to matters of alcohol consumption and intimacy.
98 Iakimov, 'Podzhog,' 32.
99 See Frierson's discussion of the practice in *All Russia Is Burning*, 153–8.
100 Frank, *Crime, Cultural Conflict and Justice*, 134–6.
101 GARO, f. R-4, op. 3 (1925), d. 6, l. 176.
102 GARO, f. R-4, op. 3, d. 13, l. 585.
103 GARO, f. R-5, op. 2, d. 5, ll. 702–3.
104 Ibid., ll. 723–4.
105 GARO, f. R-5, op. 2. d. 4, ll. 444–5.
106 GARO, f. R-5, op. 2, d. 5, l. 957.
107 Ibid., ll. 1086–8, 1124–5, 1245–6.
108 Ibid., l. 1562.

10. Pitelino

1 GARO, f. 5, op. 2, d. 5, l. 607.
2 Ibid., l. 295. See also ll. 251, 281.
3 For information on the recruitment drive and collectivization in general, see Viola, *Best Sons*.
4 For more on Bauman and his attitude to collectivization in Riazan, see Danilov, Manning, and Viola, *Tragediia Sovetskoi derevni*, 2:385–7; and R.W. Davies, *Socialist Offensive*, 113, 215, 262–3.
5 *Statisticheskii spravochnik po Riazanskomu okrugu za 1927–28–29*, 2–3. The male/female discrepancy can be attributed to losses in the First World War and the Civil War and to an exodus of migrant labour from the region.
6 GARO, f. 5, op. 2, d. 5, l. 404.
7 Ibid., ll. 286–286 ob.
8 Ibid., ll. 286–286 ob., 398. The peasantry was divided by state doctrine into poor (*bedniak*), middle (*seredniak*), and wealthy (kulak) households. Only the wealthy peasants were officially targeted for persecution and 'dekulakization.' In reality, the labels were used fluidly to punish resistance.
9 Ibid., ll. 403–4. See Hoch, *Serfdom and Social Control*, 175, for a reference to estate workers using this same punishment against women in the days of serfdom.
10 Tsentral'nyi arkhiv FSB Rossiiskoi Federatsii, hereafter FSB [TSD], f. 2, op. 8, d. 40, l. 97. (This unpublished document and all subsequent FSB references are from the draft for Danilov, Manning, and Viola, *Tragediia Sovetskoi derevni*, vol. 2, and was shown to me by Lynne Viola, with the permission of the editors.)
11 GARO, f. 5, op. 2, d. 5, ll. 404, 406. It is interesting to note the striking similarities as well as some of the differences between this unrest and the post-Emancipation unrest explored by Daniel Field, *Rebels in the Name of the Tsar*, in the village of Bezdna in 1861. In a telegram from the local governor of Kazan to the Ministry of Internal Affairs, the governor wrote, '*Pomeshchiki* and officials are not being touched, but Bezdna is surrounded by peasants on horseback, who don't allow anyone in; yesterday there were already more than 2,000 people in Bezdna' (38). In another different and noteworthy telegram to the Ministry of Internal Affairs, the Kazan governor reported that the 'peasant women have been sent out of the village' (40). As we know, women played a crucial role in resisting collectivization. See Viola, '*Bab'i Bunty* and Peasant Women's Protest,' 23–42. Pitelino peasants built on the traditions of resistance to serfdom and of the Civil War period. For remarkably similar accounts of peasant tactics of resistance, see Figes, *Peasant Russia Civil War*, 321–53; and Penner, 'Pride, Power, and Pitchforks,' 78–103. In

many of their examples, it was the behaviour of food-procurement brigades that sparked violent unrest.

12 GARO, f. 5, op. 2, d. 5, l. 407. The black flag is usually associated with anarchy and the Socialist Revolutionaries.

13 It is important to note that it was Sunday. The detachment could not have picked a worse day, as the peasants of Gridino and Veraivo had recently demanded the return of their church for religious services, and many had gathered to attend them. Moreover, February and March are replete with religious holidays and saints' days, including Maslenitsa and Lent. See Brown, *A Biography of No Place*, 263n79; and Tul'tseva, *Riazanskii mesiatseslov*, 72–95.

14 Siniukino in contemporary atlases.

15 FSB [TSD], f. 2, op. 8, d. 40, l. 97.

16 Rossiiskii gosudarstvennyi voennyi arkhiv (hereafter RGVA), f. 33987, op. 3, d. 332, l. 81. Report of the commander of the Moscow okrug military forces to K.E. Voroshilov, 2 Mar. 1930, published in *Tragediia sovetskoi derevni* 2:279.

17 Ol'khin was head of the RAIZO (district land department), and Kosyrev was chairman of the local collective farm.

18 GARO, f. 5, op. 2, d. 5, l. 426.

19 Ibid., l. 425.

20 Ibid., ll. 426, 403–4.

21 Ibid., ll. 425–6.

22 Ibid., l. 429.

23 Ibid., l. 424.

24 Ibid., ll. 426, 428.

25 Ibid., ll. 439–40. On the posters, see GARO, f. 5, op. 2, d. 5, l. 429.

26 FSB [TSD], f. 2, op. 8., d. 40, l. 98.

27 The report added that she was the wife of a church elder, perhaps as an attempt to justify her murder.

28 GARO, f. 5, op. 2, d. 5, l. 440. Interestingly enough, there was no further mention of this incident in the OGPU reports.

29 FSB [TSD], f. 2, op. 8., d. 40, l. 97.

30 GARO, f. 5, op. 2, d. 5, ll. 441, 486.

31 Ibid., l. 887.

32 Ibid., ll. 617–617 ob. Quotation, l. 887.

33 Ibid., ll. 342–4, 528. Peasants poured out of the collective farms, and not only in Pitelino District, but in neighbouring districts as well.

34 Ibid., l. 290.

35 GARO, f. 2, op. 1, d. 66, l. 124.

36 The OGPU feared the spread and impact of the Pitelino rebellion on neigh-

bouring districts. See GARO, f. 5, op. 2, d. 5, l. 379. About mass exodus, see ll. 357–8. About the impact of unrest in Pitelino and Ranenburg as important factors creating tension among peasants in other areas, see l. 329.

37 Ibid., l. 887.

38 I found this kind of report only for Pitelino District, suggesting that it was the only district in Riazan to experience such a crisis as early as June.

39 GARO, f. 5, op. 2, d. 4, l. 260.

40 Ianin, 'Vtoroe kulatskoe vosstanie i ego likvidatsiia,' 4 303n5.

41 GARO, f. 2, op. 1, d. 216, ll. 35–6.

42 FSB [TSD], f. 2, op. 8, d. 40, l. 87.

43 Ianin, 'Vtoroe kulatskoe vosstanie,' 298.

44 Ibid., 299.

45 An editorial note in *Minuvshee* claimed that there was no such member in the first Duma, although there was a Nikita Grigor'evich Osichkin from Tambov in the second. Ianin, 'Vtoroe kulatskoe vosstanie,' 299n2. In Pitelino in August 1929 an I.M. Os'kin was recorded in an OGPU report as someone who complained about state bonds (*zaem*), that workers were treated better than peasants, and about the war with China. See GARO, f. R-4, op. 3, d. 11, l. 20.

46 Ianin, 'Vtoroe kulatskoe vosstanie,' 298–9. For a similar example of blaming traditional enemies for peasant rebellion, see Hobsbawn and Rude, *Captain Swing*, 239–50.

47 Ianin, 'Vtoroe kulatskoe vosstanie,' 299.

48 Ibid., 299–300.

49 Ibid., 300.

50 See Lahusen, 'Socialist Realism Revisited,' 102–3.

51 Ianin, 'Vtoroe kulatskoe vosstanie,' 300.

52 Ibid. Ellipses in original.

53 Ibid., 301.

54 GARO, f. 2, op. 1, d. 15, ll. 53–7, 32–6.

55 Ibid., ll. 31–5.

56 See Hughes, *Stalinism in a Russian Province*. Hughes argues that the 'social influence' policy, as he dubs it, actually worked to some degree; see esp. 69, 202–9.

57 GARO, f. 5, op. 2, d. 5, ll. 149, 151. There were still a few scattered reports of poor peasant support for dekulakization in February 1930, but they were few and far between; see GARO, f. 5, op. 2, d. 5, l. 288.

58 Here I agree with Shanin, *Awkward Class*, 196–7.

59 As the first big push for collectivization got underway, Riazan peasants engaged in types of protest that have already been detailed in other studies

of collectivization. Because the catalogue of resistance has already been explored elsewhere, I touch on it only briefly here to show the degree to which the behaviour of Riazan peasants fits into the common patterns of protest against collectivization, before moving on to focus on an aspect of resistance to collectivization that I think has been overlooked in the literature. See Fitzpatrick, *Stalin's Peasants*; Hughes, *Stalinism in a Russian Province*; and Viola, *Peasant Rebels under Stalin.*

60 GARO, f. 5, op. 2, d. 5, l. 126.

61 Ibid., l. 191.

62 Ibid., ll. 309–10, 411.

63 GARO, f. 5, op. 2, d. 4, l. 20.

64 GARO, f. 5, op. 2, d. 5, l. 295.

65 Ibid., 189; GARO, f. 2, op. 1, d. 213, ll. 74–5; and GARO, f. 5, op. 2, d. 5, ll. 341–2, 348.

66 GARO, f. 5, op. 2, d. 5, l. 204, and l. 279.

67 Ibid., l. 568.

68 Ibid., ll. 475–6. The reference to the 'old life' is on l. 286 ob. and references to blood drinking can be found in GARO, f. 5, op. 4, d. 4, l. 153; GARO, f. 5, op. 2, d. 5, ll. 571, 584.

69 GARO, f. 5, op. 2, d. 5, ll. 506–7, 562–73.

70 See Danilov and Krasil'nikov, eds., *Spetspereselentsy v Zapadnoi Sibirii*; Davies, *Socialist Offensive*; Fitzpatrick, *Stalin's Peasants*; Hughes, *Stalinism in a Russian Province*; Viola, *Best Sons of the Fatherland*; Viola, *Peasant Rebels under Stalin*; and Viola et al., eds., *Riazanskaia derevnia v 1929–1930 gg.*

71 One historian who looks at peasant response to collectivization acknowledges the challenge: 'The uneven distribution of protest, the reason why riots erupt in one village and not in others, is an intractable problem' (Hughes, *Stalinism in a Russian Province*, 94). It is curious that one of the most rebellious villages in Hughes's study is called Riazan. It would be fascinating to discover whether or not these peasants resettled from Riazan. In fact, the village of the Siberian Riazan was the headquarters for a revolt that spread to seventeen villages in just over two weeks (ibid., 178–9).

72 For more on internal colonization, see Gouldner, 'Stalinism'; and Viola, *Peasant Rebels under Stalin*, esp. 3, 14–19. Frank's work on the nineteenth-century countryside looks at the problem in a development context and suggests the Tsarist regime behaved as a colonizing force as well; see *Crime, Cultural Conflict and Justice.* Gouldner sees internal colonization as a Stalinist phenomenon. Viola has a more nuanced approach, which pays attention to both the developmental side of colonization and the socialist content.

73 See Viola, '*Bab'i Bunty*,' 23–42.

74 GARO, f. 2, op. 1, d. 85, l. 45. The villagers of Zakharevo sang to the tune of the Internationale: 'Save, lord, your people' (*spasi, gospodi, liudi tvoi*).
75 RGVA, f. 33987, op. 3, d. 332, l. 81, published in *Tragediia sovetskoi derevni*, 2:279.
76 GARO, f. 2, op. 1, d. 85, l. 45.
77 Hughes claims that rape was a common weapon in Siberia. *Stalinism in a Russian Province*, 191. There are only a few such references in the Riazan materials.
78 GARO, f. 5, op. 2, d. 5, l. 168.
79 GARO, f. 4, op. 3, d. 11, ll. 258–62, 114–17.
80 Ibid., l. 108.
81 GARO, f. 5, op. 2, d. 5, l. 57.
82 GARO, f. 2, op. 1, d. 216, ll. 35–6; GARO, f. 5, op. 2, d. 5, ll. 393–4, 545–55.
83 GARO, f. 5, op. 2, d. 5, ll. 80–3.
84 Ibid., l. 10.
85 Ibid.; and GARO, f. 5, op. 2, d. 5, ll. 162–8. See also the bizarre letter from a worker in Baku in GARO, f. 2, op. 1, d. 306, ll. 301–301 ob., about the 'unlawful behaviour of his family village's rural soviet chairman who slaughtered his animals before entering the collective farm and warned his brother to sell his horse quickly because "no matter what, they would be dragged into the collective farm."'
86 GARO, f. 5, op. 2, d. 5, l. 162.
87 GARO, f. 4, op. 2, d. 5, ll. 302–6.
88 GARO, f. 5, op. 2, d. 5, ll. 392–3.
89 Ibid.
90 The Zabelino rural soviet collected oats at ten pounds 'per eater' and flax at three pounds per eater. The Iarnovskii rural soviet collected grain of all kinds 'by eater' (*po edokam*), the same from the kulaks as from the bedniaks. In both cases, the rural soviet members implicated were tried for violating the class line; see GARO f. 5, op. 2, d. 5, ll. 434–5 od.
91 Ibid.
92 GARO, f. 5, op. 2, d. 5, l. 607. See also Druzhnikov, *Informer 001*, for an excellent illustration of the precarious position of rural soviet chairmen in the person of Pavel Morozov's father.
93 GARO, f. 5, op. 2, d. 5, ll. 393–6. Similar examples were given for other villages and districts.
94 Ibid.
95 Ibid.
96 To be fair to Male, he does suggest the rural soviet may have played this role, but he does not explore the possibility. *Russian Peasant Organisation*, 114.

97 GARO, f. 5, op. 2, d. 5, l. 436.
98 Scott, *Moral Economy of the Peasant.*
99 GARO, f. 2, op. 1, d. 213, l. 75.
100 The representative 'fictional' villages of the novel are Tikhanovo, Gordeevo, and Veret'e. I suspect the proximity to Gridino and Veraievo is not accidental. Gordeevo may be a reference to the martyr Gordyi, who is celebrated on 3 January. A reading associated with Gordyi is Matthew 10:16–22, eerily appropriate verses for the rebellion itself:

> I am sending you out like sheep among wolves. Therefore be as shrewd as snakes and as innocent as doves. Be on your guard against men; they will hand you over to the local councils and flog you in their synagogues. On my account you will be brought before governors and kings as witnesses to them and to the Gentiles. But when they arrest you, do not worry about what to say or how to say it. At that time you will be given what to say, for it will not be you speaking, but the Spirit of your Father speaking through you. Brother will betray brother to death, and a father his child; children will rebel against their parents and have them put to death. All men will hate you because of me, but he who stands firm to the end will be saved.

Gordyi or Gordias was born at the end of the third century. A centurion, he stood up against the prefect of his city for persecuting Christians. He was tortured and beheaded for his troubles. Gordeevo may also be a reference to the word for pride (*gordost'*). And while a Veret'e can be a dry place in a swamp, it may also be an allusion on Mozhaev's part to the word for faith (*vera*). See Vladimir Dal', *Tolkovyi slovar' zhivogo velikorusskogo iazyka*, vol. 1 (rpr.; St Petersburg: Diamant, 1996).
101 Volume 1 was finished in 1976 and published in 1980. Volume 2 was finished in 1980, but not published until 1987. L. Vil'chek, 'Vot moia derevnia …,' in Mozhaev, *Izbrannye prozvedeniia*, 1:3. See also Gillespie, 'History, Politics, and the Russian Peasant,' 184, 192–3.
102 For an excellent exploration of the creation of a classic Soviet language, see Gorham, *Speaking in Soviet Tongues.*
103 Boris Mozhaev, *Muzhiki i baby*, 106.
– Кнут, а ты когда-нибудь влюблялся?
– Чаво?
– Почему не женишься?
– Устарел я, девки.
– Кнут, а ето правда, будто у мужиков, которые боятся баб, отсыхает?

– Чаво?

– Поливалка...

– У меня, девки, ишо хватит на семейку.

– Воды, что ли?

– Ах вы забубенные!

Knut's 'chavo' is indicative of a strong akanie in Riazan speech.

104 Ibid., 395.

– Что ж, выходит, у Тараканихи классовое лицо, ежели над ней смеятся нельзя?

– А какая у нее задница?

105 Ibid., 207.

106 Ibid., 226.

107 Ibid., 65–6.

108 Ibid., 326.

109 Ibid., 614.

110 Ibid., 76.

111 Ibid., 650. 'Я не белый и не красный, Мама. Я слишком русский.'

112 'Kruglyi stol': istoricheskaia nauka v usolviiakh perestroika,' *Voprosy istorii* 3 (Mar. 1988): 3–57. V.P. Danilov's contribution is entitled, 'Tret'ia vol'na,' 22.

113 See works by David Gillespie, and the dissertation by Holihan, 'Collectivization and the Utopian Ideal in the Works of Boris Andreevich Mozhaev,' esp. 210. Both note traces of anti-Semitism in Mozhaev's work.

114 Mozhaev, *Muzhiki i baby*, 646–7. Translation is Gillespie's in 'History, Politics, and the Russian Peasant,' 202.

115 See Katarina Clark, 'Changing Historical Paradigms in Soviet Culture,' in *Late Soviet Culture: From Perestroika to Novostroika*, ed. Lahusen with Kuperman, 300.

116 See Davies, *Soviet History and the Gorbachev Revolution*, for an excellent exploration of this process.

117 For a start, see Danilov, Manning, and Viola, *Tragediia sovetskoi derevni*, vol. 1–5; and Viola et al., *Riazanskaia derevnia v 1929–1930*.

118 The film *Uprising* was the result.

119 Portelli, *The Death of Luigi Trastulli and Other Stories*, 55. I am grateful to Ben Eklof for directing me to Portelli's work. There is obviously a developed literature on how to engage in oral history, its contributions, and its limitations etc. For a start, see Ritchie, *Doing Oral History*; and Thompson, *The Voice of the Past*.

120 Portelli, *Death of Luigi Trastulli*, 47.

121 Ibid., 53. Emphasis in the original.

122 As a starting point, see Le Goff, *History and Memory*; Klein, 'On the Emer-

gence of *Memory* in Historical Discourse,' which begins, 'Welcome to the memory industry'; Nora, 'Between Memory and History'; and Winter, *Remembering War.*

123 For two sides of the debate and a good introduction to the literature, see the works of Cathy Caruth and Ruth Leys, including Caruth's introduction to her edited collection, *Trauma: Explorations in Memory*; Caruth, *Unclaimed Experience: Trauma, Narrative, and History*; Caruth, 'Violence and Traumatic Survivals,' 24–25; Leys, *Trauma: A Genealogy*. Much of this literature focuses on memory of the holocaust. See also Young, 'Social Suffering.' In the Soviet context, Polly Jones applies literature on trauma to memories of the purges during the period of the thaw. She finds individuals trapped between the memories of trauma and offical pressure to heal and to rid themselves of 'gloomy thoughts.' 'Memories of Terror or Terrorizing Memories?

124 See Wang, *Illuminations from the Past*, 11, for reference to such studies on modern China.

125 Wachtel, 'Memory and History: Introduction,' 210–11.

126 See the introduction by Natalie Zemon Davis and Randolph Stern in 'Memory and Counter-Memory,' 5.

127 Portelli notes, 'If the interview is constructed skillfully and its purposes are clear to the narrators [those being interviewed] it is not impossible for them to make a distinction between present and past self, and to objectify the past self as other than the present one.' *Death of Luigi Trastulli*, 53. Anna Petrovna repeatedly made such a distinction.

128 Portelli explains, 'Many stories are told over and over, or discussed with members of the community; formalized narrative, even meter, may help to preserve a textual version of an event.' Ibid., 52.

129 GARO, f. R-5, op. 2, d. 5, l. 288, published in Viola et al., *Riazanskaia derevnia v 1929–1930*, 238.

130 For more on millers as targets during collectivization, see Fitzpatrick, *Stalin's Peasants*, 56, 158–9, 161; Viola, 'The Second Coming,' 73; and Viola, *Peasant Rebels under Stalin*, 41.

Conclusion

1 Stephen Kotkin makes this point in '1991 and the Russian Revolution': 'In any event, the new social history sources – diaries, unsolicited letters, sent to newspapers and officials, and political mood summaries (svodki) – have rendered far easier the efforts to get beyond high politics. For that task, the abundant published sources, especially the newspaper issued by

almost every institution, provide a local record sometimes unmatched by the archives. Indeed, notwithstanding the hypersecrecy, the new society proclaimed in the USSR could not stop talking about itself. The materials it generated are staggering. Everything depends on the questions asked and the reason for asking them' (392).

2 As Michael Gorham points out,

> Notions of purification, spoiling, mangling, regional, obsolete, real and classical – when used in conjunction with language – all functions as broader moral and ideological signifiers, indications of a certain dynamic of power and authority. If a language is 'spoiled,' 'impure,' 'defiled,' 'marginal,' and 'outdated,' someone, or some group, is most likely perceived as the source of the spoiling, contamination and marginalization, and thereby the target of 'cleansing,' or 'purification.' Similarly, someone or some group must serve as the linguistic 'purifier,' the creator and perpetuator of the 'real' Russian language. Language 'purism,' as it is commonly termed, more often than not indicates an underlying struggle for power and authority on the part of social and cultural representatives who see themselves as 'guardians' of an established language tradition, defending it against the forces whom they perceive to be alien, detrimental, and threatening to the integrity of the national tongue, and, by extension the nation itself. (Gorham, 'Mastering the Perverse, 139)

3 The standard spelling of the village name is Ermolovo. The spelling captures local pronunciation.

4 RGAE, f. 396, op. 3, d. 521, l. 10.

Bibliography

Archival Sources

Citations of archival materials are by *fond, opis', delo,* and *list,* and are abbreviated f., op., d., and l.

GARF (Gosudarstvennyi arkhiv Rossiiskoi Federatsii / State Archive of the Russian Federation)

Fond 393, NKVD

GARO (Gosudarstvennyi arkhiv Riazanskoi Oblasti / State Archive of Riazan Oblast)

Fond R-2, Okruzhskoi komitet sekter informatsii

Fond R-4, Riazanskii gubernskii ispolnitel'nyi komitet soveta rabochikh, krest'ianskikh i krasnoarmeiskikh deputatov 1917–1929 gg.

Fond R-5, Riazanskii gubernskii ispolnitel'nyi komitet soveta rabochikh, krest'ianskikh i krasnoarmeiskikh deputatov 1917–1929 gg.

Fond R-55, Otdel upravleniia ispolnitel'nogo komiteta Pronskogo uezdnogo soveta rabotnikh, krest'ianskikh i krasnoarmeiskikh deputatov

Fond R-61, Admintodel Riazanskogo ispolnitel'nogo komiteta i krasnoarmeiskikh deputatov Riazanskogo ispolnitel'nogo komiteta

Fond R-63, Adminotdel

Fond R-85, Finansovyi otdel isponitel'nogo komiteta Kasimovskogo uezdnogo soveta

Fond R-88, Finansovyi otdel isponitel'nogo komiteta Riazshskogo uezdnogo soveta

fond R-298, Riazanskoe gubernskoe otdelenie Narodnogo Komissariata raboche krest'ianskoi inspektsii

Fond R-343, Zemel'noe upravlenie ispolnitel'nogo komiteta Riazanskogo gubernskogo soveta rabochikh, krest'ianskikh i krasnoarmeiskikh deputatov

Fond R-2461, Riazan gubsud
Fond R-2462, Riazan gubsud
Fond R-2526, Narsud 8-go uchastka Riazhskogo uezda
Fond R-2534, Narsud 3-go uchastka Riazanskogo uezda
Fond R-2535, Narsud 4-go uchastka Riazanskogo uezda
Fond R-2541, Narsud 10-go uchastka Riazanskogo uezda
RGAE (Rossiiskii gosudarstvennyi akhiv ekonomiki / Russian State Archive of the Economy)
Fond 396, Krest'ianskaia gazeta
Fond 478, Narkomzem
RGASPI (Rossiiskii gosudarstvennyi arkhiv sotsial'no-politicheskoi istorii / Russian State Archive of Socio-Political History)
Fond 17, Tsentral'nyi komitet VKP(b)

Russian Journals and Newspapers

Administrativnyi vestnik
Bednota
Delegatka
Derevenskaia gazeta
Ezhenedel'nik sovetskoi iustitsii
Izvestiia
Kollektiv
Krest'ianskaia gazeta
Krest'ianskii iurist
Na agrarnom fronte
Otechestvennaia istoriia
Pravda
Pravo i zhizn'
Problemy istorii SSSR
Problemy prestupnosti
Proletarskii sud
Rabochii klich
Rabochii sud
Revoliutsiia prava
Sovetskaia derevnia
Sovetskoe stroitel'stvo
Sud idet
Sudebnaia praktika
Vlast' sovetov

Law Codes

Lesnoi Kodeks, RSFSR, 1918
Ugolovnyi kodeks, RSFSR, 1923
Ugolovnyi kodeks, RSFSR, 1934

Collections of Archival Documents

Danilov, V.P., R.T. Manning, and L. Viola. *Tragediia Sovetskoi derevni: Kollektivizatsiia i raskulachivanie: Dokumenty i materialy v 5 tomakh, 1927–1939*. Moscow: Rosspen, 2000–6.

Kriukova, S.S., ed. *Krest'ianskie istorii: rossiiskaia derevnia 1920-kh godov v pis'makh i dokumentov*. Moscow: Rosspen, 2001.

Livshin, A.Ia., and I.B. Orlov, eds. *Pis'ma vo vlast' 1917–1927*. Moscow: Rosspen, 1998.

Sokolov, A.K., ed. *Golos naroda: Pis'ma i otkliki riadovykh sovetskikh grazhdan o sobytiiakh 1918–1932*. Moscow: Rosspen, 1998.

Viola, Lynne, Sergei Zhuravlev, Andrei Mel'nik, and Tracy McDonald, eds. *Riazanskaia derevnia v 1929–1930: Khronika golovokruzheniia*. Moscow: Rosspen, 1998.

Other Primary Sources

Agitprop TsKRKP(b). *Agitatsiia i propaganda v derevne*. Leningrad: Priboi, 1925.

Alekseev, V.N. *Derevnia Kurovo, Dmitrovskogo uezda*. Moscow: Gub-izd., 1923.

Bakhtin, Mikhail. *Rabelais and His World*. Translated by Helene Iswolsky. Bloomington: Indiana University Press, 1984.

Balzac, Honore de. *The Peasants*, translated by Elen Marriage. New York: Fertig, 2004.

Bol'shakov, A.M. *Sovetskaia derevnia (1917–1924): Ekonomika i byt*. Leningrad: Priboi, 1924.

– *Derevnia posle Oktiabria*. Leningrad: Priboi, 1925.

– *Derevnia 1917–1927*. Moscow: Rabotnik prosveshcheniia, 1927.

– *Kraevedcheskoe izuchenie derevni*. Leningrad: Rabotnik prosveshcheniia, 1930.

Borders, Karl. *Village Life under the Soviets*. New York: Vanguard, 1927.

Braude, I.D. *V ugolovnom sude: Iz zapisok zashchitnika 1922–1929*. Moscow: Pravo i zhizn', 1927.

Brykin, N. *V novoi derevne: Ocherki derevenskogo byta*. Leningrad: Gos-izd., 1925.

Chaianov, A.V. *Krestianskoe khoziaistvo*. Moscow: Ekonomika, 1989.

Chugunov, S.I. *Voprosy organizatsii i deiatel'nosti sel'skikh sovetov*. Leningrad: Gos-izd., 1925.

Danilov, V.P., and Teodor Shanin, eds. *Krest'ianskoe vosstanie v Tambovskoi gubernii v. 1919–1921 gg. 'Antonovschchina' dokumenty i materialy.* Tambov: Izd-vo MINTS, 1994.

Fenomenov, M.Ia. *Sovremennaia derevnia.* Vols 1 & 2. Moscow: Gos-izd., 1925.

Fitzpatrick, Sheila, and Yuri Slezkine, eds. *In the Shadow of Revolution: Life Stories of Russian Women from 1917 to the Second World War.* Princeton: Princeton University Press, 2000.

Gernet, M. 'Statistika gorodskoi i sel'skoi prestupnosti.' *Problemy prestupnosti* 2 (1927): 15–40.

Gertsenzon, A.A. 'K metodike individual'no-sotsiologicheskogo izucheniia pravonarushitelei.' *Prestupnik i prestupnost,'* 2 (1927): 152–64.

Goliakov, I.T. *Sbornik dokumentov po istorii ugolovnogo zakonodatel'stva SSSR i RSFSR, 1917–1952 gg.* Moscow: Gosudarstvennoe izdatel'stvo iurodicheskoi literatury, 1953.

Golubykh, M. *Ocherki glukhoi derevni.* Moscow: Gos-izd., 1926.

Gorky, Maxim. 'On the Russian Peasantry.' *Journal of Peasant Studies* 4, no. 1 (October 1976): 11–28.

Gurari, E.L. 'Chto dalo ukrupnenie volostei v Tsentral'no-Promyshlennoi oblasti?' *Novaia volost' raion,* 45–60. Moscow: Izd. Gosplana SSSR, 1925.

Ianin, A.N. 'Vtoroe kulatskoe vosstanie i ego likvidatsiia.' *Minuvshee* 4 (1998): 298–304.

Igorov, K. 'Predislovie: Organizatsionnoe Biuro Tsentral'no-Promyshlennoi oblasti.' *Novaia volost' raion,* 3–6. Moscow: Izd. Gosplana SSSR, 1925.

Ilf, Ilia, and Evgenii Petrov. *The Twelve Chairs.* Translated by John H.C. Richardson. Evanston: Northwestern University Press, 1997.

Irashi, M. *Narodnyi sud v derevne (Ocherki derevenskoi praktiki).* Moscow: Gos-izd., 1924.

Isaev, M. 'Khuliganstvo.' In *Khuliganstov i khuligany,* edited by V.N. Tolmachev, 11–19. Moscow: Izd. NKVD, 1929.

Ivnitskii, N.A., T.V. Sorokina, and E.A. Tiurina, eds. *Nalogovaia politika v derevne* (1928–1937). Moscow: Sobranie, 2007.

Izdanie offitsial'noe. *Razdel 1, Rukovodiashchie ukazaniia po pereustroistvu i pod"emu sel'skogo khoziaistvo Riazanskogo okruga; Razdel 2, O rasshirenii prav sel'sovetov na territorii Riazaskogo okruga. s.-kh. proizvodstvennykh soveshchaniiakh i proch. materialy, sviazannye s rashireniem prav sel'sovetov.* 1929.

Kabanov, S.F. *Borba s ugolovnoi prestupnost'iu v derevne.* Edited by Narodnyi otdela ugolovnogo rozyska TsAU NKVD N.I. Nikolaevskii. Moscow: NKVD RSFSR, 1928.

Kataev, Valentin. *Time Forward!* Translated by Charles Malamuth. Evanston: Northwestern University Press, 1995.

Krylenko, N.V. 'Chto takoe khuliganstvo?' In *Khuliganstvo i prestuplenie: Sbornik statei*, edited by N.V. Krylenko, 11–55. Moscow: Izd. Rabochi sud, 1927.

– *Sud i pravo v SSSR, chast' pervaia: Osnovy sudoustroistvo.* Moscow: Gos-izd., 1927.

Lagovier, N. *O Samosudakh.* Moscow: Gos-izd., 1927.

Lahusen, Thomas, Veronique Garros, and Natalia Korenevskaya. *Intimacy and Terror: Soviet Diaries of the 1930s.* New York: New Press, 1995.

Lenin, V.I. *Collected Works.* Vol. 30, *September 1919–April 1920.* Moscow: Progress, 1965.

Les krest'ianam: Sbornik besplatnoe prilozhenie. Biulleteniu marobika, 1924.

Les: Sbornik statei: Pomeshchennykh v gazete 'Sovetskaia mysl'' ko 'dniu lesa.' Moscow: Sovetskaia mysl', 1924.

Liakhova, V.A. *Finansovo-nalogovaia rabota volosti: Rukovodstvo dlia volostnykh i sel'skikh finansovykh rabotnikov.* Moscow: Fin-izd., 1926.

Liublinskii, P. 'Khuliganstvo i ego sotsial'no-bytovye korni.' In *Khuliganstvo i khuligany*, edited by V.N. Tolmachev, 38–62. Moscow: Izd. NKVD, 1929.

Man'kovskii, B.S. 'Derevenskaia ponozhovshchina.' In *Khulganstvo i ponozhovshchina*, 113–29. Moscow: Mosrabototdela, 1927.

Mayakovsky, Vladimir. *Selected Verse.* Translated by Peter Tempest. Moscow: Raduga, 1985.

Moskovskii gubernskii sud i moskovskii kabinet po izucheniiu lichnosti prestupnika i prestupnosti. *Khuliganstvo i ponozhovshchina.* Moscow: Mosrabototdela, 1927.

Mozhaev, Boris. *Muzhiki i baby.* Moscow: Sovremennik, 1988.

Murugov, N., and A. Kolesnikov. *Apparat nizovykh sovetskikh organov: Po materialam obsledovaniia NK RKI RSFSR.* Moscow: Gos-izd., 1925.

Narodnyi Komissariat Raboche-Krest'ianskoi Inspektsii RSFSR. *Lesa mestnogo znacheniia: Po materialam obsledovaniia NKRKI RSFSR.* Moscow: Izd. NKRKI SSSR, 1925.

Olenetskii Gubpolitprosveta. *Lesozagotovitel'naia kampaniia 1921–22 operativnogo goda v Olenetskoi gubernii: Rukovodstvo dlia propagandov.* Petrozavodsk, 1921.

Orshanskii, L.G. 'Khuligan (Psikhologicheskii ocherk).' In *Khuliganstvo i prestuplenie: Sbornik statei*, edited by N.V. Krylenko, 55–82. Moscow: Izd. Rabochi sud, 1927.

Otchet prokuratury RSFSR prezidiumu VTsIK za 1925. Moscow: Iuridicheskoe izd. NKIu RSFSR, 1926.

Otdel Pechati TsK VKP(b). *Sovetskaia derevnia i rabota sel'korov: Sbornik statei.* Moscow: Gos-izd., 1927.

Platonov, Andrei. *Chevengur.* Translated by Anthony Olcott. Ann Arbor: Ardis, 1978.

Promyshlenno-Geograficheskogo otdela KEPS. *Les ego izuchenie i ispol'zovanie pervyi lesnoi sbornik.* Petrograd, 1922.

Rezunov, M. *Sel'skie sovety i zemel'nye obshchestva.* Moscow: Izd-vo Kommunisticheskoi akademii, 1928.

Riazanskaia gubernskaia planovaia komissiia. *Materialy k planu narodnogo khoziaistva Riazanskoi gubernii.* Vol. 4, *Ocherk lesov Riazanskoi gubernii.* Riazan, 1927.

– *Materialy k planu narodnogo khoziaistva Riazanskoi gubernii.* Vol. 5, *Sotsial'no-ekonomicheskaia struktura krest'ianskogo khoziaistva Riazanskoi gubernii.* Riazan, 1928.

Riazanskaia okruzhnaia organizatsionnaia komissiia. *Materialy k organizatsii Riazanskogo okruga.* Riazan, 1929.

RSFSR Narodnyi Komissariat Zemledeliia. *Lesnoe khoziaistvo RSFSR i Perspektivy ego razvitiia.* Vol. 1. Moscow: Iskra Revoliutsii, 1924.

RSFSR Narodnyi Komissariat Zemledeliia Upravlenie Lesami. *Lesnoe khoziaistvo RSFSR i perespektivy ego razvittia.* Vol. 2. Moscow, 1927.

– *Meropriiatiia po lesnomu khoziaistvo RSFSR.* Leningrad: Gublit, 1927.

– *Lesnoe khoziaistvo RSFSR v 1927–28 godu.* Moscow: Novaia Derevnia, 1928.

Segalov, T. 'P'ianye draki v gorode i derevne.' In *Problemy prestupnosti,* 88–99. Moscow: Gos-izd., 1927.

– 'Prestupnoe khuliganstvo i khuliganskie prestupleniia,' In *Khuliganstvo i khuligany,* edited by V.N. Tolmachev, 63–74. Moscow: Izd. NKVD, 1929.

Shestakova, A. 'Prestupleniia protiv lichnosti v derevne.' In *Problemy prestupnosti,* 1:215–23. Moscow: Gos-izd., 1926.

Sokolov, S., and P. Uvarov. *Geografiia SSSR po raionam i gosplana.* Moscow: Gosplan, 1924.

Solts, A., and S. Fainblit. *Revoliutsionnaia zakonnost' i nasha karatel'naia politika.* Moscow: Moskovskii rabochii, 1925.

Statisticheskii ezhegodnik Riazanskoi gubernii za 1923–1924 gg. Riazan, 1925.

Statisticheskii ezhegodnik Riazanskoi gubernii za 1926–1927 gg. Riazan, 1928.

Statisticheskii spravochnik po Riazanskomu okrugu za 1927–28–29 gg. Riazan, 1930.

Tan-Bogoraz, B.G., ed. *Staryi i novyi byt.* Leningrad: Gos-izd., 1924.

Tarnovskii, E. 'Konokradstvo v nastoiashchee vremia i v dovoennuiu epokhu.' In *Problemy prestupnosti,* 100–9. Moscow: Gos-izd., 1927.

Tomskii, M.P. 'Bor'ba s khuliganstvom i klubnaia rabota,' In *Khuliganstvo i prestuplenie: Sbornik statei,* edited by N.V. Krylenko, 3–9. Moscow: Izd. Rabochii sud, 1927.

Trotsky, Lev. *Literature and Revolution.* Ann Arbor: University of Michigan Press, 1960.

Uritskii, S. *Chto dolzhen znat' krest'ianin o nalogakh.* Moscow: Izd. Krasnaia Nov', 1924.
Vertov, Dziga. *Kino-Eye: The Writings of Dziga Vertov,* edited by Annette Michelson, translated by Kevin O'Brien. Berkeley: University of California Press, 1984.
Voprosy Sovetskogo stroitel'stva: Tezisy vnosimy prezidiumom gubispolkoma k VIII Riazanskomy gubernskomy s"ezdu sovetov rabochikh, krestianskikh i krasnoarmeiskikh deputatov. Riazan, 1920.
Voronov, D.N. *O Samogone.* Moscow: Gosudarstvennoe meditsinskoe izdatel'stvo, 1929.

Films

Accordion (*Garmon'*). Directed by Igor Savchenko. Moscow: Mezhrabpomfilm, 1934. 66 mins.
General Line (*General'naia liniia*), aka *Old and New* (*Staroe i novoe*). Directed by Sergei Eisenstein and Grigorii Aleksandrov. Moscow: Sovkino, 1929. 90 mins.
Happiness (*Schast'e*). Directed by Aleksandr Medvedkin. Moscow: Sovkino, 1934. 65 mins.
Kino-Eye (*Kino-Glaz*). Directed by Dziga Vertov. Moscow: Goskino, 1924. 78 mins.
Third World Cop. Directed by Chris Browne. Jamaica: Hawk's Nest Production, 1999. 98 mins.
Uprising. Directed by T. McDonald. Toronto: Chemodan Films, 2006. 19 mins.
Village Schoolteacher (*Sel'skaia uchitel'nitsa*). Directed by Mark Donskoi. Moscow: Soiuzdetfilm, 1947. 100 mins.
Women of Riazan (*Baby Riazanskye*). Directed by Olga Preobrazhenskaia, 1927. Moscow: Sovkino. 67 mins.

Secondary Sources

Alexopoulos, Golpho. 'The Ritual Lament: A Narrative of Appeal in the 1920s and 1930s.' *Russian History / Histoire Russe* 24, nos. 1–2 (1997): 117–29.
– *Stalin's Outcasts: Aliens, Citizens, and the Soviet State, 1926–1936.* Ithaca: Cornell University Press, 2003.
Anderson, David M., and David Killingray. 'Consent, Coercion and Colonial Control: Policing the Empire, 1830–1940.' In *Policing the Empire: Government, Authority and Control, 1830–1940,* edited by David M. Anderson and David Killingray, 1–15. Manchester: Manchester University Press, 1991.
Anthony, Robert J. 'Peasants, Heroes and Brigands: The Problems of Social Banditry in Early Nineteenth-Century South China.' *Modern China* 15, no. 2 (April 1989): 123–48.

Archer, John E. *By a Flash and Scare: Incendiarism, Animal Maiming, and Poaching in East Anglia 1815–1870*. Oxford: Clarendon, 1990.

Arnold, David. 'Crime and Crime Control in Madras, 1858–1947.' In *Crime and Criminality in British India*, edited by Anand A. Yang, 62–88. Tucson: University of Arizona Press, 1985.

Atkinson, Dorothy. *The End of the Russian Land Commune, 1905–1930*. Stanford: Stanford University Press, 1983.

Attridge, Steve. *Nationalism, Imperialism and Identity in Late Victorian Culture: Civil and Military Worlds*. London: Palgrave Macmillan, 2002.

Barr, Brenton M., and Kathleen E. Braden. *The Disappearing Russian Forest: A Dilemma in Soviet Resource Management*. Totowa: Rowman & Littlefield, 1988.

Beattie, J.M. *Crime and the Courts in England 1660–1800*. Princeton: Princeton University Press, 1986.

Blok, Anton. *The Mafia of a Sicilian Village 1860–1960: A Study of Violent Peasant Entrepreneur*. London: Oxford University Press, 1974.

– 'The Peasants and the Brigand: Social Banditry Reconsidered.' *Comparative Studies in Society and History* 14, no. 4 (October 1972): 494–503.

Bohac, Rodney D. 'Widows and the Russian Serf Community.' In *Russia's Women: Accommodation, Resistance and Transformation*, edited by Barbara Clements, Barbara Engel, and Christine Worobec, 95–112. Berkeley: University of California Press, 1991.

Bonhomme, Brian. *Forests, Peasants, and Revolutionaries: Forest Conservation and Organization in Soviet Russia, 1917–1929*. East European Monographs. Boulder: Distributed by Columbia University Press, 2005.

Brooks, Jeffrey. *When Russia Learned to Read*. New Jersey: Princeton University Press, 1985.

Brown, Kate. *A Biography of No Place: From Ethnic Borderland to Soviet Heartland*. Cambridge: Harvard University Press, 2003.

Brown, Nathan. 'Brigands and State Building: The Invention of Banditry in Modern Egypt.' *Comparative Studies in Society and History* 32, no. 2 (April 1990): 258–81.

– *Peasant Politics in Modern Egypt: The Struggle against the State*. New Haven: Yale University Press, 1990.

Buck-Morss, Susan. *Dreamworld and Catastrophe: The Passing of Mass Utopia in East and West*. Cambridge: MIT Press, 2000.

Burbank, Jane. *Russian Peasants Go to Court: Legal Culture in the Countryside, 1905–1917*. Bloomington: Indiana University Press, 2004.

Burds, Jeffrey. *Socialism in One Country 1924–1926*. Vol. 2. London: Macmillan, 1959.

– 'The Social Control of Peasant Labor in Russia: The Response of Village

Communities in Labor Migration in the Central Industrial Region, 1861–1905.' In *Peasant Economy, Culture and Politics in European Russia, 1800–1921*, edited by Esther Kingston-Mann and Timothy Mixter, 52–100. Princeton: Princeton University Press, 1990.

Bushnell, John. *Mutiny amid Repression: Russian Soldiers in the Revolution of 1905–1906*. Bloomington: Indiana University Press, 1985.

Carr, E.H. *Socialism in One Country 1924–26*. 2 vols. London: Macmillan, 1958.

Caruth, Cathy. *Trauma: Explorations in Memoir.* Baltimore: Johns Hopkins University Press, 1995.

– *Unclaimed Experience: Trauma, Narrative, and History*. Baltimore: Johns Hopkins University Press, 1996.

– 'Violence and Traumatic Survivals.' *Assemblage* 20 (April 1993): 24–5.

Clark, Katarina. 'Changing Historical Paradigms in Soviet Culture.' In *Late Soviet Culture: From Perestroika to Novostroika*, edited by Thomas Lahusen with Gene Kuperman, 289–306. Durham: Duke University Press, 1993.

Cobb, Richard C. *The Police and the People: French Popular Protest 1789–1820*. Oxford: Clarendon, 1970.

Coe, Steven. 'Struggles for Authority in the NEP Village: The Early Rural Correspondents Movement, 1923–1927.' *Europe-Asia Studies* 48, no. 7 (1996): 1151–71.

Cohen, Stephen F. *Bukharin and the Bolshevik Revolution: A Political Biography, 1888–1938*. Oxford: Oxford University Press, 1980.

Cohn, Bernard S. 'History and Anthropology: The State of Play.' *Comparative Studies in Society and History* 22 (1980): 198–221.

Costlow, Jane. 'Imaginations of Destruction: The "Forest Question" in Nineteenth-Century Russian Culture.' *Russian Review* 62 (January 2003): 91–118.

– 'Who Holds the Axe? Violence and Peasants in Nineteenth-Century Russian Depictions of the Forest.' *Slavic Review* 68, no. 1 (Spring 2009): 10–30.

Cox, Terry. 'Awkward Class or Awkward Classes? Class Relations in the Russian Peasantry before Collectivization.' *Journal of Peasant Studies* 7, no. 1 (October 1979): 70–85.

Cresswell, Tim. *Place: A Short Introduction*. Oxford: Blackwell, 2004.

Danilov, V.P. 'Sovetskaia nalogovaia politika v dokolkhoznoi derevne.' In *Oktiabr' i sovetskoe krest'ianstvo, 1917–1927*, edited by Volkov, 164–91. Moscow: Izd. Nauka, 1977.

– *Rural Russia under the New Regime*. Translated by Orlando Figes. Bloomington: Indiana University Press, 1988.

– 'Istoki i nachalo derevenskoi tragedii.' In *Tragediia sovetskoi derevni: Kollektivizatsiia i raskulachivanie; Dokumenty i materialy*. Vol. 1, *Mai 1927–noiabr' 1929*, edited by V.P. Danilov R. Manning, and L. Viola, 13–67. Moscow: Rosspen, 1999.

Darnton, Robert. *The Great Cat Massacre and Other Episodes in French Cultural History*. New York: Vintage, 1985.

Das, Veena, and Deborah Poole, eds. *Anthropology in the Margins of the State*. Delhi: Oxford University Press, 2004.

David-Fox, Michael. 'What Is Cultural Revolution?' *Russian Review* 58, no. 2 (April 1999): 181–201.

Davies, R.W. *The Development of the Soviet Budgetary System*. Cambridge: Cambridge University Press, 1958.

– *The Socialist Offensive: The Collectivization of Soviet Agriculture 1929–1930*. Cambridge, MA: Harvard University Press, 1980.

– *Soviet History and the Gorbachev Revolution*. Bloomington: Indiana University Press, 1989.

Davies, Sarah. *Popular Opinion in Stalin's Russia*. Cambridge: Cambridge University Press, 1997.

Davis, Natalie. *The Return of Martin Guerre*. Cambridge, MA: Harvard University Press, 1983.

– 'Charivari, Honor and Community in Seventeenth-Century Lyon and Geneva.' In *Rite, Drama, Festival, Spectacle: Rehearsals toward a Theory of Cultural Performance*, edited by J. MacAloon, 42–57. Philadephia: Institute for the Study of Human Issues, 1984.

Davis, Natalie Zemon, and Randolph Stern. 'Memory and Counter-Memory.' Special issue, *Representations* 26 (Spring 1989): 1–6.

Davis, Robert C. *The War of the Fists: Popular Culture and Public Violence in Late Renaissance Venice*. Oxford: Oxford University Press, 1994.

Duara, Prasenjit. *Culture, Power and the State in Rural North China 1900–1942*. Stanford: Stanford University Press, 1988.

Druzhnikov, Yuri. *Informer 001: The Myth of Pavlik Morozov*. New Brunswick: Transaction, 1997.

Edgerton, William, ed. and trans. *Memoirs of Peasant Tolstoyans in Soviet Russia*. Bloomington: Indiana University Press, 1993.

Eklof, Ben. *Russian Peasant Schools*. Berkeley: University of California Press, 1986.

– 'Ways of Seeing: Recent Anglo-American Studies of the Russian Peasant.' *Jahrbucher für Geschichte Osteuropas* 36 (1988): 57–79.

Engel, Barbara Alpern. *Between the Fields and the City: Women, Work and the Family in Russia, 1861–1914*. New York: Cambridge University Press, 1994.

– 'Russian Peasant Views of City Life, 1861–1914.' *Slavic Review* 52, no. 3 (Fall 1993): 446–59.

Engelstein, Laura. 'Combined Underdevelopment: Discipline and the Law in Imperial and Soviet Russia.' *American Historical Review* 98 (April 1993): 338–53.

Fainsod, Merle. *Smolensk under Soviet Rule.* 2nd ed. London: Unwin Hyman, 1989.

Fanon, Frantz. *The Wretched of the Earth.* New York: Grove, 1968.

Farnsworth, Beatrice. 'The Litigious Daughter-in-Law: Family Relations in Rural Russia in the Second Half of the Nineteenth Century.' In *Russian Peasant Women,* edited by Beatrice Farnsworth and Lynne Viola, 89–106. New York: Oxford University Press, 1992.

Field, Daniel. *Rebels in the Name of the Tsar.* London: Unwin Hyman, 1989.

Figes, Orlando. *Peasant Russia, Civil War: The Volga Countryside in Revolution (1917–1921).* Oxford: Clarendon, 1989.

– *A People's Tragedy: A History of the Russian Revolution.* New York: Viking Penguin, 1997.

Fitzpatrick, Sheila. 'The Civil War as a Formative Experience.' In *Bolshevik Culture: Experiment and Order in the Russian Revolution,* edited by Abbott Gleason, Peter Kenez, and Richard Stites, 57–76. Bloomington: Indiana University Press, 1985.

– *The Cultural Front: Power and Culture in Revolutionary Russia.* Ithaca: Cornell University Press, 1992.

– *Stalin's Peasants: Resistance and Survival in the Russian Village after Collectivization.* New York: Oxford University Press, 1994.

– 'Readers Letters to Krest'ianskaia Gazeta, 1938.' *Russian History / Histoire Russe* 24, nos. 1–2 (Spring–Summer 1997): 149–70.

Frank, Stephen P. 'Popular Justice, Community and Culture among the Russian Peasantry, 1870–1900.' *Russian Review* 46 (1987): 239–65.

– 'Confronting the Domestic Other: Rural Popular Culture and Its Enemies in Fin-de-Siècle Russia.' In *Cultures in Flux: Lower-Class Values, Practices, and Resistance in Late Imperial Russia,* edited by Stephen Frank and Mark Steinberg, 74–107. Princeton: Princeton University Press, 1994.

– *Crime, Cultural Conflict and Justice in Rural Russia, 1856–1914.* Berkeley: University of California Press, 1999.

Frank, Stephen P., and Mark D. Steinberg, eds. *Cultures in Flux: Lower-Class Values, Practices, and Resistance in Late Imperial Russia.* Princeton: Princeton University Press, 1994.

French, R.A. 'Russians and the Forest.' In *Studies in Russian Historical Geography,* edited by James H. Bater, 1:23–44. London: Academic Press, 1983.

Frierson, Cathy. 'Crime and Punishment in the Russian Village: Rural Concepts of Criminality at the End of the Nineteenth Century.' *Slavic Review* 46, no. 1 (Spring 1987): 55–69.

– '"I Must Always Answer to the Law": Rules and Response in the Reformed Volost' Court.' *Slavonic and East European Review* 75, no. 2 (1997): 308–34.

– 'Of Red Roosters, Revenge, and the Search for Justice: Rural Arson in European Russia in the Late Imperial Era.' In *Reforming Justice in Russia, 1864–1996: Power, Culture and the Limits of Legal Order*, edited by Peter H. Solomon Jr, 107–30. New York: Sharpe, 1997.

– *All Russia Is Burning! A Cultural History of Fire and Arson in Late Imperial Russia.* Seattle: University of Washington Press, 2002.

Frietag, Sandria B. 'Collective Crime and Authority in North India.' In *Crime and Criminality in British India*, edited by Anand A. Yang, 140–63. Tucson: University of Arizona Press, 1985.

Fulin, Iu.V. 'Fevral'skie dni 1917 g. v Riazani.' In *Nekotorye voprosy kraevedeniia i otechestvennoi istorii: Uchenye zapiski.* 3:3–17. Riazan: Riazanskii Gosudarstvennyi Pedagogicheskii Institut, 1972.

– 'Raspredelenie chastnovladel'cheskikh zemel' i inventaria pomeshchich'ikh imenii v Riazanskoi gubernii v 1918 godu.' In *Nekotorye voprosy kraevedeniia*, 52–72. Riazan, 1974.

Gallant, Thomas W. 'Honor, Masculinity, and Ritual Knife Fighting in Nineteenth-Century Greece.' *American Historical Review* (April 2000): 359–82.

Gaudin, Corinne. *Ruling Peasants: Village and State in Late Imperial Russia.* DeKalb: Northern Illinos University Press, 2007.

– '"No Place to Lay My Head": Marginalization and the Right to Land during the Stolypin Reforms.' *Slavic Review* 57 (Winter 1998): 747–73.

Geary, Roger. 'The Dragon and the Flame: An Analysis of the Welsh Arson Campaign.' *Contemporary Review* 264 (1994): 80–7.

Geertz, Clifford. *The Interpretation of Cultures.* New York: Basic Books, 1973.

– *Local Knowledge: Further Essays in Interpretive Anthropology.* New York: Basic Books, 1983.

Getty, J. Arch., and Oleg V. Naumov. *The Road to Terror: Stalin and the Self-Destruction of the Bolsheviks, 1932–1939.* New Haven: Yale University Press, 1999.

Gille, Zsuzsa. 'From Nature as Proxy to Nature as Actor.' *Slavic Review* 68, no. 1 (Spring 2009): 9.

Gillespie, David. C. 'History, Politics, and the Russian Peasant: Boris Mozhaev and the Collectivization of Agriculture.' *Slavonic and East European Review* 67, no. 2 (April 1989): 183–210.

– 'Ironies and Legacies: Village Prose and Glasnost.' *Forum for Modern Language Studies* 27, no. 1 (1991): 70–84.

Ginsburg, Carlo. *The Cheese and the Worms: The Cosmos of a Sixteenth-Century Miller.* Baltimore: Johns Hopkins University Press, 1980.

Glebov, Sergei. 'Interview with Peter Sahlins: Subjecthood That Happens to Be Called "Citizenship," or Trying to Make Sense of the Old Regime on Its Own Terms.' *Ab Imperio* 4 (2006): 39–58.

Goffman, Erving. *Encounters*. London: Lane, 1972.

Gorham, Michael S. 'Mastering the Perverse: State Building and Language "Purification" in Early Soviet Russia.' *Slavic Review* 58, no. 1 (Spring 2000): 132–53.

– *Speaking in Soviet Tongues: Language Culture and the Politics of Voice in Revolutionary Russia*. DeKalb: Northern Illinois University Press, 2003.

Gorshkov, Boris, and Alexander Martin. 'Debating "Backwardness" in Russian History.' *Newsnet* 47, no. 2 (March 2007): 1, 2, 4, 10.

Gorsuch, Anne. *Youth in Revolutionary Russia: Enthusiasts, Bohemians, Delinquents*. Bloomington: Indiana University Press, 2000.

Gouldner, Alvin W. 'Stalinism: A Study of Internal Colonialism.' *Telos* 54 (Winter 1977–8): 5–48.

Graziosi, Andrea. *The Great Soviet Peasant War: Bolsheviks and Peasants, 1917–1933*. Cambridge, MA: Ukrainian Research Institute, Harvard University, 1996.

Greenburg, Amy Sophia. 'Fights/Fires: Violent Firemen in the Nineteenth-Century American City.' In *Men and Violence. Gender, Honor and Ritual in Modern Europe and America*, edited by Peter Spierenburg, 159–89. Columbus: Ohio State University Press, 1998.

Guha, Ramachandra. *The Unquiet Woods: Ecological Change and Peasant Resistance in the Himalaya*. Berkeley: University of California Press, 2000.

Guha, Ranajit. *Elementary Aspects of Peasant Insurgency in Colonial India*. Delhi: Oxford University Press, 1983.

Gunst, Laurie. *Born Fi' Dead: A Journey through the Jamaican Posse Underworld*. New York: Holt, 1995.

Hagenloh, Paul. *Stalin's Police: Public Order and Mass Repression in the USSR, 1926–1941*. Washington, DC: Woodrow Wilson Center Press, 2009.

Hasegawa, Tsuyoshi. 'The Formation of the Militia in the February Revolution: An Aspect of the Origins of Dual Power.' *Slavic Review* 32, no. 2 (1973): 302–22.

Haimson, Leopold H. 'The Problem of Social Identities in Early Twentieth Century Russia.' *Slavic Review* 37, no. 1 (Spring 1988): 1–20.

Harris, James R. 'The Growth of the Gulag: Forced Labor in the Urals Regions, 1929–1931.' *Russian Review* 56 (April 1997): 265–80.

Harrison, Mark. 'Chaianov and the Economics of the Russian Peasantry.' *Journal of Peasant Studies* 4, no. 2 (January 1977): 127–61.

Harrison, Robert Pogue. *Forests: The Shadows of Civilization*. Chicago: University of Chicago Press, 1992.

Hay, Douglas, Peter Linebourgh, John G. Rule, E.P. Thompson, and Carl Winslow. *Albion's Fatal Tree: Crime and Society in Eigtheenth-Century England*. New York: Pantheon, 1975.

Hazard, John. *Settling Disputes in Soviet Society.* New York: Columbia University Press, 1960.

Heinzen, James W. *Inventing a Soviet Countryside: State Power and the Transformation of Rural Russia, 1917–1929.* Pittsburgh: Pittsburgh University Press, 2004.

Hindus, Maurice. *Red Bread: Collectivization in a Russian Village.* Bloomington: Indiana University Press, 1988.

Hobsbawm, E.J. *Primitive Rebels.* New York: Praeger, 1965.

– *Bandits.* London: Weidenfeld and Nicolson, 1969.

Hobsbawm, Eric, and George Rude. *Captain Swing: A Social History of the Great English Agricultural Uprising of 1830.* London: Lawrence and Wisehart, 1970.

Hoch, Steven L. *Serfdom and Social Control in Russia.* Chicago: University of Chicago Press, 1986.

Hoffmann, David L. 'Land Freedom and Discontent: Russian Peasants of the CIR prior to Collectivization.' *Europe-Asia Studies* 46, no. 4 (1994): 637–48.

– *Peasant Metropolis: Social Identities in Moscow, 1929–1941.* Ithaca: Cornell University Press, 1994.

– *Stalinist Values: The Cultural Norms of Soviet Modernity, 1917–1941.* Ithaca: Cornell University Press, 2003.

Hoffmann, David L., and Yanni Kotsonis, eds. *Russian Modernity: Politics, Knowledge and Practices.* New York: St Martin's, 2000.

Holihan, David Michael. 'Collectivization and the Utopian Ideal in the Works of Boris Andreevich Mozhaev.' PhD diss., University of Bath, 1994.

Holquist, Peter. 'Information Is the Alpha and Omega of Our Work.' *Journal of Modern History* 69 (September 1997): 415–50.

– *Making War, Forging Revolution: Russia's Continuum of Crisis, 1914–1921.* Cambridge: Harvard University Press, 2002.

– 'New Terrains and New Chronologies: The Interwar Period through the Lens of Population Politics.' *Kritika: Explorations in Russian and Eurasian History* 1, no. 4 (2003): 163–75.

– 'State Violence as Technique: The Logic of Violence in Soviet Totalitarianism.' In *Landscaping the Human Garden: Twentieth-Century Population Management in a Comparative Framework,* edited by Amir Weiner, 19–23. Stanford: Stanford University Press, 2003.

Holzman, Franklin D. *Soviet Taxation.* Cambridge: Harvard University Press, 1955.

Hughes, James. *Stalinism in a Russian Province.* London: Macmillan, 1996.

Humphries, Stephen. *Hooligans or Rebels? An Oral History of Working-Class Childhood and Youth, 1889–1939.* Oxford: Oxford University Press, 1981.

Hyden, Goran. *Beyond Ujamaa in Tanzania: Underdevelopment and an Uncaptured Peasantry.* London: Heinemann Educational Books, 1980.

Ingerflom, Claudio Sergio. 'Les Représentations Religieuses du Pouvoir dan la Russe Soviétique et Post-Soviétique.' *Societés Contemporaines* 37 (2000): 53–70.

Iz istorii kollektivizatsii sel'skogo khoziaistva Riazanskoi oblasti (1927–1935 gg.). Riazan, 1962.

Izmozik, V.S. 'Voices from the Twenties: Private Correspondence Intercepted by the OGPU.' *Russian Review* 55 (April 1996): 287–308.

Johnson, Robert Eugene. *Peasant and Proletarian: The Working Class of Moscow in the Late Nineteenth Century*. New Brunswick: Rutgers University Press, 1979.

Jones, Polly. 'Memories of Terror or Terrorizing Memories? Terror, Trauma and Survival in Soviet Culture of the Thaw.' *Slavonic East European Review* 86, no. 2 (April 2008): 346–71.

Joseph, Gilbert. 'On the Trail of Latin American Bandits.' *Latin American Research Review* 25, no. 3 (Summer 1990): 7–53.

Kabanov, V.V. 'Dokumentatsiia sel'skogo skhoda v pervye gody sovetskoi vlasti (1917–1920).' *Arkheograficheskii ezhegodnik za 1985* (1986): 113–23.

Keep, John. *The Russian Revolution: A Study in Mass Mobilization*. New York: Norton, 1976.

Keller, Shoshana. 'Islam in Soviet Central Asia, 1917–1930: Soviet Policy and the Struggle for Control.' *Central Asian Survey* 11, no. 1 (1992): 25–50.

Khoroshilov, G.V. 'Sozdanie material'no-tekhnicheskikh i politicheskikh predposylok massovoi kollektivizatsii sel'skogo khoziaistva 1927–1929 gg.' In *Pobeda kolkhoznogo stroia na Riazanskoi zemle*, 44–82. Riazan, 1976.

Kingston-Mann, Esther, and Timothy Mixter, eds. *Peasant Economy, Culture, and Politics of European Russia, 1800–1924*. New Jersey: Princeton University Press, 1991.

Klein, Kerwin Lee. 'On the Emergence of *Memory* in Historial Discourse.' *Representations* 69 (Winter 2000): 127–50.

Kotkin, Stephen. *Magnetic Mountain: Stalinism and a Civilization*. Berkeley: University of California Press, 1995.

– '1991 and the Russian Revolution.' *Journal of Modern History* (June 1998): 384–425.

Kotsonis, Yanni. '"Face-to-Face": The State, the Individual, and the Citizen in Russian Taxation, 1863–1917.' *Slavic Review* 2 (Summer 2004): 221–46.

– *Making Peasants Backward: Agricultural Cooperatives and the Agrarian Question in Russia, 1861–1914*. New York: St Martin's, 1999.

– '"No Place to Go": Taxation and State Transformation in Late Imperial and Early Soviet Russia.' *Journal of Modern History* 76 (September 2004): 531–77.

Kowalsky, Sharon A. '"Who's Responsible for Female Crime?" Gender, Deviance, and the Development of Soviet Social Norms in Revolutionary Russia.' *Russian Review* 62, no. 3 (2003): 366–86.

Koznova, I.E. 'Krestianskaia pozemel'naia obshchina 20-kh godov v sovetskoi literature.' *Problemy istorii SSSR* 11 (1980): 292–308.

Krylova, Anna. 'The Tenacious Liberal Subject in Soviet Studies.' *Kritika: Explorations in Russian and Eurasian History* 1, no. 1 (2000): 119–46.

Ladurie, Leroy. *Montaillou: The Promised Land of Error.* New York: Vintage, 1979.

Lahusen, Thomas. 'Socialist Realism Revisited: Or the Reader's Searching Melancholy.' *South Atlantic Quarterly* 90, no. 1 (Winter 1991): 87–109.

Landis, Erik C. *Bandits and Partisans: The Antonov Movement in the Russian Civil War.* Pittsburgh: University of Pittsburgh Press, 2008.

LaPierre, Brian. 'Making Hooliganism on a Mass Scale: The Campaign against Petty Hooliganism in the Soviet Union, 1956–1964.' *Cahiers du Monde Russe* 47 nos. 1–2 (2006): 349–75.

– 'Private Matters or Public Crimes: The Emergence of Domestic Hooliganism in the Soviet Union, 1939–1960.' In *Borders of Socialism: Private Spheres of Soviet Russia,* edited by Lewis H. Siegelbaum, 191–207. New York: Palgrave, 2006.

– 'Redefining Deviance: Policing and Punishing Hooliganism in Khrushchev's Russia, 1953–1964.' PhD diss., University of Chicago, 2006.

Laslett, Peter. *The World We Have Lost.* New York: Scribner, 1965.

Lefebvre, Georges. *The Great Fear of 1789: Rural Panic in Revolutionary France.* Princeton: Princeton University Press, 1973.

Lefebvre, Henri. *The Production of Space.* Translated by Donald Nicholson-Smith. Oxford: Blackwell, 1991.

Le Goff, Jacques. *History and Memory.* Translated by Steven Rendall and Elizabeth Claman. New York: Columbia University Press, 1992.

Lenoe, Matthew E. 'Letter-Writing and the State: Reader Correspondence with Newspapers as a Source for Early Soviet History.' *Cahiers du Monde Russe* 40, nos. 1–2 (January–June, 1999): 139–70.

Lewin, Moshe. *Russian Peasants and Soviet Power: A Study of Collectivization.* New York: Norton, 1975.

– *The Making of the Soviet System: Essays in the Social History of Interwar Russia.* New York: Pantheon, 1985.

Leys, Ruth. *Trauma: A Genealogy.* Chicago: University of Chicago Press, 2000.

Li, Tania Murray. 'Beyond "the State" and Failed Schemes.' *American Anthropologist* 107, no. 3 (2005): 383–94.

Lin, George. 'Fighting in Vain: The NKVD RSFSR in the 1920s.' PhD diss., Stanford University, 1997.

Linebaugh, Peter. 'Karl Marx, the Theft of Wood, and Working-Class Composition: A Contribution to the Current Debate.' *Crime and Social Justice* 6 (Fall–Winter 1976): 5–16.

Litvak, K.V. 'Samogonovarenie i potrebelenie alkogolia v rossiiskoi derevne 1920-kh godov.' *Otechestvennaia istoriia* 4 (July–August 1992): 74–88.

Male, D.J. *Russian Peasant Organisation before Collectivization: A Study of Commune and Gathering 1925–1930*. Cambridge: Cambridge University Press, 1971.

Mallon, Florencia E. 'The Promise and Dilemma of Subaltern Studies: Perspectives from Latin American History.' *American Historical Review* 99, no. 5 (1994): 1491–1515.

Mally, Lynn. *Culture of the Future: The Proletkult Movement in Revolutionary Russia.* Berkeley: University of California Press, 1990.

Mann, Michael. 'The Autonomous Power of the State: Its Origins, Mechanisms and Results.' In *States in History*, edited by John A. Hall, 109–36. Oxford: Blackwell, 1986.

Margulis, U.L., G.V. Lebedeva, and G.I. Tumarkina, eds. *Krest'ianskoe dvizhenie v Riazanskoi gubernii v gody pervoi russkoi revoliutsii. Dokumenty i materialy.* Riazan, 1960.

Mar'iankhin, G.L. *Ocherki istorii nalogov s naseleniia v SSSR.* Moscow: Izd. Finansy, 1964.

Marx, Karl. *Collected Works of Marx and Engels.* Vol. 1. London: Lawrence and Wishart, 1975.

McKee, W. Arthur. 'Sobering Up the Soul of the People: The Politics of Popular Temperance in Late Imperial Russia.' *Russian Review* 58, no. 2 (April 1999): 212–33.

Melancon, Michael. *The Socialist Revolutionaries and the Russian Anti-War Movement, 1914–1917*. Columbus: Ohio State University Press, 1990.

Moeller, Robert G., ed. *Peasants and Lords in Modern Germany: Recent Studies in Agricultural History.* Boston: Allen and Unwin, 1986.

Mooser, Josef. 'Property and Wood Theft: Agrarian Capitalism and Social Conflict in Rural Society, 1800–1850; A Westphalian Case Study.' In *Peasants and Lords in Modern Germany: Recent Studies in Agricultural History*, edited by Robert G. Moeller, 52–80. Boston: Allen and Unwin, 1986.

Muchembled, R. 'The Anthropology of Violence in Early Modern France.' In *Violence and the Absolutist State*, edited by S.T. Christensen, 47–73. Copenhagen: Akademisk Forlag, 1990.

Naiman, Eric. 'The Case of Chubarov Alley: Collective Rape, Utopian Desire and the Mentality of NEP.' *Russian History / Histoire Russe* 17, no. 1 (Spring 1990): 1–30.

– 'Of Crime, Utopia, and Repressive Complements: The Further Adventures of the Ridiculous Man.' *Slavic Review* 50, no. 3 (Fall 1991): 512–20.

– *Sex in Public.* New Jersey: Princeton University Press, 1997.

Neuberger, Joan. *Hooliganism: Crime, Culture and Power in St Petersburg, 1900–1914*. Berkeley: University of California Press, 1993.

Newcity, Michael A. *Taxation in the Soviet Union.* New York: Praeger, 1986.

Nora, Pierre. 'Between Memory and History: Les Lieux de Memoire.' *Representations* 26 (Spring 1989): 7–24.

Northrop, Douglas. *Veiled Empire: Gender and Power in Stalinist Central Asia.* Ithaca: Cornell University Press, 2004.

Nove, Alex. *An Economic History of the USSR.* London: Penguin, 1969.

Nye, Robert A. *Crime, Madness, and Politics in Modern France: The Medical Concept of National Decline.* Princeton: Princeton University Press, 1984.

O'Malley, Pat. 'Social Bandits, Modern Capitalism and the Traditional Peasantry: A Critique of Hobsbawm.' *Journal of Peasant Studies* 6, no. 4 (July 1979): 489–501.

Pallot, Judith. 'Forced Labour for Forestry: The Twentieth-Century History of Colonisation and Settlement in the North of Perm Oblast.' *Europe-Asia Studies* 54, no. 7 (2002): 1055–83.

Park, Ehren, and David Brandenberger. 'Imagined Community? Rethinking the Nationalist Origins of the Contemporary Chechen Crisis.' *Kritika: Explorations in Russian and Eurasian History* 5, no. 3 (Summer 2004): 543–60.

Pathak, Akhileshwar. *Contested Domains: The State, Peasants and Forests in Contemporary India.* Thousand Oaks, CA: Sage, in association with the Book Review Literary Trust, 1994.

Pearson, Geoffrey. *Hooligan: A History of Respectable Fears.* London: Macmillan, 1983.

Penner, D'Ann Rose. 'Pride, Power and Pitchforks: Farmer–Party Interaction on the Don, 1920–1928.' PhD diss., University of California, Berkeley, 1995.

Perov, I.F., and M.V. Kuznetsov. *Istoriia Riazanskoi militsii.* Vol. 1. Riazan: Uzoroch'e, 2001.

Phillips, Laura L. *Bolsheviks and the Bottle: Drink and Worker Culture in St Petersburg, 1900–1929.* DeKalb: Northern Illinois University Press, 2000.

Pipes, Richard. *The Russian Revolution.* New York: Knopf, 1990.

Popkins, Gareth. 'Popular Development of Procedure in a Dual Legal System: "Protective Litigation" in Russia's Peasant Courts, 1889–1912.' *Journal of Legal Pluralism* 43 (1999): 57–87.

– 'Code versus Custom? Norms and Tactics in Peasant Volost Court Appeals, 1889–1917.' *Russian Review* 59 (July 2000): 408–24.

– 'Peasant Experiences of the Late Tsarist State: District Congresses of Land Captains, Provincial Boards and the Legal Appeals Process, 1891–1917.' *Slavonic and East European Review* 78, no. 1 (January 2002): 90–114.

Popov, I.P., E.S. Stepanova, E.G. Tarabrin, and Iu.V. Fulin. *Dva veka Riazanskoi istorii.* Riazan, 1991.

Portelli, Alessandro. *The Death of Luigi Trastulli and Other Stories: Form and Meaning in Oral History*. New York: State University of New York Press, 1991.
Rabinowitch, Alexander. *The Bolsheviks Come to Power: The Revolution of 1917 in Petrograd*. New York: Norton, 1978.
– *Prelude to Revolution: The Petrograd Bolsheviks and the July 1917 Uprising*. Bloomington: Indiana University Press, 1978.
Radkey, Oliver. *The Elections to the Russian Constituent Assembly of 1917*. Cambridge: Harvard University Press, 1950.
Raleigh, Donald J., ed. *Provincial Landscapes: Local Dimensions of Soviet Power, 1917–1953*. Pittsburgh: University of Pittsburgh Press, 2001.
Rees, E.A. *State Control in Soviet Russia: The Rise and Fall of the Workers' and Peasants' Inspectorate, 1920–1934*. New York: St Martin's, 1987.
Retish, Aaron. *Russia's Peasants in Revolution and Civil War: Citizenship, Identity and the Creation of the Soviet State, 1914–1922*. Cambridge: Cambridge University Press, 2008.
Riazanskaia entsiklopediia: Spravochnyi material. Vol. 1. Riazan, 1992.
Rigby, T.H. *Lenin's Government: Sovnarkom 1917*–1922. Cambridge: Cambridge University Press, 1979.
– *Political Elites in the USSR: Central Leaders and Local Cadres from Lenin to Gorbachev*. Aldershot: Gower, 1990.
Ritchie, Donald A. *Doing Oral History*. New York: Twayne, 1995.
Rittersporn, Gabor Tamas. *Stalinist Simplifications and Soviet Complications: Social Tensions and Political Conflicts in the USSR, 1933–1953*. Chur: Harwood, 1991.
Robinson, David M. 'Banditry and the Subversion of State Authority in China: The Capital Region during the Middle Ming Period (1450–1525).' *Journal of Social History* 33, no. 3 (Spring 2000): 527–63.
Robinson, F. Bruce. 'Bandits and Rebellion in Nineteenth-Century Western India.' In *Crime and Criminality in British India*, edited by Anand A. Yang, 48–61. Tucson: University of Arizona Press, 1985.
Rodman, Margaret C. 'Empowering Place: Multilocality and Multivocality.' *American Anthropologist* 94, no. 3 (September 1992): 640–56.
Rogan, Eugene L. *Frontiers of the State in the Late Ottoman Empire: Transjordan, 1850–1921*. Cambridge: Cambridge University Press, 1999.
Rogers, Douglas. 'Historical Anthropology Meets Soviet History.' *Kritika: Explorations in Russian and Eurasian History* 7, no. 3 (Summer 2006): 633–49.
Sahlins, Peter. *Forest Rites: The War of the Demoiselles in Nineteenth-Century France*. Cambridge: Harvard University Press, 1994.
Said, Edward. *Orientalism*. New York: Vintage, 1978.
Sanborn, Joshua A. *Drafting the Russian Nation: Military Conscription, Total War, and Mass Politics 1905–1925*. DeKalb: Northern Illinois University Press, 2003.

– 'The Mobilization of 1914 and the Questions of the Russian Nation: A Reexamination.' *Slavic Review* 59, no. 2 (Summer 2000): 267–89.

Sant Cassia, Paul. 'Banditry, Myth and Terror in Cyprus and Other Mediterranean Societies.' *Comparative Studies in Society and History* 35, no. 4 (October 1993): 773–95.

Schapiro, Leonard. *The Communist Party of the Soviet Union.* London: Methuen, 1975.

– *Political Elites in the USSR: Central Leaders and Local Cadres from Lenin to Gorbachev.* Aldershot: Gower, 1990.

Schulte, Regina. *The Village in Court: Arson, Infanticide and Poaching in the Court Records of Upper Bavaria, 1848–1910.* Translated by Barrie Selman. New York: Cambridge University Press, 1994.

Schwarz, Bill. 'Night Battles: Hooligan and Citizen.' In *Modern Times: Reflections on a Century of English Modernity*, edited by Mica Nava and Allan O'Shea, 101–28. London: Routledge, 1996.

Scott, James. *The Moral Economy of the Peasant: Rebellion and Resistance in Southeast Asia.* New Haven: Yale University Press, 1976.

– *Domination and the Arts of Resistance: Hidden Transcripts.* New Haven: Yale University Press, 1990.

– *Seeing like a State: How Certain Schemes to Improve the Human Condition Have Failed.* New Haven: Yale University Press, 1998.

– 'Afterforeword to "Moral Economies, State Spaces, and Categorical Violence."' *American Anthropologist* 107, no. 3 (2005): 400.

Seregny, Scott. 'Peasants, Nation, and Local Government in Wartime Russia.' *Slavic Review* 59, no. 2 (Summer 2000): 336–42.

– 'Zemstvos, Peasants, and Citizenship: The Russian Adult Education Movement and World War I.' *Slavic Review* 59, no. 2 (Summer 2000): 290–315.

Shanin, Teodor. *The Awkward Class.* Oxford: Clarendon, 1972.

– *Russia as a Developing Society.* Vol. 1. New Haven: Yale University Press, 1986.

– *Peasants and Peasant Societies.* London: Penguin, 1988.

– *Defining Peasants.* Oxford: Blackwell, 1990.

Sharpe, James. 'The People and the Law.' In *Popular Culture in Seventeenth-Century England*, edited by Barry Reay, 244–70. London: Croom Helm, 1985.

Shearer, David R. 'Crime and Social Disorder in Stalin's Russia: A Reassessment of the Great Retreat and the Origins of Mass Repression.' *Cahiers du Monde Russe* 39, nos. 1–2 (January–June 1998): 119–48.

– 'Modernity and Backwardness on the Soviet Frontier: Western Siberia in the 1930s.' In *Provincial Landscapes: Local Dimensions of Soviet Power, 1917–1953*, edited by Donald J. Raleigh, 194–216. Pittsburgh: University of Pittsburgh Press, 2001.

– 'Elements Near and Alien: Passportization, Policing, and Identity in the Stalinist State, 1932–1952.' *Journal of Modern History* 76 (December 2004): 835–81.

Shelley, Louise I. *Policing Soviet Society: The Evolution of State Control.* New York: Routledge, 1996.

Shentalinsky, Vitaly. *Arrested Voices: Resurrecting the Disappeared Writers of the Soviet Regime.* New York: Free Press, 1996.

Singelmann, Peter. 'Political Structure and Social Banditry in Northeast Brazil.' *Journal of Latin American Studies* 7 (1975–6): 59–83.

Sivaramakrishnan, K. 'Introduction to "Moral Economies, State Spaces, and Categorical Violence."' *American Anthropologist* 107, no. 3 (2005): 321–30.

Slezkine, Yuri. 'Imperialism as the Highest Stage of Socialism.' *Russian Review* 59 (April 2000): 227–34.

Snow, George E. 'Alcoholism in the Russian Military: The Public Sphere and the Temperance Discourse, 1883–1917.' *Jahrbucher für Geschichte Osteuropas* 45 (1997): 417–31.

Solomon, Peter. 'Criminalization and Decriminalization in Soviet Criminal Policy, 1917–1941.' *Law and Society Review* 16 (1981–2): 9–43.

– *Soviet Criminal Justice under Stalin.* New York: Cambridge University Press, 1996.

Stepanova, E.S. 'Riazanskoe krest'ianstvo v gody vtoroi revoliutionnoi situatsii.' In *Nekotorye voprosy kraevedeniia i otechestvennoi istorii,* 5–32. Riazan: Riazanskii Gosudarstvennyi Pedagogicheskii Institut, 1974.

– 'Sel'skoe khoziaistvo i derevnia v XIX veke.' In *Riazanskaia entsiklopediia,* 1:518–19. Riazan, 1995.

Stites, Richard. *Revolutionary Dreams: Utopian Vision and Experimental Life in the Russian Revolution.* New York: Oxford University Press, 1989.

Sumpf, Alexandre. 'Confronting the Countryside: The Training of Political Educators in 1920s Russia.' *History of Education* 4–5 (July–September 2006): 475–98.

Suslov, A.I. 'Bor'ba za khleb v Riazanskoi gubernii v pervye gody sovetskoi vlasti (1917–1918).' In *Nekotorye voprosy kraevedeniia i otechestvennoi istorii. Uchenye zapiski,* 73–92. Riazan: Riazanskii Gosudarstvennyi Pedagogicheskii Institut, 1974.

Taniuchi, Yuzuru. *The Village Gathering in Russia in the Mid-1920s.* Birmingham: University of Birmingham, 1968.

Tanner, Harold M. 'The Offense of Hooliganism and the Moral Dimension of China's Pursuit of Modernity, 1979–1996.' *Twentieth-Century China* 26, no. 1 (2000): 1–40.

Thompson, Paul. *The Voice of the Past: Oral History*. Oxford: Oxford University Press, 1978.

Tilly, Charles. 'Reflections on the History of European State-Making.' In *The Formation of National States in Western Europe*, edited by Charles Tilly, 3–83. Princeton: Princeton University Press, 1975.

Tirado, Isabel A. 'The Village Voice: Women's Views of Themselves and Their World in Russian *Chastushki* of the 1920s.' Carl Beck Paper, no. 1008, Pittsburgh: REES, University of Pittsburgh, 1993.

Treplyakov, V.K., et al. *A History of Russian Forestry and Its Leaders*. Pullman: Washington State University Press, in cooperation with the Federal Forest Service of Russia and the Pacific Northwest Station of the USDA Forest Service, 1998.

Trotsky, Lev. *Literature and Revolution*. New York: Russell & Russell, 1957.

Tucker, Robert. *Stalin as a Revolutionary, 1879–1929: A Study in History and Personality*. New York, Norton, 1973.

– *Stalin in Power: The Revolution from Above*. New York: Norton, 1990.

Tul'tseva, L.A. 'Obshchina i agrarnaia obriadnost' Riazanskikh krest'ian na rubezhe XIX–XX vv.' In *Russkie: semeinyi i obshchestvennyi byt*, edited by S.V. Vlasova, M.M. Gromyko, and L.A. Listova, 45–62. Moscow: Nauka, 1989.

– *Riazanskii mesiatselov: Kruglyi god prazdnikov, obriadov, i obychaev Riazanskikh Krest'ian*. Riazan, 2001.

Turner, Victor. *From Ritual to Theatre: The Human Seriousness of Play*. New York: Performing Arts Journal Publication, 1982.

Uchenye zapiski. Vol. 18. Riazan: Riazanskii Gosudarstvennyi Pedagogicheskii Institut, 1957.

Vandergeest, Peter. 'Real Villages: National Narratives and Rural Development.' In *Creating the Countryside: The Politics of Rural and Environmental Discourse*, edited by E. Melanie DuPuis and Peter Vandergeest, 279–302. Philadelphia: Temple University Press, 1996.

Venturi, Franco. *Roots of Revolution: A History of the Populist and Socialist Movements in 19th-Century Russia*. Translated by Francis Haskell. London: Weidenfeld and Nicolson, 1960.

Verner, Andrew. *The Crisis of Russian Autocracy: Nicholas II and the 1905 Revolution*. Princeton: Princeton University Press, 1990.

Viola, Lynne. 'The Campaign of the 25,000ers: A Study of the Collectivization of Soviet Agriculture.' PhD diss., Princeton University, 1984.

– '*Bab'i Bunty* and Peasant Women's Protest during Collectivization.' *Russian Review* 45, no. 1 (1986): 23–42.

– *The Best Sons of the Fatherland: Workers in the Vanguard of Collectivization*. New York: Oxford University Press, 1987.

– *Peasant Rebels under Stalin: Collectivization and the Culture of Peasant Resistance.* New York: Oxford University Press, 1996.

– 'Popular Resistance in the Stalinist 1930s: Soliloquy of a Devil's Advocate.' *Kritika: Explorations in Russian and Eurasian History* 1, no. 1 (Winter 2000): 45–69.

– 'The Role of the OGPU in Dekulakization, Mass Deportations, and Special Resettlement in 1930.' Carl Beck Paper, no. 1406, Pittsburgh: REES, University of Pittsburgh, 2000.

– 'The Second Coming: Class Enemies in the Soviet Countryside, 1927–1935.' In *Stalinist Terror: New Perspectives,* edited by J. Arch Getty and Roberta Manning, 65–98. New York: Cambridge University Press, 1993.

– *The Unknown Gulag: The Lost World of Stalin's Special Settlements.* Oxford: Oxford University Press, 2007.

Viola, Lynne, V.P. Danilov, N.A. Ivnitskii, and Denis Kozlov, eds. *The War against the Peasantry 1927–1930.* New Haven: Yale University Press, 2005.

Wachtel, Nathan. 'Memory and History: Introduction.' *History and Anthropology* 2, no. 2 (1986): 207–24.

Wade, Rex. *Red Guards and Workers' Militias in the Russian Revolution.* Stanford: Stanford University Press, 1984.

Wang, Ban. *Illuminations from the Past: Trauma, Memory, and History in Modern China.* Stanford: Stanford University Press, 2004.

Waxmonsky, Gary Richard. 'Police and Politics in Soviet Society, 1921–1929.' PhD diss., Princeton University, 1982.

Weber, Max. *The Theory of Social and Economic Organization.* New York: Free Press, 1964.

Weiner, Amir. 'Nature, Nurture, and Memory in Socialist Utopia: Delineating the Soviet Socio-Ethnic Body in the Age of Socialism.' *American Historical Review* 104, no. 4 (October 1999): 1114–55.

Weiner, Douglas. *Models of Nature: Ecology, Conservation, and Cultural Revolution in Soviet Russia.* Bloomington: Indiana University Press, 1988.

Weissman, Neil. 'Rural Crime in Tsarist Russia: The Question of Hooliganism, 1905–1914.' *Slavic Review* 37, no. 2 (1978): 228–40.

– 'Regular Police in Tsarist Russia, 1900–1914.' *Russian Review* 44, no. 1 (1985): 45–68.

– 'Prohibition and Alcohol Control in the USSR: The 1920s Campaign against Illegal Spirits.' *Soviet Studies* 37, no. 3 (July 1986): 349–68.

– 'Policing the NEP Countryside.' In *Russia in the Era of NEP: Explorations in Soviet Society and Culture,* edited by Sheila Fitzpatrick, Alexander Rabinowitch, and Richard Stites, 174–91. Bloomington: Indiana University Press, 1991.

Werth, Nicholas. 'Une source ineditée: Les svodki de la Tcheka-OGPU.' *Revue des Études Slaves* (November 1993): 17–27.

Wheatcroft, Stephen G. 'Grain Production and Utilisation in Russia and the USSR before Collectivization.' PhD diss., University of Birmingham, 1980.

Whited, Tamara L. *Forests and Peasant Politics in Modern* France. New Haven: Yale University Press, 2000.

Winter, Jay. *Remembering War: The Great War between Memory and History in the Twentieth Century*. New Haven: Yale University Press, 2006.

Wolf, Eric R. *Peasants*. New Jersey: Prentice-Hall, 1966.

Worobec, Christine. 'Horse Thieves and Peasant Justice in Post-Emancipation Russia.' *Journal of Social History* (Winter 1987): 281–93.

– *Peasant Russia: Family and Community in the Post-Emancipation Period*. Princeton: Princeton University Press, 1991.

– 'Witches, Sorcerers, and Demons in a Remote Corner of Contemporary Northern Russia.' Paper presented at the Workshop on Russian Witchcraft, University of Michigan, 1–2 April 2005.

Yaney, George L. *The Systematization of Russian Government: Social Evolution in the Domestic Administration of Imperial Russia 1711–1905*. Urbana: University of Illinois Press, 1973.

– *The Urge to Mobilize: Agrarian Reform in Russia, 1861–1930*. Urbana: University of Illinois Press, 1982.

Yang, Anand. 'A Conversation of Rumors: The Language of Popular Mentalites in Late Nineteeth-Century Colonial India.' *Journal of Social History* 20 (Spring 1987): 485–505.

– ed. *Crime and Criminality in British India*. Tucson: University of Arizona Press, 1985.

– *The Limited Raj: Agrarian Relations in Colonial India, Saran District 1793–1920*. Berkeley: University of California Press, 1989.

Young, Allan. 'Social Suffering.' *Daedalus* 125, no. 1 (Winter 1996): 245–60.

Young, Glennys. *Power and the Sacred in Revolutionary Russia: Religious Activists in the Village*. University Park: Pennsylvania, 1997.

Zhevniak, A.V., ed. *Atlas Riazanskoi oblasti*. Riazan: Rinvest, 1995.

Index

An italic *f* following a page reference indicates the presence of an illustration; an italic *m* indicates a map; an italic *t* indicates a table.